Literary Cultures and Childhoods

Series Editor
Lynne Vallone
Department of Childhood Studies
Rutgers University
Camden, NJ, USA

Scholarly interest in the literary figure of the child has grown exponentially over the last thirty years or so due, in part, to the increased attention given to children's literature within the academy and the development of the multidisciplinary field of Childhood Studies.

Given the crucial importance of children to biological, social, cultural and national reproduction, it is not surprising that child and adolescent characters may be found everywhere in Anglo-American literary expressions. Across time and in every literary genre written for adults as well as in the vast and complex array of children's literature, 'the child' has functioned as a polysemous and potent figure. From Harry Potter to Huck Finn, some of the most beloved, intriguing and enduring characters in literature are children.

The aim of this finite five-book series of edited volumes is to chart representations of the figure of the child in Anglo-American literary cultures throughout the ages, mapping how they have changed over time in different contexts and historical moments. Volumes move chronologically from medieval/early modern to contemporary, with each volume addressing a particular period (eg 'The Early Modern Child', 'The Nineteenth Century Child' etc). Through the aggregate of the essays, the series will advance new understandings of the constructions of the child and the child within different systems (familial, cultural, national), as communicated through literature. Volumes will also serve, collectively, as an examination of the way in which the figure of the child has evolved over the years and how this has been reflected/anticipated by literature of the time.

More information about this series at
http://www.palgrave.com/gp/series/15353

Andrew O'Malley
Editor

Literary Cultures and Eighteenth-Century Childhoods

palgrave
macmillan

Editor
Andrew O'Malley
Ryerson University
Toronto, ON, Canada

Literary Cultures and Childhoods
ISBN 978-3-319-94736-5   ISBN 978-3-319-94737-2   (eBook)
https://doi.org/10.1007/978-3-319-94737-2

Library of Congress Control Number: 2018956866

This Palgrave Macmillan imprint is published by the registered company Springer Nature Switzerland AG
The registered company address is: Gewerbestrasse 11, 6330 Cham, Switzerland

ACKNOWLEDGMENTS

I would like to thank the series editor, Lynne Vallone, for approaching me to be the editor of this volume; she has afforded me a wonderful opportunity to work with many scholars whose research I already admired and to get to know others whose scholarship has been an exciting revelation to me. In the editing of this volume, I have benefitted greatly from the assistance of two research assistants from the Literatures of Modernity graduate program at Ryerson University: Erin Della Mattia and Danielle Waite. Thank you both for your careful and attentive work on these chapters. I would also like to acknowledge the Faculty of Arts at Ryerson University for its support in the completion of this volume. Finally, I want to express my gratitude to my wife, Nima Naghibi, and our children, Safianna and Cyrus; it is as always your love and support that makes everything possible.

CONTENTS

NOTES ON CONTRIBUTORS

Adriana Benzaquén is an Associate Professor in the Department of History at Mount Saint Vincent University (Halifax, Canada). She is the author of *Encounters with Wild Children: Temptation and Disappointment in the Study of Human Nature* (McGill-Queen's University Press, 2006) and of articles on children and youth, health and medicine, human science, and friendship in early modern and Enlightenment Europe. Her current research project is a study of children and child-adult relations in England in the late seventeenth and early eighteenth centuries, focusing on the children in John Locke's circle of friends and acquaintances.

Richard De Ritter is a Lecturer in the School of English at the University of Leeds. He has published on a range of eighteenth-century and Romantic writing, including articles on James Boswell, Maria Edgeworth, and Elizabeth Hamilton. His book, *Imagining Women Readers, 1789–1820: Well-Regulated Minds*, was published by Manchester University Press in 2014. He is currently working on a new book project entitled *Domesticating Wonder: Women Writing for Children, 1778–1832*.

Jessica R. Evans received her Ph.D. in English Literature at the University of Kentucky. Currently, she is an Instructor of English in Humanities and Social Sciences and Sigma Kappa Delta Faculty Sponsor at Columbia State Community College. She teaches, lectures, and writes on a variety of topics, such as eighteenth-century British literature, development of the Gothic mode, and children's literature.

Louise Joy is a Fellow and Senior Lecturer in English at Homerton College, University of Cambridge. She is the co-editor of two volumes of essays, *Poetry and Childhood* (2010) and *The Aesthetics of Children's Poetry: A Study of Children's Verse in English* (2017). Her first monograph, *Literature's Children: The Critical Child and the Art of Idealisation*, will be published later this year by Bloomsbury Academic. She has published widely on topics relating to eighteenth-century literature, to children's literature, and to the history of the emotions. Her articles have appeared in journals including *Studies in Romanticism*, *Children's Literature Association Quarterly*, *History of European Ideas*, *Philosophy and Literature*, and *European Romantic Review*.

Susan Manly is a Reader in English at the University of St Andrews and the author of *Language, Custom and Nation in the 1790s: Locke, Tooke, Wordsworth, Edgeworth* (2007). She is currently writing a book on late eighteenth- and early nineteenth-century radical and reformist writing for children, *Schools for Treason*, and a political and intellectual biography of Maria Edgeworth. She is also the editor of Maria Edgeworth's *Harrington* and *Practical Education* and the co-editor of *Helen* and *Leonora*, all in the 12-volume *The Novels and Selected Works of Maria Edgeworth* (1999–2003), and the editor of *Maria Edgeworth: Selected Tales for Children and Young People* (Palgrave, 2013).

Teresa Michals is an Associate Professor at George Mason University. Her publications include *Books for Children, Books for Adults: Age and the Novel from Defoe to James* (Cambridge, 2014) and "'Experiments Before Breakfast': Toys, Education, and Middle-Class Childhood" in Dennis Denisoff (Ed.) *The Nineteenth-Century Child and Consumer Culture* (Ashgate, 2008). She studies the history of children's literature, representations of disability, and eighteenth- and nineteenth-century British novels. Her work has appeared in journals such as *Eighteenth-Century Studies*, *Studies in Eighteenth-Century Culture*, *Disability Studies Quarterly*, *Nineteenth-Century Literature*, and *NOVEL: A Forum on Fiction*.

Sebastian Mitchell is a Senior Lecturer in English Literature at the University of Birmingham, UK. He has written widely on literature and art in the eighteenth century. His book *Visions of Britain, 1730–1830: Anglo-Scottish Writing and Representation* (2013) was shortlisted for the Saltire Society Research Book of the Year. He has recently guest edited a special issue on Ossian for the *Journal for Eighteenth-Century Studies*. His study *Utopia and Its Discontents* will be published by Bloomsbury Press in 2019.

Anja Müller is a Full Professor of English Literature and Cultural Studies at the University of Siegen, where she is a co-chair of the faculty's research group on European Children's Literature (EKJL). Her research interests range from eighteenth-century literature and culture to contemporary drama, fantasy, intertextuality and adaptation, (historical) childhood studies, and children's literature. Her publications in the latter fields include *Fashioning Childhood in the Eighteenth Century: Age and Identity* (ed., Ashgate, 2006), *Framing Childhood in Eighteenth-Century English Periodicals and Prints, 1689–1789* (Ashgate, 2009, ChLA Honor Book), *Childhood in the English Renaissance* (ed., Wissenschaftlicher Verlag Trier, 2013), *Adapting Canonical Texts in Children's Literature* (ed., Bloomsbury 2013), and *Canon Constitution and Canon Change in Children's Literature* (ed., with Bettina Kümmerling-Meibauer, Routledge, 2016). Together with Bettina Kümmerling-Meibauer and Astrid Surmatz, she is co-editing the book series Studies in European Children's Literature (Heidelberg: Winter).

Cheryl Nixon is a Professor of English and an Associate Provost at the University of Massachusetts Boston. Her research focuses on literary representations and legal restructurings of the family; her current project connects the development of family law to the eighteenth-century rise of the domestic novel. Her recent books include *The Orphan in Eighteenth-Century Law and Literature: Estate, Blood, and Body* and *Novel Definitions: An Anthology of Commentary on the Novel, 1688–1815*. These works and her articles feature archival research that interweaves print and manuscript literary and legal materials. In an attempt to make archival research and the early novel accessible to a broader public, she has worked with students to create rare books exhibitions for the Boston Public Library, including "Crooks, Rogues, and Maids Less than Virtuous: Books in the Streets of 18th-Century London" and "The Imaginative Worlds of Daniel Defoe: *Robinson Crusoe, Moll Flanders*, and the Early Novel."

Andrew O'Malley is Associate Professor of English at Ryerson University in Toronto. He is the author of *The Making of the Modern Child: Children's Literature and Childhood in the Late Eighteenth Century* (Routledge, 2003) and of *Children's Literature, Popular Culture, and* Robinson Crusoe (Palgrave, 2012).

Lissa Paul is a Professor at Brock University in St. Catharines Ontario, Canada, an Associate General Editor of *The Norton Anthology of Children's Literature* (2005), and a co-editor of *Keywords for Children's Literature* (2011). *The Children's Book Business: Lessons from the Long Eighteenth Century*, her first book on Eliza Fenwick, was published in 2011. Her new biography, *Eliza Fenwick (1766–1840): A Life Rewritten*, will be published by the University of Delaware Press in January 2019, in their Early Modern Feminisms Series. Lissa's research is generously funded by the Social Sciences and Humanities Research Council (SSHRC) of Canada.

Ann Wierda Rowland is an Associate Professor of English at the University of Kansas. She is the author of *Romanticism and Childhood: The Infantilization of British Literary Culture* (Cambridge University Press, 2012) and the co-editor, with Paul Westover, of *Transatlantic Literature and Author Love in the Nineteenth Century* (Palgrave, 2016). She has also published articles on John Keats, William Wordsworth, Walter Scott, the Romantic ballad revival, the Romantic novel, and sentimental fiction.

Donelle Ruwe is the author of *British Children's Poetry in the Romantic Era: Verse, Riddle, and Rhyme* (Palgrave Macmillan, 2014) and the editor of a collection of essays, *Culturing the Child 1660–1830: Essays in Memory of Mitzi Myers* (Scarecrow, 2005), and the forthcoming *Children, Childhood, and Musical Theater*. She has published numerous scholarly articles on Romantic poetics, women writers, and children's writing in *Eighteenth-Century Life, Writing Women, Children's Literature, Nineteenth-Century Contexts*, and others. Ruwe is the co-president of the eighteenth- and nineteenth-century British Women Writers Association and has been the chair of the Scholarly Edited Collection award for the Children's Literature Association. She has received research awards including a National Humanities Center Summer Program Fellowship, the RMMLA Faculty Travel Award, the Fleur Cowles Fellowship at the Harry Ransom Research Center, and an Ahmanson Fellowship from UCLA. Ruwe is a published poet, and her chapbook *Condiments* won the Kinloch Rivers Award in 1999, and her chapbook *Another Message You Miss the Point Of* won the Camber Press Prize in 2006.

Jennifer Thorn is an Associate Professor of English and Director of the Interdisciplinary Minor in Gender Studies at Saint Anselm College (New Hampshire). She works in the transatlantic eighteenth and nineteenth centuries, with a special focus on the history of childhood, class, and race, and is the author of many book chapters and articles on early American and eighteenth-century British texts. The editor of the collection *Writing British Infanticide: Child-Murder, Gender, and Print, 1722–1859* (2003), she is at work on a book, *Black Children, Slavery, and Piety in Early New England,* which focuses in part on Phillis Wheatley, about whose life and writings she has published four articles.

LIST OF FIGURES

CHAPTER 1

Introduction: Eighteenth-Century Childhoods and Literary Cultures

Andrew O'Malley

The eighteenth century has long been regarded as a watershed period in the history of both childhood and children's literature. It saw the rapid growth of a specialized text industry addressing young readers,[1] and at the same time, the child became increasingly visible and important in a range of 'adult' discourses. Philippe Ariès's now more than a half-century-old assertion that the child, as differentiated subject with its own needs and material culture, did not exist in Europe before the seventeenth century has rightly and usefully been critiqued,[2] as has J. H. Plumb's famous celebration of a 'new world of children' in the eighteenth century.[3] Yet the fact remains that, certainly and most notably within the more privileged segments of English society, experiences of childhood for many changed significantly in the period this volume considers, as did the ways in—and extent to—which the child circulated within literary culture.

There has been considerable scholarship, including new research to appear in the other volumes of the *Literary Cultures and Childhoods* series, demonstrating that the generations before the period considered here produced or adapted texts for the use of child readers. Likewise, 'the child' had already accrued a variety of cultural meanings in the literary

A. O'Malley (✉)
Ryerson University, Toronto, ON, Canada
e-mail: aomalley@ryerson.ca

© The Author(s) 2018
A. O'Malley (ed.), *Literary Cultures and Eighteenth-Century Childhoods*, Literary Cultures and Childhoods,
https://doi.org/10.1007/978-3-319-94737-2_1

imagination. One significant change in the long eighteenth century, however, is the ubiquity of childhood both in terms of the print materials marketed to people at this stage of life and in terms of the discourses in which it becomes an important consideration and significant trope. Both cases owe a great deal, of course, to changing demographics in Britain during the period, which saw considerable growth in the number of young people, and to economic growth that helped increase literacy rates and spurred a rapidly expanding text industry that quickly identified the opportunities afforded by the greater numbers of parents with disposable income.[4] Added in this period to the existing juvenile corpus of hornbooks, battledores, chapbooks, devotional texts, fables, and conduct books was a remarkable range of reading material designed and marketed specifically for children: long-form fiction modelled on the novel for adult readers; periodicals; dramas for home theatricals; books of verse (particularly by the end of the century); and non-fiction works covering such subjects as the natural sciences, technological innovations, local and world geography and history, mathematics, and biography.

As children increasingly became subjects for whom adults wrote, they similarly became subjects about whom adults wrote with greater frequency. Pedagogical treatises and systems proliferated in the period, penned by some of the key luminaries of the age, most famously John Locke and Jean-Jacques Rousseau.[5] Medical experts devoted greater attention to repairing and sustaining the health of young people, producing treatises for fellow practitioners, along with advice books for parents anxious to safeguard the immediate and future well-being of their offspring.[6] The legal status of the child likewise became a matter of greater concern, and this interest manifested itself in novels and plays centring on issues of inheritance and apprenticeship, as Cheryl Nixon's chapter in this volume discusses. As Susan Manly and Sebastian Mitchell demonstrate in their chapters, childhood also became a powerful trope that could be mobilized for different political agendas, while Ann Wierda Rowland, also a contributor to this volume, has shown elsewhere the extent to which theorizing about the child extended into theories of poetics and language.[7]

When we speak of changes in the realm of childhood, in the eighteenth century or in any other period, it is worth keeping in mind, as Adrienne Gavin notes, that these are never adopted uniformly or universally; it is a mistake to assume 'each new – or seemingly new – construction of childhood neatly and irrevocably replaces its predecessor.'[8] Likewise, such changes are rarely as unequivocally positive as is sometimes suggested by the accounts of children's 'progress' common to later twentieth-century histories on the subject.[9] Taking into account a variety of literary and print forms—novels, poetry, legal writing, periodicals, pamphlets, personal letters, graphic prints, along with the literature produced specifically for young readers—the authors of this volume explore the complex and sometimes paradoxical ways in which childhood was approached and represented in the period. To account for this complexity, this volume looks at eighteenth-century childhoods from a variety of angles: as a set of expectations, desires, concerns, limitations, and capacities adults sought to address in their writing for young people; as a trope or symbol that performed a range of cultural work in the writings adults produced for adult readers; as a lived, embodied experience children recorded and actively shaped. Then as now, the meanings of childhood were not always stable, and the boundaries—such as age—used to demarcate it were at times fluid, as Teresa Michals's chapter here demonstrates. Childhood tended, as it still tends, to be invoked with purpose and its definition relies on the contexts in which it is being addressed. One of the fundamental contradictions of childhood within our culture illustrates this instability, and it is a contradiction that begins to take shape in the eighteenth century: that the child embodies, sometimes simultaneously, the promise of futurity as well as an ideal of, and longing for, a lost past. Childhood became a category equally suited to Enlightenment ideas of progress and improvement and to the sentimental and nostalgic ideas associated with what has come to be known as the 'Romantic child.'

The study of historical children's literature and childhood has not always co-habited easily with the modern field of 'child studies.' Peter Hunt famously and controversially insisted that current children's literature scholarship should keep to works produced for children who are 'recognizably' like today's children.[10] At the same time, as Matthew Grenby recounts, bibliographers such as Brian Alderson, with deep investments in the historical particulars of children's book publishing, have expressed frustration over recent trends in children's literature criticism, 'especially any criticism based on literary theory.'[11] This volume attempts to attend to the demands of rigorous historical analysis while remaining wholly aware of the theoretical concerns child studies as a discipline has raised over the problems of child-adult relations and of the constructedness of 'childhood' as a category. The essays here also acknowledge and build on recent methodological developments specific to the field of eighteenth-century children's literature and culture, such as: the ideological readings of children's texts pioneered by Isaac Kramnick and Alan Richardson; the feminist recuperations and reassessments Mitzi Myers helped initiate; and more recently reader-focused investigations of the sort pursued by Matthew Grenby.[12]

The thirteen chapters contained in this collection are arranged into three sections that correspond to some of the key aspects of child studies this introduction has tried to identify: definitions and experiences of childhood; children's reading and pedagogy; and representations of childhood in adult discourse. Several offer fresh insights into texts and authors with considerable existing criticism: Jessica Evans's look at pedagogy in Ann Radcliffe, or Richard De Ritter's treatment of wonder in Arnaud Berquin, Anna Laetitia Barbauld, and others. They also bring to light now-obscure aspects of the period's print culture, as in the case of Donelle Ruwe's investigation into debates around the use of the 'chiroplast' in musical training. Some, such as Anja Müller's recasting of child-adult power dynamics, bring new theoretical approaches to the field, while others, specifically Adriana Benzaquén's study of children's letter-writing, inform us about how young people in the period understood themselves within the system of family relations. Although the focus of this volume is very much on texts and discourses for and about childhood in the British context (more so than I had originally hoped would be the case), two of the essays here reach beyond England, to look at questions of race and childhood in the American context (Jennifer Thorn), and at British ex-patriot Eliza Fenwick's efforts to forge a transatlantic pedagogy (Lissa Paul).

For a volume that concerns itself with English-language literary cultures, such a concentration on Britain is to be expected. There is, however, a growing body of scholarship on American childhoods and children's literature in the eighteenth century.[13] As well, childhoods in the Irish and Scottish, as well as the English provincial and labouring-class, contexts are certainly deserving of greater consideration; this proved regrettably not possible in this volume. Finally, while Jennifer Thorn's essay makes an important contribution to scholarship on African-American childhood, much more remains to be investigated in this area, as well as in colonial and Indigenous childhoods.

Section I, 'Status and Contexts of Childhood,' gathers essays that situate childhood socially in the eighteenth century and explore its definitional contours. In 'Age, Status, and Reading in the Eighteenth Century,' Teresa Michals offers a careful reading of the period's most influential text about children, Locke's *Some Thoughts Concerning Education*, which seeks to untangle ideas of age, dependence, social status, and the idea of 'age-appropriate' reading. As she reveals, the age-levelled reading we now assume to have a natural and obvious correspondence to children's needs and capacities was also profoundly rooted in structures of social hierarchy. Anja Müller looks at one of the early eighteenth century's most generative textual sites for discourses of childhood: widely read periodicals such as *The Tatler* and *The Spectator*. Her essay, 'Circulating Childhood in Eighteenth-Century England,' proposes a theoretical framework new to historical child studies, Bruno Latour's actor-network theory, to re-evaluate the adult-child relationship. Instead of viewing childhood as merely the subject on which adult power is exercised, Müller proposes a more fluid dynamic in which its meanings are governed by networks of association between a variety of different actors.

In 'Wards and Apprentices,' Cheryl Nixon investigates the surprising complexity of the period's family structures and the child's legal status, especially within non-nuclear arrangements. Eighteenth-century England recognized a broad range of biological, marriage, and work alignments in its family structures, and the period's literary texts were often preoccupied with wards and apprentices and how these dependent household members tested the limitations of the legally defined child. Adriana Benzaquén provides an intimate look into the family dynamics revealed in personal letters (John Locke's friend and the dedicatee of *Some Thoughts Concerning Education*) Edward Clarke, his wife, and children wrote one another over many years. 'Pray lett none see this impertinent Epistle' offers unique insight into how children understood themselves within the network of family relations and how they moved between formal and familiar registers depending on the content and addressees of their correspondences.

The essays in Section II, 'Reading, Pedagogy, and the Child's Mind,' focus primarily on writers for and educators of young people, what they saw as the stakes involved in literary production for child readers, and how they understood children as learners. Ann Wierda Rowland, in 'Learned Pigs and Literate Children,' considers the phenomenon of the famous 'learned pig' who exhibited mathematical and spelling prowess in the 1780s and became emblematic in the period's elite literature of growing anxiety over popular print culture and the state of traditional social order. The pig, who makes an appearance in one of the period's most renowned children's books, Sarah Trimmer's *Fabulous Histories*, raises issues about literacy as a marker of difference not just between human and animal, but between adult and child as well. In 'Eighteenth-Century Children's Poetry,' Louise Joy examines what poetry written for young readers in the period reveals about their mental capacities and how they acquire knowledge. The value of poetry as a pedagogical tool was widely debated in the period, as were concerns over the debasement of an elevated aesthetic form that producing a lower, child's version entailed. Isaac Watts's *Divine Songs*, however, remained in print throughout the century and demonstrated both the utility of poetry to overall learning and the complex cognitive processes the young mind could perform.

The nature of the child's mind, how it acquired information and knowledge, was a subject of considerable interest in the period. While Locke's *tabula rasa* was decidedly the most influential psychological model across the eighteenth century, Susan Manly discusses a radical alternative in 'Powers Expanding Slowly.' Progressive writers, such as Mary Wollstonecraft and Anna Laetitia Barbauld, posited—instead of a blank slate to be judiciously filled by an adult authority—an 'innate' rationality, which when 'unfolded' and liberated could offer socially transformative possibilities. If the mind was the primary site of pedagogical efforts, Donelle Ruwe reminds us in her essay, 'Mediocrity: Mechanical Training and Music for Girls,' of the importance of the physical training involved in the acquisition of the polite accomplishment of music. In so doing, Ruwe revisits the period's concerns over rote and experiential learning, while elucidating how music training for girls conflicted with gender and class expectations around performance and labour.

The children's literature of the late eighteenth century has been branded 'rational-moralist' and regarded as overly didactic; it was reviled by contemporaries Charles Lamb and Wordsworth, and by generations of (mostly male) scholars of children's book history as the enemy of childhood imagination and wonder.[14] Yet as Richard De Ritter argues in 'From Wild Fictions to Accurate Observations,' wonder remained an integral part of the period's books for the young. Indeed, it is a mistake to consider 'wondrous' and 'rational' as binary terms; the rationalist writers of the day did not jettison the one in favour of the other, but instead 'domesticated' the former by locating the wondrous in the commonplace and familiar. Lissa Paul's essay, 'To Communicate Energy,' which rounds out this section, traces the journey of Eliza Fenwick, an important early nineteenth-century children's writer and educator who brought her experience and pedagogical ideas developed in England to the Caribbean and North America, where she established a series of schools. Fenwick's often trying experiences supporting a family as an educator highlight not only the resilience of a woman inspired by and contributing to progressive pedagogical theories, but how the transatlantic migration of these theories—and practices—necessitated adaption to their new context.

The essays in the final section of the volume address the period's 'Shifting Representations and Meanings of Childhood' in genres and discourses primarily directed at adults. Looking at satirical prints in his essay, 'In the Margins,' Sebastian Mitchell considers the different cultural and aesthetic functions the figure of the child served in popular visual culture. Mitchell notes that while the child is a more prominent figure in sentimental prints than in satirical prints, suggesting the increasing affective investment in childhood, slippage in childhood's meaning does however occur between the implied associations of child, innocence, and sentiment, and of adult, experience, and satire. In 'Redefining the Gothic Child,' Jessica Evans takes up the figure of the child in the popular Gothic fiction of Ann Radcliffe. The Gothic, with its wild improbabilities and excesses of sentiment and sensibility, has conventionally been regarded as the antithesis of rational pedagogy. Radcliffe's portrayals of young women developing rational judgement and critical thinking, however, align surprisingly well with the work of such advocates for rational female education as Mary Wollstonecraft and Maria Edgeworth. Finally, Jennifer Thorn's chapter invites, like the others in this section and others throughout this volume, a reconsideration of one of the givens of historical child studies: that the children's literature and child-rearing practices of the Puritan/Congregationalist faiths were conspicuous for their oppressiveness. In 'Lemuel Haynes and "Little Adults,"' Thorn investigates what she calls the 'levelling tendency of original sin' and how this religious community's focus on piety instead of reason enabled some subversion of adult authority over children. The same doctrine also allowed for the possibility, albeit always in a contained way, of African-American spiritual superiority, as the case of the Black minister Lemuel Haynes demonstrates. Thorn's analysis allows for a reconsideration of how structures of authority operate in the contexts of race and of age.

While this volume cannot aspire to a comprehensive view of the exciting research being done on the child and children's literature in the eighteenth century, it does hope at least to convey some of the diversity of the work being undertaken in the field. In an effort to showcase the interdisciplinarity of the field, the essays here come from scholars working in a range of disciplines, including literary and cultural studies, history, education, and visual culture. The motivation to collect work from different disciplines comes in part from a desire to see the study of childhood more fully integrated into other areas of scholarly concern. As Andrea Immel and Michael Witmore have noted, 'it is just as important to connect those issues of particular relevance to a child's situation to those circulating in the wider culture. Children's studies cannot be an island, although it may have sometimes seemed so during the years following the publication of *Centuries of Childhood*.[15] Immel and Witmore are right to call the exchange between 'childhood and the broader social categories that have shaped the more "elevated realms of European culture"' a 'two-way traffic,'[16] just as Kimberley Reynolds is right to assert that children's literature's 'long history and the fact that writing for children straddles domestic and institutional, official and unofficial, high and mass cultures' make it 'a particularly valuable source of historical information' about a wide range of subjects.[17] Yet the siloing of child studies, and what Brian Sutton-Smith famously identified almost fifty years ago as 'the triviality barrier' erected around the study of subjects related to childhood, still continues for reasons both institutional and cultural.[18] Tremendous strides have been made to correct this attitude, and this volume hopes humbly to contribute to that important, ongoing work.

NOTES

1. Debates over whether or not the 'origins' of children's literature can be found in eighteenth-century England have been, at least to my mind, resolved satisfactorily enough that a short note should suffice here. It is certainly very likely that children have been reading something for as long as there have been reading materials—if perhaps not 'ever since there were children,' as Seth Lerer has claimed (*Children's Literature: A Reader's History* [Chicago: University of Chicago Press, 2008], 1). However, as Matthew Grenby has argued, it is not until the eighteenth century that a self-consciously aware *genre* for child readers gained widespread recognition: 'a set of texts specifically commissioned, written and marketed for the use of the young' (*The Child Reader, 1700–1840*, Cambridge: Cambridge University Press, 2011), 4.

2. See Ariès, *Centuries of Childhood: A Social History of Family Life* (Trans. Robert Baldick, New York: Vintage Books, 1962). Medieval scholars in particular have taken issue with, and gone to considerable lengths to disprove, Ariès's claim that 'in medieval society the idea of childhood did not exist' (125). See, for example, Nicholas Orme, *Medieval Children* (New

Haven: Yale UP, 2003) and Sally Crawford, *Childhood in Anglo-Saxon England* (Stroud, UK: Allan Sutton, 1999).

3. See Plumb, 'The New World of Children in Eighteenth-Century England' (*Past and Present* 67.1 (1975): 64–95). Ludmilla Jordanova, in 'New Worlds for Children in the Eighteenth Century: Problems of Historical Interpretation' (*History of the Human Sciences* 3.1 (1990): 69–83), takes Plumb to task for an overly rosy view of the period's childhood that elides the experiences of the majority of children for whom the rich new material culture Plumb describes was not accessible.

4. The demographic, economic, and print culture expansions I mention here have been thoroughly documented by many historians; Morag Styles and Evelyn Arizpe offer a particularly useful short summary related specifically to juvenile reading and publishing in *Reading Lessons from the Eighteenth Century: Mothers, Children and Texts* (Shenstone: Pied Piper Publishing Ltd., 2006); see esp. Chap. 2, 'The Changing World of Books and Reading in the Eighteenth Century.'

5. *Some Thoughts Concerning Education* (1693) and *Emile* (1762) are of course the most famous and influential examples. There were many more that followed, however; these include Mary Wollstonecraft's *Thoughts on the Education of Daughters* (1787), Catharine Macaulay's *Letters on Education: With Observations on Religious and Metaphysical Subjects* (1790), Joseph Priestley's *Miscellaneous Observations Relating to Education* (1778), and Erasmus Darwin's *A Plan for the Conduct of Female Education in Boarding Schools* (1797).

6. A few examples by notable physicians of the period include: William Buchan's *Advice to Mothers on the Subject of Their Own Health, Strength, and Beauty of Their Offspring* (1803); William Cadogan's *An Essay upon Nursing, and the Management of Children, from Their Birth to Three Years of Age* (1748); and Thomas Beddoes's *A Guide for Self-Preservation, and Parental Affection* (1793).

7. See Rowland's *Romanticism and Childhood: The Infantilization of British Literary Culture* (Cambridge: Cambridge University Press, 2012), a study she describes as a 'rhetorical history of childhood' in which she charts how 'new ideas of childhood made possible new ways of thinking about language, literature, history and culture' (11).

8. Adrienne E. Gavin, 'The Child in British Literature: An Introduction,' *The Child in British Literature: Literary Constructions of Childhood, Medieval to Contemporary* (Houndmills: Palgrave, 2012), 3.

9. Plumb's account subscribes largely to a historical model of steady improvement, while Lloyd deMause, in *The History of Childhood* (New York: Psychohistory Press, 1974), posits a 'psychohistorical' trajectory of increasing parental empathy resulting in incremental improvements to

the lives of children. David Rudd has observed that histories of children's books also tended to follow this 'humanist' and 'presentist' ethos until the intervention of poststructuralism in children's literature scholarship; see 'The Development of Children's Literature' in *The Routledge Companion to Children's Literature* (ed. David Rudd, Abingdon: Routledge, 2010): 3–13.

10. Peter Hunt, *Criticism, Theory, and Children's Literature* (Oxford: Blackwell, 1991, 61). For a useful discussion of Hunt's assertion, see M. O. Grenby, *Children's Literature* (2nd Edition, Edinburgh: Edinburgh University Press, 2014), 2–3.

11. Matthey Grenby, 'Bibliography,' *International Companion Encyclopedia of Children's Literature* (2nd edition, vol. 1, Peter Hunt, ed., Abingdon: Routledge, 2004), 203.

12. See Isaac Kramnick's 'Children's Literature and Bourgeois Ideology: Observations on Culture and Industrial Capitalism in the Later Eighteenth Century' (*Studies in Eighteenth-Century Culture* 12 [1983]: 11–44) and Alan Richardson's *Literature, Education, and Romanticism: Reading as Social Practice, 1780–1832* (Cambridge: Cambridge University Press, 1994); one of the most influential of Mitzi Myers's many contributions is 'Impeccable Governesses, Rational Dames, and Moral Mothers: Mary Wollstonecraft and the Female Tradition in Georgian Children's Books' (*Children's Literature* 14 [1986]: 31–56); using a variety of documents, including children's marginalia in their books, Grenby explores the child's experience of reading in *The Child Reader*.

13. See, for example, Anna Mae Duane's *Suffering Childhood in Early America: Violence, Race, and the Making of the Child Victim* (Athens: University of Georgia Press, 2010) and Courtney Weikle-Mills's *Imaginary Citizens: Child Readers and the Limits of American Independence, 1640–1868* (Baltimore: Johns Hopkins University Press, 2013).

14. Lamb famously referred to Barbauld and her peers as 'those blights and blasts of all that is human in man and child' (*The Life, Letters, and Writings of Charles Lamb*, 6 vols., ed. Percy Fitzgerald [1876; reprint, Freeport, N.Y.: Books for Libraries, 1971], I: 421). Wordsworth offers a lengthy lament for the child trained in rational pedagogy in Book V of *The Prelude*.

15. Andrea Immel and Michael Witmore, 'Little Differences: Children, Their Books, and Culture in the Study of Early Modern Europe,' *Childhood and Children's Books in Early Modern Europe, 1550–1800* (New York: Routledge, 2006), 3.

16. Ibid., 10.

17. Kimberley Reynolds, *Children's Literature: A Very Short Introduction* (Oxford: Oxford University Press, 2011), 4.

18. Brian Sutton-Smith, 'The Psychology of Childlore: The Triviality Barrier,' *Western Folklore* 29.1 (1970): 1–8. Sutton-Smith remarks on how all things connected to childhood—play, imagination, irrationality—are relegated to the realm of the 'unserious.'

Status and Contexts of Childhood

CHAPTER 2

Age, Status, and Reading in the Eighteenth Century

Teresa Michals

Imagine walking through a bookstore that has no sections labeled 'Teens,' 'Kids,' 'Fiction,' 'Romance,' or 'Thrillers,' a bookstore that is instead divided up into sections labeled 'Masters' and 'Everybody Else'—and one very small, very new room labeled 'Children of the Aspiring Middle Class.' Finding our way in the eighteenth-century book market is a similarly disorienting experience. In our own time, the difference between books for children and books for adults seems natural. It shapes the publishing and marketing choices of presses and the curricula of schools and universities, as well as the floor plans of libraries and bookstores, and the software through which we try to control access to the Internet. When we turn back a few centuries, however, writing, marketing, and readership look quite different, because age itself worked quite differently. While we may consider age differences to be fundamental and differences in social status to be relatively superficial, much writing up through the early eighteenth century sees social status as the fundamental difference, often imagining age itself in the likeness of social status. To this way of thinking, children are like servants and servants are like children. Subordinate status defines them both. John Locke's enormously influential manual on how to bring

T. Michals (✉)
George Mason University, Fairfax, VA, USA
e-mail: tmichals@gmu.edu

© The Author(s) 2018   15
A. O'Malley (ed.), *Literary Cultures and Eighteenth-Century Childhoods*, Literary Cultures and Childhoods,
https://doi.org/10.1007/978-3-319-94737-2_2

up a young gentleman, *Some Thoughts Concerning Education* (1693), is rightly recognized for eventually playing an important role in the rise of democratizing impulses in educational theory. But this fate is an ironic one. In Locke's own time, his book was remarkable instead for the rigour with which it attacks longstanding links between gentlemen's children and their social subordinates.

Social historians argue that age is in large part an effect of culture, not biology. Consider our ideas of racial or sexual difference. They tend to be a combination of simple physical differences and the complex meanings that history and culture have given to those differences. Similarly, when we think about age, what matters is the wide range of meanings that a different set of physical differences may or may not have at a given place and time. 'Age categories are not natural,' Stephen Mintz asserts; instead, 'they are imbued with cultural assumptions, meaning, and values.'[1] Similarly, Andrea Immel and Michael Witmore point out that, in practice, age is generally understood through its close connection with other social categories: 'it is usually a bundled set of associations—childishness with, say, servitude or femininity—that structures action and perception at any given time.'[2] This essay will argue that English childhood and servitude were traditionally part of the same 'bundled set of associations'—and that in the mid-eighteenth century the new genre of children's literature began to pick this bundle apart. Locke tried to separate young gentlemen from actual servants and from servile or 'slavish' qualities of character. Borrowing some of Locke's ideas and his cultural authority, the new children's literature extended this attempt into a broader revision of childhood itself.

Although society in the United States today is far from equal, we associate adulthood with personal autonomy in everyday life, with freedom from childlike deference to the authority of others. At a minimum, for citizens today, an eighteenth birthday automatically brings an expansive set of rights. Much of our thinking about education and literacy aims to prepare young people for this sharp break with childhood, for the moment when, ready or not, they gain the legal and political autonomy of adulthood. Moreover, when we consider inequality, we tend to hope that education works against it, that school offers everyone a chance to rise. Up through the beginning of the eighteenth century, however, England was largely a paternalist society in which the great majority of people did not gain such autonomy no matter how old they became. Society was not composed of politically equal citizens but rather organized on the model of a family. A handful of gentlemen of property at the top acted with a father's authority, and everyone else—men and women, old and young—remained all their lives in the position of children, with a child's duty to obey.[3]

For instance, in 1771, an Anglican minister blandly states that most people 'must ever in a great degree be … mere children; and pay of course a due submission to the authority of their political elders.'[4] Similarly, 'The authority of fortune,' Adam Smith matter-of-factly notes in 1776, 'is very great … much greater than that either of age or of personal qualities.' According to Smith, age determines who has power over whom *only* 'among those who are in every other respect equal and among whom, therefore, there is nothing else to regulate.'[5] The flipside of the property-less person's perpetual childhood was the propertied person's early ascension to the status of 'political elder.' In 1667, a 13-year-old named Christopher Monk was elected to Parliament, served on committees, and made important floor speeches. The son of a powerful Devon family, Monk was one of a number of similarly wealthy and well-connected teen-aged MPs.[6] When property trumps age so effectively in deciding who has authority over whom, simple numerical age does not mean what we expect it to mean. *→ gender?*

Carolyn Steedman reminds us that in the eighteenth century, the relationship between master and servant was a 'great social fact … one of the most widely experienced in society.' Domestic servants were then the single largest occupational group in England. Not only were children part of the same bundle of associations as servants, but at times servants became a model for how to understand—and to legislate about—childhood. As Steedman points out, the foundational English jurist Sir William Blackstone states that the master-servant contract was the first of the 'three great relations of private life.' The other two legal relations, that between husband and wife and parent and child, were 'founded on this first and primary one.'[7]

Both childhood and servitude meant being subject to physical coercion. Authority takes many subtle forms, but in the master-servant relationship there was nothing subtle about who had the legal right to hit whom. In his *Commentaries on the Laws of England*, Blackstone sums up this aspect of the law of master and servant when he differentiates 'correction' from 'assault': 'A MASTER may by law correct his apprentice or servant for negligence or other misbehavior, so it be done with moderation … But if any servant, workman, or labourer assaults his master or dame, he shall suffer one year's imprisonment, and other open corporal punishment, not extending to life or limb.'[8] Similarly, sermons and conduct books differed over how violently a father should beat his children, but the consensus was clear that it was his duty to do so when confronted with disobedience, while the duty of a child forbade raising his hand against his father. We should remember that, in addition to domestic servants such as footmen and cooks, anyone who worked for someone else for payment traditionally fell under the law of master and servant and was subject to some extent to the paternalist implications of this relationship. It was not until 1857, for example, that a court denied an employer the right to seize and lock up a potter who wished to leave his employment.[9] Under the law of master and servant, adulthood does not mean what we now might expect it to mean.

Paternalist ideas of age included paternalist ideas of literacy. Up to the eighteenth century, education meant either the education of the soul to achieve eternal salvation, which was equally the obligation of each Christian, rich or poor—or education for life in this world, which varied radically according to one's social status. Because of their belief that all people must save their own souls through reading the Bible, the Puritans and their Dissenting heirs had a passion for literacy, and the debt children's literature owes them in this regard has been widely acknowledged.[10] It is no coincidence that the materials traditionally used to teach the basics of English literacy also taught the basics of Christianity. Locke sums them up: 'nothing that I know has been considered of this kind out of the ordinary road of the horn-book, primer, psalter, Testament, and Bible.'[11] M.O. Grenby stresses that this earliest reading cut across the usual distinctions of social status: 'Perhaps only about 50 per cent of the population were taught to read in the first half of the [eighteenth] century, but within this group rich and poor travelled along Locke's "ordinary Road" to literacy together, the great majority of them using some combination of the hornbook, primer, psalter, testament and Bible.'[12] Once basic literacy was achieved, however, young gentlemen set off on a different road entirely, embarking on a specialized education that was all about distancing them from the shared vernacular world. This education focused on the literature of a very different place, the ancient world. It consisted of learning to read, translate, and compose in Latin—and, at an even more elite level, in Greek—at an exclusive boarding school. This process was long and expensive. It began with boys as young as seven or eight, and required years of rote memorization enforced by beatings and the threat of more beatings.

The kind of gentlemanly education that Locke proposes uses new methods, but its political end remains unchanged. In his account, education is more rigorously differentiated by social status than by gender. His stated purpose is to educate 'a gentleman's son' (178), although he casually suggests that much of what he advocates may well be appropriate to a gentleman's daughter: 'where the difference of sex requires different treatment, 'twill be no hard matter to distinguish' (27). Scholars often see Locke as a democratizing force in educational history, pointing in particular to his sense of the malleability of the child's mind. Locke indeed claims that young minds are as easily turned as water or, like white paper or wax, are 'to be moulded and fashioned as one pleases' (179), and this claim does indeed, eventually, become important to democratizing or egalitarian theories about the influence of environment on individual development.[13] This impact, however, was indirect and unintentional, and made possible only through a process of reception and adaptation that Locke did not anticipate. The emergence of children's literature as a commercially viable genre played an important role in this process, as we shall see.

Some Thoughts is a rich and complex book. Locke ranges from constipation, wet feet, and cold baths to the relations between words, images, and things. He is fascinated by how the mind apprehends the world. I want to focus here, however, on two points that Locke finds particularly exasperating, and that I find particularly relevant to the history of age and reading. In Locke's opinion, gentlemen are far too quick to flog Latin into their sons, and far too slow to stop their sons from fraternizing with servants. Both of these practices contradict what Locke argues is the true end of education: the mastery of the self through reason. Flogging and fraternizing produce instead a grown man who is servile and who therefore is childish.

Some Thoughts began as a series of letters from Locke to his friend, Edward Clarke, Esquire, of Chipley, Somerset, advising Clarke on how to educate his son. 'It never occurred to him that every child should be educated or that all those to be educated should be educated alike,' Peter Gay reminds us; 'Locke addressed his little book on education to a gentleman, on the subject of the education of that gentleman's son and in the hope that other gentlemen would read it.'[14] Edward Clarke was unambiguously a gentleman,[15] born to land and power. On inheriting his estate, he distinguished himself by ornamenting the manor house's '120-foot-long north–south front with an ashlar doric frontispiece,' became an active Member of Parliament, and left about £17,000 at his death, principally in Bank and East India stock.[16]

Locke's exclusion of most children from the kind of education he outlines is based on a certain set of pedagogical and political principles. He
argues that reason is the only master a gentleman should recognize. But
while gentlemen need to learn how to be ruled by reason, everyone else
needs to learn how to be ruled by gentlemen. Locke does not see literacy
as a universal perquisite for citizenship or a tool for rising to a higher position in society. Rather, he believes that children are generally born to the
social positions they should occupy in life. And as the ones who 'bring all
the rest into order,' those born to the position of gentleman are of primary
importance to England: 'that most to be taken care of is the gentleman's
calling. For if those of that rank are by their education once set right, they
will quickly bring all the rest into order' (24). He aims to teach young
gentlemen how to gain control of the body's impulses through reason
because the future masters of England must first learn to master their own
fear of pain and attraction to pleasure: 'the great principle and foundation
of all virtue and worth is placed in this, that a man is able to deny himself
his own desires, cross his own inclinations, and purely follow what reason
directs as best, though the appetite lean the other way' (29).

In 'An Essay on the Poor Law,' Locke offers his recommendations for
what to do with children at the lower end of the social scale. He argues
that by the age of three the children of the working poor should properly
be seen as small labourers. Their status as workers shapes his understanding of their numerical age. Indeed, he is a reformer only in taking this
principle farther than was customary. Twelve or 14, the usual age to begin
working, is to Locke's mind far too old: the 'children of labouring people
are an ordinary burden to the parish, and are usually maintained in idleness,
so that their labour is also generally lost to the public till they are 12 or
14 years old':

> we therefore humbly propose ... working schools be set up in each parish,
> to which children of all such as demand relief of the parish, above 3 and
> under 14 years of age, whilst they live at home with their parents, and are
> not otherwise employed for their livelihood by the allowance of the over-
> seers of the poor, shall be obliged to come.[17]

The bodies and minds of these children would be 'inured' early to the
physical labour that is their destiny in life: they would 'from infancy be
inured to work, which is of no small consequence to the making of them
sober and industrious all their lives after' (190). Although Locke calls the

institutions he proposes 'working schools,' what he describes are factories filled with workers ranging from 3 to 13 years old. He admits that the very youngest children are unlikely to be efficient workers at first. Nevertheless, he imagines that as a group, the children will be productive enough to pay for their own bread, water, and gruel, 'with an overplus' that will profit the parish (192). In the fantasy of economically profitable tots that Locke indulges in here, the social reality of 12- and 14-year-old labourers that he takes for granted, and the education for young gentlemen that he outlines, age does not work as we expect it to. In Mintz's words, it is shaped by the 'cultural assumptions, meaning, and values' of Locke's own time and social position.

My point here is not that Locke was elitist or inhumane. As Natasha Gill demonstrates, scholars have long wrestled with the paradox that Locke 'opened the door to the idea of universal education' by describing the child's mind as malleable even as he 'denied the application of this idea.' Moreover, achieving anything close to real equality in education remains a 'central dilemma' today, long after Locke.[18] The point I wish to focus on here, rather, is that that the poor are not in fact as neatly quarantined from Locke's ideas of gentlemanly education as the stark differences between *Some Thoughts* and 'An Essay on the Poor Law' might at first suggest. For example, Gay claims that 'as for the poor, they do not appear in Locke's little book at all.'[19] However, the poor do appear in *Some Thoughts*. They are present in Locke's little book just as they were present in Edward Clarke's household: in the person of servants. As Carolyn Steedman has pointed out, servants in the long eighteenth century are often overlooked, but always essential. And they are surprisingly troublesome to their masters.[20]

The greatest obstacle to teaching young gentlemen to obey their reason rather than their appetites, according to Locke, is the fact that a gentleman's children spend their days with his servants, who do not act according to reason: 'The great difficulty here is, I imagine, from the folly and perverseness of servants, who are hardly to be hindered from crossing herein the design of the father and mother.' Education in reason is undone by 'the caresses of those foolish flatterers' (41). Although he is clear that servants are a terrible influence, Locke is much less clear about how this influence is to be countered: 'But how this inconvenience from servants is to be remedied, I can only leave to parents' care and consideration. Only I think it of great importance; and that they are very happy, who can get discreet people about their children' (42).

Perhaps the most dramatic example of how servants undermine the power of reason is fear of the dark. For Locke, this fear is not a natural human trait, but rather a sure sign that servants have infected a child's mind with their favourite superstitions:

> be sure to preserve his tender mind from all impressions and notions of spirits and goblins, or any fearful apprehensions in the dark. It being the usual method of servants to awe children, and keep them in subjection, by telling them of Raw-Head and Bloody-Bones, and such other names, as carry with them the ideas of some hurtful, terrible things inhabiting darkness, this must be carefully prevented. (106)

Locke returns to the claim that servants control gentlemen's children through fear of unreal things:

> I think it inconvenient that their yet tender minds should receive early impressions of *goblins, spectres,* and *apparitions,* wherewith their maids and those about them are apt to fright them into a compliance with their orders, which often proves a great inconvenience to them all their lives after, by subjecting their minds to frights, fearful apprehensions, weakness and superstition.... (160, emphasis in original)

When darkness falls 'all their lives after,' the minds of such gentlemen reveal themselves to be weak, fearful, and irrational, the minds of servants or children.

The more Locke considers the problem of servants, the less hopeful he becomes about solving it:

> [A gentleman's children] are wholly, if possible, to be kept from such conversation: for the contagion of these ill precedents, both in civility and virtue, horribly infects children, as often as they come within reach of it.... 'Tis a hard matter wholly to prevent this mischief. You will have very good luck, if you never have a clownish or vicious servant, and if from them your children never get any infection. (48)

Locke's book as a whole is an upbeat exhortation to leave absolutely nothing in education to 'good luck,' so his sense of defeat on this point is striking: 'In the whole business of education, there is nothing like to be less hearkened to, or harder to be well observed' than preserving children from bad company, he notes glumly (71).

Locke rouses himself to offer a few practical suggestions for limiting the infection of servants' company, proposing instead the novel idea that children should spend their time in the company of their parents: 'But yet, as much must be done towards it, as can be … to make them in love with the company of their parents, they should receive all their good things there, and from their hands' (48–49). But he feels no confidence in his own advice: 'Having named company, I am almost ready to throw away my pen, and trouble you no farther on this subject. For since that does more than all precepts, rules, and instructions, methinks 'tis almost wholly in vain to make a long discourse of other things, and to talk of that almost to no purpose' (49). Although he does not quite throw away his pen, at this point Locke interrupts himself by imagining a hypothetical gentleman who protests against being oppressed by the company of his son: 'For you will be ready to say, What shall I do with my son? If I keep him always at home, he will be in danger to be my young master …' (49).

To solve this problem, Locke advises elite parents to pay whatever it costs to secure a supremely virtuous and attentive tutor to live with their son. Rather than teaching any particular body of knowledge, this tutor will cultivate intellectual curiosity and critical thinking: 'his business is not so much to teach [his student] all that is knowable, as to raise in him a love and esteem of knowledge; and to put him in the right way of knowing and improving himself when he has a mind to it' (164). This kind of teaching is a more labour-intensive business than instruction in Greek or Latin. It requires constant close observation of the individual student and exquisite responsiveness to his strengths and weaknesses:

> He therefore that is about children should well study their natures and aptitudes, and see by often trials what turn they easily take, and what becomes them; observe what their native stock is, how it may be improv'd, and what it is fit for; he should consider what they want, whether they be capable of having it wrought into them by industry, and incorporated there by practice; and whether it be worthwhile to endeavor it. (46)

Although children's minds are malleable, it seems Locke is aware that in practice what can be 'wrought into them' has its limits and varies according to individual 'natures and aptitudes.' This version of elite education differed sharply from the rote memorization of Christian basics, even more sharply than did the young gentleman's traditional rote memorization of the classics. That is, Locke does not think of reading as a skill that must be gained so that a crucial mass of information—either God's commandments or the Latin grammar—could be memorized, but rather as part of the developing 'capacity' of the individual young mind.

Elite parents who fail to engage such a tutor will be obliged to fall back on boarding school to save their sons from their servants. And Locke has very little good to say about this traditional method of breeding up gentlemen. He acknowledges that there is no doing without Latin: 'Latin I look upon as absolutely necessary to a gentleman,' he acknowledges (126). Like later social historians, however, Locke seems to see Latin as 'absolutely necessary' more as a marker of status than as training for the mind. Social historians argue that a shared familiarity with these elite texts marked gentlemanly status. Although classical learning is the hallmark of a gentleman, Locke claims that it is of little use to him in any other way: 'Latin and learning make all the noise,' he writes, 'and the main stress is laid upon his proficiency in things a great part whereof belong not to a gentleman's calling; which is to have the knowledge of a man of business, a carriage suitable to his rank, and to be eminent and useful in his country, according to his station' (75).

In our imaginary bookstore representing the eighteenth-century book market, Latin and Greek texts occupy the shelves of honour in the section for masters of all ages.[21] Whether or not a gentleman continued to read Virgil once he left school, there was no literature for him to grow into as he aged that was considered better or more 'adult' than the classics he had first encountered as a schoolboy. The Latin authors a public schoolboy first read at 7 or 8 years old were what, in principle, he ought still to be reading at 70 or 80, together, perhaps, with vernacular works of history, political philosophy, and poetry.

While Locke admits 'there is no doing without Latin' for these reasons, the way boys traditionally learn Latin and Greek—memorization enforced by beatings—contradicts the central principle that he advocates for elite education, government of the self through reason. He argues it is time to stop flogging young gentlemen, declaring that 'the usual lazy and short way [of teaching] by chastisement and the rod, which is the only instrument of government that tutors generally know, or ever think of, is the most unfit of any to be us'd in education' (36). Because it depends on fear of pain, education through flagellation works against the cultivation of reason: 'This kind of punishment contributes not at all to the mastery of our natural propensity to indulge corporal and present pleasure, and to avoid pain at any rate, but rather encourages it ...'(36). Locke complains that he 'can hardly forbear thinking that the parents of children still live in fear of the school-master's rod, which they look on as the only instrument of education; as a language or two to be its whole business.' Paradoxically, parents who support traditional elite education are themselves childlike and servile: they 'still live in fear of the school-master's rod' (114).

Because the rejection of corporeal punishment has become a commonplace of liberal childrearing and education, I want to stress the ideas about age and authority that shape Locke's own position. The problem with beating these particular schoolboys is that they are not supposed to grow up into the sort of men who remain subject to regular beatings. That is, Locke rejects the practice of flogging elite schoolboys, not because it is developmentally inappropriate for children as a group, but rather because beating is appropriate to servants, not to masters. 'Such a sort of slavish discipline makes a slavish temper,' he warns (37). Locke stresses that 'beating them, and all other sorts of slavish and corporal punishments, are not the discipline fit to be used in the education of those we would have wise, good, and ingenuous men' (37). Like fraternizing with servants, flagellation creates a servile and, therefore, a permanently childish mind.

Alexander Pope points to this same tension within a traditional public school education when he describes Members of Parliament as whipped schoolboys in his *Dunciad*. The target of Pope's satire is the limitations of contemporary scholarship, but in the course of attacking the intellectual dullness of his time, he enjoys unmanning 'Westminster's bold race' by calling up the spectre of a flagellating school-master. Like the unreasonable and childish parents Locke criticizes, Pope's MPs still live in fear of the school-master's rod:

When lo! a spectre rose, whose index-hand
Held forth the virtue of the dreadful wand;   *140*
His beaver'd brow a birchen garland wears,
Dropping with infants' blood and mothers' tears.
O'er ev'ry vein a shudd'ring horror runs,
Eton and Winton shake thro' all their sons.
All flesh is humbled, Westminster's bold race   *145*
Shrink, and confess the Genius of the place:
The pale boy-senator yet tingling stands,
And holds his breeches close with both his hands.

While Pope wants to humiliate the old boys of Eton and Winchester by reminding them of how they were once flogged, Locke wants to preserve

the dignity of the young gentleman's mind and body from such experiences.[22] 'All flesh is humbled' by beating or the memory of beating, Pope
claims, but Locke argues that such humiliation is appropriate only to those
born to a humble station in life.

In contrast to *Some Thoughts'* recommendation to stop beating gentlemen's sons, Locke's 'Essay on the Poor Laws' enthusiastically supports
beating the children of the poor: 'If any boy or girl, under 14 years of age,
shall be found begging out of the parish where they dwell (if within five
miles distance of the said parish), they shall be sent to the next working
school, there to be soundly whipped, and kept at work till evening' (187).
Beating is the remedy not only for poor children who beg in the wrong
places, but also for those who beg 'at any other hour than those allowed':
'they shall be sent immediately, if they are under 14 years of age, to the
working school to be whipped' (198). For Locke, flagellation is the perfect form of discipline for those who must remain in a childlike state of
subordination throughout their lives.

Locke's complaints about servants were not new. Educational theorists
had lamented long and ineffectually the fact that the children of elite families were brought up by their servants. In his 1570 *The Scholemaster*, for
example, Roger Ascham describes meeting a gentleman's four-year-old
son who knows no prayers but many curse words, a sure sign that he has
been not only living among servants but also learning from them: 'This
Child using much the company of serving men, and giving good ear to
their talk, did easily learn, which he shall hardly forget, all days of his life
hereafter.'[23] In the eighteenth century, however, the emergence of a children's book market would provide a wealth of images, stories, and direct
instructions that promoted a new answer to elite parents' question of what
they should do with their children. This market would re-envision parents
themselves—particularly mothers—as Locke's ideal tutor, and family life
as an extended educational enterprise.[24] In doing so, it would identify elite
children as a certain kind of consumer, separate at last from servants and
other semi-literate readers. To return to the image of the eighteenth-
century book market with which this essay began, this way of thinking
would add, at last, a separate children's section to the shop, one carefully
roped off from all other readers.

In Locke's time, neither gentlemen nor ordinary people moved through
a deliberately constructed hierarchy of age-levelled vernacular fiction,
starting with stories written specially for the very young and culminating
in 'adult' novels, as students do today. This does not mean, however, that

children read nothing but primers, the Bible, and Greek and Latin classics. As part of his call to break with 'old custom' (179), Locke urges that the young gentleman be supplied with 'some easy pleasant book, suited to his capacity' because such children are instead amusing themselves with 'useless trumpery [full of] vice and folly.' Cheap, flashy, vicious, and quite possibly superstitious, these trumpery books sound like a certain kind of reading that servants and masters—especially young masters—both enjoyed: the chapbook. Small and flimsy, crudely printed and illustrated, and remarkably cheap (some cost as little as a penny), chapbooks featured old chivalric romances, bawdy tales, crude jokes, and fairy tales, which themselves often contained generous amounts of sex and violence.

Sold by a network of travelling packmen largely based in London, chapbooks were considered 'hopelessly plebian.'[25] To return to our imaginary eighteenth-century bookshop, these tiny pamphlets (4 × 6 inches or smaller) would load the shelves of the section marked 'Everybody Else.' They were priced to be affordable to working people. Eventually, this lowness helped make the chapbook suspect reading for a new kind of child. As Andrew O'Malley argues, it was the chapbook's 'plebeian fantasies of miraculous social advancement, its subversions of the social order, and its unrepentant portrayals of drunken ribaldry and even criminal activity that middle-class pedagogues of the late eighteenth century considered so potentially vicious an influence on their young.'[26] Earlier, however, chapbooks were typical childhood reading. Through the early eighteenth century, they were 'commonly used by middle- and upper-class families as their children's first books.'[27] That is, rather than reading different sets of works specialized to fit the different interest of adults and children, or their different psychological and intellectual stages of development, semiliterate people of all ages read the same accessible, exciting, trashy little books. In a gentleman's household in 1693, the master's heir and his servants might be reading the same chapbook.

These are the ideas of age, status, and reading that Locke takes on in *Some Thoughts Concerning Education*. Having struggled to separate the gentleman's child from his servants and from the kind of discipline that is proper to servants, Locke proceeds to the problem of separating this child from the servants' books. He claims that learning should be fun, but it must be the right kind of fun:

> When by these gentle ways he begins to read, some easy pleasant book, suited to his capacity, should be put into his hands, wherein the entertainment

that he finds might draw him on, and reward his pains in reading, and yet not such as should fill his head with perfectly useless trumpery, or lay the principles of vice and folly.

As we have noted, the 'perfectly useless trumpery' and 'vice and folly' that Locke rejects here suggest the kind of fun traditionally found in superstitious, sensational chapbooks. This description of abundant and silly books suggests the wealth of popular reading traditionally associated with semiliterate people such as servants and children:

> What other books there are in English of the kind of those above-mentioned, fit to engage the liking of children, and tempt them to read, I do not know: but am apt to think, that ... this sort of useful books, amongst the number of silly ones that are of all sorts, have yet had the fate to be neglected. (156)

In reimagining education, Locke rejects the opposition of gentlemanly classics and plebian chapbooks of his own day in favour of age-levelled reading, the foundation of children's literature today.

Locke describes the gentleman's son in terms of developmental stages leading to an adulthood defined by rational self-mastery. To do so, I have argued, he must attack more traditional ideas about age categories. To give primary importance to the development of mental and psychological 'capacity,' Locke must separate ideas about numerical age from traditional ideas about status. A child defined in terms of steady progress through a series of well-established intellectual and psychological stages is a very different kind of person than a child defined in terms of paternalism's life-long social hierarchy.[28]

Such change did not happen overnight. Separating childhood and its proper reading from servants and their reading took longer than Locke hoped, and came about through larger social changes than he could imagine. Although *Some Thoughts Concerning Education* was widely praised, the print landscape that it describes did not change much for half a century. Individual parenting varied, but as a class, aristocratic parents did not throng to shops full of easy, pleasant books for young readers any more than they stopped leaving their children with their servants or packing them off to boarding school. For decades, there was no commercially viable response to Locke's call to turn elite infancy, early childhood, and youth into a very long and intensive tutorial experience closely supervised by a superhumanly even-tempered and vigilant adult, one armed with a wealth of age-appropriate playthings and reading materials. Young masters continued to grow up on a combination of gentlemanly classics and the plebian popular reading consumed by readers all ages.

However, in the 1740s, a wave of publishers—including John Newbery, who invoked the authority of 'the great *Mr. Locke*'—began to cater to a new demographic: the middle-class child reader. That is, the kind of reading Locke called for appears as a commercially successful genre only half a century or so after his death in 1704, produced for a kind of people he never knew: England's rising middle class. The emergence of children's literature as a 'distinct and secure branch of print culture' depended on many factors, as Grenby has noted. In addition to the tastes and reading habits of the individual child readers that Grenby seeks to recover, his list of key factors includes 'enterprising entrepreneurs, talented authors and illustrators, and technological innovations … also shifting cultural constructions of childhood, demographic changes, and socio-economic transformations' (1). Not having inherited anything close to Edward Clarke's Chipley estate, middle-class parents were not the audience Locke had in mind. Nevertheless, they aspired to the status of gentlemen and gentlewomen, and this aspiration helped make them central to the market for children's literature: 'most anecdotal evidence suggests that the new children's literature of the Newbery era was purchased by what we can think of as the upper middle class' (76).

Grenby stresses the care with which the new genre positioned itself in terms of social status. Newbery and his rivals criticized well-off parents whose children still followed older, promiscuous reading habits: 'the offending titles were usually novels, chapbooks or fairy tales, publications not designed especially for children' (265). A story about good children being rewarded by a visit to Mr. Alphabet's bookstore for children at St. Paul's Church-Yard puffed Newbery's shop, presenting it as an 'attractive and respectable place' (147). These books promoted themselves and each other; more broadly, however, they promoted the new category of literature exclusively for children. As Heather Klemann points out, in contrast to traditional chapbooks, Newbery's books are 'self-referentially [codified] as virtuous objects in his stories, imbuing with moral virtue the act of sharing and reading these books.'[29]

Even once these changes were in motion, however, age and social status remained blurry categories when it came to eighteenth-century reading. The middle-class child reader emerges clearly, but the rest of the reading world and the fiction it enjoyed remained less rigorously divided by age than it is today. Childishness and low social status remained linked in many general discussions of novel-reading and pleasure. Even Locke does not see books for children and books for adults as totally separate. Although he rejects chapbooks, he wants young gentlemen to continue reading one traditional and accessible kind of story: the fable. Locke's point is that although children's literature must be adapted to a child's capacities, it must not be childish. We now associate didacticism, in one form or another, most strongly with children's literature. Although we are more likely to talk about role models than morals, we still hope children's books will teach useful lessons. The distinction is far from absolute, but today 'adult' novels—at least elite literary ones—are more free to end ambiguously, for example, with good intentions overwhelmed by unforgiving environments or an irresolvable moral quandary.[30] For Locke, however, a clear didactic message about virtue rewarded or vice punished is what raises entertaining fiction above the level of servants' trash—for readers of all ages. A didactic message, relevant to old and young, elevates the time-honoured best-seller *Aesop's Fables* above mere entertainment:

> To this purpose, I think Aesop's Fables the best, which being stories apt to delight and entertain a child, may yet afford useful reflections to a grown man; and if his memory retain them all his life after, he will not repent to find them there, amongst his manly thoughts and serious business. (116)

Aesop and the fables of Reynard the Fox are at once easy, pleasant, and conducive to manly thoughts. That is, here the father of age-levelled reading argues that moral fables are good for a young gentleman because they are also appropriate to a grown gentleman, one immersed in manly thoughts and serious business.

In 1744, John Newbery followed Locke's lead on didacticism, as well as cashing in on the still massive prestige of the classics, when he gave his landmark children's book, *A Little Pretty Pocket-Book*, a motto borrowed from Horace: *Delectando Monemus*, 'Instruction with Delight.' Similarly, *Rambler* No. 4, Dr. Samuel Johnson's famous 1750 essay on novels, shares a version of the same Horatian epigraph: 'And join profit and delight in one.' Although Johnson sees young people as central to the novel's audience, this motto sums up his idea of what good novels should do for readers of all ages. For Johnson as for Locke, good fiction is by definition didactic: 'These books are written chiefly to the young, the ignorant, and the idle, to whom they serve as lectures of conduct, and introductions into life.'[31]

In promoting children's literature as a commercially viable genre, John Newbery did not merely call attention to the natural developmental needs of the child reader. Rather, like the great Mr. Locke himself, he helped to distinguish ideas about numerical age from ideas about social subordination. To some extent, however, age and social status remain 'bundled' together even today. Locke's contemporaries tended to think of unequal social status as a natural and compelling way of organizing their world. They often describe relations between old and young people along the lines of relations between those of high and low social position. The reverse may be true for us, as Beverley Lyon Clarke has pointed out.[32] When reviewers today praise an elite literary work as showing a truly 'adult' understanding of life, or damn a popular one for childishness, they are in part using a language of psychological age difference, a language that we find natural and compelling, to describe the differences in education and literacy that accompany differences in status in an unequal society.

NOTES

1. Steven Mintz, 'Reflections on Age as a Category of Historical Analysis,' *Journal of the History of Childhood and Youth* 1 (2008): 5.
2. Andrea Immel and Michael Witmore, 'Introduction,' in *Childhood and Children's Books in Early Modern Europe*, eds. Andrea Immel and Michael Witmore (New York: Routledge, 2006), 5.
3. For a fuller discussion of the disconnect between chronological age and the 'childishness' of servitude, see Philippe Ariès's *Centuries of Childhood: A Social History of Family Life* (New York: Vintage Books, 1965) and the Introduction to Teresa Michals, *Books for Children, Books for Adults: Age and the Novel from Defoe to James* (Cambridge: Cambridge University Press, 2014).
4. Quoted in Holly Brewer, *By Birth or Consent: Children, Law, and the Anglo-American Revolution in Authority* (Chapel Hill: U North Carolina Press, 2005), 107.
5. Adam Smith, *An Inquiry into the Nature and Causes of the Wealth of Nations* (Oxford: Clarendon Press, 1976), vol. I, 2.
6. Keith Thomas, *Age and Authority in Early Modern England* (London: Oxford University Press, 1976), 231.
7. Carolyn Steedman, 'Servants and Their Relation to the Unconscious,' *Journal of British Studies* 42 (2003): 320.

8. Sir William Blackstone, *Commentaries on the Laws of England: In Four Books* (Chicago: University of Chicago Press, 1979, 1765), Book 1, Chap. 14 'Of Master and Servant,' 416.

9. Robert J. Steinfeld, *The Invention of Free Labor: The Employment Relation in English and American Law and Culture, 1350–1870* (Chapel Hill: University of North Carolina Press, 1991), 18.

10. On the connection between Protestantism and literacy, see, for example, C. John Sommerville, *The Discovery of Childhood in Puritan England* (Athens: University of Georgia Press, 1992).

11. John Locke, *Some Thoughts Concerning Education*, ed. John Adamson (NY: Dover, 2007), 156. Further references are made parenthetically and are to this edition.

12. M.O. Grenby, *The Child Reader 1700–1840*, Cambridge: Cambridge University Press (2011), 70. Further references will be made parenthetically.

13. On Locke's complex relationship to existing educational theorists, and his distinctive cultural impact, see Margaret Ezell, 'John Locke's Images of Childhood: Early Eighteenth Century Response to *Some Thoughts Concerning Education*,' *Eighteenth-Century Studies* 17 (1983): 139–155.

14. Peter Gay, 'Locke on the Education of Paupers,' in *Philosophers on Education*, ed. Amélie Rorty (Routledge, 1998), 189.

15. See Adriana Benzaquén's 'Pray lett none see this impertinent Epistle': Children's Letters and Children in Letters at the Turn of the Eighteenth Century' in this volume for a discussion of the Clarke family.

16. 'Edward Clarke,' *Oxford Dictionary of National Biography*, and *History of Parliament Online*.

17. *Locke: Political Essays*. ed. Mark Goldie (Cambridge: Cambridge University Press, 1997), 190. Further references are to this text and are given parenthetically.

18. Natasha Gill, *Educational Philosophy in the French Enlightenment: From Nature to Second Nature* (Routledge, 2016).

19. Gay, 'Locke on the Education of Paupers,' 189.

20. See, for example, Carolyn Steedman, *Labours Lost: Domestic Service and the Making of Modern England* (Cambridge: Cambridge University Press, 2009).

21. John Chandos notes the survival of this principle well into the nineteenth century: 'What a classical education was designed to do was to forge a bond of shared thought, sensibility and manners between gentlemen of all ranks, uniting in one caste—the caste of a gentleman—nobility, gentry, and their kin, the professional classes, requisite to the ordering of society.' John Chandos, *Boys Together: 1800–1864* (New Haven: Yale University Press, 1984), 32.

22. Alexander Pop, *The Dunciad* (Auckland, New Zealand: The Floating Press, 2016), 47.
23. Roger Ascham, *The Schoolmaster: Or, a Plain and Perfect Way of Teaching Children to Understand, Write, and Speak the Latin Tongue* (London: Cassell &Co., 1895), 53.
24. On the mother as a kind of quasi-professional educator, see Mitzi Myers, 'Impeccable Governesses, Rational Dames, and Moral Mothers: Mary Wollstonecraft and the Female Tradition in Georgian Children's Books.' *Children's Literature* 14, 1 (1986): 31–59.
25. On chapbooks and their audiences, and their relation to the new children's literature of the eighteenth century, see William St. Clair, *The Reading Nation in the Romantic Period* (Cambridge: Cambridge University Press, 2004); M.O. Grenby, 'Before Children's Literature: Children, Chapbooks and Popular Culture in Early Modern Britain,' in *Childhood and Children's Books in Early Modern Europe*, eds. Andrea Immel and Michael Witmore (New York: Routledge 2006), 25–46, and Bennett A. Brockman, 'Robin Hood and the Invention of Children's Literature,' *Children's Literature: Annual of the Modern Language Association Division on Children's Literature and The Children's Literature Association* 10 (1982): 5.
26. Andrew O'Malley, 'The Coach and Six: Chapbook Residue in Late Eighteenth-Century Children's Literature,' *The Lion and the Unicorn* 24 (2000): 20. See also Andrew O'Malley, *The Making of the Modern Child* (New York: Routledge, 2003) and *Children's Literature, Popular Culture, and Robinson Crusoe* (New York: Palgrave Macmillan, 2012).
27. Gary Kelly, 'Introduction' to *Street Gothic: Female Gothic Chapbooks*, vol. II of *Varieties of Female Gothic*, general ed. Gary Kelly, 6 vols. (Pickering and Chatto, 2002), xi.
28. On the eventual link between this idea of individual human development and stadial theories of society's development that were popular in the Enlightenment, see Ann Wierda Rowland's *Romanticism and Childhood: The Infantilization of British Literary Culture* (Cambridge: Cambridge University Press, 2012).
29. Heather Klemann, 'The Matter of Moral Education: Locke, Newbery, and the Didactic Toy-Book Hybrid,' *Eighteenth-Century Studies* 44 (2011): 225.
30. On this point, see Beverly Lyons Clark, *Kiddie Lit: The Cultural Construction of Children's Literature in America* (Baltimore and London: Johns Hopkins UP, 2003); and Teresa Michals, *Books for Children, Books for Adults*.
31. Samuel Johnson, *Dr. Johnson's Works*, ed. Arthur Murphy. Oxford English Classics (New York: AMS Press, 1970), vol. iv, 175.
32. Beverly Lyon Clark, *Kiddie Lit: The Cultural Construction of Children's Literature in America* (Baltimore: Johns Hopkins University Press, 2003).

CHAPTER 3

Circulating Childhood in Eighteenth-Century England: The Cultural Work of Periodicals

Anja Müller

INTRODUCTION

The following chapter seeks to gauge the contribution of eighteenth-century English periodicals to the circulation of ideas about childhood. Without a doubt, these early mass media were instrumental for the formation of tastes and the shaping of English morals, manners, political convictions, and mentalities.[1] The enormous success of Joseph Addison and Richard Steele's collaborative productions *The Tatler*, *The Spectator*, and *The Guardian* (all published between 1709 and 1714)[2] is also reflected in the various imitations they inspired (among them *The Female Tatler* and Eliza Haywood's *The Female Spectator*).[3] Each of these periodicals addresses to a considerable extent topics connected with childhood, such as family values, the relationship between parents and children, child care or educational matters. Featuring not only child-related topics but also children in their exemplary tales, the periodicals identify childhood as a highly relevant topic for English society. In an earlier monograph (Müller 2009),

A. Müller (✉)
University of Siegen, Siegen, Germany
e-mail: anja.mueller@anglistik.uni-siegen.de

© The Author(s) 2018
A. O'Malley (ed.), *Literary Cultures and Eighteenth-Century
Childhoods*, Literary Cultures and Childhoods,
https://doi.org/10.1007/978-3-319-94737-2_3

I explored in detail the role of those early printed mass media in establishing a veritable discourse on childhood in eighteenth-century England. Informed by Foucauldian theories of discourse, knowledge, and power, I argued that a major function of those periodicals was to convey and popularize ideologies of childhood that were mostly shared by and supported the moral claims of the rising middle classes.[4] The perspective of this earlier study was therefore framed by the questions of what kind of childhood was constructed in eighteenth-century English periodicals and by the possible motivations and purposes behind this construction. Accordingly, the child and childhood were perceived in those texts as social units. The periodicals themselves obviously appeared to perform ideological work, instilling attitudes towards childhood among their readers that should hitherto be regarded as normative. However, the very frequency of admonitions and criticism those periodicals voice about the many existing practices that deviate from the rules they seek to establish raise at least some doubts about the pervasive efficiency of this ideologizing. If the actual ideological effect of eighteenth-century periodicals cannot ultimately be gauged, what can we, then, say about the function and role of those still highly popular texts?

The present chapter approaches this question by taking its cue from some assumptions of Bruno Latour's actor-network theory (henceforth abbreviated as ANT). Eschewing a search for strategies and causalities behind the childhood construct conveyed in eighteenth-century English periodicals, I intend to do something fairly simple, yet nonetheless thoroughly relevant: I will enquire into the dynamics of the cultural work performed by those periodicals when circulating information about childhood as facts and truths. To this end, the periodicals mentioned above will be treated as agents in their own right, instead of mere printed matter employed by Addison and Steele to voice their Whiggish middle-class opinions.[5] Since periodicals do affect the behaviour of their readers, or at least purport to do so, a claim for their agency is certainly justified. One can assume that the cultural work of early eighteenth-century periodicals consists in offering thick descriptions of imagined actors—among them children and parents. In order to assess this work, it is necessary to describe, in turn, these descriptions. As a consequence, I am going to examine different levels on which the circulation of childhood concepts operates in the periodicals in question. After a brief introduction to the core concepts and terminology of Latour's ANT, I shall first assess a selection of tales and reflections on family relationships, as an example of fictional actor networks involving children and childhood, which both—as will be demonstrated—can be treated as actors or actants according to ANT. From these case studies, I will proceed to look at how the periodicals' narrators themselves reflect on the function of the texts they inhabit. These observations on the periodicals' self-reflexive stance will finally lead to a general conclusion drawn about the function of periodicals as actors in an actor network construing childhood. I shall argue that the cultural work of early eighteenth-century English periodicals emerges as that of a mediator for the circulation of a childhood concept which has enjoyed a considerable durability right up to our present time through the constant repetition of its pattern.

A Brief Introduction to ANT Terminology

Before engaging with the periodicals themselves, a few words need to be said to clarify the terminology of my theoretical framework, because Bruno Latour's use of the terms "actor" and "network"—as, for instance, outlined in his seminal *Reassembling the Social* (2005)—is not entirely congruent with our everyday use of these words. Latour does not restrict the notion of an actor to human or even animate beings: '[A]ny thing that does modify a state of affairs by making a difference is an actor–or, if it has no figuration yet, an actant.'[6] Hence, the decisive question identifying an actor is: 'Does it [the actor] make a difference in the course of some other agent's action or not?'[7] An actor, therefore, can never be alone in acting—quite like an actor on stage, who requires fellow actors, props, and an audience with and to which to perform. Nor is an actor simply the 'source of an action but the moving target of a vast array of entities swarming towards it' as well (46). Actors are thus defined by their relationships to and with other actors and, most importantly, by effecting a transformation of sorts in the course of that encounter. Agency eventually consists in producing such transformations (52).

Moreover, Latour distinguishes between what he calls intermediaries and mediators. Whereas an intermediary 'transports meaning or force without transformation [so that] defining its input is enough to define its output,' mediators have a transformative effect, modifying 'the meaning or the elements they are supposed to carry' (39). As a result, the output they produce is unpredictable.[8] With regard to these core elements, Latour's view of what is perceived as a 'social unit' is largely characterized by associations and relationships, because the actors assembling into the social will inevitably have to establish attachments and interact in such a transformative, modifying manner.[9] In other words, they establish actor networks.

'Everything and everyone is profoundly relational'[10]—this quintessential statement of ANT, which regards itself as 'fundamentally a theory of relationality,'[11] contains a number of premises and consequences that will be helpful for analysing the circulation of concepts of childhood in eighteenth-century periodicals. All contributors to interactions in this network, be they persons, media, or concepts, are actants or actors with their own agency, with their different forms of material appearance or history.[12] If we take this into account, periodicals (or literature at large) can certainly be considered to be such actors. They are neither mere projection screens of writers' opinions, nor do they simply repeat or reiterate what is sometimes referred to as hegemonic discourse. By viewing eighteenth-century periodicals as actors *sensu* Latour, one can instead appreciate the transformative impact and cultural work performed by these texts through their own agency—a work the outcome of which is essentially unpredictable.

Before commenting on this unpredictability, it is important to keep in mind that actor networks exist only in performance. Actors become visible only when their performance is being observed. Networks always construct their objects and, with them, their participants, too.[13] By analysing and describing the attachments, relations, and transformations between the actors in a network, ANT can help to gauge 'knowledge circulation as the process through which the social construction of truths takes place.'[14] These 'truths' emerge 'by travelling through networks in patterned ways that imbue the piece of knowledge with authority and relevance.'[15] In other words: An actor network acquires stability if its performances are recurrently repeated in patterns. The success of such networking is manifest in the number of actors a network can mobilize and absorb. The larger a network, the more effort it takes to alter its course and to challenge the 'truths' it produces—thus, 'the more *real* it appears and the lesser the chances that attempts to subvert it will arise, or, if they do, will be successful.'[16]

It ought to be clear by now that applying such a conception of dynamic social processes can prove fruitful for studying historical conceptualizations of childhood. Besides, analysing the circulation of such concepts in literary texts such as eighteenth-century periodicals may add a new dimension to previous studies that were concerned with identifying the discourses, causalities, and ideologies presumably underlying childhood concepts, yet never could satisfyingly explain them entirely. An ANT approach at first sight pursues a modest goal, as it seeks to identify the actors involved and to describe the attachments they form. Yet as soon as one considers the many actors involved in the actor network(s) constructing childhood in the eighteenth century, such a modest endeavour soon proves to be quite vast. My chapter will therefore restrict itself to a limited selection of actors as well as to a comparatively tiny section of the childhood actor network. Of the periodicals mentioned above, I shall particularly refer to *The Spectator, The Female Spectator, The Guardian*, and *The Female Tatler*. I scrutinize these texts for passages representing the fictional actor networks these periodicals present when commenting on family relationships. My aim is to identify the actors involved, their relationships, and—finally—to examine how the periodicals include themselves as actors in this actor network.

Fictional Actor Networks in Eighteenth-Century Periodicals: A Case Study of Family Relations

The periodicals mentioned above teem with fictional accounts of family relations. For the conceptualization of childhood, these family fictions are integral, because, as I have contended elsewhere, '[w]ithin the family the child becomes the object through which the family manifests itself and by which it asserts its function.'[17] Since the family is a relational pattern in itself, constituted by attachments of various sorts and quality, it is certainly an ideal test case to probe the applicability of ANT for our purpose. In fact, when looking at the examined periodicals, the family features as a veritable actor network constructing both the (nuclear) family and the child within the larger actor network of childhood.[18] Within this actor network, several actors and attachments are clearly identifiable and receive a stable, authoritative meaning through constant repetition.

One crucial actor in the actor network of the family is parental care, since parental care is essential for circulating the concept of the affectionate family. The relations and attachments between the actors in the network are, consequently, defined by mutual affection, gratitude, care, and love rather than genealogically determined blood relationships. Indeed, the affectionate family seems to be a particularly suitable pattern to conceive of the family as an actor network in the first place. After all, it requires mutually transformative actions among the family members, thus perceiving parents (both as a unit and in their distinct roles as father or mother) and children as actors.

According to an exemplary tale in issue number 14 of *The Guardian* (27 March 1713), about two sons of noble parents who are largely left to their own devices, the transformative effect of parental care including a rational education is nothing less but humanization, quenching or at least curbing 'the Animal Life' in the children. Issue number 189 of *The Spectator* (6 October 1711), for instance, describes how the favours, love, and care parents bestow on their children ought to produce, on the one hand, an affective, relational bonding between those actors and—more importantly—a modification in children's attitudes towards their parents because they ought to react to the latter's care with gratitude:

> I think it is one of the greatest Reflections upon Human Nature that Paternal Instinct should be a stronger Motive to Love than Filial Gratitude; that the receiving of Favours should be a less Inducement to Good-will, Tenderness and Commiseration, than the conferring of them; and that the taking Care of any Person should endear the Child or Dependant more to the Parent or Benefactor, than the Parent or Benefactor to the Child or Dependant; yet so it happens, that for one cruel Parent we meet with a thousand undutiful Children.[19]

If this desirable line of cause and effect occurred automatically, parental care would be an intermediary, for its output would be predictable. However, the reader learns from *The Spectator*'s continuous lament on children's ingratitude that such an output cannot be taken for granted. The modification parental care will have for the child is unpredictable and, therefore, a veritable mediator.

According to *The Spectator* no. 120 (18 July 1711), this unpredictability is even identified as a distinctive human feature. In the animal world, by contrast, parental care does have an intermediary function, because animals instinctively respond to parental care in an unchangeable chain of cause and predictable effect:

> This natural Love [parental love] is not observed in Animals to ascend from the Young to the Parent, which is not at all necessary for the Continuance of the Species: Nor indeed in reasonable Creatures does it rise in any Proportion, as it spreads itself downwards; for in all Family-Affection, we find Protection granted and Favours bestowed, are greater Motives to Love and Tenderness, than Safety, Benefits, or Life received.[20]

By representing affection as a biological necessity and a moral imperative, *The Spectator* seeks to transform human parental care into an intermediary, as well. If that project were successful, the resulting family structure would no longer classify as an actor network, for at least part of its constituents, namely, the children, would lose their transformational agency and become mere recipients of a causal order. The imperative voiced by *The Spectator*, therefore, would, if heeded, deprive the child of its agency as an actor in the family actor network.

One apparently encounters a paradox in this fictional actor network in *The Spectator*: On the one hand, the child is perceived as an actor in the family actor network, for its presence as an actor is necessary to establish the family network in the first place. On the other hand, the child's position of an actor is contested because the agency of this pivotal actor is considered to be dangerous and in need of monitoring. If parental affection, however, is unmasked as sheer egotistical self-love (as in issue 11 of *The Female Tatler* [29 July–1 August 1709] 22), such indulgence becomes useless and tedious for society. This ambiguity is apparent, for instance, in *The Spectator* no. 192 (10 October 1711):

> The Survivorship of a worthy Man in his Son, is a Pleasure scarce inferior to the Hopes of the Continuance of his own Life. That Man is happy who can believe of his Son, that he will escape the Follies and Indiscretions of which he himself was guilty, and pursue and improve every thing that was valuable in him. The Continuance of his Virtue is much more to be regarded than that of his Life....
>
> It is the most beautiful Object the Eyes of Man can behold, to see a Man of Worth and his Son live in an entire unreserved Correspondence. The mutual Kindness and Affection between them give an inexpressible Satisfaction to all who know them. It is a sublime Pleasure which encreases [sic] by the Participation. It is as sacred as Friendship, as pleasurable as Love, and as joyful as Religion.[21]

Relegating the continuity of family values to the child, *The Spectator* once more resorts to ideologizing, assigning to (the parent-child relationship in) the family an intermediary function, as children growing up in an affectionate family are supposed to continue the values of their family automatically. Yet simultaneously, the praise the author bestows on the quasi-religious bond between father and son can be productive only if both are actors in a relational network instead of remaining the isolated social units which they would be, according to ANT, in a merely biologically defined family structure.

In the periodicals, the relational network of the family is not restricted
to the attachments of parents and children, be they imagined as single
(father, mother, daughter, son, etc.) or collective actors (parents, children,
siblings, etc.). Several *Spectator* papers clearly include other actors, too.
Although those actors do not immediately belong to the nuclear family,
they form part of the actor network constructing this social unit. Of particular interest in this context is the inclusion of the community as an
actant—either in the figuration of a clan, a village, or even a country. One
prominent example is given in *The Spectator* no. 189 (6 October 1711):

> It is Father *Le Compte*, if I am not mistaken, who tells us how want of Duty
> in this Particular is punished among the *Chinese*, insomuch that if a Son
> should be known to kill or so much as to strike his Father, not only the
> Criminal, but his whole Family would be rooted out, nay the Inhabitants of
> the Place where he lived would be put to the Sword, nay the Place it self
> would be razed to the Ground, and its Foundations sown with Salt: For, say
> they, there must have been an utter Depravation of Manners in that Clan or
> Society of People, who could have bred up among them so horrible an
> Offender. To this I shall add a Passage out of the first Book of *Herodotus*.
> That Historian in his Account of the *Persian* Customs and Religion tells us,
> it is their Opinion that no Man ever killed his Father, or that it is possible
> such a Crime should be in Nature; but that if any thing like it should ever
> happen, they conclude that the reputed Son must have been Illegitimate,
> Supposititious, or begotten in Adultery. Their Opinion in this Particular
> shews sufficiently what a Notion they must have had of Undutifulness in
> general.[22]

Including a community collective into the actor network, as an actor particularly affected by modifications of the child as actor, the nuclear family
comes to appear in a different light. Whereas this family model is usually
regarded as segregated from the community, withdrawing into a separate
private sphere, an ANT approach to this passage reveals the nuclear family
as an actor network that must include actors outside the narrow boundaries of the nuclear family as a social unit in order to underscore the authoritative claim of this family structure to serve as a model for the
community.[23]

A further, even more prominent extension of the family actor network
surfaces if one examines more closely the actors involved in the notion of
parental care. Since parental care can appear in different figurations, what
the periodicals call 'care' or 'provision' eventually implies different possi-

ble actors. Two exemplary tales from Eliza Haywood's *The Female Spectator* may serve to illustrate this point. In the story of Jemima (*Female Spectator* no. 22), parental material provision in the form of money, food, or clothing becomes an important actor in the relational actor network including the child Jemima, her father, her siblings, her mother, and the community. Once this actor is missing, the attachments between the human actors will have to be rearranged since the child will form new attachments with actors outside her biological family. In a similar vein, a passage in *The Female Spectator* no. 3 suggests that the presence of the actor's father, provisions, and child is the desirable norm for the family actor network:

Nurturing Parents ⇒ *expectations of parents*
✗

> Children, being Part of ourselves, are born to share our Possessions; and nothing is more absurd, in my Opinion, than the Saying of some People, that their Children may labour for themselves as they have done. – How are such Parents certain they will be able so to do? A thousand Accidents may happen to render the utmost Efforts they can make of no Effect; and, when that is the Case, how hardly must a Son think of a Father, who, by a profuse and riotous Manner of Living, has reduced to starving those who derive their being from him?[24]

Provision can either figure in the shape of materials (especially money) or education. Issue no. 165 of *The Guardian* (19 September 1713) very drastically depicts a dysfunctional family actor network, in which the actors father and mother fail to connect with the actant education—hence the network produces a detrimental intermediary effect on the child:

Education ✗

> I have been very often secretly concerned, when I have seen a Circle of pretty Children cramped in their natural Parts, and prattling even below themselves, while they are talking after a couple of silly Parents. The Dulness of a Father often extinguishes a Genius in the Son, or gives such a wrong Cast to his Mind, as it is hard for him ever to wear off. In short, where the Head of a Family is weak you hear the Repetitions of his insipid Pleasantries, shallow Conceits, and topical Points of Mirth, in every Member of it.[25]

Nevertheless, education is largely seen in material terms, too, namely, as the necessary means of acquiring the abilities to obtain material provisions independently. Considering this constellation, the emphasis on material actors in the family network is striking. After all, one could have imagined affection to be integral for the construction of the nuclear family. The fictional actor networks circulated in the periodicals, however, regularly emphasize the attachments of genealogically and materially defined actors. With their relational cluster of parents, material provision, and child, the periodicals construe an economically informed family actor network that is well-suited to become embedded into the actor network of the consumer society.

If we look more closely at the role and position of the child in this network, the child is an actor by necessity: its attachment to material provision, to possessions, and commodities transforms the child into a consumer and paves the way for its becoming a citizen, whose integrity is defined by its owning of property. Moreover, the attachment of the child to parental care in terms of affection transforms the child into part of a genealogical chain with mutual responsibilities and obligations. By interlinking the concomitant actor networks, the periodicals enlarge and stabilize the actor network of childhood they are establishing, thus making it harder to change the patterns of this network and, eventually, rendering it more authoritative.

The significance of extending the family actor network to include elements of the community and of economy becomes particularly meaningful in passages referring to the marriage market. In view of marriage, the fictions presented in the periodicals tend to imply highly inclusive actor networks, comprising the family, parents, father, mother, child, material provision, education, community, affection, the prospective spouse, the spouse's family, provision, and so on. The child actor in this actor network is often gendered, since in most cases the stories are concerned with daughters' marriage choices. Stories of arranged or clandestine marriages construe highly complex fictional actor networks as they deal with questions of marriage choices and parental consent. The contributor to *The Guardian* no. 57 (16 May 1713) uses his case story to forward several propositions concerning the arrangement of marriages, negotiating the rights of the female child versus her parents in marriage affairs. Due to the contractual concept of marriage on which those proposals are based, the legal status of each family member is reconsidered. The general tenor of the proposals suggests strengthening the individual rights of the daughter by ranking her individual interest over that of the social unit of the family, which is represented by the parents. The agency of the child within this actor network is here being foregrounded and even given a legal foundation. The periodicals thus raise awareness for the multifarious attachments to which the child as actor is connected and which illustrate impressively that the eighteenth-century child was by no means segregated from society into the secluded realm of a nuclear family. As such factors as the community, money, class, contracts, and dynastic considerations come into play in those stories, an ANT approach to the construction of childhood can help to highlight how thoroughly the child as an actor in these fictional actor networks is related to actors that are generally perceived as 'public.'

Finally, some words ought to be said on the role of blood in the fictional actor networks of the family and childhood in eighteenth-century periodicals. The notion of a transition from blood relations to affective bonding is often remarked on in studies on the rise of the affective nuclear family in the eighteenth century.[26] This, however, can be slightly qualified if one observes this development through the lens of ANT, which does not reveal a linear development from one type of attachment to another. Instead, the accounts of affective family attachments in the periodicals always also imply, either explicitly or implicitly, blood as only one actor alongside affection and care. The difference between the consanguineal and the affectionate concept of the family consists in a restructuring of the family actor network insofar as the attachments between the different actors do not acquire different qualities but different priorities. Whereas blood relations reconnect the child to the other family members (and, if figuring as a clan, to the community), care, provision, and other figurations of affection potentially offer a greater variety of attachments, connecting the child not only with a greater number of different actors but to other actor networks, as well (e.g. consumer society). With its greater complexity and flexibility, this new type of relationship is far more suitable for establishing the stability which this conceptualization requires to become truly pervasive.

PERIODICALS AS ACTORS—THE CULTURAL WORK OF PERIODICALS

Ironically, this powerful potential of actor networks, in conveying and circulating knowledge as truth, appears to have gone largely unnoticed by the periodicals themselves. The narrator figures of the periodicals—the self-declared spectators or tatlers—all insist on their didactic agendas, foregrounding their roles as moral educators. Their professed goal is to establish their fictional family stories as exemplary, cautionary tales with the function of intermediaries: Their readers ideally should follow the stories' precepts, reiterate the underlying norms, and thus help to establish and stabilize the concomitant ideological framework. The periodicals as a particular form of mass media are supposed to fulfil this purpose, as well. Nevertheless, apart from the raised moral index of the periodicals, there is also the silent acknowledgement that the readers, in fact, may not comply with this wish. In an essay on notions of spectatorship and performance in *The Spectator* and *The Female Spectator*, I have explained how both *Spectator* journals profess a panoptical paradigm of inculcating morals through fictional presentation (for instance, through exemplary tales). Yet in addition to that, they also imply, again and again, the possibility of deviance. The journals thus construe for themselves the role of an intermediary as an ideal; that is, their goal is to provide input for one particular, monitored, predictable output of desirable moral behaviour. Simultaneously, however, they give evidence of their actual function as mediators, because what they really do is affect readers in a way that engenders a transformation: they instigate conversations and communications (for instance, letters to the editors), they may even have influence on their readers' behaviour, but the character of these outputs remains unpredictable.

From an ANT perspective, the periodicals are arguably actors in a literary sphere, forming part of an actor network as they establish relationships between the journals and their readers as well as among readers. Especially with regard to childhood and the family, they come to define family via its affective relationships, focussing on and evolving around the child as a pivotal actor. This agency of the child is to be seen in terms of a structural function: The child construed in the periodicals is an actor that makes a difference. Reading eighteenth-century periodicals with Latour, one can appreciate these popular and highly influential texts as something other than manipulative power instruments employed to impose and consolidate certain middle-class ideologies. Instead, their cultural work consists in bringing forth actor networks on the fictional level of communication (in the fictional actor networks) as well as on the level of communication between reader and periodical. Describing the intricate structures of these networks and the dynamics of the relationships that constitute them can prove more fruitful than the attempt to discover supposed causalities or ideologies behind perceived power structures.

'Information becomes facts by travelling through networks in patterned ways that imbue the piece of knowledge with authority and relevance.'[27] This statement by Latour definitely applies to the processes that have been described in this chapter with regard to the circulation of child-hood in eighteenth-century periodicals. If one wants to gauge the cultural work of these periodicals, one needs to analyse the structure of the emerging networks and how they allocate authority and certainty. A significant part of this work apparently consists in making the child visible as a constitutive actor in various actor networks, most notably the family actor network. By reiterating stories, by expanding the fictional actor networks and attaching them in ever-new constellations, the periodicals achieve a durability for their concepts of childhood. The cultural work of eighteenth-century periodicals, therefore, consists in establishing, circulating, and stabilizing these patterns. With this work, these periodicals are media-tors in the process of circulating childhood concepts. While the causalities behind this circulation may be debated, what one can certainly say is that historical differences between childhood concepts may be accounted for by shifts in the relationships and relational density of the actor networks involving the child as actor.

NOTES

1. See, for instance, Roy Porter, *Enlightenment: Britain and the Creation of the Modern World* (London: Penguin, 2000), 80–82; and Erin Mackie, *Market à la Mode: Fashion, Commodity, and Gender* in *The Tatler* and *The Spectator* (Baltimore: Johns Hopkins University Press, 1997).
2. For a discussion of the relation of the success of the periodicals to the rise of a leisure society, see J.H. Plumb, 'The Public, Literature, and the Arts in the Eighteenth Century,' in *The Emergence of Leisure*, ed. Michael R. Marrus (New York: Harper & Row, 1974), 18–22. Samuel Baudry, Scott Black, Scott Paul Gordon, and Pierre Morère explore the rhetorical strategies supporting this function. In a particular view of *The Spectator*, Michael Ketcham has stated most pointedly: 'The *Spectator* essayists [...] create these conventions in order to establish rather than question an idea of social order [...], they create conventions which will, in turn, create a self-confirming system of values' (*Transparent Designs: Reading, Performance, and Form in the* Spectator *Papers* [Athens: University of Georgia Press, 1985]), 5. For a comprehensive study of *The Spectator*, see Donald J. Newman ed., *The Spectator: Emerging Discourses* (Newark: University of Delaware Press, 2005). See also Alain Bony's annotated bibliography on Steele's and Addison's periodicals, 'Addison & Steele et l'essai périodique: bibliographie critique,' *Bulletin de la société d'études anglo-américaines des XVIIe et XVIIIe siècles* 49 (1999): 111–58. Donald

F. Bond estimates a number of about 3000–4000 copies of *The Spectator* circulating per day. Even when sales dwindled to 50 per cent of the former numbers, after the Stamp Act of 1712, *The Spectator* remained one of the few papers to survive the stamp tax at all. The increasing number of advertisements and the letters posted at the lion's head, erected at Button's Coffee-House for this purpose in 1713, attest to an impressive readership whose diversity can be deduced from the subscription lists for the bound editions. Bound sets of the three periodicals were sold shortly after the papers had been launched. Even the comparatively less-successful *Guardian* already appeared in a fifth edition in 1729; a collection of selections from the three periodicals had reached its 18th edition by 1765. For further figures and information on the success story of these papers see Bond's introductions to the Clarendon editions of *The Tatler* and *The Spectator* as well as Stephens's introduction to the critical edition of *The Guardian* by the University of Kentucky Press.

3. Published from July 1709 to March 1710, with two rival issues from numbers 19 to 44, *The Female Tatler* was the most enduring of *The Tatler* offshoots. Its authorship is still under discussion; it has frequently been attributed to Mary Delarivière Manley, Susanna Centlivre, Thomas Baker, and Bernard de Mandeville (for the latter two see the recent edition by Maurice Goldsmith). My quotations refer to Fidelis Morgan's edition of the complete text.

To date, there is no critical edition of the full text of Eliza Haywood's *The Female Spectator*. My quotations refer to the electronic edition of the first bound London edition of 1745, hosted by *The Spectator Project*, http://www2.scc.rutgers.edu/spectator/haywood/index.html

4. This confirmed, albeit based on another textual corpus, Andrew O'Malley's observations on the contribution of eighteenth-century children's literature to 'the making of the modern child.' See his excellent monograph *The Making of the Modern Child: Children's Literature and Childhood in the Late Eighteenth Century* (New York: Routledge, 2003).

5. On Addison's and Steele's Whiggish leanings, see William Walker, 'Ideology and Addison's Essays on the Pleasures of the Imagination,' *Eighteenth-Century Life* 24, no. 2 (2000): 65–84.

6. Bruno Latour, *Reassembling the Social: An Introduction to Actor-Network Theory* (Oxford: Oxford University Press, 2005), 71. Emphasis in the original. By figuration, Latour means the shape an action takes (Latour, *Reassembling the Social*, 53–4). Within the actor network of the family, for instance, childhood can thus be regarded as an actant, because it is not only related to the other actors in that network (such as father, mother, other relatives, but also child care, education, material provisions like toys, books, etc.); it also engenders transformations, for example, while establishing

the particular affective and material conditions, dynamics, and bonds within a nuclear family—as opposed to other family types.

7. Ibid., 71.
8. Latour illustrates this distinction by contrasting a computer (which may appear highly complex but will, if working properly, process its input predictably according to the algorithms it has been programmed with) with a face-to-face conversation (which may appear simple and banal, but offers various points of possible interpretations or misunderstandings, from which unpredictable consequences my bifurcate). See Latour, *Reassembling the Social*, 39.
9. David J. Krieger and Andréa Belliger, *Interpreting Networks: Hermeneutics, Actor-Network Theory and New Media* (Bielefeld: Transcript, 2014): 58, 73.
10. Latour, *Reassembling the Social*, 163.
11. Ibid., 164.
12. Ibid., 164–65.
13. Krieger and Belliger, *Interpreting Networks*, 99.
14. Latour, *Reassembling the Social*, 169.
15. Ibid., 170.
16. Krieger and Belliger, *Interpreting Networks*, 113–14. Emphasis in the original.
17. Anja Müller, *Framing Childhood in Eighteenth-Century English Periodicals and Prints, 1689–1789* (Farnham: Ashgate, 2009), 113. In the fourth chapter of *Framing Childhood*, I have elaborated at length on the ways in which eighteenth-century periodicals contributed to a theorization of the family by explaining and determining the child's place within this social unit.
18. Further actors can be added to this network, such as the mother or the father, whose roles are equally constructed through this network. Moreover, it needs to be mentioned at this point that actor networks are by no means isolated entities, but that an actor network such as the family can itself be an actor in another actor network—such as childhood—and vice versa.
19. *The Spectator*, 1711–14. 5 vols. ed. Donald F. Bond (Oxford: Clarendon, 1965), 2:243–44.
20. *The Spectator* 120,1:491. Later in the century, John Huddlestone Wynne's *Choice Emblems, Natural, Historical, Fabulous, Moral and Divine; For the Improvement of Youth* opens with an emblem 'Of Filial Duty and Affection,' which draws on the belief that young storks repay the care they received by carrying their old parents on their backs when the latter are too weak for the journey into southerly regions. See John Huddlestone Wynne, *Choice Emblems, Natural, Historical, Fabulous, Moral and Divine; For the Improvement of Youth*, 2nd ed. (London, 1775).

21. *The Spectator*, 2:253, 255. This patriarchal tableau has a feminine counterpart in issues 31 (16 April 1713) and 150 (2 September 1713) of *The Guardian*, which, respectively, describe blissful scenes of mothers encircled by their daughters (*Guardian* pp. 131 and 490–491, respectively).
22. *The Spectator*, 2:244.
23. Once again one can discern the tension between the nuclear family as a mediator—with its unpredictable effect on its members as well as on the community—and the desire of the periodicals to reduce the complexity of this actor network, rendering it a mere intermediary.
24. Eliza Haywood, *The Female Spectator*, 4 vols. (London 1745. Rutgers University Libraries: The Spectator Project), 1:150–51. http://www2.scc.rutgers.edu/spectator/haywood/index.html
25. *The Guardian*, 536–537.
26. On a critical position towards this acclaimed narrative, see Ruth Perry, 'De-familiarizing the Family; or, Writing Family History from Literary Sources,' in *Eighteenth-Century Literary History: An MLQ Reader*, ed. Marshall Brown (Durham: Duke University Press, 1999), 159–71.
27. Latour, *Reassembling the Social*, 169–70.

CHAPTER 4

Wards and Apprentices: The Legal and Literary Construction of the Familial Position of the Child

Cheryl Nixon

Eighteenth-century fiction often places its underage characters in temporary families, only to move them to new families that prove equally flawed or fragmented. Simply put, storytelling structure proves reliant on family structure. For example, in many of the century's most popular novels, although the child searches for a lost nuclear family, the plot seems most interested in the many replacements he or she inhabits during that search. Within the first few pages of Daniel Defoe's *Moll Flanders* (1722), Moll is born in Newgate Prison, taken in by a group of gypsies, placed into the home of a poor school teacher, and integrated into the household of the mayor's wife, where she is famously seduced by one son and marries another. In Frances Burney's *Evelina* (1778), the eponymous heroine leaves her protective guardian Villars to travel to London with the Mirvan family, where she is reclaimed by her grandmother before being able to reunite with her father. In Jane Austen's *Mansfield Park* (1814), Fanny is adopted into the Bertram household by her aunts; when she returns to her nuclear family, she realizes that she no longer feels at home there and

C. Nixon (✉)
University of Massachusetts Boston, Boston, MA, USA
e-mail: Cheryl.Nixon@umb.edu

© The Author(s) 2018
A. O'Malley (ed.), *Literary Cultures and Eighteenth-Century Childhoods*, Literary Cultures and Childhoods,
https://doi.org/10.1007/978-3-319-94737-2_4

51

returns to the Bertram's. These well-known heroines' shifting familial positions encourage us to reexamine the place the child inhabits within the household and to account for the non-biological family that recreates itself to accommodate the child. Taking its cue from the experiences of Moll, Evelina, and Fanny, this essay focuses on the economic and emotional roles the child plays in the flexible family that is under construction, and compares eighteenth-century legal definitions of the child, captured in the terminology of the legal treatise, to literary dramatizations of the child, central to the plotting of novels, plays, conduct books, and children's literature. This comparison of factual and fictional understandings of the child reveals the law's equation of the child with relationships of economic obligation, while the literary work emphasizes the child's questioning of those obligations and plots his or her escape from them, often as part of a trajectory of self-realization. The law, quite predictably, is interested in positioning the child within stable family structures defined by legal devices such as contracts, while the literary work is interested in the dramatic possibilities provided by the disrupted, fragmented family, and highlights both the challenges and opportunities it affords the child.

Eighteenth-century common law and equity address the child when he or she needs further regulation or when the family he or she inhabits needs official restructuring. The law can then characterize the child as a legal person, worthy of definition, protection, or supervision. The legal child most typically takes one of two forms: (1) the parentless ward who is placed, along with his or her property, in a surrogate guardian/ward family that requires legal monitoring and accounting, and (2) the working child who is placed as a servant or apprentice in a contractual family defined by economic exchange. These legal categories reveal class distinctions; if his or her family is disrupted, the child with property will be placed in a guardianship structure that protects both the child and the estate, while the working-class child will leave his or her biological family to live with another in order to be prepared for a trade, ranging from being trained to become a skilled tradesperson to engaging in service, a lower-class designation. Legal treatises and guides, which reference, digest, and explain precedent-setting cases, can be used to locate the legal vocabulary applied to the child, reconstruct the factual definition of the child, and reveal the ideological conceptualization of the child's role in the non-nuclear household.

These two legal 'types' of the child can also be uncovered in imaginative literature, showing how legal definitions of the child's obligations are both embraced and questioned by fiction. As brief considerations of plays, novels, and conduct books demonstrate, the fictional child appropriates the terminology associated with legal understandings of the child, but revises, subverts, or critiques those understandings. Most interestingly, children's literature also critiques the legal definition of the child, often emphasizing the child's moral understanding of the family as preferable and even superior to that of the law. Literary representations of the ward and the apprentice typically emphasize gender in addition to class, often depicting the female child as restructuring her position from within the family by becoming the object of a domestic romance, while showing the male apprentice as escaping his position by leaving the family and enjoying picaresque adventures. Two mid-century plays, David Garrick's *The Guardian* (1759) and Arthur Murphy's *The Apprentice* (1756), can serve as touchstones for the literary rewriting of the legal definition of the child.[1] These short plays reveal central attributes of the family plotting enabled by the legal child; the literary imagination heightens the conflicts within the family by emphasizing, in extreme form, the economic and emotional obligations the law places on the child and dramatizing, in equally extreme form, the child's choice of submission or flight.

As it aligns imaginative texts with legal texts, this essay emphasizes the eighteenth century's creation of a rich set of possibilities for defining the child. Many of these possibilities involve non-biological familial relationships. As now-classic studies by historians such as Linda Pollock, Ralph Houlbrooke, Margaret Hunt, and Randolph Trumbach, more recent studies by Joanne Bailey, Patricia Crawford, and Hugh Cunningham, and recent collections by Helen Berry and Elizabeth Foster, and David Kertzer and Marzio Barbagli have shown, the early modern child was a valued member of the family, central to both its emotional and economic functions.[2] This essay builds on that research by examining the child's position in the non-nuclear family, relying on Naomi Tadmor's important expansion of the definition of the family.[3] In *Family and Friends in Eighteenth-Century England*, Tadmor explains, 'Very often when English people spoke or wrote about "families," it was not the nuclear unit that they had in mind. "Family" in their language could mean a household, including its diverse dependents, such as servants, apprentices, and co-resident relatives' (19). As Tadmor shows, the eighteenth-century household was a porous, flexible structure that often changed its shape and self-definition. Reconceptualizing the family as the household 'illuminates a wide canvas of social action; for example, when people left households or joined them, as servants, apprentices, wards, or even long-term guests, their actions were very often understood as familial actions' (ibid., 20). As Tadmor's listing of apprentices and wards reveals, the child is central to the non-nuclear family and its household functions, and a focus on the household allows for a better understanding of the 'wide canvas' of activities defining the child. Tadmor's research investigates the language used to define these familial structures; 'In order to understand concepts of the family current in the eighteenth century we … need to turn our attention to the language in which familial and social terms were coined, expressed, and negotiated' (10). This essay connects the vocabulary of law and literature, locating the eighteenth-century child in legal definitions and literary plottings of the ward and apprentice. The eighteenth-century household affords the child space for the active negotiation of his/her position as a ward or apprentice, and that negotiation is best traced in both fictional and legal sources.

THE LEGAL CHILD IN THE ECONOMIC HOUSEHOLD: LEGAL TREATISES

An investigation of the legal child necessitates a focus on the child who is defined in terms other than that of a blood relationship to a parent. When delineating laws relating to the child, legally termed an 'infant' due to being a minor under age 21, eighteenth-century legal commentaries start by positioning the child within the biological family structure and defining his or her dependency on and responsibility to that structure; they then quickly move beyond these considerations and examine the child's position within non-biological family structures, emphasizing the ward, defined by structures of property, and the apprentice, defined by structures of work. A brief examination of a few of the most influential legal treatises highlights the legal language used to define the non-nuclear family and the child's place within it. This terminology reveals that the family is understood as transactional, with duties, interests, responsibilities, and powers defining connections between the ward and guardian or master and servant. These relationships are obviously economic in nature, but are framed as obligations that both benefit and bind the two parties. In addition, these relationships focus on exchanges that are strictly regulated, defined by legal contracts, accounts, remedies, and restraints.

In eighteenth-century treatises, the economic 'interests' of familial structures are paramount. Matthew Hale's *Analysis of the Law* (1713), an early attempt at outlining the logic of the English law, defines the family by contrasting the 'Political Relations' of the king and the state with 'Oeconomical Relations' that encompass husband/wife, parent/child, and master/servant relationships, and 'Civil Relations' that encompass ancestor/heir, lord/tenant, and guardian/pupil relationships.[4] Hale expands the boundaries of the family to include figures such as servants by positioning it as an economic and civil structure defined by mutual 'interests' (49). For example, the father has an interest in the child's custody or wardship, the value of the child's marriage, and the disposal of the child's education; in turn, the child has an interest in being maintained by the father (ibid.). In his five-volume, alphabetically organized *A New Abridgment of the Law* (1736–66), Matthew Bacon's account of the non-nuclear family emphasizes the unequal power relations that accompany these interests.[5] The chapter on guardianship opens by explaining, 'A Guardian is one appointed by the Wisdom and Policy of the Law to take Care of a Person and his Affairs who by ... Want of Understanding is incapable of Acting for his own Interest' (II, 672), while the chapter on apprenticeship opens by noting 'The Relationship between a Master and a Servant' is defined by 'the Superiority and Power which it creates on the one Hand, and Duty, Subjection, and as it were Allegiance on the other' (III, 544). The guardianship chapter emphasizes the guardian's custody of the body and land of the underage child, which gives him 'Authority' over and 'Interest' in both (II, 682). It also explains the actions he may take to 'bind the Infant' or control his property (II, 682). The child gains agency in a section on 'The Infant's Remedy Against His Guardian for Abuses by Him,' which addresses the 'waste' or mismanagement of the infant's land. Here, the 'account' proves all-important; the guardian must show his records of the estate's profits and losses to the court, being held 'accountable to the Infant' (II, 687). Similarly, the chapter on 'Master and Servant' emphasizes the regulation of a reciprocal relationship based on 'interests' that benefit both master and child, explaining that both apprenticeship and service are an 'implied Trust or Confidence' (III 555, 564). However, in both, 'the Acts of' the child 'are deemed the Master's of which the Master may take Advantage' (III, 545), and if the apprentice 'misbehave[s] himself, the Master may correct him ... or complain to a Justice of Peace, to have him punished' (III, 547). The master may similarly 'correct and punish' a servant (III, 566). The position of the servant and apprentice is defined by his or her 'hiring,' 'binding,' 'discharging,' 'assigning,' and 'turning over' to the master for contracted work (III, 555–563).

As these brief overviews of Hale's and Bacon's treatises reveal, an examination of the legal positioning of the child within the family requires an expansive definition of the family that moves beyond equating it with biological parenthood. Tadmor similarly finds that the 'boundaries of the household-family are not those of blood and marriage, they are boundaries of authority and household management.'[6] She determines that 'household organization' is built on two key criteria: 'co-residence' and 'submission to the head of the household' (ibid., 27). The law's interest in regulating the child's 'co-residence' in a non-nuclear family furthers this definition of 'submission': the legal treatise reveals that the child is defined by the guardian or master's expression of 'interest,' 'authority,' and 'power' through acts of claiming 'custody,' keeping an 'account,' 'correcting' and 'punishing,' and 'binding' and 'discharging.' The treatise's vocabulary supports Tadmor's emphasis on three defining features of the household: 'the contractual, instrumental, or occupational nature of the household-family relationships' (29). Tadmor focuses on the apprentice indenture and service contract, explaining that these contracts ensure that the household is defined by 'instrumental' relationships that involve an exchange of work and material benefits. In addition, because they involve work, the household can be understood as 'occupational,' in which 'family members had specific occupational tasks, such as cooking, cleaning, working in the shop, or nursing an invalid' (28).

Emphasizing the economic structuring of the family, the eighteenth-century legal treatise typically defines the guardian/ward and master/servant as relationships of reciprocal exchange, but also reveals that exchange to be dependent on the subservience of the child. The child enacts a contractual, instrumental, or occupational relationship that presumes his or her disempowerment. This is clearly illustrated by William Blackstone's famous *Commentaries on the Laws of England* (1765–69), which includes chapters on the 'private oeconomical relations' of master/servant, husband/wife, parent/child, and guardian/ward.[7] In 'Of Parent and Child,' Blackstone emphasizes a reciprocal relationship defined by three 'natural' duties: the parent must maintain, protect, and educate the legitimate child (435). In exchange, 'the power of parents over their children is derived from … their duty,' which gives them the right to 'keep the child in order and obedience' (40). The children owe to their parent 'subjection and obedience during [their] minority, and honor and reverence ever after' (441). When defining the biological parent's powers, Blackstone resorts to legal forms of the non-biological family—guardianship and apprenticeship—and their overt definition of the family's economic relations. He states, 'A father has no other power over his son['']s estate, than as his trustee or guardian; for, though he may receive the profits during the child's minority, yet he must account for them when he comes of age. He may indeed have the benefit of this children's labour while they live with him, and are maintained by him: but this is no more than he is entitled to from his apprentices or servants' (441). As Blackstone demonstrates, familial structures are legally defined rather than naturally assumed.

Blackstone's explanation 'Of Parent and Child' points to his 'Master and Servant' and 'Guardian and Ward' chapters. The guardian is a 'temporary parent' responsible for 'the maintenance and education of the minor' and 'the care of the fortune' (ibid., 448). After outlining the legal forms of guardianship dictated by land tenures, Blackstone explains that the guardian holds the child's estate in trust until he or she comes of age. 'The power and reciprocal duty of a guardian and ward are the same, *pro tempore*, as that of a father and child,' Blackstone notes, but with the additional responsibility that 'the guardian, when the ward comes of age, is bound to give him an account of all that he has transacted on his behalf' (450–451). As a result of this mandate to outline income and expenses relating to the child's estate, many guardians 'indemnify themselves by applying to the court of chancery …, and accounting annually' (451). Blackstone provides few other details relating to the guardian/ward household, but focuses on the child's limited abilities to engage in lawsuits, deeds, and contracts.

The relationship of a master and servant articulates even more clearly the contractual, instrumental, and occupational understanding of the household. As Blackstone explains, these relationships encompass domestic service, in which men and women work as contracted 'menial servants' starting as young as age 12, and apprenticeship, in which men and women 'are bound for a term of years, by deed indented or indentures, to serve their masters, and be maintained and instructed by them' (413–14). The servant is defined by a 'contract' that spans at least a year and aims at 'the promotion of honest industry' (413). The apprentice is defined by the indenture, in which the master is paid 'in order to learn their art and mystery' (414); in exchange, the servant and apprentice both gain settlement in the parish, and the apprentice 'after seven years of servitude' earns the 'exclusive right to exercise that trade' (415) while the servant is 'entitled to wages' (416). Blackstone emphasizes that the servant and apprentice 'live *intra moenia*, as part of the family' (414).

By the end of the century, specialized guardianship and apprenticeship legal guides started to appear, such as James Bird Barry's *Laws Respecting Wills* (1799) and *Laws Respecting Masters and Servants* (1795).[8] Barry is less interested than Blackstone in emphasizing reciprocity within these relationships of exchange. In his guide to last wills, Barry employs the hierarchical terminology of 'authority' to explain the guardian's position, noting, 'All other lawful acts done by the guardian during the infant's minority … take effect by virtue of his authority … which … is general and absolute,' although those acts must be done 'for the infant's benefit' (ibid., 81–82). The ward may seek 'redress' against the guardian for any mismanagement of the estate and the guardian is 'bound' to give the ward an account of the estate (84). Similarly, in his guide to servants and apprentices, Barry stresses the master's 'interest' in and 'power' and 'authority' over them, including the right to 'correct and punish' them (34). In return, as outlined in the chapter on servants, the master is 'answerable' for acts of the servant, including his errors, injuries, and misbehaviour (6–8). The chapter on apprenticeship further equates work with exchange. The 'apprentice is one who is bound by indenture to another … for the purpose of being taught his master's trade or profession' (16); in exchange, the 'master has a right to the labour of his apprentice during the whole term of his apprenticeship' and is 'entitled to all the apprentice might earn' (32–33).

The eighteenth-century legal treatise emphasizes the economic structuring of the non-nuclear family, detailing the contracts, accounts, and transactions it oversees. The treatise does not use emotional terminology to explain familial responsibilities, but develops a vocabulary of 'interest,' 'authority,' 'power,' and 'submission.' More specifically, as these treatises demonstrate, guardianship is defined by the 'maintenance and education' of the child and the management of the estate, which is secured by 'accounting.' Service and apprenticeship is defined by a 'contract' or 'indenture' that secures 'wages' or 'instruction' in exchange for 'labour.' As these treatises' key words reveal, the surrogate family confines the child to a household defined by the contractual language of exchange. Literature rewrites this understanding of the legal child.

The Legal Ward: Guardianship in Literary Fiction

Eighteenth-century literature counters the treatise's definition of the family as primarily economic by emphasizing the emotional relationships that bind the child to the household. This prioritizing of the emotional content of the non-biological family is given its clearest expression in representations of the guardian/ward relationship. While apprenticeship and service relationships are defined by work and are inherently occupational, guardianship more closely mimics the parental relationship and more readily introduces issues of emotional care to the household. Literary fiction not only uses the guardian/ward relationship to dramatize the family as a structure of emotional obligation, but reimagines the family by subverting its legal definitions.

Little demographic information is available on the eighteenth-century guardian/ward relationship, as it is not recorded in, for example, a centrally held register. In the eighteenth century, guardianship is created primarily through the last will and testament, in which the father is legally empowered to name his successor; successful testamentary guardianships simply follow from a last will that is not contested. If a child who owns property is not afforded a testamentary guardian or if the guardianship is unclear or contested, the case would be heard in the Court of Chancery and decided by the Chancellor. In the absence of a guardianship-specific survey of last wills or Chancery Court decisions, more general demographic findings on orphaning can prove helpful.[9] A compilation of historians' work on orphans reveals that, at any one time, 20–30 per cent of families would have experienced orphaning, and any one individual child would have approximately a 50 per cent chance of losing one parent before turning 21.[10] For example, in a study of Bristol tax records from 1696, J.R. Holman finds that 23.7 per cent of the city's children were orphans.[11] In a study of late seventeenth-century marriage registers in Manchester, Peter Laslett finds that approximately 50 per cent of brides were described as fatherless at first marriage.[12] Orphaning also figures into apprenticeship relationships, with Joan Lane citing eighteenth-century orphaning rates ranging from 8 to 34 per cent for different occupations.[13] Due to this high rate of orphaning, the need for surrogate family structures was clear—and accounts for both law and literature's interest in the child's placement in non-nuclear families.

As seen, this essay turns to legal treatises to remedy this lack of more specific historical information, maintaining that treatises provide valuable insight into the conceptual understanding of guardianship. Most treatises divide the guardian's powers into the control of the child's 'person' and the child's 'estate.' Blackstone's *Commentaries* (1765–69) emphasizes the guardian's care for the child's 'maintenance and education' and care for the child's 'fortune.'[14] Blackstone explains the source of these powers: 'The guardian ... performs the office both of the *tutor* and *curator* of the Roman laws; the former of which had the charge of the maintenance and education of the minor, the latter the care of his fortune; ... the *tutor* was the committee of the person, the *curator* the committee of the estate' (I, 448). Similarly, Sir John Comyns's *A Digest of the Laws of England* (1762–67) outlines 'The Power of a Guardian' and explains that a father can give to a guardian, 'the custody and tuition of his child, or children ... till their respective ages of 21 years' and the 'custody, to the use of such child, all profits of lands ... of such child, and his goods, chattels, and personal estate.'[15] Comyns's treatise provides few details on the care of the child's person, but provides explanations of how the guardian holds the child's estate in trust, manages the rents and profits of the estate, and provides yearly accounts of the estate to Chancery. Even when outlining the maintenance of the child, the treatise emphasizes 'maintenance-money.' The treatise lacks any exploration of exactly what the care of the 'person' would encompass in emotional, psychological, or social terms (IV, 287).

This vacuum is filled by literary texts that emphasize the care of the person of the child, rather than the care of the estate. A two-act comedy that features a simplified plot, Garrick's *The Guardian* presents guardianship as centrally concerned with emotional obligation rather than economic exchange. While the guardian/ward relationship enacts the contractual household—the guardian offers authoritative protection, while the ward offers submission to his power—the play critiques and revises this contract. It focuses on the (predictably) young, attractive, and well-behaved ward Harriet, who has recently come to live with her guardian, Mr. Heartly. She must resist the advances of the vain, foppish Mr. Clackit, himself living in a ward-like relationship with his uncle, Sir Charles. Through a series of misunderstandings, the characters come to believe that Harriet loves Clackit and plans to accept his marriage proposal. Ultimately, it is revealed that Harriet loves her guardian and the play concludes with him realizing her love, expressing his astonishment, and asking her to marry him. The replacement of the guardian/ward relationship with the husband/wife relationship is summarized in the play's last lines, 'For you, my Harriet, Words cannot express my Wonder or my Joy; my future Conduct must tell you what a Sense I have of my happiness, and how much I shall endeavor to deserve it,' and its concluding couplet, 'My friendly Care shall change to grateful Love,/And the fond Husband still the GUARDIAN prove.'[16]

Harriet's goal is to restructure the family while remaining within it, meeting its expectations while changing them. In order to win her guardian's love, she must fulfil her obligation to remain obedient and submissive, accepting his power as head of the household. Yet, at the same time, she must resist his efforts to marry her to Clackit. One of the legal powers exercised by the guardian is the exchange of the ward in marriage, and Heartly's attempt to enact that exchange—while his ward simultaneously submits to and rebels against it—provides the plot's central conflict. Heartly aims to follow Harriet's choice in marriage, explaining 'Miss Harriet's Will is a Law to me' (ibid., 19). Harriet's challenge is to communicate her love to him without breaking the rules of decorum; she cannot declare her emotions outright, but must convey them to her guardian before he marries her to Clackit. She creates a sophisticated solution, playing a language game that allows her to express her hidden emotions. She asks Heartly to write a letter that she dictates to him; her dictation and Heartly's repetition of her words reveals her love for Heartly while seeming to address Clackit. For example, she asks him to write, 'It is in vain for me to conceal, from one of your Understanding, the Secrets of my Heart ... Tho' your Humility and Modesty will not suffer you to perceive it,' and 'To convince you, that you owe much more to my Affections ... I wish that I had not experienced ... Your tender Care of me in my Infancy' (35–7).

Ultimately, Harriet expresses an obligation to the family by solidifying rather than questioning its structures. Contrasting the apprenticeship plot, which often features an attempt to escape the family, Harriet redefines the guardian/ward household in a way that allows her to remain within it. She denies the external exchange of the daughter-figure in marriage and instead secures an 'internal' exchange in which her wardship is transformed into a spousal relationship. Guardianship allows a unique reworking of the courtship plot: a surrogate father/daughter relationship can be transformed into a husband/wife relationship, which both titillatingly mirrors incestuous desire and reassuringly conforms to patriarchal familial authority. The gendering of this plot is obvious; it is aligned with the female daughter-figure who is defined by her domestic relationships—and her ability to reimagine them.

Like *The Guardian*, many eighteenth-century novels—including Delarivier Manley's *The New Atalantis* (1709), Eliza Haywood's *Love in Excess* (1719–20), Sarah Scott's *Millenium Hall* (1762), Henry Mackenzie's *The Man of the World* (1773), and Ann Radcliffe's *The Mysteries of Udolpho* (1794)—are structured by guardian/ward plots that reconstruct the parental relationship as a love relationship, some resulting in a happy marriage and others in tragic seduction. Analysing the attractions of the plot, Eleanor Wikborg argues: 'To depict the feelings and actions of a lover—and future husband—as intimately related to the care of a father/guardian for a dependent woman is a way of highlighting the close links between patriarchy and matrimony that characterized the legal and emotional structure of eighteenth-century marriage.'[17]

To take just one example of a well-known guardian/ward plot, Elizabeth Inchbald's *A Simple Story* (1791) demonstrates that the equation of the legal and emotional characterizes parental and not just matrimonial structures.[18] The first half of the novel features the tumultuous relationship between the guardian Mr. Dorriforth and his ward Miss Milner, which results in marriage; the second half of the novel focuses on his need to provide a home for their daughter, Matilda, whom he refuses to see after Milner has an adulterous affair and dies. The novel's most compelling drama occurs in the first half of the novel, which focuses on Dorriforth's attempt to control the 'person' of the rebellious Milner by creating a series of household regulations that limit her provocative social activities. An overdetermined father-figure, Dorriforth is a Jesuit priest (before being released from his vows) as well as a surrogate parent; he thus embodies the idea of paternal authority expressed as household law. Miss Milner refuses to submit to that authority, purposefully disobeying Dorriforth's orders, attending parties unchaperoned, encouraging potential suitors, and causing Dorriforth to fight a duel on her behalf.

In *A Simple Story*, the guardian's imposition of familial laws of obligation and the ward's refusal to submit to those laws lead to a dramatic reversal of power. Rather than emphasize the ward's need to maintain a submissive position within the family, as seen in legal treatises and *The Guardian*, Milner uses her transformation from daughter into lover to proclaim her power over her guardian. For example, she declares, 'Are not my charms even more invincible than I ever believed them to be? Dorriforth, the grave, the sanctified, the anchorite Dorriforth, by their force is animated to all the ardour of the most impassioned lover—while the proud priest, the austere guardian, is humbled, if I but frown, into the veriest slave of love.'[19] When she decides to attend a masquerade against his orders, she explains, 'if he will not submit to be my lover, I will not submit to be his wife' (ibid., 145). She repeatedly states that she 'demands … submission' (156). Although she seems to occupy the disempowered position of ward, Milner uses her understanding of the guardian's desire to restructure the household to secure her interests and power within it. The guardian and ward come to an impasse; as one will not fully submit to the other, the exchange of emotion dramatically stops. Their friend, Sanford, recognizes that pride has not allowed them to admit their love and forces them to come together and marry. *A Simple Story* provides a particularly provocative example of the novel's ability to question the structuring of the household and afford the legal child unexpected forms of power within it.

THE LEGAL APPRENTICE: THE WORKING CHILD IN LITERARY FICTION

While eighteenth-century treatises articulate the legal understanding of apprenticeship and service as a household structure of contractual exchange, literature actively reimagines that relationship. As Tadmor makes clear, the apprentice and servant are integral parts of a household defined by instrumental and occupational relationships. Like Tadmor, Ilana Krausman Ben-Amos expands this description of apprenticeship by emphasizing its contractual definition of labour and its incorporation of the child into an economy that values the acquisition of skills and training in social responsibility.[20] Through apprenticeship, the child is integrated into a household that mimics some forms and functions of the nuclear family, but is most concerned with the economic rather than emotional structuring of the child.

As analysed in detail by Lane in *Apprenticeship in England, 1660–1914*, 'the legal theory of apprenticeship was that the master became for the time of the apprenticeship the parent of the apprentice; he exercised the same rights and was liable to the same obligations as a father, and the apprentice became a member of his household.'[21] When a child reached between 11 and 14 years of age, he or she could undertake an apprenticeship for the expected term of 7 years. As specified in apprenticeship indentures, the master was contracted to train the child in a specific field in exchange for an apprenticeship premium and for the earnings of the apprentice. As

Lane emphasizes, 'In response to the master's personal obligation to teach, the apprentice's primary duty was "duly and truly to serve"' (ibid., 3). In addition to training the child in a trade, the master was expected to provide the apprentice with food, lodging, clothes, and washing. Legal statutes outline the specific skilled trades (often termed a 'craft' or 'mystery') that require the extended training of apprenticeship. While apprenticeship covers the expected labouring trades, such as those of the blacksmith, carpenter, cooper, goldsmith, mason, saddler, shoemaker, or weaver, the upper classes could apprentice sons to more prestigious trades, such as working for a surgeon or attorney (131–36). In contrast, pauper apprentices would be placed in accordance with the Poor Law; parish administrators would contract children to masters to engage in low-skilled labour (89).

Eighteenth-century legal treatises use the vocabulary of a 'covenant' or contract to define the apprentice, emphasizing 'obligation' and loyalty on the part of the child and 'interest' and 'authority' on the part of the master. For example, the first legal treatise devoted to children, *The Infants Lawyer* (1697), dedicates a chapter to the apprentice and explains, 'The Relation betwixt a Master and an Apprentice ... differs from all other Minors; not only of the Master towards his Apprentice, by reason of such Relation, but also in respect of Obligation' which binds the infant.[22] The treatise explains, 'One is put Apprentice to a Master for Seven years, and the Master covenants to instruct him in the Trade, and to find him with Meat and Drink' (193); in return, 'In the Indenture the words are, That the Infant shall be *Loyal and Faithful* ... [and] it was Resolved that the words imply a Covenant' (198). At the end of the century, Bird's *The Laws Respecting Masters and Servants* emphasizes the 'necessity of serving [as] an apprenticeship' in order for the child to earn 'Qualification to practice a Trade or Profession' and also stresses, in return, 'the interest which a master has in the service of his apprentice' and 'the authority a master has over his apprentice.'[23] Bird outlines the legal contract, explaining that the apprenticeship requires a written indenture signed by the child and duty stamped (ibid., 29–30). He further overviews the responsibilities on each side of the relationship, making the terms of the exchange clear; while the apprentice gains the legal right to practise a trade, it comes at a cost: he or she is 'compelled to ... continue his service till the expiration of this term,' and if he 'absent[s] himself' or 'refuse[s] to serve,' he can be 'committed to a house of correction' (32–33).

Literary fiction positions the apprentice and servant as individuals who can reorganize the household, precisely because, although bound by legal contracts, they are not bound to the family through fixed biological ties. Although he or she cannot completely overturn the hierarchy of the master/servant relationship, the fictional child can restructure that relationship. The fictional working male child, typically an apprentice, can escape the constraints of the household, running away and returning to critique or question it. In contrast, the working female child, typically a servant, often remains within a household position, but recreates the relationships defining it.

Murphy's play *The Apprentice: A Farce* offers a comic expression of the male apprentice's desire to escape the family and its relationships of obligation and exchange. The play features an apprentice, Dick, who has run away from his commitment to train to be an apothecary because he hopes to be an actor. At the play's end, Dick ultimately returns to and accepts his apprentice position because his master also promises to allow his daughter, Charlotte, to marry him. The play's Prologue and Epilogue make the play's conservative message clear; the Prologue provides the admonition 'mind your Trade,' while the Epilogue's last lines advise, 'Be timely wise, for oh! Be sure of this!—/A shop with Virtue, is the Height of Bliss.'[24] And yet, the play's comic energy results from Dick's replacement of his apprenticeship family's hierarchical relationships with a communal fraternity of young apprentices who create an 'Honorable Society of Spouters,' in which members practise their acting, reciting lines from famous plays to each other (ibid., 21). The club substitutes the imagination of the actor for the physical work of the apprentice. For example, one member says to another, '[W]as not I the first that took compassion on you, when you lay like a sneaking Fellow under the Counter, and swept your Masters Shop in a Morning? When you read nothing but the *Young Man's Pocket-Companion*, or the *True Clerk's Vade Mecum*, did not I put *Chrononhotonthologos* in your Hand?' (21). One of the rules of the Society is that attendance at acting sessions is mandatory and disobeying parents and masters is to be expected, 'Business, or want of Money, shall not be received as an Excuse for Non-Attendance, nor the Anger of Parents or other Relations, nor the complaints of our Masters be ever heard' (22).

Dick has followed these rules in extreme fashion. The play opens with him having absconded from his apprenticeship, 'a whole Month missing, and no Account of him far or near,'[25] and been arrested while travelling with 'a Company of Strollers, who were taken up by the Magistrate, and committed, as Vagabonds, to Jail' (5). The play dramatizes his return, after which he steals a fancy laced coat from his father, is arrested again for debt, and then convinces Charlotte to leave her home with him. Dick explains that he has loftier ambitions than being an apprentice, proclaiming 'An Apothecary!—make an apothecary of me!—what cramp my Genius over a Pestle and Mortar, or mew me up in a Shop... –No no!' (18). Dick refuses to accept the definitions of his familial position offered by both his master and father and this rejection is represented in his rebellious use of language; he speaks only by quoting plays that neither understands. For example, in response to his father's admonition to be useful, he quotes *Hamlet* and replies, 'How weary, stale, flat, and unprofitable seem to me all the Uses of this World!' (11). In contrast, his apothecary master speaks the language of the profession Dick should be learning, explaining that he will cure Dick: 'I shall alter the morbid State of the Juices, correct his Blood, and produce laudable Chyle.'[26] Dick's father speaks the language of economic self-advancement, explaining, 'I made my own Fortune, and I could do the same again ... you read Shakespear!— Get *Cocker's Arithmetic* ... best Book that was ever wrote' (ibid., 10). Although Dick capitulates to the demands of his apprenticeship, the play's comic emphasis is on his ability to imagine—and almost speak into being— an alternative life for himself.

The Apprentice humorously captures literature's emphasis on the child's desire to restructure the contractual household. In so doing, it draws on an understanding of the apprentice and servant formed by novels such as Samuel Richardson's *Pamela* (1740) and Henry Fielding's *Joseph Andrews* (1742); both novels feature working minors who successfully rewrite the master/servant relationship: Pamela parlays her servant status into marriage to her master, Mr. B., while the apprentice Joseph is turned out of his household when he refuses the advances of his mistress, Lady Booby. *The Apprentice* also draws on a wealth of little-studied literature that features the wayward apprentice and his connections to the playhouse, fashion, and crime. It mimics popular depictions of the character of the 'beau apprentice' that appear, for example, in Edward Ward's *The Reformer* (1701). In this short character sketch, the 'beau apprentice' is mocked because he is a 'Half-Man, Half-Boy,' who aims to 'Ape a Gentleman, [while] in the Bondage of a pair of Indentures' and proves himself to be 'all *Noise* and *Nonsense* ... His Wisdom terminates only in the repetition of some part of a *Play*.'[27] The figure of the 'beau apprentice' was well-known enough to be referenced by Henry Fielding in his poem, 'A Description of

U[pto]n G[rey] …,' in which he describes a playhouse and the 'lace' that 'decks some Beau Apprentice out for Balls.'[28] Dick's exploits also echo the actions of the apprentice that exists at the opposite end of the social spectrum: the criminal apprentice, a staple of popular sensationalistic accounts of crime and execution. For example, a 1742 account of Robert Ramsey's crimes explains that he was an 'Apprentice to a Chymist' before being introduced to a life of robbery and forgery; similarly, a 1752 account of the life of Nicholas Mooney opens with a description of his work as an apprentice to a paper-maker, followed by him eloping, going to sea, joining and deserting the army, and becoming a highwayman.[29]

The Apprentice satirizes another widely read form that overtly addresses the working life of the apprentice: the conduct book or instructional guide. Throughout the eighteenth century, numerous guidebooks were aimed at the apprentice; Murphy's play names the *Young Man's Pocket-Companion*, or the *True Clerk's Vade Mecum*, referencing the first publication of the novelist Samuel Richardson: *The Apprentice's Vade Mecum: or Young Man's Pocket-Companion* (1734). Richardson's guide uses the notion of 'obligation' to connect a contractual understanding of work to the moral structuring of the family. The guide's first pages outline the contract, emphasizing the 'Obligation on the Part of the Apprentice' and the apprentice's need to serve in a 'faithful, dutiful, and obliging Manner as a good Servant and willing Learner ought.'[30] It then moves directly onto explaining that the apprentice must protect his master's secrets, which Richardson interprets as family secrets and not just trade secrets: the apprentice must keep 'All those Secrets which relate to his Family-Affairs or Business … There is a good English Proverb, That a Man's House would be his Castle; intimating the inviolable Regard which Servants taken into a Man's Family, and who are become a Part of it, ought to have to whatever may tend to the Reputation or Profit thereof' (ibid., 2–3). The guide contains numerous instructions in good behaviour including an extended section warning the apprentice against going to the theatre and experiencing its 'deplorable depravity' (12) and a section teaching the apprentice to seek out true friendship that creates a 'reciprocal' relationship (42). *The Apprentice's Vade Mecum* revises the legal understanding of apprenticeship by imagining the apprentice as a moral force who not only belongs to but protects the family. The literary imagination can position the child as the best critic or the best defender, and often both, of the household he or she joins.

The Legal Child in the Moral Household: Children's Literature

Children's literature presents the legal child—a child living in a household defined by relationships other than a blood relationship to a parent and by, to use legal treatises' terms, contracts, responsibilities, duties, and interests—and provides a compelling redefinition of that child as a moral agent able to reshape the family. Just as eighteenth-century imaginative literature aimed at the adult reader comments on the legal definition of the child without referencing specific legal regulations, eighteenth-century children's literature critiques the legal subordination that defines the ward's and apprentice's familial position without overtly citing the testamentary or contractual agreements of guardianship and apprenticeship. Because it addresses the child it dramatizes, children's literature reveals the impulses informing the fictional rewriting of the legal child— and is thus a fitting place to conclude a consideration of fiction's investment in that child and his or her place within the constructed family. In children's literature, the child's replacement of an economic structuring of household obligations with a moral structuring proves all-important. As Mitzi Meyers demonstrates, the moral tale for children often features the child's acts of 'domestic heroism;' similarly, pedagogical works often feature children seeking, as Andrew O'Malley argues, the improvement of self and society, and as Lissa Paul argues, the liberation offered by literacy.[31] O'Malley examines works that overtly depict the law as a source of the self-regulating subject; for example, 'Richard Johnson's *Juvenile Trials* … describes a model of peer regulation of behavior in which children hold mock trials, judge each other, and hand down appropriate sentences for infractions' (ibid., 95). Here, the child is not just a legal subject, but a legal agent, even if that agency furthers self-disciplining. Children's literature thus clarifies eighteenth-century fiction's critique of the law: although the law can structure the family's contractual, instrumental, and occupational relationships, it cannot structure the moral relationships that are essential to the success of the family—and those moral relationships prove surprisingly dependent on the actions and insights of the child.

Featuring one of the eighteenth-century's best-known orphan figures, *Little Goody Two Shoes* (1765) opens and closes with scenes that depict corrupt applications of the law and throw into relief Goody's superior moral understanding. In the story's first scenes, Goody's father dares to support 'the poor at the Parish Meetings' against the wishes of Sir Timothy Gripe, with the result that Sir Timothy engages him in a series of costly legal cases. The narrator exclaims, 'we brag of Liberty and boast of our Laws; but the Blessings of the one and the Protection of the other, seldom fall to the Lot of the Poor ... how can he plead his Cause ... when our Laws are so obscure and so multiplied that an Abridgement of them cannot be contained in fifty Volumes in Folio?'[32] Goody's father dies of 'care and discontent,' with her mother dying a few days later of a 'broken Heart' (ibid., 13). In a guardian-like arrangement, Goody is taken in by the kind Smith family until Sir Timothy forces her to be removed from the parish. Self-reliant Goody becomes a 'trotting Tutoress' or travelling teacher, instructing students in moral lessons, such as 'tell no Lies; but be honest and just,' that are reprinted in the story (28, 37). At the end of the story, Goody is legally charged with witchcraft for helping her neighbours efficiently mow their grass during good weather; her witchcraft is her use of a barometer. The judge dismisses the witchcraft case as a 'scandal to our Religion, to our Laws, to our Nation, and to common Sense' (125). These legal cases provide a narrative frame in which the law is, perversely, used as a source of injustice and a contrast to Goody's development from innocent orphan into a kind, virtuous, self-possessed, and intelligent schoolteacher.

The young ward's moral fortitude, which empowers her to reshape her family and community, is also central to a collection of short narratives for children by John Aikin and Anna Laetitia Barbauld, *Evenings at Home; or the Juvenile Budget Opened* (1792–96). Echoing the play *The Guardian*, the story 'The Landlord's Visit' reimagines the female ward by giving her unexpected power to transform household structure through willful submission. The story is presented as a drama in which the Landlord comes to visit his farmer tenant's home; while there, he praises the children's industriousness and inquires about a child he does not recognize. The farmer's wife, Betty, explains that the young woman, Fanny, 'is a stranger, from a great way off' who was left an orphan due to a wagon accident and has been taken in by the family.[33] Betty reveals the child's last name, Welford, which leads the Landlord to question the child; he realizes they are related and declares, 'I am your kinsman' (ibid., 21–2). He quickly determines that he should 'take the child home for a companion to my wife and daughters' (24).

Because she has grown to love their son, Thomas, Fanny is hesitant to leave her surrogate parents for this advantageous form of guardianship. Even though she has been discovered by a wealthy father-figure who wants to adopt her into her household, Fanny remains loyal to Thomas and explains to the Landlord, 'Thomas offered me his service when he thought me a poor friendless girl ... He gained my good-will, which no change of circumstances can withdraw.'[34] She asks that she be allowed to fulfill her 'duty' to the Landlord, 'without going to live in a way so different from what I have been used to' (ibid., 27). The Landlord admires her 'propriety and good sense' and rewards it with the gift of a farm to Thomas, a payment to Fanny, and his 'free consent' to the marriage (26–7). In return, she pledges her 'most grateful obedience' (27). Fanny promises to submit to her new father-figure, but wins admiration by transferring that submission to her surrogate family. Like *The Guardian*'s Harriet, Fanny refuses external exchange and restructures the household in accordance with her emotions. She rejects the economic definition of the family embodied by the wealthy Landlord and instead enacts a moral equation of familial obligation with love and loyalty.

Apprentices prove to be popular figures in children's literature, most likely because they afford an obvious opportunity for providing instruction on the virtues of hard work. For example, *The Child's Friend* (1800?) is comprised of a series of disconnected wood cut images that are explained by short one-page descriptions. The descriptions inculcate religious values; the child has the obligation to be industrious, but that work will result in God's notice and reward. One image of a young chimney sweep looking up at an adult is explained: 'this poor boy who follows his master, lost his parents when he was an infant; and was brought up by the parish, and put an apprentice to this low employment, which however is an honest calling, and far superior to idleness and dishonesty'; the description then gives the moral lesson, 'God tempers the wind to the shorn Lamb, and fits the back to Burthen; so much for the Sweep.'[35] As another example, Hannah More devoted a set of her *Cheap Repository* tracts to a story featuring two young men contracted to serve as apprentices to a shoemaker. The five-part *The Two Shoemakers* (1795?) compares the idle Jack Brown to the dutiful and pious yet poor James Stock. By the end of the tale, Stock proves successful and is able to impart lessons to his own apprentice on the importance of seeing work as an expression of Christianity. The story conveys moral sentiments such as 'God commands us to be industrious, and if we love him, the desire of pleasing him should be the main spring of our industry.'[36]

Even if a story is not overtly religious, the child's obligation to work can be equated with the obligation to be virtuous. Thomas Day's *The History of Little Jack* (1788) features an orphaned boy who is raised by an old man (and, quite humorously, a goat). When the old man dies, Jack shifts through a series of servant and apprentice-like positions including being taken in by a farmer, working in a forge that melts iron, serving a wealthy family in their stable and taking up blacksmith and carpentry work, and filling the occupation of a sailor. The story details his work obligations; for example, when he works for the wealthy family, 'His business was, to help in the stables, to water the horses, to clean shoes, to perform errands, and to do all the jobs of the family; in the discharge of these services, he soon gave universal satisfaction.'[37] This listing of chores is immediately followed by the virtues he brings to that work; 'He was indefatigable in doing what he was ordered, never grumbled, or appeared out of temper, and [was] quiet and inoffensive in his manners' (ibid., 54).

As literature crafted for the child reader demonstrates, the non-nuclear household and the child's place in it provide opportunities for dramatic storytelling. The non-nuclear family also provides opportunities for reimagining the family—and gives the child the power to do that reimagining. Children's literature offers perhaps the clearest example of how imaginative literature shapes eighteenth-century understandings of the family: the child is able to revise the contractual, instrumental, and occupational definitions of the family articulated in legal treatises. Children's literature often takes this revision of the family one step further, dramatizing the child's overt rejection of these legal definitions' powerful articulation of a moral construction of the family. In literature, the legal child can actively negotiate his or her position in the household, aligning it with emotional rather than economic exchange; the ward and the apprentice can recreate the family and recreate the child in the process.

NOTES

1. David Garrick, *The Guardian. A Comedy* (London: J. Newberry, 1759) and Arthur Murphy, *The Apprentice, A Farce* (London: P. Valliant, 1756).
2. Joanne Bailey, *Parenting in England, 1760–1830: Emotion, Identity, and Generation* (Oxford: Oxford University Press, 2012); Helen Berry and Elizabeth Foster, eds. *The Family in Early Modern England* (Cambridge: Cambridge University Press, 2011); Patricia Crawford, *Blood, Bodies, and Families in Early Modern England* (New York: Routledge, 2004); Hugh Cunningham, *Children and Childhood in Western Society Since 1500* (New York: Routledge, 2005); Ralph Houlbrooke, *The English Family, 1450–1700* (London: Longman, 1984); Margaret R. Hunt, *The Middling*

Sort: Commerce, Gender, and the Family in England, 1680–1780 (Berkeley: University of California Press, 1996); David I. Kertzer and Marzio Barbagli, *Family Life in Early Modern Times, 1500–1789* (New Haven, Yale University Press, 2001); Linda Pollock, *Forgotten Children: Parent-Child Relations from 1500 to 1700* (Cambridge: Cambridge University Press, 1984) and *A Lasting Relationship: Parents and Children over Three Centuries* (Lebanon, NH: University Press of New England, 1990); Randolph Trumbach, *The Rise of the Egalitarian Family: Aristocratic Kinship and Domestic Relations in Eighteenth-Century England* (New York: Academic Press, 1978). For a textbook-like overview of current research, also see Will Coster, *Family and Kinship in England 1450–1800*, 2nd ed. (New York: Routledge, 2016).

3. Naomi Tadmor, *Family and Friends in Eighteenth-Century England: Household, Kinship, and Patronage* (Cambridge: Cambridge University Press, 2001).

4. Matthew Hale, *The Analysis of the Law* (London: John Nutt, 1713), 45, 51. Subsequent citations appear parenthetically.

5. Matthew Bacon, *A New Abridgement of the Law* (London: E. and R. Nutt, 1736–66). Subsequent citations appear parenthetically.

6. Tadmor, *Family and Friends*, 24.

7. William Blackstone, *Commentaries on the Laws of England* (Oxford: Clarendon Press, 1765), I: 410. Subsequent citations appear parenthetically.

8. James Barry Bird, *The Laws Respecting Wills, Testaments, and Codicils, and Executors, Administrators, and Guardians*. Third Edition (London: W. Clarke, 1799); James Barry Bird, *The Laws Respecting Masters and Servants; Articled Clerks, Apprentices, Journeymen and Manufacturers* (London: W. Clarke, 1795).

9. Guardianship demographics could be traced though a survey of a series of wills copied in local probate registers or proved in the Prerogative Court of Canterbury or through a survey of guardianship decisions that are recorded in Chancery's incomplete (and unreliable) manuscript 'Decree Rolls.'

10. I explain how these orphaning numbers are generated in *The Orphan in Eighteenth-Century Law and Literature: Estate, Blood, and Body* (Burlington, VT: Ashgate, 2011), 50–51.

11. J.R. Holman, 'Orphans in Pre-Industrial Towns: The Case of Bristol in the Late 17th Century,' *Local Population Studies* 15 (Autumn 1975): 40–44.

12. Peter Laslett, *Family Life and Illicit Love in Earlier Generations* (Cambridge: Cambridge University Press, 1977), 160–73. See Chap. 4, 'Parental Deprivation in the Past: A Note on Stepparenthood in English History.'

13. Joan Lane, *Apprenticeship in England, 1660–1914* (London: Routledge, 1996), 62.

14. Blackstone, *Commentaries*, 448.

15. Sir John Comyns, *A Digest of the Laws of England. The Third Edition...by Stewart Kyd* (London: A. Strahan, 1792), IV: 281.
16. David Garrick, *The Guardian. A Comedy* (London: J. Newberry, 1759), 54.
17. Eleanor Wikborg, *The Lover as Father Figure in Eighteenth-Century Women's Fiction* (Gainesville: University Press of Florida, 2002), 20.
18. Elizabeth Inchbald, *A Simple Story* (New York: Penguin, 1991).
19. Inchbald, *A Simple Story*, 131–32.
20. Ilana Krausman Ben-Amos, *Adolescence & Youth in Early Modern Europe* (New Haven: Yale University Press, 1994), 85.
21. Lane, *Apprenticeship in England, 1660–1914*, 2–3. Lane provides sample apprenticeship documents in her Appendix 1, 249–251. For additional studies of servants and apprentices, see Jonathan Barry and Christopher Brooks, eds. *The Middling Sort of People: Culture, Society and Politics in England, 1550–1800* (London: Palgrave, 1994); Peter Earle, *The Making of the English Middle Class: Business, Society and Family Life in London 1660–1730* (London: Methuen, 1989); J. Jean Hecht, *The Domestic Servant in Eighteenth-Century England* (London: Routledge, 1980); Carolyn Steedman, *Master and Servant: Love and Labour in the English Industrial Age* (Cambridge: Cambridge University Press, 2007); Denys Van Renen, *The Other Exchange: Women, Servants, & the Urban Underclass in Early Modern English Literature* (Lincoln: University of Nebraska Press, 2017).
22. *The Infants Lawyer: Or, the Law (Ancient and Modern) Relating to Infants* (London: Robert Battersby, 1697), 192–3.
23. Bird, *The Laws Respecting Masters and Servants*, 17, 32–33.
24. Murphy, *The Apprentice*, 48.
25. Ibid., 1.
26. Ibid., 8–9.
27. Edward Ward, *The Reformer, Exposing the Vices of the Age in Several Characters. The Fourth Edition* (London: J. How [1701?]), 30–31. This work is also published under the title *The Libertines: Or, the Vices of the Age Expos'd, In Several Characters* (1720).
28. Henry Fielding, 'A Description of U—n G—, (alias New Hog's Norton) in Com. Hants' in *The Wesleyan Edition of the Works of Henry Fielding: Miscellanies, Volume I*, ed. Henry Knight Miller (Oxford: Oxford University Press, 1972), 54.
29. *A Compleat, True and Genuine Account of the Life, Adventures, and Transactions of Robert Ramsey, alias Sir Robert Gray* (London, H. Goreham, 1742); *The Life of Nicholas Mooney, alias Jackson* (Dublin, E. Golding, 1752).
30. Samuel Richardson, *The Apprentice's Vade Mecum: or Young Man's Pocket-Companion* (London: J. Roberts, 1734), 2.

31. Mitzi Myers, 'Romancing the Moral Tale: Maria Edgeworth and the Problematics of Pedagogy,' *Romanticism and Children's Literature in Nineteenth-Century England*. Ed. James Holt McGavran, Jr. (Athens: University of Georgia Press, 2009), 101; Andrew O'Malley, *The Making of the Modern Child: Children's Literature and Childhood in the Late Eighteenth Century* (New York: Routledge, 2003), 122–123; Lissa Paul, *The Children's Book Business: Lessons from the Long Eighteenth Century* (New York: Routledge, 2011), 71–75.

32. Anon., *The History of Little Goody Two Shoes: The Third Edition* (London: J. Newbery, 1766), 9.

33. John Aikin and Anna Laetitia Barbauld, *Evenings at Home; or the Juvenile Budget Opened* (6 vols. London: J. Johnson, 1793), III: 16.

34. Ibid., 26.

35. *The Child's Friend or Careful Guardian* (London: J. Mackenzie [1800?]), 21.

36. Hannah More, *Cheap Repository. The Two Shoemakers in Five Parts* (London: J. Evans [1795?]), 36.

37. Thomas Day, *The History of Little Jack* (London: J. Stockdale, 1788), 54.

CHAPTER 5

'Pray lett none see this impertinent Epistle': Children's Letters and Children in Letters at the Turn of the Eighteenth Century

Adriana Benzaquén

'Pray lett none see this impertinent Epistle,' wrote 16-year-old Betty Clarke to her father's steward, John Spreat, in November 1698: 'I was in such a vein of writt this morning that I could not stop my pen.'[1] Betty's letters to Spreat were long and chatty, full of personal news and witty observations, unlike her letters to her father, the Somerset landowner and politician Edward Clarke (John Locke's closest friend for more than two decades), which were short and formal, primarily expressions of her duty to him. In the history of childhood as a scholarly field, which is generally seen as beginning in 1960 with the publication of Philippe Ariès's *Centuries of Childhood*, the problem of sources has been a recurring topic of debate and concern.[2] Whereas literary texts, works of art, educational and medical treatises, and official and institutional records offer useful evidence of past concepts of childhood and attitudes towards children, to write history from 'a child-centred perspective,' to recreate children's lives in the past, what is required, as Claudia Jarzebowski and Thomas Max Safley suggest, is 'either that available sources be read in new ways or that new sources be

A. Benzaquén (✉)
Department of History, Mount Saint Vincent University, Halifax, NS, Canada
e-mail: adriana.benzaquen@msvu.ca

© The Author(s) 2018   75
A. O'Malley (ed.), *Literary Cultures and Eighteenth-Century Childhoods*, Literary Cultures and Childhoods,
https://doi.org/10.1007/978-3-319-94737-2_5
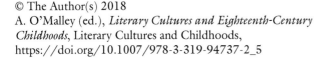

exploited.'[3] This chapter approaches childhood and children in England at the turn of the eighteenth century by exploring (and exploiting) one type of source: personal letters, namely, the letters written by and about Betty Clarke and her siblings.

Between 1676 and 1694, Edward Clarke's wife Mary gave birth to 11 children, 8 of whom survived infancy.[4] The circumstances of their lives made the exchange of letters essential both to the Clarkes' practical and emotional survival and to their collective identity as a gentry family. Edward and Mary wrote to each other by virtually every post during the long months they spent apart, when one of them was in London (usually Edward, a member of Parliament from 1690 until his death in 1710) and the other at Chipley, the family estate.[5] The Clarkes belonged to the first generations of wealthy but non-noble English families who were able to engage in extensive and regular correspondence, something that would become much more common throughout the eighteenth century. The correspondents included all the members of the immediate family, other relatives, friends, and acquaintances, and an assortment of people who provided services for the Clarkes: servants, tutors, medical practitioners, craftspeople, and merchants. Children were featured in the Clarkes' correspondence in two different ways. The adult members of the Clarkes' circle wrote about the children constantly and assiduously. Indeed, it was for Edward Clarke's eldest (living) son and heir, Ward, that Locke wrote the letters on education that he later published as *Some Thoughts Concerning Education.*[6] The letters written by the children themselves, at different ages and stages of their lives, varied in style and content depending on whom they were addressed to and for what purpose. Children's letters could be a means to express obedience or affection, to demonstrate educational progress, to convey information or record important events, or simply to keep in touch.

What can we learn about children in the past from the study of personal letters, and especially from the study of the Clarkes' letters? What makes letters so valuable as historical sources is their immediacy. They are 'unintentional records,'[7] private and intimate, written for a specific reader and, with few exceptions (like Locke's letters on the education of Ward Clarke), with no expectation of eventual publication. Steven Ozment claims that what letters 'lack in representativeness they more than make up for in depth and opportunity for precise analysis.'[8] Letters have some drawbacks, though. Their very existence depends on distance and physical separation. Just as the letters between Edward and Mary Clarke were written when one was in London and the other at Chipley, Locke's letters on Ward's education were sent while he was in exile in Holland, and the Clarke children wrote to their parents when they were away at school or staying at the homes of friends or relatives. When the Clarkes (and their friends) were living in the same house or city, the letters stopped.[9] Moreover, that personal letters were not intended for wide circulation or publication may complicate their interpretation. As Locke himself noted, 'The Nature of Epistolary Writings in general, disposes the Writer to pass by the mentioning of many Things, as well known to him to whom his Letter is address'd, which are necessary to be laid open to a Stranger, to make him comprehend what is said.' For this reason, 'a well Penn'd Letter which is very easy and intelligible to the Receiver' may be 'very obscure to a Stranger, who hardly knows what to make of it.'[10] Most of the Clarkes' letters were not meant for others but only for those to whom they were addressed, and the common knowledge assumed by writer and receiver must be reconstructed or inferred. Epistolary conventions, learned in childhood and varying over time, both facilitated and constrained what could be written to different addressees and in different circumstances.[11] Finally, the survival of personal letters is far from guaranteed. The Clarkes and their friends held on to the letters they received and painstakingly carried them with them when they travelled (from London to Somerset, from Holland to England), but the fate of those letters after the recipient's death was uncertain. Many letters written to Locke were preserved with his other papers and manuscripts because by the time of his death he was already famous, but most of those written by him have been lost.[12] While hundreds of letters written by and to Edward and Mary Clarke and their children have survived, as many or more are missing. In many cases we can ascertain that a letter was written, and deduce some of its content, through references in other letters. Most of the missing letters were no doubt unintentionally or accidentally lost, casually thrown out, or damaged by water, fire, vermin, or the passage of time, but some were purposely destroyed, whether at the time, by the recipients, or much later, by the Clarkes' descendants or other people. Letters may have been destroyed because they were deemed unimportant—or too important. Not just individual letters but entire series of letters on particular topics may have been deliberately destroyed. Some letters were meant to be destroyed, but were not. 'Adieu burn this if you thinke fitt,' Betty asked at the end of another letter to Spreat.[13] It gives the historian a bittersweet thrill to be able to read these words.

These limitations and methodological concerns notwithstanding, the Clarke family letters provide a wealth of information about the children's lives and shed light on their relationships with their parents, siblings, servants, relatives, teachers, and friends. They make it possible both to study the experiences of the Clarke children in detail and to distinguish elements that were common to many childhoods in this period from those that varied, even within a single family, based on gender, birth order, ability, and personality.

* * *

The adults in the Clarkes' circle habitually wrote about the children in connection with several practical matters: health and illness, education and preparation for adult life, and purchases of clothes and other items. References to the state of the children's health were ubiquitous throughout the correspondence.[14] Mary worried about the children's health all the time and she consulted Locke about their ailments in her own letters to him or through her husband's. In early 1695, anxious because two-year-old Sammy 'dont Gett strankth as I could wish,' she suspected his weakness might be a sign of rickets.[15] Locke urged Mary to abide by the advice of the local doctor, who 'will be the better able to judg what is fitest to be done for yt wch y^u apprehend to be ye rickets, & will be at hand to help or alter his course if any thing given him should not agree well with him.'[16] But it was not only anxious mothers who expressed concern about, and reported on, young children's health and illnesses. Fathers' letters could show them to have been just as caring, affectionate, and involved. In one of the few surviving letters about Mary Clarke's own childhood, her father, Samuel Jepp, informed his wife Elizabeth, then in London, 'that yor daughters Cough was almost gon and that greatest paines was breedinge teeth.' After proclaiming that the child was 'well recovered, and as Merry as ever she was when y^u weare heare,' Samuel reassured Elizabeth that 'their shalbe nothinge wantinge of my part (God willinge) for my care in lookeinge after her health.'[17] In June 1680, Mary herself was away from home, and her husband thought his letter would be very welcome to her, 'since it brings you this Account that at my Returne home ffryday night … I found my Deare little Gyrle verie well … ffor shee hath not had any of those ffaint sweates since I came home that shee was formerly troubled with, and is extreamely well pleased wth. her being annoynted every night, And sleepes well & quietly.'[18]

Aside from those that became part of *Some Thoughts Concerning Education*, numerous letters from and to Edward and Mary Clarke dealt with the education of their children. These letters raised questions and requested guidance about educational methods and appropriate programmes of study, inquired about prospective tutors and schools, supplied detailed progress reports, and scrutinized the children's abilities, behaviour, character, and faults. As the children reached adolescence, attention turned to planning and preparation for their future lives, which might include travel (in Ward's case), training for a lucrative career as a merchant (in Jack's case), or marriage negotiations (in Betty's case).[19] The Clarke letters reveal the extraordinary lengths to which wealthy parents went to enlist the assistance of their friends and acquaintances and employ people outside the family to ensure their children's 'preservation' and give them an education suitable to their individual inclinations and future social prospects. This was not a matter of elite parents delegating or abrogating responsibility for their children's care and wellbeing, but of sharing the burden and mobilizing a wide network at a time when the state and state institutions delivered few or no services for children or support to families.

Relatives and friends participated in the children's upbringing and rejoiced in their attainments. Ursula Venner, Clarke's widowed sister and neighbour, kept an eye on the children at Chipley when their parents were in London. In December 1693 she let her brother know that Jack and his tutor 'were here last night.' She hoped Clarke would 'find my Godson [Jack], & all yᵉ rest, to answare yʳ desirs, they are very Good & obliging & deligent in ther bussines, which is a very great Blessing, & sattisfaction to all ther frends, & pertticulerly to me.'[20] When Mary's friend Ann Levinz saw 12-year-old Nanny shortly after the girl arrived in London to enter a boarding school in Hackney, her praise was unstinted: 'your pretty Daughter, is so much grown, & so much a Woman in every thing, that your son [Ward] had much ado to peswade me, twas she; certainly I never saw any thing so much improvd, & we all thought her fitter to instruct others, than to learn any thing att a Boarding-School; I am sure you would have been of yᵗ opinion, if you had seen how exactly she behaved her self, in a room ful of company, wᶜʰ we happen'd to have att that time.' She promised to visit Nanny at school and tell Mary 'all yᵉ observations I am able to make of her, & her Mistris; I am sure I ought to endeavour to be serviceable to you & her there, if I can.'[21] In the Clarkes' network, children were a major element in the exchange of favours and services between adults. Locke's lengthy letters on Ward's education, for example, were a means to acknowledge or repay Clarke's help with the management of Locke's financial affairs in England during his years of exile.[22]

Mary's letters to her husband in London frequently contained requests to buy fabric, clothes, and accessories for the children. In January 1695 the children were in need of mourning clothes (for the queen's death), and Mary was 'Extreemly oblidged' to her husband 'for the paine and troble you take in bying those things we want which I know is a worke very disagreable to you.'[23] The children's tutors sent requests as well. In May 1687 Mary asked Clarke, on behalf of Ward's tutor, to 'bye Littletons dictionary and bring done with you which he tells me is much wanted and will be of Great use to Master [Ward].'[24] Some of Mary's letters conveyed the children's own requests. In the letter that carried the instructions for mourning clothes, she added that 'the Girles' desired that John Spreat, then in London with Clarke, would buy them 'a paire or 2 of battle-dors and shuttle cockes to exercise themselfes thiss Cold wether' and 'the play of Don quicksett both parts If it is printed.'[25]

Although in the adults' letters practical matters pertaining to the children's physical, moral, and material wellbeing were paramount, in many of them we discern glimpses of the children as individuals with unique traits and personalities. As infants, the Clarke children lived with their wetnurse, Mrs. Trent, in Ditton, near London, and it was her husband George who corresponded with the parents. About Molly, Trent wrote: 'Mis is grown a lettele woman Shee now frownes to have any body to lead har for shee goes perfectly a lone and very strongly with har duch hatt.' Trent's account both placed Molly into her group (all the Clarke children who had been nursed by his wife) and individualized her: 'I am as much In har favor as ever I was in any of har brothers or Sisters for I have often har hand, to kiss.'[26] The presence of such details suggests that Trent knew the parents expected and would appreciate them. While the extant letters do not state the reasons why Mary did not breastfeed her children herself, they offer strong evidence of the high value she and her husband placed on the warm relationship between their children and the Trents, whose services the Clarkes employed from 1681 to 1696.[27] Other letters touched on the relations between the Clarke siblings. When Jack had just turned five, Mary wanted her husband to have a conversation with Locke about beginning Jack's education, 'for now hee Growes Bigger I find what a maid Can teach him signifyes very Little and he teatches his Little sister [Molly] to doe all sorts of Dangerouse boy Like trickes Just as his Brother Edward did his other 2 sisters [Betty and Nanny] before him, and she will venture as far to breake her neack with him as she is able.'[28] When Nanny was on her way to London with her father to attend boarding school, she briefly met Betty, who was spending a year with the Clarkes' friends Thomas and Jane Stringer at Ivy Church, near Salisbury. Clarke described the meeting: 'The two sisters were much surprised to meete Each other, and Nanny offered to Exchange wth. Betty, and to stay at Ivy church wth. M[r]. Stringer, soe as Miss: Betty would take her Place to London, theire Dialogue upon that Subject was pleasant Enough as was most of theire other Conversation.' In her reply, Mary asked 'whether the sisters Cried att meetting or parting.'[29]

Locke's educational programme had been conceived for Ward, the heir, yet it was Betty who, from early childhood, became Locke's favourite. In the letters, she was singled out as Locke's 'little mistress' and later as his 'wife.'[30] When the Clarkes visited Locke in Holland in the summer of 1688, it was Betty whom they took with them. In letters to her husband from Chipley, Mary recounted anecdotes that show both Betty's intelligence and wit and the important role Locke played in her imagination and emotional life. In February 1690, Betty was 'much trobled' because she had not heard from Locke: 'she tells me she Expects a Letter Every post she haveing writt 2 to him and If he doss not write quickly she is not able to bare it but beleves she shall Come after him.'[31] A few months later, when Ward saw Mary pull out his father's watch from a drawer he was 'very desirouse that he might be soe much a man as to have the keeping of it' until Clarke's return, and Mary agreed 'apon Condision that he would be soe in all things Else and take care of it.' Betty, not wanting to be any less than her brother, became 'soe impatient for a watch two that nothing would serve her but she would write to her ffather by the very next post to desire him to by her one allsoe but we all perswaded her it would be to noe purpose for that he had soe many uses for his money that he would not doe it.' Then Betty had another idea: she would write to her father in French, knowing he could not understand the language, 'and then she sed you must shew it to m[r]. Locke to interpret it by which meanes he would know she had a mind to such a thing and If you did not Bye it she beleved he would, she pleased her selfe much with thiss peice of Craft but I tell her it will never take.' Mary's outward sternness and her insistence that neither Clarke nor Locke would accede to Betty's superfluous entreaty cannot conceal her amusement, and even pride, at her daughter's ingenuity.[32] Letters like these ones indicate that adults paid attention to, and enjoyed, displays of individuality and creativity in children. In them, even if written by adults, we hear echoes of children's own words and voices.

*   *   *

The Clarke children's letters allow us to examine the relationships between the children and other people—especially their parents, to whom most of them were addressed—and to observe the children themselves developing over time: their identities as individuals and as writers. In *Some Thoughts Concerning Education* Locke posited the writing of letters as an essential element of a child's, or more accurately a gentleman's son's, education. Letters being critical 'in all the occurrences of Humane Life,' and having both a practical and a social purpose, a gentleman could not 'avoid shewing himself in this kind of Writing,' which, 'besides the Consequences, that in his Affairs, his well or ill managing of it often draws after it, always lays him open to a severer Examination of his Breeding, Sense, and Abilities, than oral Discourses.'[33] As soon as the Clarke children learned how to read and write, they wrote letters to their parents whenever they were apart. The number of people with whom the children corresponded increased as they grew older and their social circles expanded.

The children's earliest letters had a twofold purpose: they were expressions of deference, obedience, duty and gratitude, and demonstrations of educational achievement. When Ward was six-and-a-half, Clarke notified Locke that the French tutor he had hired for his son, following Locke's advice, had begun to teach him writing 'in y^e. Method you Advised … to y^e. End Hee may in time bee able … to thanke you wth. His own Hand for yor. Extraordinary and tender care of Him.'[34] The promised letter was forwarded six months later, and Clarke trusted Locke would 'thereby see what good Effects the following of yor. Methods in teaching y^e. Child to Write, as well as all other things, hath allready produc'd.'[35] Locke encouraged Clarke to make the boy feel proud of his 'pretty letter … that he may take a pleasure betimes in writing.'[36] The deferential and educational purpose of the Clarke children's early letters is apparent in Ward's first extant one, to his father, written in French (and most likely dictated by his tutor). Ward and his father had quarrelled just before Clarke had left Chipley for London, and in his letter Ward apologized profusely and pledged to show himself deserving of the effort and money being devoted to his education. Satisfied, Clarke declared that if Ward kept his word he would 'not only bee forgiven all that is past, but Restored to the former Place you had in y^e. tender Love & Affection of yor. best ffreind as well as ffather.'[37]

The children's letters to their parents were addressed to their 'Honored Father' or 'Honored Mother' and subscribed 'Your obedient son,' 'Your ever dutiful son,' 'Your most Dutifull and Obedient Daughter,' or a variation thereof. Only a few of the letters received by the children have survived, and in them they were addressed as 'Deare Betty' or 'Deare Jack' by 'yor. truly Affectionate ffather' or 'your affecttionate and Tender Mother.'[38] As the children became more experienced and confident letter-writers, they were expected to adopt a simple and unaffected style. A letter from Betty gave Locke a reason to criticize and correct the Clarkes' tutor's teaching: 'They make children write high unnatural complem^ts. for good breeding as if it could be civility in any one to say what could not be beleived. To teach them to write as they should, one ought to make them write their own thoughts as they can & then to correct that a litle & by this means teach them to creep & not to vault, before they can goe.'[39] For Locke, naturalness and sincerity marked the mature, 'civil' writer.[40] The children still felt compelled to demonstrate their educational progress and thank their parents for their investment in them. In April 1697 Ward was studying law at the Temple in London, following on his father's footsteps, and he let his mother know that Clarke 'by much pains & Industry' had found him a convenient chamber and 'a very honest & sober partner.' His father's care having 'so far overcome me as to exceed my expressions for y^e: same,' he vowed 'to use my utmost diligence in answering both your expectations which will be all y^e: recompence I can make for what is expended for me.'[41] Likewise, when Jack was at school in Holland he was 'very Glad to heare' that his father was 'So wel pleased wth my Writing & Drawing' and hoped he would be able to give him 'as good Satisfaction in every thing else that I undertake.'[42]

The children's letters had other purposes as well: they were a means to keep in touch and maintain familial and friendship ties through the distance; they manifested concern about others' health and attested to the writer's own; they conveyed news, gossip, and requests; and they established and confirmed affection, intimacy, and closeness. Ample space was dedicated, in most letters, to the topic of letter-writing itself. Writers voiced their frustration and impatience when letters were delayed or lost in the mail and apologized for not writing often enough or for writing too often, for letters being too short or too long, or hastily written and full of mistakes. Ward spent the winter of 1696 at Oates with Locke and Lady

Masham. In January, he wrote to his father that he was 'in great hopes you receiv'd my last letter, but on y^e: tother hand I am mightily affrai'd it miscarried because I have hear'd nothing of it neither from you nor by M^r: Lock's Letters; wherefore I hope this will have better Luck.' He knew he should have written 'oftener' but was 'so taken up with y^e. good company we enjoy hear y^t. it makes me something more Backward in writing then I shou'd to manifest & acknowledge ye duty I owe you.' He also knew his letter should have been longer but was 'straitened in time because y^e. Man stays to carry the Letters,' so he concluded by asking his father 'to cast a favorable eye upon this hasty Scrall.'[43] His apology to his mother for not writing sooner after moving to the Temple was more flowery: 'I wou'd have answer'd your last obleigeing Letter before now, had not my removal into y^e: Temple prevented me; Indeed it has cast me so far behind hand with you, not only for what civility requires, but for what duty forceth me to, that had I not an assurance of your Goodnesse in easy pardoning greater offences than my silence, I shou'd Labour under greater difficultye in makeing my excuse & in humbly craving your pardon y^t: I came thus late to doe it.'[44]

Since the arrival of a letter usually confirmed that the writer was alive and in good health, the absence of letters could be a source of intense anxiety and fear. Children away from home worried about their parents' health. When the young Edward Clarke was a student at Oxford in the late 1660s, he 'humbly petition[ed]' his stepmother Elizabeth to command his sisters or a servant 'to write oftener unto mee, for I have not heard from home this eight weeks' even though he had written several letters himself, 'for which I am not a little troubled.'[45] His letters to his father, Edward Clarke senior, included thorough reports about health and illness in general, and the smallpox in particular, at his college and in the city. He ended most of his letters 'who am in good health,'[46] and when he was not, he described his distempers and medical treatments at length. In Holland, almost 40 years later, Jack grew uneasy when he did not hear from his father for some time: 'I have Wrote you 2 or 3 Letters & have yett received no Answer to either wch. makes me afraid they are miscaried or y^t. you are Indisposed, wch. I should be Extraordinary Sorry to hear.'[47]

The children's letters also relayed news and gossip. In November 1694 Mary wished to know the whereabouts and goings-on of several relatives and acquaintances, but realizing her busy husband might not have time to write 'these little historys,' she 'should be Glad to heare them from your sone.'[48] In one letter, Ward apprised Mary of his recent visit to Nanny at school and of the current situation of two of the Clarkes' former servants who had left their service in search of better opportunities. Grassemare, one of the French tutors, 'now lives with one M^r: Scudamore in Herefordshire, but … Hee is already weary of y^t: place, being prejudic'd by Levity, (that innate & natural property of the French) for he hath lately wrote a Letter to my ffather desiring him to try to get him some place if possible . . ., but above all intimateing how glad he shou'd be to serve him & you again.' Ward (then barely 16) reflected on the tutor's fate: 'Perhaps since Fortune hath deny'd him in bettering himselfe as he did imagine, it may work a reformation upon him, & make him grow **OLDER and WISER**.'[49] Most of the letters Betty wrote to her father during the year she lived at Ivy Church with the Stringers were brief and to the point: 'I received the fine petycoate you were pleased to send me for which as well as all other your favours I return you my humble thankes, I should be very glad if any of my indeavours to please you may deserve the lesst of your kindness towards me, I know Sir you are very full of busyness soe a long letter would be troublesome to you soe I shall conclude with my true love to my Brothers and Sister and my most humble Duty to your self.'[50] But Betty knew her aunt Ursula, unlike her harried father, welcomed longer letters. At first, Betty's news was confined to her siblings: 'My sister Ann desires me to present you her services and hearty thankes for her token …, and is larning to wright as fast as she can, to be able to doe it her selfe, my brother Edward is still att S^r. ffrancis Mashams, but I heare he is well, and soe is my brother Jepp, and has too teeth.'[51] A few years later, when Ursula was at Bath for her health, Betty kept her abreast of local gossip and neighbours' and servants' marriages, births, christenings, and deaths.[52]

Requests for permission, clothes, books, and money were yet another frequent component of the children's letters. In February 1692 Ward sought his father's approval to extend his visit to Oates: 'my Lady and M^r. Locke are so willing to have me stay here that I hope you will not take it amise that my mother hath given me Leave.'[53] Later that year it was Betty's turn to spend time at Oates, but she needed 'a paire of shoes, and here is none to be got,' so she asked her mother, 'if it wont be to much trouble,' to send her one by Locke's servant.[54] From school, Nanny beseeched her father to forward her letters to Chipley and buy her 'an english byble and comonpraer book.'[55] In December 1696, when she received an invitation to spend the Christmas holiday at a school friend's home, her mistress would not allow her to go without Clarke's consent. She also needed 'cloth for shifs' and money, both because her pocket was 'at present very empty' and because if she went to her friend's she must have 'some money exterordinary for to give to ye servants; & to have in my pocket if I should play at cards.'[56]

Although duty and respect loomed so large in the Clarke children's letters, love and affection had a central place in them too. In their letters to their parents, in fact, duty and affection were often intertwined. In letters to their father, the children's feelings could be implied and contained rather than openly displayed, as when Nanny wrote 'I shall be very glade S^r to se you hear as soon as your business will give you leave.'[57] The opposite was the case in this letter from the young Edward Clarke to his stepmother: Edward was moved when he heard of her 'kissing ... my letters representing my person, which I account is to mee the greatest honour imaginable and certainly is a most perfect sumptome of your great affection towards mee,' but learning about

> the continuation of your sickness ... imediately banished all that joye ... and left mee in the darke Grots of solitude, where mallancolly imediatly layd her ugly claws uppon mee, and presently after the heaviness of my imaginations closed upp my distracted senses in a little sleep, but then did my dreams likewise (representing your danger) become my tormentors, and when I awaked, new forms but still of the same miseries seized uppon my mind, and my heart seemed then to remaine within mee for noe other cause, but at every pant to count the clock of my miseries.[58]

The overblown style of this letter, so uncharacteristic of the sensible and down-to-earth adult Clarke, does not make the emotions expressed in it any less sincere. For comparison, here is a letter from Ward to his mother, written almost three decades later and exhibiting a similar admixture of respect and overstated affection:

> If in adventuring to expresse my Poore sentiments of y^or: Vertue or Prudence, I have been induc'd at any time to write any thing to you, w^ch: Looks like complement or flattery, I am sure t'is what was verie farr from my Intentions; It being my Opinion y^t: to complement a true friend, is to denye one's self the freedome & Liberty y^e: State of friendship allows to all; And 'tis under y^e: protection of y^t: State, I clayme a right of attributeing what is so justly due to you, And I hope you will not denye mee y^e: satisfaction of admireing y^e: affection and tendernesse you manifest to us all, and therefore whatever thoughts I have of y^t. kind, I hope you will pardon me if I express them with sincerity, and make due acknowledgments of your favors as farr as my Talent reaches.[59]

Ward flattered his mother in terms that were in all likelihood learned, not spontaneous, yet he insisted that his feelings and his admiration were genuine.

In other letters, affection and intimacy were displayed in less formal ways. In February 1694, when Mary's dog Mustard died at Chipley while she was in London, Betty wished to reassure her mother that the dog's death was not due to negligence—and to prove that, as the eldest daughter (even if she was just 11 at the time), she was a capable manager of household and servants: 'I can so far Justify my selfe that No care of mine Was wanting, for I caused Dorcas [a servant] every day to make him pottage when his Teeth ware not strong enongh to eat nor his Stomack to disgest bones, & the day he dyed I saw him eat a good mess theirof.' What followed exposed Betty's witty, playful side and hinted at the close and friendly relationship between her and her mother: 'though (tis true) he lived long enough to dye of old age, yet Not satistyed so, I thought it nesicary to call a jurry, to inquire into the reason of his suden Death.' This 'jury' was made up of some of the Clarkes' servants: 'D^r. Isaac was of the opinion he dyed of an appoplexy, but the corroner M^r. Thomas Verdict was y^t. it was occasioned by eating of a toad, He beeing very much swelled; … Heer was some advised Me to Ring his Funerall Knell, but my heart was too heavy for such an office, Humphry would faine have burryed him under the Vine But I Knew you would never more have eat of the grapes, So he was buryed in the parke Without any Cerimony.'[60] Betty's letters to Locke, however, were more restrained and also combined deference and affection. In July 1701 she wrote to him from Chipley 'to renew our conversation (tho if I mistake not it is on your side it rest's)' and to welcome him to town: 'I am much pleased at your being there Master of So much more health, then you are used to bee; & I know nothing could add to the pleasure I received with the News, but it's being confirmed by you, when your Leasure will permitt; for you daily have my best wishes, I being devoted to you, by gratitude as well as by inclination.' Betty then mentioned that she had just reread 'Telemaque, & La Fontaine wth as much pleasure … as at ye first time.' Her intelligence and love of books were key to Betty's continuing special bond with her by then famous friend.[61]

The Clarke children wrote not only to adults but also to other children. Still, the few letters between the Clarke siblings and to and from their friends that have survived—from Betty to Jack, from Betty's friend Elizabeth Duke to Betty, and between Jack and his friend Arent Furly—do not bear out Amy Harris's argument that young people's letters to each

READ

other disclose 'an informal world of adolescent camaraderie.'[62] Betty was a versatile writer, and none of her siblings could match the sparkle and humour in some of her letters; those to her 'Dearest Brother' in Holland, however, were among her most stilted and exaggerated. 'I am so brim full of good Wishes for you,' she wrote in February 1701, 'that I fear I should burst did I not Somtimes take this way of unloading My person, & assuring you of my affection's; wch thô you Should bee many Yeares out of my presence, & at as great distance as ye East is from the West, can never bee in ye Least worn out.' She wished Jack 'health, & good Luck in all your undertakeaing's, & in whatever disapointment's you meett wth, a Chearfull Mind.'[63] Elizabeth Duke's letters to Betty showed a similar affectation (which, as I suggested above, need not be seen as insincerity). In May 1695 Elizabeth sent Betty a piece of embroidery to thank her for her friendship and favours: 'I long for some opportunity of returning some of the many obligations I have received from you, & especially, Madam, when I had the happiness to wait on you at Chipley, which I should perform with as much pleasure as I receiv'd them with, being extreamly ambitious to approve my self Your most humble servant.'[64] Several years later Elizabeth was still thanking Betty for her friendship and favours:

> To acknowledge in the manner I ought the favour of such agreable company, so much goodness as you have shewn in passing by my deffects, & accepting my good will, & so very civil & kind a letter as you have lately oblig'd me with; is more than I can pretend to do in the midst of company . . . Yet if through my extreme haste, I should write but thankfull nonsense, it would be more pardonable then a longer ommission, nor am I so much concern'd what may be thought of my sense, as to give you a just opinion of my friendship & gratitude.

Betty would always keep the place she had in Elizabeth's heart 'for I hope, I shall never be so unreasonable as to bestow it on any of less merit, & I don't expect to meet with one of greater.'[65]

The children's letters to the Clarkes' most loyal servants, and in particular Betty's to the steward John Spreat when she was in London with her parents in 1698–1699, were a different matter altogether. Betty addressed Spreat formally ('Mr Spreat') and signed 'Your reall friend' or 'Your reall friend att command,' but before the subscription she sometimes referred to him by the nickname 'Pom.' In one occasion Betty apologized for what she thought would be a short letter: 'I have not News enough to make a long letter ... if this proves very shorte you should not take it as a peece of unkindness but purely for want of a subject.' Once she got going, though, she could not stop. First she embarked on a long and detailed account of a visit to Kensington Palace. Everything was 'as fine as can bee imagined, the rooms lofty & statly, the furniture Magnificent, & the gardens a perfect paradice. & amongst the rest of the fine things there is a noble present, from the King of France; (since the peace) to King W^m. it is the largest looking-glass that ever was seen.' She was deeply moved when she toured 'the poor Queens apartment': 'it is impossible for mee to tell you, how dismall [it] looked, for want of her to grace it, and by his Majesty's order (since her death) the house has been all turned and his coach goes in by another court, he not being able to bear the sight of any thing, that belong'd to her.' She concluded with another apology ('I believe I have tired you') and gossip about former servants and a former tutor who had left the Clarkes' service seeking better positions but were 'still discontented & roving' (like Ward, Betty thought this was 'a punishment for people that wont know when they are Well'). She then covered the entire other side of the sheet with postscripts: she sent her duty, love, and service to everyone at Chipley, 'not forgetten Punch, Treby, & tity' (presumably the dogs), wrote more about the visit to the queen's apartments, and sent news of her siblings who were then in London.[66] In another letter, Betty apologized 'for not answering your Kind letter, till now,' adducing lack of time, and offered, as compensation, to write 'a long letter ... & tell you all the news I can thinke on.' The news included the celebrations for the king's birthday (the ball at court and the Clarkes' private celebration at home) and for Betty's own birthday (which she thanked Spreat and the rest of the 'family' at Chipley for remembering): her cousin Hopkins had invited her to play cards and have supper at her house and her mother took her to see the Lord Mayor's show for the first time (Betty did not find it as impressive as she expected and 'never desire to see it again').[67] In the relationship between Betty and Spreat, who served her family for decades and, for the children, acted as a caregiver, surrogate father, and friend, familiarity was possible because the discrepancy in age and gender was compensated, in some measure, by the difference in class and status.[68] The pleasure Betty felt writing her long, spontaneous, gossipy and 'impertinent' epistles is evident. Spreat's answers, unfortunately, have not been preserved.

* * *

Lingering traces of the Clarke children's lives are inscribed in the letters written by them and the adults who cared for them. This chapter considered a sample of these letters, to illustrate their range and variety and the multiple purposes they served. Analysis of the letters exposes both what lives and letters had in common (arising from similarities and differences in age, class, and gender) and what was unique about them (stemming from a child's individuality, personality, and creativity). I have focused on relationships between the children and other people—parents, siblings, other relatives, friends, tutors and teachers, servants—and suggested that, to a large extent, for an English gentry family at the turn of the eighteenth century it was the constant, persistent exchange of letters that made relationships possible. Stylistically, the children's letters covered a broad spectrum, from stiff and formulaic to spontaneous and informal. They also covered a wide spectrum of emotions, even if, to appreciate them, we need to set aside our own assumptions and expectations regarding how emotions are properly expressed. Thus, as I have argued, affection expressed in affected, pretentious language was not necessarily fake. Especially in the case of children, whose writing voice and identity were in process of being formed, it would be futile to imagine a raw, natural feeling that existed before, or outside, its expression in a particular (learned, acceptable) style or discourse. Some historians of childhood assert that the 'authentic' voice of the child can only be detected in utterances or writing that are 'unconstrained by the adult eye': private or between children.[69] For Harris, it is in 'examples of young people writing each other' that we may hear '"authentic" young people's voices outside of their efforts to please adults.'[70] In the surviving Clarke family letters, however, exchanges between children were as contrived and 'artificial' as many (but by no means all) of the exchanges between children and adults. This should not surprise us, as children strive to please each other (through excessive civility, in the Clarkes' time; through a 'naturalness' and informality that are no less learned, in our own) just as much as, or more than, they do adults.

Letters are not transparent windows into past lives, experiences, or emotions, but because they played such a central role in the Clarke children's lives, experiences, and emotions, they allow us to glimpse not that illusory construct, 'the authentic child,' but a web of relationships as they were being learned, negotiated, and reconfigured. We see that following rules and conventions did not unavoidably mean dissimulation or insincerity; that the expectation of obedience, deference, and duty did not preclude warmth and affection; and that closeness in age did not necessarily lead to informality or spontaneity, nor class difference always create a barrier to intimacy. The children's voices are everywhere in the Clarke letters, but to hear them we must attend to the nuances of different discourses and circumstances and suspend the Rousseauian, Romantic idea of an authentic self—or child.

NOTES

1. Betty Clarke to John Spreat, November 5, 1698, Somerset Archives and Local Studies (hereafter SALS) DD\SF 7/1/14. The original punctuation, spellings, abbreviations, and contractions of the manuscript letters have been retained throughout. This chapter is part of a larger project tentatively titled *Locke's Children: Children and Adults in England, 1660–1720*. I gratefully acknowledge the funding provided by the Social Sciences and Humanities Research Council of Canada and Mount Saint Vincent University.

2. Philippe Ariès, *Centuries of Childhood: A Social History of Family Life*, trans. Robert Baldick (New York: Vintage, 1962), originally published as *L'enfant et la vie familiale sous l'Ancien Régime* (Paris: Plon, 1960); Colin Heywood, *A History of Childhood: Children and Childhood in the West from Medieval to Modern Times* (Cambridge: Polity, 2001), 6.

3. Claudia Jarzebowski and Thomas Max Safley, 'Introduction,' in *Childhood and Emotion Across Cultures 1450–1800*, ed. Claudia Jarzebowski and Thomas Max Safley (London: Routledge, 2014), 6.

4. Following the early deaths of their first three children, Edward, Elizabeth, and Anne, the Clarkes gave the same names to their next three (nicknamed Ward, Betty, and Nanny, born in January 1681, October 1682, and November 1683, respectively). The other children were John (Jack), Mary (Molly), Jepp, Samuel (Sammy), and Jane (Jenny).

5. There were three weekly posts between London and Somerset in this period, and letters normally took two days to reach their destination. On the history of the Post Office and English letters in the long eighteenth century, see James How, *Epistolary Spaces: English Letter Writing from the Foundation of the Post Office to Richardson's Clarissa* (Aldershot: Ashgate, 2003); Susan Whyman, *The Pen and the People: English Letter Writers 1660–1800* (Oxford: Oxford University Press, 2009).

6. John Locke, *Some Thoughts Concerning Education*, ed. John W. Yolton and Jean S. Yolton (Oxford: Clarendon Press, 1989); Adriana Benzaquén, 'Locke's Children,' *Journal of the History of Childhood and Youth* 4, no. 3 (Fall 2011): 382–402 and '"No greater Pleasure in this Life": The Friendship of John Locke and Edward Clarke,' in *Friendship and Sociability*

in Premodern Europe: Contexts, Concepts and Expressions, ed. Amyrose McCue Gill and Sarah Rolfe Prodan (Toronto: Centre for Reformation and Renaissance Studies, 2014), 43–70.

7. Mathias Beer, 'Private Correspondence in Germany in the Reformation Era: A Forgotten Source for the History of the Burgher Family,' *Sixteenth Century Journal* 32, no. 4 (Winter 2001), 950.

8. Steven Ozment, *Ancestors: The Loving Family in Old Europe* (Cambridge: Harvard University Press, 2001), 106. For other studies of early modern European children and families that use personal letters as the main sources of evidence, see Mary Joe Hughes, 'Child-Rearing and Social Expectations in Eighteenth-Century England: The Case of the Colliers of Hastings,' *Studies in Eighteenth-Century Culture* 13 (1984): 79–100; Miriam Slater, *Family Life in the Seventeenth Century: The Verneys of Claydon House* (London: Routledge & Kegan Paul, 1984); Steven Ozment, *Three Behaim Boys: Growing Up in Early Modern Germany* (New Haven: Yale University Press, 1990); Vivienne Larminie, *Wealth, Kinship and Culture: The Seventeenth-Century Newdigates of Arbury and their World* (Woodbridge: Royal Historical Society and Boydell, 1995); Benjamin Roberts, *Through the Keyhole: Dutch Child-Rearing Practices in the 17th and 18th Century, Three Urban Elite Families* (Hilversum: Verloren, 1998); Christine Adams, *A Taste for Comfort and Status: A Bourgeois Family in Eighteenth-Century France* (University Park: Pennsylvania State University Press, 2000); Willemijn Ruberg, 'Children's Correspondence as a Pedagogical Tool in the Netherlands (1770–1850),' *Paedagogica Historica* 41, no. 3 (June 2005): 295–312 and 'Epistolary and Emotional Education: The Letters of an Irish Father to His Daughter, 1747–1752,' *Paedagogica Historica* 44, no. 1–2 (February–April 2008): 207–18; Henry French and Mark Rothery, '"Upon Your Entry into the World": Masculine Values and the Threshold of Adulthood Among Landed Elites in England 1680–1800,' *Social History* 33, no. 4 (November 2008): 402–22; Amy Harris, '"This I Beg My Aunt May Not Know": Young Letter-Writers in Eighteenth-Century England, Peer Correspondence in a Hierarchical World,' *Journal of the History of Childhood and Youth* 2, no. 3 (2009): 333–60; Sara Mendelson, 'Anne Dormer and Her Children,' in *Gender and Early Modern Constructions of Childhood*, ed. Naomi J. Miller and Naomi Yavneh (Farnham: Ashgate, 2001), 117–26; Emily C. Bruce, '"Each Word Shows How You Love Me": The Social Literacy Practice of Children's Letter Writing (1780–1860),' *Paedagogica Historica* 50, no. 3 (2014): 247–64; Valentina Sebastiani, 'Childhood and Emotion in a Printing House (1497–1508),' in *Childhood and Emotion Across Cultures*, ed. Jarzebowski and Safley, 143–56. Anthony Fletcher's *Growing Up in England: The Experience of Childhood 1600–1914* (New Haven: Yale University Press, 2008) relies

on correspondence and diaries to reconstruct childhood and family life in England.

9. After his return to England in February 1689, Locke resided either in London or at Oates, the house of his friends Sir Francis and Lady Damaris Masham in Essex.

10. John Locke, 'An Essay for the Understanding of St Paul's Epistles by Consulting St Paul Himself,' in *John Locke: Writings on Religion*, ed. Victor Nuovo (Oxford: Clarendon Press, 2002), 51.

11. See Roger Chartier, Alain Boureau, and Cécile Dauphin, *Correspondence: Models of Letter-Writing from the Middle Ages to the Nineteenth Century*, trans. Christopher Woodall (Princeton: Princeton University Press, 1997); William Merrill Decker, *Epistolary Practices: Letter Writing in America Before Telecommunications* (Chapel Hill: University of North Carolina Press, 1998); Whyman, *The Pen and the People*.

12. E.S. de Beer, 'Introduction,' in *The Correspondence of John Locke*, 8 vols., ed. E.S. de Beer (Oxford: Clarendon Press, 1976–1989), I:xxxv–xli.

13. Betty Clarke to Spreat, January 6, 1699, SALS DD\SF 7/1/78.

14. See Hannah Newton, *The Sick Child in Early Modern England, 1580–1720* (Oxford: Oxford University Press, 2012), 23–4. While religion was everywhere present and assumed in the Clarke letters, mostly in relation to health and death, it was not a major topic of discussion in either the adults' or the children's letters.

15. Mary Clarke to Edward Clarke, January 21, 1695, SALS DD\SF 7/1/31 and February 9, 1695, SALS DD\SF 7/1/67.

16. Locke to Mary Clarke, March 22, 1695, Bodleian Library (hereafter BL) MS. Locke b. 8, no. 170 (also in *Correspondence*, V:296). On Locke as a practising physician see Kenneth Dewhurst, *John Locke (1632–1704) Physician and Philosopher: A Medical Biography with an Edition of the Medical Notes in His Journals* (London: Wellcome Historical Medical Library, 1963).

17. Samuel Jepp to Elizabeth Jepp, June 24, 1659, SALS DD\SF 10/3/20.

18. Edward Clarke to Mary Clarke, June 9, 1680, SALS DD\SF 7/1/53. The child mentioned in this letter was the first Elizabeth, born in July 1678, who died soon after.

19. On the education of Ward and Jack, see Benzaquén, 'Locke's Children' and 'Educational Designs: The Education and Training of Younger Sons at the Turn of the Eighteenth Century,' *Journal of Family History* 40, no. 4 (Fall 2015): 462–84. On marriage negotiations for Betty, see Bridget Clarke, 'The Marriage of John Locke's "Wife," Elizabeth Clarke,' *Locke Newsletter* 22 (1991): 93–114.

20. Ursula Venner to Edward Clarke, December 6, 1693, SALS DD\SF 7/1/22.

21. Ann Levinz to Mary Clarke, December 7, 1695, SALS DD\SF 7/1/60.
22. See Benzaquén, "'No greater Pleasure.'"
23. Mary Clarke to Edward Clarke, January 27, 1695, SALS DD\SF 7/1/31. Clarke had been Mary I's auditor since 1689. He recorded his purchases in his London account book, SALS DD\SF 6/2/3.
24. Mary Clarke to Edward Clarke, May 14, 1687, SALS DD\SF 7/1/30. Adam Littleton's Latin dictionary was first published in 1673 and went through several editions.
25. Mary Clarke to Edward Clarke, January 18, 1695, SALS DD\SF 7/1/60. The play was Thomas D'Urfey's *The Comical History of Don Quixote* (1694).
26. George Trent to Mary Clarke, [September 1689?], SALS DD\SF 7/1/2.
27. On negative and positive interpretations of the practice of wetnursing in early modern Europe, see Rudolf Dekker, *Childhood, Memory and Autobiography in Holland: From the Golden Age to Romanticism* (Houndmills: Macmillan, 2000), 25–7, 34–5, 91–100; Heywood, *A History of Childhood*, 63–9.
28. Mary Clarke to Edward Clarke, December 22, 1690, SALS DD\SF 7/1/31.
29. Edward Clarke to Mary Clarke, November 9, 1695, SALS DD\SF 7/1/60; and Mary Clarke to Edward Clarke, November 12, 1695, SALS DD\SF 7/1/31. On siblings, see Amy Harris, *Siblinghood and Social Relations in Georgian England: Share and Share Alike* (Manchester: Manchester University Press, 2012).
30. See, for instance, Locke to Mary Clarke, February 28/March 8, 1688, *Correspondence*, III:386 and December 12, 1689, BL MS. Locke b. 8, no. 30 (also in *Correspondence*, III:751–2).
31. Mary Clarke to Edward Clarke, February 9, 1690, SALS DD\SF 7/1/22.
32. Mary Clarke to Edward Clarke, October 14, 1690, SALS DD\SF 7/1/31. In his endorsement, Clarke mentioned 'Betty's Contrivance to gett a Watch of Mr Locke.' On children and watches, see Rudolf Dekker and Arianne Baggerman, 'Otto's Watch: Enlightenment, Virtue, and Time in the Eighteenth Century,' in *Childhood and Children's Books in Early Modern Europe, 1550–1800*, ed. Andrea Immel and Michael Witmore (New York: Routledge, 2006), 277–303.
33. Locke, *Some Thoughts*, 243.
34. Edward Clarke to Locke, September 29, 1687, BL MS. Locke c. 6, f. 38 (also in *Correspondence*, III:275–6).
35. Edward Clarke to Locke, March 16, 1688, BL MS. Locke c. 6, f. 47 (also in *Correspondence*, III:415). None of Ward's letters to Locke have survived.
36. Locke to Edward Clarke, May 6/16, 1688, *Correspondence*, III:450.

37. Ward Clarke to Edward Clarke, November 29, 1689; and Edward Clarke to Ward Clarke, c. December 5, 1689, copy, SALS DD\SF 7/1/15.
38. The letters Jack received in Holland, where he was sent in October 1700 to go to school and be apprenticed to a merchant, were returned to the family with Jack's belongings after his death in June 1705.
39. Locke to Edward Clarke, November 23, 1694, SALS DD\SF 9/1/5; see also *Some Thoughts*, 242–3.
40. Eve Tavor Bannet discusses the paradox, in eighteenth-century letter manuals, of an ideal of naturalness and sincerity that had to be achieved by learning a set of rules and conventions; *Empire of Letters: Letter Manuals and Transatlantic Correspondence, 1688–1820* (Cambridge: Cambridge University Press, 2005), 42–6. There is no indication in the surviving Clarke correspondence that any of the Clarkes owned or used a letter manual.
41. Ward Clarke to Mary Clarke, April 27, 1697, SALS DD\SF 7/1/2.
42. Jack Clarke to Edward Clarke, May 4/15, 1703, SALS DD\SF 7/1/15.
43. Ward Clarke to Edward Clarke, January 13, 1696, SALS DD\SF 7/1/15.
44. Ward Clarke to Mary Clarke, April 27, 1697, SALS DD\SF 7/1/2.
45. Edward Clarke to Elizabeth Clarke, January 13, 1668, SALS DD\SF 7/1/15.
46. See, for instance, Edward Clarke to Edward Clarke senior, March 31, 1668, SALS DD\SF 7/1/15.
47. Jack Clarke to Edward Clarke, March 28/April 8, 1704, SALS DD\SF 7/1/2.
48. Mary Clarke to Edward Clarke, November 3, 1694, SALS DD\SF 7/1/31.
49. Ward Clarke to Mary Clarke, March 6, 1697, SALS DD\SF 7/1/2.
50. Betty Clarke to Edward Clarke, November 4, 1696, SALS DD\SF 7/1/15.
51. Betty Clarke to Ursula Venner, April 21, 1692, SALS DD\SF 7/1/63.
52. Betty Clarke to Ursula Venner, July 10, 1697, SALS DD\SF 7/1/77, and July 19, 1697, SALS DD\SF 7/1/63.
53. Ward Clarke to Edward Clarke, February 25, 1692, SALS DD\SF 7/1/2.
54. Betty Clarke to Mary Clarke, November 21, 1692, SALS DD\SF 7/1/46.
55. Nanny Clarke to Edward Clarke, December 13, 1695, SALS DD\SF 7/1/15
56. Nanny Clarke to Edward Clarke, December 1, 1696, SALS DD\SF 7/1/15.
57. Nanny Clarke to Edward Clarke, December 13, 1695, SALS DD\SF 7/1/15.
58. Edward Clarke to Elizabeth Clarke, February 5, 1668, SALS DD\SF 7/1/15.
59. Ward Clarke to Mary Clarke, February 18, 1697, SALS DD\SF 7/1/15.
60. Betty Clarke to Mary Clarke, February 12, 1694, SALS DD\SF 7/1/52.

61. Betty Clarke to Locke, July 5, 1701, BL MS. Locke c. 6, ff. 157–8 (also in *Correspondence*, VII:358–9). Betty was corresponding with Locke by early 1692. Ten of her letters to him have survived, written between September 1697 and August 1704 (two months before Locke's death). From time to time Locke sent Betty presents of books.

62. Harris, "'This I Beg My Aunt May Not Know,'" 334.

63. Betty Clarke to Jack Clarke, February 3, 1701, SALS DD\SF 7/1/84.

64. Elizabeth Duke to Betty Clarke, May 15, 1695, SALS DD\SF 7/1/68.

65. Elizabeth Duke to Betty Clarke, May 2 [1704?], SALS DD\SF 7/1/68. I discuss the correspondence between Jack Clarke and Arent Furly in 'Educational Designs.'

66. Betty Clarke to Spreat, August 9, 1698, SALS DD\SF 7/1/80.

67. Betty Clarke to Spreat, November 5, 1698, SALS DD\SF 7/1/14.

68. Spreat's proven loyalty exempted him, in Edward and Mary Clarke's eyes, from the anxieties raised by closeness between upper-class children and servants; see, for instance, Locke to Edward Clarke, April 19/29, 1687, BL MS. Locke b. 8, no. 23 (also in *Correspondence*, III:172–84) and Locke, *Some Thoughts*, 126–7.

69. Fletcher, *Growing Up in England*, 291.

70. Harris, "'This I Beg My Aunt May Not Know,'" 340.

Reading, Pedagogy, and the Child's Mind

CHAPTER 6

Learned Pigs and Literate Children: Becoming Human in Eighteenth-Century Literary Cultures

Ann Wierda Rowland

In the winter of 1785, after a successful summer tour of provincial cities, the Learned Pig made its London debut to great acclaim and sensation. Touted for its erudition and clever methods—'he reads, writes, and casts accounts by means of typographical cards, in the same manner that a printer composes and by the same method'—the performing pig quickly became a fashionable attraction, moving to Sadler's Wells in the summer as the main act.[1] Evidence of the pig's popularity comes from a variety of contemporary diaries, letters and press accounts; as the anonymous author of *London Unmask'd* declares, 'it would be quite monstrous and ill-bred not to follow the *ton*, and go see the wonderful Learned Pig; it being the trite question in all polite circles, Pray, my Lord, my Lady, Sir John, Madam, or Miss, have you seen the Learned Pig?'[2]

In fact, the spectacle of the Learned Pig and his alphabet cards caused such a sensation in the mid-1780s that one finds this reading pig popping up in English writings over the next 20 years as a shared cultural reference. William Wordsworth includes the pig in his catalogue of London's freakish

A. W. Rowland (✉)
University of Kansas, Lawrence, KS, USA
e-mail: arowland@ku.edu

© The Author(s) 2018
A. O'Malley (ed.), *Literary Cultures and Eighteenth-Century Childhoods*, Literary Cultures and Childhoods,
https://doi.org/10.1007/978-3-319-94737-2_6

spectacles in the *Prelude*: 'All moveables of wonder from all parts / Are here, Albinos, painted Indians, Dwarfs, / The Horse of Knowledge, and the learned Pig.'[3] In 1807, Robert Southey's prime example of the 'indiscriminate curiosity' and credulity of the English is the very same 'erudite swine': 'the learned pig was in his day a far greater object of admiration to the English nation than ever was sir Isaac Newton.'[4] And Samuel Taylor Coleridge, writing in 1816, also turned to the pig when musing on what he found to be the rather strange phrase, 'the Reading Public':

> But the phrase ... brings to my mind the mistake of the lethargic Dutch traveller, who returning highly gratified from a showman's caravan, which he had been tempted to enter by the words, THE LEARNED PIG, gilt on the pannels, met another caravan of a similar shape, with THE READING FLY on it, in letters of the same size and splendor. 'Why, dis is voonders above voonders!' exclaims the Dutchman, takes his seat as first comer, and soon fatigued by waiting, and by the very hush and intensity of his expectation, gives way to his constitutional somnolence, from which he is roused by the supposed showman at Hounslow, with a *'In what name, Sir! was your place taken? Are you booked all the way for Reading?'* – Now a Reading Public is (to my mind) more marvellous still, and in the third tier of 'voonders above voonders.'[5]

Coleridge's riff on voonderful acts of reading comes in a footnote at a moment of reflection on his own preferred readers. He has not, he insists, courted what he considers a 'promiscuous audience' but rather writes for men of 'that *'sound book learnedness'* into which our old public schools still continue to initiate their pupils,' men with 'occasional impulses at least to philosophic thought.'[6] Coleridge's elitism here betrays a strong anxiety about popular culture and mass literacy, about the extent to which 'our Readers' have 'multiplied exceedingly' into a 'vast company' that is 'dieted at the two public *ordinaries* of Literature, the circulating libraries and the periodical press.'[7]

Indeed, in the decades around the turn of the nineteenth century the Learned Pig became a favorite image for evoking the dangers and confusions of popular consumer culture. Wordsworth's pointed contrast of the 'moveable' wonders of London to the 'steady form' and 'forms / Perennial' of the 'ancient hills' hints at the anxiety caused by the unstable, ever-shifting, 'undistinguishable world' of the city; the freaks and monsters of Bartholomew Fair are threatening precisely because they are odd and disorderly mixtures of disparate things, 'jumbled up together,' 'melted and reduced / To one identity, by differences / That have no law, no meaning, and no end.'[8] Creatures and their categories become muddled and distinctions are collapsed in the fair's 'blank confusion.'[9] Paul Keen describes the particular taxonomic confusions on display at showings of the Learned Pig and other popular animal acts in the late eighteenth century as a 'set of spectatorial reversals': slavishly following after the latest novelty, people crowd to watch the performances of seemingly rational animals and, in so doing, display their own bestial tendencies. As Keen writes: 'the more these performing animals succeeded in appearing human-like, the more starkly their obvious discipline and training contrasted with the misplaced energies of those whose habits they had learned to mimic.'[10] As animals acted like humans, humans acted like animals, suggesting that one of the most disquieting aspects of the modern city's 'blank confusion' was a fundamental collapse of distinction between human and animal, between people and pigs.

What interests me in the case of the Learned Pig is that *reading* plays such a critical role in the definition and confusion of human and animal. Coleridge signals this most clearly in the connections he makes between 'the Reading Public' and the reading pig. The idea of widespread popular literacy brings to his mind the image of an animal reading, or, more specifically, the image of a credulous and torpid man stupidly marveling at the spectacle of a reading animal. For Coleridge, both man and pig serve as ready-to-hand examples of unthinking consumption and thus of 'illiterate readers,' that oxymoronic cultural category whose emergence Keen traces to cultural anxieties about popular print culture troubling the last decades of the eighteenth century. 'Illiterate readers' are 'those people who had mastered the mechanics of reading but were either incapable or unwilling to engage in the more arduous process of critical reflection.'[11] Thus to connect a reading pig to a reading public as Coleridge does not only begs the question of the difference between man and animal but also the question of what it means to read. What do we do when we read? Is reading a matter merely of alphabetization, of rote 'mechanics' that can be imitated, repeated and performed? Or is it a matter of rational thought and sympathetic imagination, of a subjectivity uniquely human? Can one be both literate and illiterate? Or can reading work to mark and maintain the differences between human and nonhuman animals?

The questions of what it means to be human and what it means to read became persistently tangled up in each other with the emergence of popular print culture over the course of the eighteenth century. The figure of the Learned Pig makes these entanglements evident, but an exclusive focus on the pig's appearance in adult literature and writings misses much of the complexity of the figure's cultural work. For one of the most sustained explorations of what reading is and what role it plays in distinguishing the human from the animal can be found in eighteenth-century children's literature, where the Learned Pig makes a significant appearance in Sarah Trimmer's influential *Fabulous Histories* (1786) (later published as *The Story of the Robins*). As a figure in a children's book, the Learned Pig joins a host of speaking, spelling and reading animals that populate the pages of eighteenth-century children's literature, animals that, as Tess Cosslett has argued, were central to the rise of a separate literature for children.[12] We can view the talking animals of children's literature as the liberty of a playful genre; as Cosslett points out: 'the belief ... that children are somehow "nearer" to nature and to animals than adults, means that these children's stories can explore the animal-human divide with more freedom and playfulness than literature directed at adults.'[13] But the assumption enabling this playfulness—the belief 'that children are somehow "nearer" to nature and to animals than adults'—is foundational to Enlightenment theories of the natural or animal origins of human language, suggesting that the linguistically gifted animals of children's literature are cousins to the similarly endowed animals of eighteenth-century conjectural history and philosophy.

The Learned Pig in Trimmer's *Fabulous Histories* connects the animals of children's literature and those of conjectural history and, in so doing, brings childhood literacy into focus as a critical category in the definition of the human. Infant language acquisition became newly interesting in the eighteenth century, along with infant education more generally, not only as a way to observe and influence an important phase in the formation of the human, but also as the place to monitor the differences and similarities between the human and the animal. To this end, scenes of children learning to read became newly significant as enacting another crucial step in the process of becoming human, and as animals were increasingly credited with language, it was not the ability to speak, but the ability to read and write that became important distinguishing characteristics of human beings. Literature and the scene of the child learning to read thus took their place as critical figures in the development and distinction of the human, but as such, they beg questions about what exactly qualifies as reading.[14] As the Learned Pig and other reading animals in children's literature perform the mechanical skills of spelling and reading, human literacy moves inward, and reading becomes a marker of human cognition and consciousness.

There are many reasons why British children's literature of the eighteenth century featured nonhuman animals and animal stories so extensively. John Locke, who influentially exhorted parents to make instruction amusing for their children and who specifically recommended *Aesop's Fables* as the best book to be placed in the hands of a child, played a critical role in establishing animal stories as a staple of children's literature. The stories of *Aesop's Fables*, according to Locke, were 'apt to delight and entertain a Child' and thus would 'reward his Pains in Reading' and yet not 'fill his Head with perfectly useless Trumpery, or lay the Principles of Vice and Folly.'[15] As Jayne Lewis has shown, *Aesop's Fables* would have appealed to Locke not only because of their balance of entertainment and moral instruction, but also because of the fables' well-established place in seventeenth-century school texts and particularly in educational reform efforts to 'realign primary education with the world of ... phenomenal and familiar things.'[16] The English used the animals, natural objects, concrete vocabulary and graphic illustrations of *Aesop's Fables* to naturalize textual experience and, in Lewis's words again, to 'bridge the sensible and linguistic realms.'[17] It is not surprising, then, that authors would have readily turned to Aesop's animals in writing for children who were crossing precisely that bridge between the material world and the world of signs and symbolic language, for children learning to read.

The animals of eighteenth-century children's literature may be the descendants of Aesop's beasts, but they carried new messages from the Enlightenment world of natural history and benevolent humanity, particularly as the humane treatment of animals became a central concern of eighteenth-century educational theory.[18] Locke famously warned that children who are cruel to animals will 'by degrees harden their minds even toward men' and urged mothers to encourage the kind treatment of animals in their children.[19] A book such as Sarah Trimmer's *An Easy Introduction to the Knowledge of Nature* (1770) offers lessons on the basic husbandry and habits of animals—'There is the dairy-maid milking the cows. How comfortable the cattle look grazing in the verdant meadow! I dare say the herbage is as pleasant to them as apple-pie is to you'—as well as lectures on the inhumanity of hunting, cock-fighting and trapping birds.[20] Natural histories for children drew on the bestiary tradition to present illustrated catalogues and descriptions of animals but often added moral exhortations urging children to treat animals with compassion.

Benevolence to animals, however, almost always had clear human recompense and application. As Harriet Ritvo notes, 'the animal kingdom, with man in his divinely ordained position at its apex, offered a compelling metaphor for the hierarchical human social order, in which the animals represented subordinate human groups.'[21] Lessons in kindness to animals, Andrew O'Malley argues, were often blatantly designed to be lessons in kindness to the lower orders of society; the child, typically figured as upper or middle class and male, learns his own place in the social hierarchy as he learns the moral and pragmatic benefits of treating working animals, servants, and labourers with benevolence.[22] 'It is extremely fatiguing to a poor boy, with his heavy nailed shoes, to walk by the side of a plough all day,' Mamma tells Henry in Trimmer's *Easy Introduction* when pointing to a horse, 'so I think that the least we can do is to give them plenty of oats and hay, and a warm stable at night.'[23] Trimmer's casual gestures of comparison between the animal being observed and the child being addressed— 'I dare say the herbage is as pleasant to them as apple-pie is to you'—are habitual and characteristic of how animals are used in eighteenth-century children's literature, gestures which invite the child into 'simultaneous identification with and differentiation from animals.'[24] Such mixed invitations to sympathize yet keep separate are foundational to how these texts negotiate the boundaries between human and animal, as well as how they teach the child his or her proper place in the hierarchies of human and nonhuman animals.

When the horse, cow and bird *talk*, however, such calibrations of sympathetic identification and hierarchical discrimination can quickly become skewed. Anthropomorphizing animals by giving them the capacity to speak runs the risk of promoting excessive sympathetic identification, and Trimmer was not alone in considering 'immoderate tenderness' toward animals as grave a fault as cruelty.[25] The extent to which the talking animals of eighteenth-century children's literature misrepresent or destabilize the distinctions and hierarchical orderings of human and nonhuman animals was much debated in the pages of the books themselves. Talking animals typically came with caveats insisting on their imaginary status. The stories of *Fabulous Histories*, Trimmer reminds her young readers, should be considered 'not as containing the real conversations of Birds (for that is impossible we should ever understand) but as a series of Fables.'[26] In this way, the animals that *can* talk in the pages of the child's book become an opportunity to point out the animals that *cannot* talk in the child's world. As Trimmer comments on the relationship between child and animal: 'the line of distinction should be carefully drawn.'[27]

It is, however, exactly at the point of language, at the question of who and what can talk, that other Enlightenment texts refused to hold the line. Keith Thomas describes the eighteenth century as a period in which 'popular and learned notions about animals combined to weaken the orthodox doctrine of man's uniqueness,' and this was certainly the case in discussions of language where the traditional idea of speech as what separates human beings from the rest of the animal world eroded significantly over the course of the century.[28] Philosophical histories of language increasingly located the origins of human speech in the gestures, feelings and sounds of the human body, a language of action or sensation that humans were understood to share with nonhuman animals. Some conjectural historians speculated that humans first learned language from animals, as in *Of the Origin and Progress of Language* where Lord Monboddo speculates on how man's 'inarticulate cries' develop into a 'method of communication by sound ... like a musical language formed by the imitation of birds.' Man, Monboddo insists, is 'the most imitative of all animals,' and the treatises of Enlightenment philosophers of language are filled with animals and animal language for early man to mimic.[29] Novels and poems of the sentimental literary tradition followed suit and regularly featured scenes of humans imitating and communicating with animals or birds, suggesting possibilities of sympathy and similarity between them.[30]

Children's literature incorporated these ideas about a shared natural or animal language, using animal figures to teach children the fundamentals of language and staging scenes of sympathetic interaction between children and animals, whether in tone, look, gesture or word.[31] The mother in Trimmer's *Fabulous Histories* reminds the children that 'though [animals] cannot speak our language, each kind has one of its own, which is perfectly understood by those of their own species; and so far intelligible to us, as to convince us they are susceptible of joy, grief, fear, anger and resentment.'[32] Likewise, the children in Mary Wollstonecraft's *Original Stories from Real Life* learn from their teacher, Mrs. Mason, that animals only appear 'dumb' to those 'who do not observe their looks and gestures.' God 'understands their language,' she assures her pupils, and so do these children when they respond sympathetically to the 'intelligible tones' of a mother bird whose nest has been commandeered by a naughty boy.[33] Such scenes participate in the larger Enlightenment challenge to the idea of human linguistic distinction, even if—and, perhaps, not surprisingly— Mrs. Mason's pupil immediately interrupts 'to ask, if insects and animals were not inferior to men.' 'Certainly' is the prompt reply.[34] Darren

Howard offers a compelling account of the ambivalence generated by such exchanges over the animal object: 'human dominion over and possession of animals are asserted, but the emphasis on dominion and possession sits uneasily next to the assumption of a child's sympathetic identification with animals.'[35]

The uneasiness generated by talking animals in the literary cultures of the long eighteenth century ultimately settles on the figure of the child whose state and status as a human become increasingly uncertain. Indeed, Mrs. Mason's quick assurance of man's superiority to animals turns out to have many shifting elements. Here is how the passage unfolds: 'Certainly, answered Mrs. Mason; and men are inferior to angels; yet we have reason to believe, that those exalted beings delight to do us good. You have heard in a book, which I seldom permit you to read, because you are not of an age to understand it, that angels ... wished for peace on earth, as proof of the good will they felt toward men.'[36] Here man's superiority to animals is immediately tempered by his inferiority to angels, and young children, it becomes clear, are not necessarily—or, at least, *not yet fully*—included in the ranks of men, being too young to read and understand the text which contains man's lore and laws. The stakes are high for these children trying to secure their ever-shifting and precarious place. When her pupils behave badly, Mrs. Mason refrains from scolding them and instead simply informs them that they 'are now inferior to the animals that graze on the common.' When little Mary remains skeptical about treating troublesome insects and worms with kindness, Mrs. Mason coolly comments, 'You are often troublesome – I am stronger than you – yet I do not kill you.'[37]

Understandably, the children respond to such implicit threats with only more questions. When they ask 'in what manner they were to behave, to prove that they were superior to animals,' Mrs. Mason has this reply:

> Be tender-hearted; and let your superior endowments ward off the evils which they cannot foresee. It is only to animals that children *can* do good, men are their superiors. When I was a child, added their tender friend, I always made it my study and delight, to feed all the dumb family that surround our house.... This employment humanized my heart, while, like wax, it took every impression; and Providence has since made me an instrument of good.[38]

To prove their superiority to animals, the children are urged to sympathize with them. This curiously cold formulation of sympathetic identification deserves our close attention, for the child's invitation into that paradoxical relationship of simultaneous identification with and differentiation from the animal here becomes instrumental: they are urged to identify *in order to* differentiate. This rather steely sympathetic structure, it turns out, also frames the children's relationship to 'men,' who are 'their superiors' and who thus cannot be objects of a child's compassion. It seems sympathy only flows downward and in channels that reinforce rather than resist the hierarchical classification of beings. Mrs. Mason's gesture of remembrance—'When I was a child'—somewhat mitigates the rigidity of this hierarchy, suggesting that children may become worthy adults like their 'tender friend' if they, themselves, practice being 'tender-hearted.' Growing up and out of childhood is a possibility, although not one to be taken for granted, as the process, Mrs. Mason insists, must be one of *improvement* for the children ever to be confident of superior status. 'Between angels and men,' Mrs. Mason tells the children, 'a much greater resemblance subsists, than between men and the brute creation; because the two former seem capable of improvement.'[39] Such categorical assertions about humans, angels, and animals generate increasing apprehension in children who are clearly left out of the category of 'men' when the process and effects of improvement are described as 'humanizing.' Seeking assurance that they are not animals, Mrs. Mason's pupils ultimately learn only that they are not fully human.

What we are seeing here is the anxious and even rather clumsy translation of classical and religious hierarchies of beings—in particular, the notion of the chain of being which gives every species its fixed place—into what will become the evolutionary hierarchies of the nineteenth century. Enlightenment thinkers of the eighteenth century prepared the ground for evolutionary ideas by insisting, as Harriet Ritvo notes, 'that the chain of being represented relationships that were dynamic rather than static.'[40] Indeed, Mrs. Mason's emphasis on improvement participates in the larger notion of *development* which cohered across a range of Enlightenment enquiries into the origins and progress of human institutions, including language, and which framed man's species history and man's individual development as linked and parallel processes out of animal or 'savage' origins. What emerges from this notion of a developmental and dynamic 'chain of beings' is, above all, an increasingly permeable boundary between the human and the animal at the level of both the individual and the species.[41] Howard describes this as the 'identity crisis of the enlightenment,' one which 'defines the human as an animal whose difference from other animals lies in its self-definition as not-animal.'[42] The growing consensus that humans develop out of animal origins is the crux of this crisis, how-ever, to the extent that we should instead say that the human comes to be understood as an animal whose difference from other animals lies in its self-definition as *no longer animal*. But this developmental understanding of the human leaves the child in a liminal state; neither fully human nor fully animal, the child of the eighteenth century is increasingly figured as a human-becoming animal or 'an animal object en route to becoming a human subject.'[43]

Because of episodes such as this one in Wollstonecraft's *Original Stories*, children's books became significant sites for tracing and modeling the pro-cess of human development out of animal origins, for staging scenes and teaching skills that enable the human-becoming animal that is the child to become more fully human. Animals that talk—whether they do so with words, as in any number of imaginative and fabulous tales, or in the natu-ral tones and gestures of more realistic texts—suggest that language acqui-sition is no longer that which positively distinguishes the human from the animal, but rather just a developmental step along the child's way to becoming human. The 'line of distinction' between human and animal so important to Sarah Trimmer keeps receding even as these texts try to maintain it. To this end, scenes of children learning to read become newly significant: as animals are credited with language, it is not the ability to speak, but the ability to read that is increasingly pointed to as the distin-guishing characteristic of human beings. Thus Patricia Crain identifies a recurring scene in children's primers of a child trying but failing to teach an animal the alphabet.[44] Anna Barbauld's *Lessons for Children* offers one example of the didactic weight loaded on such scenes (and, once again, of the high stakes involved for the child): 'Can Pierrot, your dog, read?' the mother asks Charles, 'No. Will you teach him? Take the pin and point to the words. No, he will not learn. I never saw a little dog or cat learn to read. But little boys can learn. If you do not learn, Charles, you are not good for half as much as a puss. You had better be drowned.'[45]

It is in this context that Sarah Trimmer introduces the Learned Pig to the pages of her *Fabulous Histories* as the subject of an adult philosophical conversation staged for the edification of little Harriet Benson. One of her mother's visitors introduces the topic by confessing 'I have ... been for a long time accustomed to consider animals as mere machines, ... but the sight of the learned pig, which has lately been shewn in London, has deranged these ideas, and I know not what to think.'[46] What exactly the

Learned Pig can do that so troubles this orthodox Cartesian is later described by Harriet's mother:

> The creature was shown for a sight in a room provided for the purpose, where a number of people assembled to view his performances. Two alphabets of large letters on card paper were placed on the floor; one of the company was then desired to propose a word which he wished the pig to spell. This his keeper repeated to him, and the Pig picked out every letter successively with his snout, and collected them together til the word was compleated.[47]

Perhaps what is so troubling about the learning of this remarkable pig, particularly when recounted in the pages of a children's book, is that the tools of his trade—alphabet cards—and the skills he performs, identifying and assembling letters to spell a word, are exactly the tools and skills of basic literacy featured in children's story books and primers. In fact, the pig's performance immediately calls to mind the canonical figure of children's literature, Little Margery, or Goody Two-Shoes, and her basket of wooden alphabet letters. Margery uses her wooden letters to teach the village children to read, asking them to identify letters and spell words in a variety of games and exercises, exercises which the young readers of *Goody Two-Shoes* are invited to imitate: 'Now, pray, little Reader, take this Bodkin, and see if you can point out the Letters from these mixed Alphabets.'[48]

What is the difference, little Harriet Benson may wonder, between the performance of the pig picking out the letters with his snout and the performance of the child picking out the letters with her bodkin? Not much, she would have to conclude if she were to turn back to her copy of *Goody Two-Shoes* in search of an answer; for when Mrs. Margery Two-Shoes becomes 'President of the A, B, C College,' she trains Ralph the Raven and Tom the Pidgeon to read, spell, and to help her manage her alphabets: 'And as the Raven *Ralph* was fond of the large Letters, *Tom* the Pidgeon took Care of the small ones, of which he composed this Alphabet.'[49] Trimmer uses the figure of the Learned Pig in *Fabulous Histories* precisely to pose such queries of difference and distinction between animal and human and to connect these questions with those about reading and literacy that swirled around accounts of the Learned Pig in other print publications: what counts as reading and what, exactly, do we do when we read? Can pigs read in the same way children read?

'Do you think, mamma,' Harriet asks, 'that the pig knows the letters, and can really spell words?' This is Mrs. Benson's reply:

> I think it possible, my dear, for the pig to be taught to know the letters one from the other, and that his keeper has some private sign, by which he directs him to each that are wanted; but that he has an idea of *spelling* I can never believe; nor are animals capable of attaining human sciences, because for these human faculties are requisite; and no art of man can *change* the nature of any thing, though he may be able to improve that nature to a certain degree, or at least to call forth to view powers which would be hidden from us, because they would only be exerted in the intercourse of animals with each other.[50]

Recognizing letters is one type of learned skill, but this, the mother contends, is not the same as spelling, and despite all sensational reports to the contrary, the mother insists that the pig does not understand how to combine letters to form words nor how to read those words. It is the phrasing of Mrs. Benson's objection, however, that we must note: the learned pig does not have the '*idea* of spelling.' With the insertion of the word 'idea,' Mrs. Benson shifts the grounds of literacy from the mechanics of alphabetization to the inner workings of cognition and consciousness, to the ways that letters and words as a system of representation enable thinking and create meaning. Of course, the implications for writing and reading are that they are not simply mechanical and gestural, not executed merely by pointing to letters and numbers, not an external, visible performance but rather an interior, unseen practice; writing and reading happen in the brain before and beyond the rudimentary alphabetic performances of animals and children.

This understanding of reading as a cognitive rather than mechanical process once again places the child in a precarious and liminal position, especially for the purposes of early reading primers. The basic literacy skills the young child learns in the pages of a children's book are the same as those of performing animals. *Goody Two-Shoes* makes this explicit when it compares the skills of Tom the Pidgeon to those of another famous bird: 'he performed all those extraordinary Things which are recorded of the famous Bird, that was some Time since advertised in the *Haymarket*, and visited by most of the great People in the Kingdom.'[51] This comparison, as well as the presence of the Learned Pig in Trimmer's *Fabulous Histories*, suggests that the reading of both animals and children is primarily performative: visible, capable of being displayed, and functioning as a repertoire of mechanical, repeated gestures primarily for the benefit of an audience. From Comenius's seventeenth-century *Orbis Sensualium Pictus* into alphabet books and primers of the eighteenth century, animals populate the pages of children's literature in order to link letters to the natural, material world and to teach children their sounds and shapes, and to facilitate the child's acquisition of basic literacy skills. But by the mid-eighteenth century, the learned animals of children's books are also staging a shared repertoire of literacy in order to insist upon and simultaneously to break down the barrier between human and nonhuman animals and, most pointedly, to figure the child as a human-becoming animal.

What becomes increasingly important and culturally productive about this precarious figure of the human-becoming child are the conversations about interiority and consciousness that it prompts. More than a decade earlier than Trimmer's discussion and attempted dismissal of the Learned Pig's powers, J. G. von Herder framed the question of animal language and literacy in surprisingly similar ways. In his *Treatise on the Origin of Language*, Herder insists that human language comes into being not through the imitation of animal sounds, as Monboddo proposes, but in that moment the human being 'collect[s] himself into a moment of alertness [to] freely dwell on a single image, pay it clear, more leisurely heed, and separate off characteristic marks for the fact that this is that object and no other.' For Herder, a child learning animal names and sounds does not merely imitate the 'baaa' of the lamb, but turns that bleat into the lamb's 'characteristic mark'; human imitations of animal sounds should not be seen as acts of mimicry, but rather as acts of recognition and representation: 'Aha! You are the bleating one!'[52] On the possibility of animals imitating and acquiring human language, Herder thus concludes: 'parrot and starling have learned enough human sounds, but have they also thought a human word?'[53] Like Trimmer, Herder uses learned animals and literate children to move language and literacy inward and to locate the origin of language in a uniquely human capacity for consciousness. To *think* a word and to have an *idea* of spelling are to enter the field of symbolic representation and 'characteristic marks.'

The notion that animals and humans share a natural language of sounds and even the basic mechanical skills of literacy puts pressure on the question of what exactly reading is that makes it a uniquely human endeavor. Over the course of the eighteenth century, reading—in reaction to the growth of literacy, popular consumer culture and theories of language that broke down distinctions between humans and animals—moves inward to be located in an interior space of human cognition, subjectivity and consciousness. What is at stake in scenes of children learning to read is not only what makes us human, but how we understand the child in relationship to this interiorized humanity. Carolyn Steedman points to the figure of the child as playing a central role in establishing the importance of interiority in late eighteenth-century notions of subjectivity: 'the interiorised self, understood to be the product of a personal history, was most clearly expressed in the idea of "childhood", and the idea of "the child".'[54] But Steedman's emphasis on the personal and individual version of the interior self misses the species history also embedded in the figure of the child: the extent to which the education and development of the child was understood as tracing and enacting the distinction and the history of the human. The scene of the child reading, even as it features a repertoire of literacy also performed by animals, also suggests a potential in the child beyond what can be seen and performed in its present state, what Herder pointed to as the 'other hidden powers sleeping in the human child.'[55] Reading then becomes a way to track the development of those otherwise hidden powers, making visible the 'human being's distinctive feature' even as that distinction moves inward and goes into hiding. Literacy thus acquires developmental stages and the highest levels of reading come to be figured as the most deeply hidden in the human mind. Over and against the material and mechanical reading performances of young children and learned animals, Trimmer uses the Learned Pig to remind her readers of a higher order of literacy, one which, immaterial and invisible in its practice, marks the threshold of the exclusively 'human sciences' and 'human faculties,' a literacy that the child must achieve in order to become fully human.

NOTES

1. Publicity handbill quoted in Richard D. Altick, *The Shows of London* (Cambridge, MA: The Belknap Press of Harvard University Press, 1978), 44. See also Paul Keen, *Literature, Commerce, and the Spectacle of Modernity, 1750–1800* (Cambridge: Cambridge University Press, 2012), 173, and Charles Royster, *The Fabulous History of the Dismal Swamp Company: A Story of George Washington's Times* (New York: Alfred A. Knopf, 1999), 308.
2. *London Unmask'd: Or the New Town Spy. Exhibiting a Striking Picture of the World as It Goes* (London: William Adlard, 1787[?]), 141–142.

3. William Wordsworth, *The Thirteen-Book Prelude*, ed. Mark L. Reed (Ithaca: Cornell University Press, 1991), 210.
4. Robert Southey, *Letters from England* (London: The Cresset Press, 1951), 340.
5. Samuel Taylor Coleridge, *The Statesman's Manual; Or The Bible the Best Guide to Political Skill and Foresight* (Burlington: Chauncey Goodrich, 1832), 51.
6. Ibid., 51.
7. Ibid., 49–50.
8. Wordsworth, *Prelude*, 210–211.
9. Ibid., 210–211.
10. Paul Keen, *Literature, Commerce, and the Spectacle of Modernity, 1750–1800* (Cambridge: Cambridge University Press, 2012), 178.
11. Keen, *Literature*, 167.
12. Tess Cosslett, *Talking Animals in British Children's Fiction, 1786–1914* (Aldershot: Ashgate, 2006), 9.
13. Ibid., 2.
14. I have discussed other aspects of literature, development and becoming human elsewhere; see Ann Wierda Rowland, *Romanticism and Childhood: The Infantilization of British Literary Culture* (Cambridge: Cambridge University Press, 2012), 109–157.
15. John Locke, *Some Thoughts Concerning Education* (1693), quoted in Jayne Lewis, *The English Fable: Aesop and Literary Culture, 1651–1740* (Cambridge: Cambridge University Press, 1996), 40. For discussions of Locke's influence on children's literature, see Cosslett, *Talking Animals*, 9–11, and Samuel F. Pickering, *John Locke and Children's Books in Eighteenth-Century England* (Knoxville: University of Tennessee Press, 1981).
16. Lewis, *The English Fable*, 40.
17. Ibid., 41.
18. Cosslett, *Talking Animals*, 1.
19. John Locke, *Letters to Edward Clarke on Education*, quoted in Cosslett, *Talking Animals*, 10.
20. Sarah Trimmer, *An Easy Introduction to the Knowledge of Nature* (London: T. Longman, 10th ed., 1799), 37.
21. Harriet Ritvo, *Noble Cows and Hybrid Zebras: Essays on Animals and History* (Charlottesville: University of Virginia Press, 2010), 37.
22. Andrew O'Malley, *The Making of the Modern Child: Children's Literature and Childhood in the Late Eighteenth Century* (London: Routledge, 2003), 51–58. See also Christine Kenyon-Jones, *Kindred Brutes: Animals in Romantic-period Writing* (Aldershot: Ashgate, 2001), 57–58; and Cosslett, *Talking Animals*, 14–15 & 18.

23. Trimmer, *Easy Introduction*, 44–45.

24. Heather Klemann, 'How to Think with Animals in Mary Wollstonecraft's *Original Stories* and *The Wrongs of Woman; or, Maria*,' *The Lion and the Unicorn* 39 (2015): 3.

25. Sarah Trimmer, *Fabulous Histories: Designed for the Instruction of Children, Respecting Their Treatment of Animals* (London: T. Longman, 1786), vii.

26. Ibid., x. Dorothy Kilner's *Rational Brutes* begins with the same cautionary reminder; see Dorothy Kilner, *The Rational Brutes; or Talking Animals* (London: Vernor and Hood, Poultry, 1799), 7.

27. Sarah Trimmer, *The Guardian of Education* (London: J. Hatchard, 1803–1806), Vol. I: 304); quoted in Darren Howard, 'Talking Animals and Reading Children: Teaching (dis)Obedience in John Aikin and Anna Barbauld's *Evenings at Home*,' *Studies in Romanticism*, 48 (Winter 2009): 644.

28. Keith Thomas, *Man and the Natural World: Changing Attitudes in England, 1500–1800* (Oxford: Oxford University Press, 1983), 135.

29. James Burnet Monboddo, *Of the Origin and Progress of Language* (Edinburgh: J. Balfour, 1774), Vol. 1, 494, 208. Vocal mimicry is still considered the basis of human language.

30. For a longer examination of Enlightenment histories of language and how this discourse defines the human, the relationship between child and animal and the philosophical conception of infancy, see Rowland, *Romanticism and Childhood*, 67–157.

31. For discussions of how alphabet books from Comenius onward used animals to usher children into language and letters, see Patricia Crain, *The Story of A: The Alphabetization of America from* The New England Primer *to* The Scarlet Letter (Stanford: Stanford University Press, 2000) 26–38, and Klemann, 'How to Think with Animals,' 4–5.

32. Trimmer, *Fabulous Histories*, 60.

33. Mary Wollstonecraft, *Original Stories from Real Life* (1791) (Otley: Woodstock Books, 2001), 12, 9.

34. Ibid., 13.

35. Howard, 'Talking Animals,' 650.

36. Wollstonecraft, *Original Stories*, 13.

37. Ibid., 30 & 5.

38. Ibid., 16–17 (emphasis in original).

39. Ibid., 14.

40. Ritvo, *Noble Cows*, 5.

41. For a more thorough discussion about the emergence of *development* in the eighteenth century as the dominant way of describing change over time, see Rowland, *Romanticism and Childhood*, 25–66.

42. Howard, 'Talking Animals,' 653.

43. Rowland, *Romanticism and Childhood*, 109–11; and Howard, 'Talking Animals,' 647.
44. Crain, *The Story of A*, 103.
45. Anna Letitia Barbauld, *Lessons for Children: Part III Being the Second for Children of Three Years Old* (London: J. Johnson, 1795), 6–7.
46. Trimmer, *Fabulous Histories*, 67.
47. Ibid., 71.
48. *The History of Little Goody Two-Shoes; Otherwise called Mrs. Margery Two-Shoes*, 3rd Edition (London: J. Newberry, 1766), 31.
49. Ibid., 72.
50. Trimmer, *Fabulous Histories*, 72.
51. *The History of Little Goody Two-Shoes*, 72.
52. Johann Gottfried von Herder, *Philosophical Writings*, translated and edited by Michael N. Foster (Cambridge: Cambridge University Press, 2002), 87–88.
53. Ibid., 95.
54. Carolyn Steedman, *Strange Dislocations: Childhood and the Idea of Human Interiority 1780–1930* (Cambridge: Harvard University Press, 1995), 5.
55. Herder, *Philosophical Writings*, 81.

CHAPTER 7

Eighteenth-Century Children's Poetry and the Complexity of the Child's Mind

Louise Joy

Isaac Watts's *Divine Songs Attempted in Easy Language for the Use of Children* (1715) was not the first volume of poems written expressly for children, but it was the first successfully to make the case that something peculiar might be achieved by addressing children through poetic form, and that in order to effectively meet the needs and capacities of a young audience, poetry needed to be shaped with those needs and capacities in mind. By the end of the eighteenth century, Watts's volume had gone through at least 14 editions, and, as Harvey Darton points out, by the end of the nineteenth century, several of the poems within it had suffered the 'misfortune' of 'being recited by children in public, year in, year out, to the mortification of the reciters and the weariness of the audience.'[1] Over the course of the eighteenth century, then, poetry that was specially written or adapted for young people came to occupy a central place in the child's life of the mind. By 1745, the notion that children ought to be conversant with the principles of poetry had become such an established one that John Newbery dedicated an entire volume of his series, *Circle of the Sciences* (1745–6), to the business of introducing young readers to excerpts of poetry and equipping them with strategies for understanding them.

L. Joy (✉)
Homerton College, University of Cambridge, Cambridge, UK
e-mail: lj214@cam.ac.uk

© The Author(s) 2018
A. O'Malley (ed.), *Literary Cultures and Eighteenth-Century Childhoods*, Literary Cultures and Childhoods,
https://doi.org/10.1007/978-3-319-94737-2_7

The pre-eminent place that adults aspired for poetry to have in children's culture can be construed from the fact that there are no equivalent volumes in the *Circle of the Sciences* series devoted to other species of literature, reflecting the engrained view of poetry's aesthetic and moral superiority to prose or drama. As John Dennis wrote in *The Advancement and Reformation of Modern Poetry* (1701), 'Poetry…is more passionate and sensual than prose,' a belief which endured throughout the period, despite concerted attempts to establish the aesthetic and moral credentials of the novel.[2] But Newbery's tacit prioritisation of poetry over prose also indicates a widespread supposition that whereas prose is self-explanatory, poetry does not readily yield itself to the reader, and it can only be understood, or at least only understood correctly, after initiation.[3] This is apparent in the use of 'Easy' in the titles both of Newbery's volume, *Poetry Made Familiar and Easy*, and Watts's *Divine Songs Attempted in Easy Language for the Use of Children*, wherein the emphasis placed on accessibility alerts us to the perceived difficulty of this art form for its intended audience. Careful examination of how these two seminal figures in the evolution of children's literature, Isaac Watts and John Newbery, manipulated subject matter and form in order to render poetry 'easy' for the child provides us with a means of viewing some of the period's most prominent ideas about children's cognitive needs and capacities and reflecting on the role established during the period for children's poetry in cultivating intellect.

In the Preface to *Divine Songs*, Watts proclaims: 'I have endeavoured to sink the language to the level of a child's understanding, and yet to keep it (if possible) above contempt.'[4] This visual metaphor of height and depth implies a scale in which, as the word 'contempt' drives home, simplicity is aligned with intellectual poverty on the one hand and complexity aligned with intellectual prowess on the other. In this respect, Watts perpetuates a customary belief in the child's ignorance as a gap that must be filled. The influence of John Locke's *Some Thoughts Concerning Education* (1693) in the early decades of the eighteenth century had weakened the dominance of the Puritan view of the child's ignorance as a sign of immorality and ungodliness, seen in the catechism *Milk for Babes* (1646) by the New England reformer John Cotton: '*Qu. How doth the Ministery of the Law bring you towards Christ?* A. By bringing me to know my sinne, and the wrath of God against me for it.'[5] Nonetheless, even in Locke's more liberal account of knowledge, ignorance carries with it the weight of shame, albeit in the secularised political sense that it signifies social redundancy rather than moral perdition. In *Some Thoughts Concerning Education*,

Locke argues that 'Curiosity in children…is but an appetite after knowledge, and therefore ought to be encouraged in them, not only as a good sign, but as the great instrument nature has provided to remove that ignorance they were born with, and which, without this busy inquisitiveness, will make them dull and useless creatures.'[6] To prevent such psychological and social waste, and to foster instead a 'sound mind in a sound body,'[7] is the primary stated aim of Locke's educational treatise. Watts's deployment of 'easy language' thus seeks to tread a delicate path between acknowledging the Lockean belief in children's native desire for intellectual stimulation and the consequent need for literary material to challenge children into readiness to negotiate complexity, while at the same time accepting that the cognitive needs of the pre- or newly literate are such that they require material devoid of unnecessary complication.

Watts reconciles, at least in part, the possible tension between these competing demands through his recognition that 'language' cannot be reduced to mere diction. Watts appreciates that since a child's vocabulary is less extensive than an adult's, poetry for children needs to favour terminology already familiar to the child. That this practice has in the centuries since become a customary feature of writing for children should not obscure its innovativeness in 1715. Watts was not responsible for inaugurating it. John Bunyan, for example, whose *A Book for Boys and Girls, or Country Rhymes for Children* (1696) went through nine editions by 1724, had made some attempts to temper his mode of address to his young readership through the incorporation of lines which refer in simple terms to instantly recognisable natural phenomena: 'This pretty Bird, oh! how she flies and sings!'[8] But lines such as these are interspersed with lines elsewhere whose comprehension requires a secure grasp of subtle theological nomenclature: 'The fallen Candles to us intimate, / The bulk of God's Elect in their lapst state.'[9] Likewise, James Janeway's prose *A Token for Children* (1672) intermittently ventriloquises distinctively childish voices, but the polysyllabic circumlocutions he attributes to his juvenile characters belie the adult machinations behind the scenes: 'O Mother…it is not any particular Sin of Omission or Commission, that sticks so close to my Conscience, as the Sin of my nature.'[10] By comparison, the vocabulary which Watts selects for his child audience is more consistently and calculatedly pared down, so much so that in the decades following the publication of *Divine Songs*, Watts came to emblematise this practice. John Wesley, in his Preface to the 1790 edition of his brother Charles's *Hymns for Children* (1763), in which he attempts to defend Charles's sophisticated phraseology, therefore refers back to Watts to set up a counterpoint. Watts, he complains, neglected to teach his readers because he adjusted language to the demands of children rather than requiring children to meet the demands of language: 'There are two ways of writing or speaking to children,' John Wesley writes; 'the one is, to let ourselves down to them; the other, to lift them up to us. Dr. Watts has wrote [sic] in the former way... leaving [children] as he found them.'[11] Similarly, Watts is the implicit target when Anna Laetitia Barbauld in her Preface to *Hymns in Prose* (1781) claims that it is an assault on poetry to adapt it to the child's ear, insisting that prose is a more suitable form for young readers until their cognitive skills are sufficiently developed to enable appreciation of ambiguity. What all of these accounts share in common is a belief that children find it simpler to deal in vocabulary that is already within their purview; what is at stake is a difference of opinion concerning the pedagogical (and, implicitly, the aesthetical and moral) advantages of catering to, versus resisting, the child's ease.

It is clear, though, both from Watts's Preface to *Divine Songs* and from the poems themselves that what Watts has in mind by 'language' is not merely *which* words are used but also *how* these words are used: that is to say, not just diction or the systems within which words function (what Ferdinand de Saussure would later term 'langue') but also the forms in, or methods by which, words are uttered ('parole').[12] Watts gauged that poetic form could be customised to render it peculiarly apposite for child readers. Believing that the key pedagogical advantage of verse over prose was its memorability—'What is learnt in verse is longer retained in memory, and sooner recollected. The like sounds and the like number of syllables exceedingly assist the remembrance' (5)—Watts made a powerful argument for the importance of repetition. Patterning the form such that a feature reappears again and again is, he suggests, a means of embedding a thought into the mind, since together recursive patterns form a memorable tune (a feature that is foregrounded by his decision to identify these poems for children as *songs*).[13] Accordingly, the metrical lines used in *Divine Songs* are strikingly unvaried and hence easy for the child to anticipate. The majority of the stanzas used are quatrains made up of alternating rhyme; most are lines of tetrameter, sometimes alternated with lines of trimeter to comprise common metre, the traditional metre of hymns. This template was taken up as the usual poetic form of choice by Watts's successors, for example, by the anonymous author of *Little Master's Miscellany*

(1767), by Christopher Smart in *Hymns for the Amusement of Children* (1771), and even by William Blake in *Songs of Innocence* (1789).[14] Its close correspondence with ballad metre, the metre of so many popular songs and verses disseminated orally during the period, meant that children would likely already be accustomed to the conventions of the form.[15] Watts hopes that encountering subject matter in a form that can be replayed again and again in the inner ear enables his reader, seemingly inadvertently, to catch hold of the ideas carried by the semantic connotations of the words: 'it may often happen, that the end of a song running in the mind may be an effectual means to keep off some temptation, or to incline to some duty, when a word of scripture is not upon the thoughts' (5). Watts's theory of children's poetry thus deals in a kind of proto-unconscious. Nearly a century before Samuel Taylor Coleridge imported the vocabulary of the unconscious into the English language, musing in his *Notebook*, 'there is a self, or consciousness of the day, and an opposing self of the night,'[16] Watts envisages that the trick of the educationalist must be to instil habits of mind without the reader even appearing to notice. Indeed, for the sleight of hand to be successful, the educator must appear to be doing the opposite, performing what today we might call *reverse psychology*, or what in his 1784 work, *Studies in Nature*, Jacques-Henri Bernardin de Saint-Pierre, the disciple of Jean-Jacques Rousseau, termed 'contrary effects': 'if the nurse wants her child to laugh, she shrouds her head in her apron; upon this the infant becomes serious.'[17] Watts aspires for his language to be 'easy,' then, in the sense that its ingestion requires a lack of effort—or at least, a lack of conscious effort—on the part of its reader.

Watts was not the first to perceive the possibilities inherent in manipulating poetic form for a child audience. For example, the anonymous author of *A Guide for the Child and Youth* (1709), identified simply as 'A Teacher of a Private School,' recognises that 'Prayers, Graces, and Instructions' must be 'fitted to the Capacity of Children' if they are to be accessible to their designated audience, and lights upon poetic form as a fertile mode for communication. However, the writing in *A Guide for the Child and Youth* wears its laboriousness in plain view, resulting in verse that is awkward to read and instantly forgettable. In one poem, the author sets up an anapaestic metre, forcing the word 'Petition' into three distinctly separate syllables in a way that causes the word to be articulated unnaturally, with the emphasis on the first syllable:

> First in the Morning
> When thou dost awake,
> To God for his Grace
> Thy Petition make. (1–4)

Whilst in so doing, the author maintains metrical consistency, we are forced to treat the word not as a carrier of semantic meaning but as a series of pulses in order to complete the line. As Alexander Pope mockingly observed in *Essay on Criticism*, 'But most by numbers judge a poet's song; / And smooth or rough, with them is right or wrong.'[18] The flexibility of the author of *A Guide for the Child and Youth* in relation to the rules of scansion leaves his poetry susceptible to outright rejection. For Watts, though, it was crucial that sound and sense were embroiled in one another in order to enable children to replay the poem to themselves on demand: 'This will be a constant furniture for the minds of children, that they may have something to think upon when alone, and sing over to themselves' (5). The elision here between thought and song reveals the ways in which Watts aspires for the one to yield to the other: the sound will bring to mind the thought, just as the thought will bring to mind the sound. Ann Wierda Rowland has recently demonstrated the ubiquitousness in the eighteenth century of the idea that primitive speech, and by extension the speech of infancy, was proximate to music.[19] Johann Gottfried von Herder's *Treatise on the Origin of Language*, for instance, refers to the 'wild, unarticulated noises' of children as a 'language of sensation' (66). Crucially, for Watts, the connection between thought and sound at play in poetry is one that not merely expresses, but moreover produces, the primal sensation of pleasure. For all that Joyce Irene Whalley has argued that 'to "like" or "enjoy" reading is a comparatively recent concept,'[20] Watts understands the necessity that the child be motivated to read by the thrill of the process itself. In Watts's account, though, such pleasure is envisaged as unwitting; indeed, it is generated precisely by the inadvertency of the child's ingestion of the text. The fact that the child does not need to try, the fact that the text burrows its way into the child's ear without the child having to make an effort to learn it, is precisely the point. This marks a clear departure from established Early Modern learning methods such as catechism, which was a key means in the period of ensuring that ideas were imprinted on the child's mind.[21] The *ease* of Watts's language, then, is not merely a token nod to the child's comparatively narrow vocabulary; it is moreover a means to ensure both the message's safe passage and the child's satisfaction from, perhaps even enjoyment of, the journey itself.

There are certain key insights that we can extrapolate from Watts's championing of easy language as the language most fit for the child reader. One is the obvious point which was largely accepted without question in the period: that the child's cognitive capacities were limited to functions that were basic. Hence, Locke had claimed:

> Children's minds are narrow and weak, and usually susceptible but of one thought at once. Whatever is in a child's head, fills it for the time, especially if set on with any passion. It should therefore be the skill and art of the teacher, to clear their heads of all other thoughts, whilst they are learning of any thing, the better to make room for what he would instil into them, that it may be received with attention and application, without which it leaves no impression. The natural temper of children disposes their minds to wander.[22]

One of Locke's many radical interventions into educational thought had been to encourage a view of the child's inability to concentrate for long periods of time as an inevitable feature of childhood cognition rather than as something to be railed against: 'Inadvertency, forgetfulness, unsteadiness, and wandering of thought,' he writes, 'are the natural faults of childhood' (132). Whilst he still labels these characteristics as 'faults,' keeping in play an association between inattention and wilful immorality, Locke's promotion of tolerance towards the child's short attention span enabled writers who, like Watts, were interested in addressing children to think with renewed focus about the kinds of poetic techniques that would best suit this cognitive feature. Watts's deployment of 'easy language' also enables us to view in clear sight another belief that pre-dominated in the period: the belief that the child might be inherently lazy or disinclined towards intellectual effort. By the beginning of the eighteenth century, this view of children had become such an established belief that it was often used as a stock motif, with numerous images of the child, both visual and verbal, emphasising a state of indolence. Advice manuals, such as the anonymously authored *Advice to a Son, Directing Him How to Demean Himself in the Most Important Passages of Life*, popular in the decade when Watts published *Divine Songs*, urged the child against idleness: 'Avoid Sloth, if thou would'st avoid Scorn; Shame is the reward of a Sluggard: Idleness will bring thee to want and beggary' (89). The most well-known of the poems in Watts's *Divine Songs*, 'Against Idleness and Mischief,' is dedicated precisely to this theme, its very susceptibility to parody, most notably by Lewis Carroll, itself an indicator of its totemic familiarity.[23]

But a radical insight underpins Watts's championing of easy language. Watts's dedication to the child's pleasure reflects a belief, or at least a hope, that intellectual effort is more effective if it is allied to reward. This belief went against the mainstream current: physical punishment was still widespread in schools, despite the fact that Locke had argued its counter-productiveness, and the belief that education was a necessary chore under-pinned much thinking on pedagogy and curriculum.[24] Centuries' worth of moral and theological thought reinforced the attitude, enshrined in scrip-ture, that 'He that spareth the rod, hateth his son; but he that loveth him, chasteneth him betimes' (Proverbs, XIII, 24), and both educational the-ory and practice largely reified it.[25] Watts does not present his modification of this position as a rejection of such moral or theological thought. Nor is it expressly an endorsement of the aesthetic valorisation of instruction through delight that Horace had immortalised in *Ars Poetica* (19 BC) and which was to prove a central guiding principle for much mid-century chil-dren's literature by John Newbery and his followers. Watts's implicit argu-ment operates instead at a logical level: the child should enjoy the play of ideas not because it is the duty of the adult to make the child happy (an idea not really articulated with any influence or forcefulness until well into the nineteenth century), but because this is a more reliable way of ensur-ing that the child learns at all. As Matthew Grenby has put it, the 'enter-tainment on offer in respectable children's books was generally understood...as a catalyst of education, but not, at least until the nine-teenth century, as an end in itself.'[26] Even in the late eighteenth century, children's writers still felt the need to justify the pleasurable elements of their children's books, by way of such arguments as Mary Ann Kilner's in her Preface to *The Adventures of a Pincushion*: 'the avidity with which children peruse books of entertainment, is a proof how much publications proper for their attention are required.'[27] Watts, then, rejects compulsion, and although he does not go as far as embracing voluntarism of the kind that the Edgeworths would later champion in *Practical Education* (1798), what Watts envisages is a kind of involuntarism, a kind of alchemy that will inevitably occur once the child is exposed to verse. Where Locke had repu-diated physical compulsion on the basis that it reinforces concern with bodily pleasure and pain, we might see here in Watts's proto-psychology an unspoken acknowledgement of the importance of bodily appetite. He builds on Locke's belief that physical drives are intuitive and that education involves learning how to harness our passions so that we become accustomed not always to pursuing sensory pleasure. Watts's *Divine Songs*, then, presents the child with an opportunity to give in to the pursuit of *jouissance* (the thrill of acoustic play) as a means to the end of education. In so doing, Watts's children's poems provide an early example of what Ellenor Fenn in her Preface to *Rational Sports* would later more explicitly refer to as the possibility for literature to 'tincture the mind' by inculcating a 'taste for rational amusement.'[28]

It is one thing to get a rhyme or rhythm into the child's head; it is something else altogether to know that the child has acknowledged the semantic content of those lines and that anything material has been learned. We see in Watts's optimism a faith in children's impressionability, their susceptibility to sensation and affect, which is a belief that recurs throughout the period, articulated by David Hartley in his 1749 *Observations*, when he remarks that children are 'more exquisitely sensible and irritable than adults.'[29] He elaborates: 'Children, and young Persons, are diverted by every little jingle, pun, contrast, or coincidence, which is level to their Capacities, even though the Harshness and Inconsistency, with which it first strikes the Fancy, be so minute as scarce to be perceived.'[30] Such impressionability carried with it heavy consequences for the educationalist, since it was widely believed that the 'impression of those ideas, which are first engraven on young minds, will influence their characters ever afterwards.'[31] In particular, it was thought that children were unusually affected by passion, and that early education takes place primarily through emotional exchange. Henry Home, Lord Kames, anticipating the connection that William Wordsworth would later draw between the ingestion of love and the ingestion of milk in his famous depiction of the primal scene in *The Prelude* (1798), wrote that an 'infant on the breast discerns good or bad humour in its nurse, from their external signs on her countenance, and from the different tones of her voice.'[32] He envisages the child as peculiarly perceptive of the 'internal passions' that are encoded in their 'external signs.'[33] Children, then, were perceived to be conspicuously susceptible to external influence. This belief carried into literary theory in the form of an anxiety about, alongside a concomitant optimism in relation to, the child's vulnerability to its reading matter. At the end of the eighteenth century, Ellenor Fenn lamented in her Preface to *School Occurrences*: 'Those who are conversant with children, know, that they are more influenced by maxims which they chance to meet with in books, than by those that are inculcated by their parents. It ought not to be *so.*— But *so* it is' (vi).

The ways in which Watts's *Divine Songs* seeks to visit 'maxims' on children, and the nature of the cognitive activity which these 'chance' encounters precipitate, or seek to precipitate, in their child readers, can best be examined through close reading of particular poems. Take, for example, 'Song 1: A General Song of Praise to God,' quoted here in full:

How glorious is our Heavenly King,
Who reigns above the sky!
How shall a child presume to sing
His dreadful majesty?

How great his power is none can tell,
Nor think how large his grace;
Not men below, nor saints that dwell
On high before his face.

Not angels that stand round the Lord
Can search his secret will;
But they perform his heavenly word,
And sing his praises still.

Then let me join this holy train,
And my first offerings bring;
Th'eternal God will not disdain
To hear an infant sing.

My heart resolves, my tongue obeys,
And angels shall rejoice
To hear their mighty Maker's praise
Sound from a feeble voice.

The poem rehearses for children a sequence of worshipping manoeuvres. Ostensibly, it appears to open with a series of questions, but grammatically the opening sentence is in fact a statement, one which is aurally indistinguishable from a question, a confusion which is exacerbated by the fact that the subsequent sentence is indeed grammatically a question. The proximity of the two kinds of sentence to one another requires the child reader not merely passively to recognise but moreover actively to experience that observation and interrogation might be bound up in one another, particularly when it comes to the contemplation of the divine. The potentially limitless consequences of this expansive thought, however, are kept in check by the contained nature of the common metre, which provides what feels like a question-and-answer format, wherein the reader is invited to treat the shorter lines of trimeter as solutions of kinds to the sonic problems posed by the longer lines of tetrameter. The poem thus provides its child readers with a means of broaching large abstract questions in a form that promises reassurance and finitude. Locke had written: 'Much less are children capable of reasonings from remote principles. They cannot conceive the force of long deductions: the reasons that move them must be obvious, and level to their thoughts, and such as may (if I may so say) be felt and touched.'[34] This poem recognises the cognitive barriers that might render it hard for children to think in the abstract by carefully managing the transitions between the particular and the general.

The delayed entry of the first-person singular in stanza four, until which point the child is subsumed within a plural first-person voice, 'we,' provides the reader with a means of identifying as a plurality, not merely of children, but of people, by virtue of an apparently shared reading experience. The invitation to feel the pulse is proffered as a means of coming together with others—of being initiated into the rites of a culture. As the American philosopher of education, John Dewey, was to observe at the beginning of the twentieth century:

> Society exists through a process of transmission quite as much as biological life. This transmission occurs by means of communication of habits of doing, thinking, and feeling from the older to the younger. Without this communication of ideals, hopes, expectations, standards, opinions, from those members of society who are passing out of the group life to those who are coming into it, social life could not survive.[35]

Watts's invitation to join in the song functions not merely in the immediate sense of asking the child to take up the same notes as the people nearby, occupying common time and place with them, but moreover in Dewey's sense as a kind of cultural transmission. It reminds us that for children, especially when literacy is not yet secure, reading is often an aural, communal experience—we read to children and they read to us. The poem emphasises this aural quality of sound in its references to 'song' and 'voice.' It offers the possibility that simply to sound a note is affirmatory, is delightful—but not in a trivial way: the sound of voice is a powerful, affecting reminder of one another's presence (the parent reading, perhaps?). And yet the poem is not just sound; it is perhaps not even sound, since poems do not have to be read aloud. Indeed, we might pause to wonder where the song of the title takes place. Is the poem the song? Is the child's response to the poem the song? As the abundant use of indicative verbs in this poem suggests, Watts's poem operates in a strange middle space between present tense and abstract idea of the present, or between present tense and future. The coming together of presentness and futurity in the poem ('Then let me') fosters a sense of belonging to a human race—human as distinct from the other creatures in this poem: saints, angels, divine—and calls upon the child actively and voluntarily to subscribe to the values of this race.

For all Watts's emphasis on simplicity in the Preface to *Divine Songs*, there is nonetheless a distinctive complexity at work here. It is a complexity, however, that is shaped by our particular awareness that the words on this page are not a child's own, or at least, not a child's alone. There is an indeterminacy in the source of the words and the source of the sounds. The poem provides a chorus in which adult voices and child voices are imagined to mingle across time. The complexity at work is thus one of vocal and temporal instability: one which comes into being precisely by virtue of the status of this work as a song for children. For the child is required to be out of time—conscious of its alterity to the ideas discussed, the words used, the script which it has not yet learnt—all of which predate the coming of the child to them. There is, then, a futurity embedded in the poem not merely by virtue of its address projected onto the child ('Let me') but by virtue of its didactic premise.[36] But in order to activate what the poem offers *in potentia*, the child does not straightforwardly (indeed, surely cannot) take up the message to 'sing'; the child must first feel the common rhythms, anticipate the rhymes, compute the question-and-answer format of the stanza pattern before he or she can know how to sound his or her voice. There is thus an irony at work here. This is a poem which commands the child to sing, but the child must infer not just from the premise of the poem but from the intricacy of its form that their task is not really to sing but in fact merely to listen: to listen now, in the present, and to sing later, in the future. That is to say that the child must perform a sophisticated mental operation; they must compute that the present tense here really signifies the future, the abstract, the general, and not the particularised now.

We can gain a sense of just how sophisticated the mental operations of child readers of poetry were deemed, or hoped, to be from the volume on poetry published by John Newbery as part of his series, *Circle of the Sciences* (1745–6). Newbery's aim in this multi-volume non-fictional work for young people was to 'diffuse a Light over their Understanding, assist their Reasoning Powers, and lead them on to such Improvements in Knowledge as are to be expected from Years of Maturity' (I.v). It contains volumes on Grammar, Arithmetic, Rhetoric, Poetry, Logic, Geography, Chronology, and ends with a Dictionary. The significance of poetry for Newbery can be estimated from the fact that over the course of his career, Newbery published at least seven books of poetry for children.[37] Close attention to *Poetry Made Familiar and Easy* provides us with insight not merely into what knowledge and skills Newbery considered it to be important for children to develop in relation to poetry, but furthermore into how he anticipated that they would acquire these skills. The volume's narrator asserts that his 'task' is 'to give the Reader some Idea of every Species of Poetry that is worth his Notice' (224). In part, then, the book aims to provide the child with exposure to poetry, the clear implication being that by gaining familiarity with the customs associated with this art, children will gain access to the culture with which these customs are associated. Throughout, the collective pronoun 'our' is used, building a sense of shared traditions, traditions whose custodian the child will one day be. But the work functions as more than merely an anthology of excerpts of poetry; it seeks also to endow children with ways of asking and answering questions about poetry such that they are left with certain knowledge about it, and such that the child is able to perform certain intellectual manoeuvres in relation to it. There are several pertinent insights that we can extrapolate from close scrutiny of this book. Firstly, its aims to tell us about why authors might have considered that children should need poetry and, specifically, what intellectual benefits it might bring. Secondly, its priorities provide us with a means of identifying what it was deemed important that children were capable of doing to or with poetry. Thirdly, its own engagement with its implied child reader equips us with a means of viewing in process how eighteenth-century authors such as Newbery envisaged that children might engage with poetic theory.

The Preface to *Poetry Made Familiar and Easy* suggests that the aim of the book is to enable children to 'soon entertain an adequate idea of [poetry's] real beauties' (n.p.)—that is to say, to inform children's taste and to pass on socially mandated ways of appreciating the complexities of poetry. It is worth noting, if only because it has become so habitual to notice the preoccupation in eighteenth-century children's literature with the child's morality, that the book presents the education of children's moral faculties as an incidental benefit rather than a primary concern: 'should any of our readers be but one virtue the better for these our honest endeavours, we shall not think our labour ill bestowed' (n.p.). And yet, while the book is impelled by a clear desire to educate, and is founded on a belief that exposure to poetic monuments plays a vital role in shaping the critical faculties of the child, its reverence towards poetry threatens at times to position poetry as a phenomenon of such cultural prestige that children could not hope to gain access to its mysteries. When Newbery insists that 'We must, in a word, be born poets; for this divine art is not to be attain'd by the most unwearied industry and application' (n.p.), the reader might be forgiven for wondering what is to be gained from the industry and application involved in reading the very book in hand. Such wondering is further fuelled by suggestions throughout that readers are born, not made: 'a person who has a tolerable ear for poetry, will have little occasion for rules concerning the pause and the accents, but will naturally so dispose his words as to create a certain harmony, without labour to the tongue, or violence to the sense' (15). The book therefore puts the child reader in a paradoxical position: children are required to want to labour to acquire the knowledge that the book promises, but simultaneously, they are encouraged to bow to the belief that if knowledge has to be attained through strenuous effort, then the pupil's poetic credentials are doubtful. As Andrew O'Malley has shown, if 'the ideal figure of the age was the productive, moral, self-disciplined, healthy, male adult governed by the faculty of reason, the child came to be viewed in many regards as its opposite: the subject interpellated through absence and difference.'[38] Newbery's reader, implicitly characterised by way of difference to the adult speaker, seems destined to be unpoetical.

The vexed position in which Newbery places his child reader is reflected in a related uncertainty that suffuses *Poetry Made Familiar and Easy*: indecision about whether the child reader is to be addressed as a future consumer or a future maker of poetry. The stated aims in the Preface make clear that appreciation of poetry is the central goal. Yet, many of the remarks throughout the book ostensibly court the poet apprentice. Questions are posed such as 'On what syllables must the accent fall in this kind of verse?' (11), and rules are supplied in answer, rules which are often more pertinent for learning how to write poetry rather than to read it. For example, 'tho' the Alexandrine verse, when rightly employ'd, has an agreeable effect in our poetry, it must be used sparingly and with judgment' (19). The steer here is towards how best to apply this knowledge in the crafting of poetry, encouraging the child to take responsibility for the safe-keeping of poetry's prosperity by writing it in accordance with cultural expectations of taste. There is thus a clear implication that in order to appreciate the genius of those who do not need to learn or practise, the child must learn and practise such that he or she is better able to feel awe at the mastery demonstrated by those with innate skill. Reading and writing are implicitly bound together, viewed as embroiled skills; imitation of the masters, it is implied, though never explicitly stated, will itself enhance understanding of them. The deference to authority that underpins this pedagogic principle is also apparent in the frequent quotation of existing commentators on the subject, such as the French historian and educationalist, Charles Rollin, invoked throughout respectfully as 'Monsieur Rollin.' The words of such figures are quoted at length and treated as gospel.

One of the striking features of the volume is its invitation to think in expansive terms. It introduces a sweeping historical scope, ranging between summaries of Greek and Roman thought and more recent examples. It therefore supposes that the child is capable of taking a long historical view and perceiving the place that our own age has in a wider temporal context. However, it recognises the inherent challenges in this task for the child, and simplifies by flattening out historical difference, making it possible for the child to view examples from radically different eras alongside one another and focus on similarity not difference. Expertise in the specifics of history or an ancient language is therefore not necessary; all is brought within the jurisdiction of a novice. More strikingly still, Newbery pre-supposes that children are capable of and interested in dealing in large, abstract philosophical ideas, including some of the seminal literary theoretical questions that have concerned philosophers for millennia. For example, he begins by asking 'What is poetry?', supplying a gratifyingly succinct answer: 'It is the art of composing poems, or pieces in verse' (1). What is potentially a question of daunting proportions, one which might require prolixity to capture the nuances inherent in even an unsatisfactory answer, is reduced to its most literal and indisputable elements by Newbery's emphasis on the fact of authorship. This tendency to foreground the material and the technical—an attitude signalled by the series title, *Circle of the Sciences*—is a key feature of the book, which quickly gets down to formal matters pertaining to scansion and the characteristics of genre. Chapters are organised around tangible matters such as 'Of the Structure of English Verse; and of Rhyme' and 'Of Satire,' and in its attempts to communicate information about these issues, it does not hold back from using technical vocabulary, providing full names of rhetorical features and succinct accounts of what they comprise. While the language in which it explains such terms might resemble that which Watts had in mind by 'easy,' Newbery deems the child capable of learning and understanding the meaning of complex terminology and furthermore assumes it to be important, indeed essential, that the child be familiar with such terms.

Newbery may make little concession to his child audience in terms of diction, but the modes of address deployed by the narrator of *Poetry Made Familiar and Easy* directly and consistently recognise the child's idiosyncratic needs. Throughout, the narrator makes use of a question-and-answer format, posing rhetorical questions such as 'how seldom do we find so many great and valuable qualifications meet in one person?' (n.p.), involving his readers in the process of abstract thought and expecting them to generate hypothetical propositions in response. The book therefore solicits its readers actively to participate in the quest for understanding, at times lapsing into the first-person voice and exemplifying the questions that the child might ask: 'Have you any other instructions to give me concerning rhyme?' (9). In this way, it gives the child space in which to be a learner, or 'Pupil,' as it frequently calls the reader—one who is currently ignorant but keen to change this plight. Indeed, the imagined curiosity of the child sometimes takes on an urgency: 'Can't you give me some examples of this?' (13). Far from casting the child's ignorance as a sin, the sympathetic alignment between the narrator and the implied reader indicates a view of ignorance as an inevitable affliction which children must bear, one which adults must compassionately seek to alleviate. Newbery's approach shows the influence of Locke's advice that children 'should always be heard, and fairly and kindly answered, when they ask after anything they could know, and desire to be informed about. Curiosity should be as carefully cherished in children, as other appetites suppressed' (85). Just as Locke counsels, Newbery's speaker does not speak down to the child but instead seeks to adapt himself to the child's cognitive and emotional needs. He recognises, therefore, that the child will become bored by explanations that are too lengthy or which veer from the main point, legitimising the child's right to experience wandering attention: 'besides, that I fear the Reader will think I have already detained him too long upon this Subject' (133–4). The speaker recognises too that the child's understanding of poetry may be impeded by a lack of contextual awareness and discreetly supplies information as needed (e.g. explaining the story of Prometheus) to help the reader fill in any gaps. In so doing, the speaker offers reassurance, implying that children are not to feel ashamed of what they do not yet know.

Indeed, far from implying that the ultimate goal is to arrive at a position of omniscience, the speaker reveals his own fallibility, for example, by admitting, in relation to an epigram by Alexander Pope: 'For my part, I am at a loss to determine whether it does more honour to the poet who wrote it, or to the nobleman for whom the compliment is designed' (38). In so doing, he leaves the child to determine what to make of the lines. Catherine Macaulay in *Letters on Education* (1790) was later to insist on the importance of the educator matching practice with theory—of parents and teachers leading by example—since, as she puts it, in youth, 'the powers of the understanding are not sufficiently strong to combat the difficulties which in this early season of life it has to encounter. Hence reason loses its energy, and becomes no more than the echo of the public voice.'[39] Newbery's speaker anticipates this demand for good practice to be modelled, extending his faith in children's capacities to assert their own voices rather than merely echo precedent by encouraging them to practise making their own judgements. He does so not in the spirit that we might associate with late twentieth-century reader-response theory, wherein readers are licensed to constitute the text howsoever they wish, but by nudging his readers to take the cue from the accumulation of judgements—often in the form of assertions offered up as objective truths: epigrams are a 'low species of poetry,' for instance (49)—which have sought to shape their taste over the course of the book. Through the process of reading this book, it is envisaged that the reader will have been made sufficiently familiar with the standards and premises of taste that the child's own instincts will start to kick in, functioning like a sensory organ, invisibly and seemingly without effort enabling the reader to make poetic discriminations.

Newbery's own poetry for children has often been dismissed as didactic, the implication being that it functions straightforwardly to direct the child's morals, situating the reader as a passive and docile recipient of textual transmission.[40] But close consideration of how his verse invites its readers to make use of the powers of discrimination which his non-fiction work seeks to impart reveals that the ease with which the child reader receives instruction through the poetic text might be rather more illusory than such critical verdicts imagine. Take, for example, the poem 'Shuttle-Cock' from *A Little Pretty Pocket-Book* (1744), quoted here in full:

> The Shuttle-Cock struck
> Does backward rebound;
> But, if it be miss'd,
> It falls to the Ground.
>
> Moral.
> Thus chequer'd in Life,
> As Fortune does flow;
> Her Smiles lift us high,
> Her Frowns sink us low.

As in Watts's 'A General Song of Praise to God,' Newbery here sets up a present moment; the poem's epigrammatic style relays an active scene, and the speedy tick-tock of the dimeter alerts us to the continuousness of the action which is apparently taking place right before us. The brevity of the poem gives a sense of a small treat; we are being offered a light slice of something fun—a vignette which offers a brief glimpse of amusement. Also like the Watts poem, it sets up a question-and-answer format, a format made explicit by the prominence of the moral, which announces itself in the second stanza. But the relationship between the two stanzas bears closer inspection. For all that it *feels* like a question posed, it is not altogether clear what problem the first stanza has laid bare; and for all that the second stanza *feels* like a reply to the first, it in fact exists in a weirdly asymmetrical relationship with it. Formally, there is a satisfying balance in length between the two evenly matched quatrains. But what is signified by the break between them? Is the one scenario an analogue for the other? If so, precisely what attributes are alike? In this analogy, who is the chequered party? The shuttle-cock? Fortune? Us? The poem's indeterminacy is generated as much by imprecision (Newbery's formula fails as a sentence, since none of the hermeneutic options it opens up are grammatically coherent) as by multiplicity. But perhaps this does not matter, for we get the general point: life, like a game of shuttle-cock, has its ups and downs; it is unpredictable; it can end in contempt, not in elation. We may not know what this poem is advising us to do or how we can alter our behaviour in response, but we have been prompted, through the comparison, to perceive a similitude—to gain a handle on an abstract idea. The two stanzas operate coterminously, and invite us to hold them both in our line of sight at once, but not because the first forces the second stanza to perform the function of explaining the first, whatever the term 'moral' might imply.

By leaving us without a singular subject position to take up, Newbery's poem, by default, prevails on us to occupy a plural, communal, and potentially general subject position. The child is being brought into a fold, membership of which is conducive to pleasure, provided that the rules have been learned. For games are fun; rhythmic language is diverting. For all that the poem presents what we might see as a simplified—an easy—view of life, one underpinned by strictures, methods, and truths, it does not coerce us into taking on these values for ourselves. Its mode, rather, is descriptive: it offers up a slice of everyday experience and a glimpse of a routine idea. It re-introduces child readers to the familiar (a shuttle-cock) and, in so doing, introduces them to the unfamiliar (the unpredictable vicissitudes of life). It is this that eighteenth-century poets for children discovered about the child's cognition: that poetic language and poetic form might enable children to yoke together what would otherwise remain apart—the particular and the general, the localised and the abstract, the knowable and the unknowable—and that inspiring children to join in the song permits access to the ongoing cultural conversation.

NOTES

1. Harvey F.J. Darton, *Children's Books in England*. 3rd edition (Cambridge: Cambridge University Press), 109.
2. John Dennis, *The Advancement and Reformation of Modern Poetry. A Critical Discourse. In Two Parts* (London, 1701), 24. For arguments in favour of the literary respectability of the novel, see, for example, Clara Reeve's *The Progress of Romance* (1785).
3. See, for example, Joseph Trapp, *Lectures on Poetry* (1742); Anon, *The Art of Poetry on a New Plan* (1762); and James Beattie, *Essays: on Poetry and Music, as they Affect the Mind* (1776).
4. Isaac Watts, *Divine Songs Attempted in Easy Language for the Use of Children*. Intro. J.H.P. Pafford (London: Oxford University Press, 1971), 6. All subsequent references are to this edition and are cited parenthetically.

5. John Cotton, *Milk for Babes, Drawn out of the Breasts of Both Testaments* (London: Henry Overton, 1646), 7.
6. John Locke, *Some Thoughts Concerning Education*. Ed. John William Adamson (Mineola, New York: Dover Publications, 2007), 93.
7. Locke, *Some Thoughts Concerning Education*, 25.
8. John Bunyan, *A Book for Boys and Girls, or Country Rhymes for Children* (London, 1686), 11.
9. Bunyan, *A Book for Boys and Girls*, 51.
10. James Janeway, *A Token for Children, being an exact account of the conversion, holy and exemplary lives and joyful deaths of several young children*. 2nd ed. (London, 1676), 6.
11. Quoted in Alisa, Clapp-Itnyre, *British Hymn Books for Children, 1800–1900: Re-Tuning the History of Childhood* (Farnham: Ashgate, 2016), 61.
12. See Ferdinand de Saussure, *Course in General Linguistics* (trans. Roy Harris, London: Bloomsbury, 2013).
13. For further discussion of children's poetry as song, see Katherine Wakely-Mulroney and Louise Joy Eds., *The Aesthetics of Children's Poetry: A Study of Children's Verse* (Abingdon: Routledge, 2018), 6–8.
14. For further discussion of the forms most frequently used in children's poetry of the period, see Donelle Ruwe, *British Children's Poetry in the Romantic Era: Verse, Riddle, and Rhyme* (Basingstoke: Palgrave Macmillan, 2014).
15. For more on the forms of popular songs and ballads in the period, see Robin Ganev, *Songs of Protest, Songs of Love: Popular Ballads in Eighteenth-Century Britain* (Manchester: Manchester University Press, 2009).
16. Samuel Taylor Coleridge, *The Notebooks of Samuel Taylor Coleridge*, Vol. 3, Ed. Kathleen Coburn (London: Routledge & Kegan Paul, 1957–1973), 4409.
17. Bernardin de Saint-Pierre, Jacques-Henri, *Studies of Nature*. Vol. 4 (London, 1796), 158.
18. Alexander Pope, *Pope: Poetical Works* (ed. Herbert Davis, intro. Pat Rogers, Oxford: Oxford University Press, 1979).
19. Ann Wierda Rowland, *Romanticism and Childhood: The Infantilization of British Literary Culture* (Cambridge: Cambridge University Press, 2012), 88.
20. Joyce Irene Whalley, *Cobwebs to Catch Flies: Illustrated Books for the Nursery and Schoolroom 1700–1900* (London: Elek, 1974), 10.
21. For more on the history of catechistic methods in the eighteenth century, see Alan Richardson, *Literature, Education, and Romanticism: Reading as Social Practice 1780–1832* (Cambridge: Cambridge University Press, 1994), 64–77.
22. Locke, 130.

23. For further discussion of this, see Katherine Wakely-Mulroney 'Isaac Watts and the Dimensions of Child Interiority,' *Journal for Eighteenth-Century Studies* 39.1 (2016): 106–07.

24. See, for example, John Chandos, *Boys Together: English Public Schools 1800–1864* (London: Hutchinson, 1984) especially Chap. 11.

25. For more on this, see, for example, Joseph H. Wicksteed, *The Challenge of Childhood: An Essay on Nature and Education* (London: Chapman & Hall, 1936) and Peter Newell Ed. *A Last Resort? Corporal Punishment in Schools* (London: Penguin, 1972).

26. Matthew Grenby, *The Child Reader 1700–1840* (Cambridge: Cambridge University Press, 2011), 262.

27. Mary Ann Kilner, *The Adventures of a Pincushion: Designed Chiefly for the Use of Young Ladies: in Two Volumes.* Vol. 1. (London: J. Marshall, 1790), iv.

28. Eleanor Fenn, *Rational Sports. In Dialogues passing among the Children of a Family* (London: J. Marshall, nd), xiii.

29. David Hartley, *Observations on Man, his Frame, his Duty, and his Expectations. In Two Parts.* (London: S. Richardson, 1749), 437.

30. Hartley, *Observations on Man,* 439.

31. Rosenberg-Orsini, Justine Gräfin, *Moral and Sentimental Essays, on Miscellaneous Subjects.* 2 vols. Volume 1. (London: J. Robson, 1785), 180.

32. William Wordsworth, *Poetical Works; with Introduction and Notes,* ed. by Thomas Hutchinson and Ernest de Sélincourt (London: Oxford University Press, 1974), 3.

33. Wordsworth, *Poetical Works,* 2.

34. Locke, 65.

35. John Dewey *Democracy and Education, 1916: The Middle Works of John Dewey 1899–1924,* Vol. 9, Ed. Jo Ann Boydston (Carbondale and Edwardsville: Southern Illinois University Press, 1985), 6.

36. See Clementine Beauvais's *The Mighty Child: Time and Power in Children's Literature* (Amsterdam: John Benjamins Company 2015) for a fascinating account of the ways in which children's literature 'addresses not just a person but also a temporality, not just a subject but also a project, not just a now but also a thereafter' (205).

37. See John Rowe Townsend's *Trade and Plumb-Cake Forever, Huzza! The Life and Work of John Newbery, 1713–1767* (Colt Books Ltd.: Cambridge, 1994), 127–134 for a list of Newbery's children's books. The educational importance of poetry to Newbery can also be seen in the nature of the volumes of poetry he printed for adults in which he sought to make poetry and its rules available to a wider audience. For example, his *A Collection of Pretty Poems for the Amusement of Children Six Feet High* (1784) seeks to

introduce to an uninitiated adult audience, construed as 'children,' ideas about poetry and seminal examples of the form.

38. Andrew O'Malley, *The Making of the Modern Child: Children's Literature and Childhood in the Late Eighteenth Century* (New York: Routledge, 2003), 11–12.

39. Catherine Macaulay, *Letters on Education. With observations on religious and metaphysical subjects* (London, 1790), 152.

40. See, for example, Geoffrey Summerfield, *Fantasy and Reason: Children's Literature in the Eighteenth Century* (London: Methuen, 1984), 93, and Patricia Demers, ed., *From Instruction to Delight: An Anthology of Children's Literature to 1850*, 4th ed. (Don Mills, Ont.: Oxford University Press, 2015), 148.

CHAPTER 8

'Powers Expanding Slow': Children's 'Unfolding' Minds in Radical Writing of the 1790s

Susan Manly

In 1790, Edmund Burke attacked the French revolutionaries for their sub-version of 'the bosom of our family affections.' In place of the 'mutually reflected charities' that bound together 'our state, our hearths, our sepul-chres, and our altars,' the French National Assembly had set up 'a school where systematically, and with unremitting perseverance, they teach prin-ciples … destructive to all spirit of subordination,' undermining the authority of government and jeopardizing the 'obedience' of 'an anarchic people.'[1] Burke's metaphors of stable familial bonds, reinforced by piety, which he opposed to this perverted schooling of a refractory and resistant infant nation, are echoed at the close of the decade by Hannah More in her attack on the 'revolutionary spirit in families.' Like Burke, More expresses disquiet at the 'spirit of independence, and disdain of control' characterizing modern children, especially girls: a moral deterioration that she ascribes to the Jacobin 'public principles' that had infiltrated homes, families, and schools. The rights of man and of woman, More argues, had led inevitably to 'the next stage of that irradiation which our enlighteners

S. Manly (✉)
University of St Andrews, St Andrews, UK
e-mail: sm32@st-andrews.ac.uk

© The Author(s) 2018   139
A. O'Malley (ed.), *Literary Cultures and Eighteenth-Century Childhoods*, Literary Cultures and Childhoods,
https://doi.org/10.1007/978-3-319-94737-2_8

are pouring in upon us ... grave descants on the *rights of children*.'[2] More's intention was to ridicule the idea of children's rights as a means of dismissing radical and reformist debate. Yet for a number of late eighteenth- and early nineteenth-century writers publishing for and about children and childhood, the idea of children's expanding powers of mind and unprejudiced view of 'things as they are' (to use William Godwin's alternative title for his Jacobin novel *Caleb Williams*) was vital. While the innocence and malleability of children was widely understood in the second half of the eighteenth century as a source of promise, several of the writers that I discuss in this chapter implicitly or explicitly contest the idea that children's minds are principally of interest for their imprintability, blank slates providing space for the designs of adult authority: a doctrine that women writers reflecting on the education of girls, such as Mary Wollstonecraft, associate with the adult colonization of children's minds. Rather than focusing on innocence or an idealized state of nature, Wollstonecraft and other radical and reformist writers emphasize children's innate rational and imaginative powers as a source of social and moral improvement. The liberation of these powers and their transformative potential, released through the unfolding of children's capacity for reason, empathy, and love, is not fatally threatened by a knowledge of human history or suffering. Indeed, these writers consider reflections on history and conflict an important part of early education, equipping children to take up their role as citizens of the future.

A reading of Helen Maria Williams's version of Bernardin de Saint-Pierre's *Paul and Virginia* suggests much to explain why the idea of children's natural innocence and the desirability of their isolation from politically driven conflict continued to be one against which this countervailing insistence on children as future citizens needed to assert itself. Written in the midst of 'the turbulence of the most cruel sensations, and in order to escape awhile from overwhelming misery,' the effects of 'the horrors of Robespierre's tyranny,' *Paul and Virginia* focuses upon the children of two mothers—one a servant, the other a rebellious aristocrat—and their attempt to escape the violence and class tyranny of *ancien régime* France on the island of Mauritius.[3] The two women work together to create a place out of time, a small community of equals living in 'simplicity and virtue,' far from the 'prejudices' and 'history of the great,' and the weight of an unhappy past that burdens the adult protagonists, a pre-established narrative that will finally reimpose its malign imperatives upon the two children.[4] Even as Williams refers to the 'soothing relief' that the 'enchanting scenes' of her imaginary escapees' island life brought her from the misery and terror of Robespierre's purges, we understand that the tale before us is to be a story of failed hopes and of a fatally fragile asylum from the violence of tyranny (vi, vii). This much is clear from the opening description of 'the ruins of two small cottages' huddled in a sheltered valley within earshot of 'the hollow murmurs of the winds that shake the neighbouring forests, and the tumultuous dashing of the waves': a premonition of the storm that eventually drowns Virginia and indirectly destroys Paul, and a visual and auditory representation of the ruination of the two women's hopes (1–2).

Margaret, the mother of Paul, has escaped to Mauritius after having been seduced and abandoned by a gentleman; Madame de la Tour, Virginia's mother, has likewise transgressed the 'laws' of marriage and class by 'descending from her rank' to marry an unsuitable man. Both women signal their rejection of the 'cruel prejudices of Europe' through their humble dress (22). Attempting to reconstruct an Edenic bliss out of their exclusion, they share all that they own: 'United by the tie of similar wants, and the sympathy of similar misfortunes, they gave each other the tender names of companion, friend, sister, – they had but one will, one interest, one table; – all their possessions were in common' (18). They go about in the 'coarse blue linen of Bengal, which is usually worn by slaves;' even their children are shared and learn to acknowledge both women equally as their mother (17). But as the passing reference to slavery in the description of the women's dress suggests, Williams's little Eden is itself already tainted by its connections to the exertion of unjust power. Yet rather than educating the children in the history that has brought about this suffering, Margaret and Madame de la Tour deliberately keep Paul and Virginia in ignorance, a lack of knowledge which the women equate with innocence. History, in particular, is forbidden to their children, as a form of knowledge that threatens to 'poison the most precious sources of our happiness,' and to menace 'the pleasures of love, and the blessings of equality' (22). The children never read about 'past times,' never enquire about the world beyond the little valley, and are spared the 'lessons of morality, superfluous to bosoms unconscious of ill' (25, 26). Williams describes this education as an 'unfolding' of 'the feelings most natural to the human mind, and which are our best support, under evil' (75). Paul and Virginia's upbringing is presented as a return to a 'state of nature,' in which '[t]heir lives seemed linked to the trees like those of fawns or dryads. They knew no other historical epochas than that of the lives of their mothers, no other chronology than that of their orchards, and no other philosophy than that of doing good, and resigning themselves to the will of heaven' (75, 86).

In its suppressions, omissions, and resignation, however, such a childhood education leaves the children ill-equipped to reflect on consequences or to resist injustice. An incident in which young Paul and Virginia attempt to help a fugitive from slavery, yet succeed only in compounding her sufferings, implicitly shows the limits of their ahistorical schooling in morality. Skeletal and almost naked, 'her body marked by deep scars from the lashes she had received,' the enslaved woman asks the 'good white people' for assistance (37–8). Unable to conceive of the oppression of slavery, or to read the marks on her body as the history of systemic injustice, Virginia has no help to offer besides returning the woman to her master and asking for his 'forgiveness' on her behalf, which predictably results in further degradation: she is later seen 'with her feet chained to a block of wood, and an iron collar with three hooks fastened round her neck' (38, 50). Virginia's feeble response—'Oh how difficult it is to do good!'—suggests the weaknesses of the 'natural,' anti-historical education designed by the two refugees from French aristocratic society (51).

Subsequently, the children, now fully grown and in love, have to face the obstacles that they have inherited from their French parents, class-specific struggles that their utopian education has left them powerless to confront. Virginia comes under pressure to wed an aged nobleman chosen for her by her malicious French aunt; Paul finds that he cannot fulfil his dream of following Virginia to France and rising by his own merits, barred by his class and his illegitimacy from realizing his ambition. They thus find themselves ill-served by their mothers' utopian, atemporal visions of equality and love. Paul later tries to read history as part of his programme of self-education, in his attempt to make himself a suitable future husband for Virginia as she is being educated and wooed back in France; but he is repelled by its messiness, the lack of morality it exposes in human society, and its seemingly irresolvable 'evils': 'wars for which there was no reason, and no object; nations without principle, and princes without humanity.' Disappointed with this dismaying picture of human beings and their acts, he turns instead to romances, preferring their depictions of pastoral life and the passions of the human heart (136). Neither Paul nor Virginia finds it possible to adapt to the moral complexity and compromise of life beyond the island, or even to find a response to the evils of slavery and local corruption closer to home; and this is in part a consequence of their 'natural' education, which is focused on nuances of feeling rather than on developing rational reflection and alert observation. The innocence that has been so fetishized in their upbringing finally brings about Virginia's death. Urged to throw off her clothes in order to stand a better chance of surfacing above the waves as she stands on the wreck of the ship bringing her home from France, she refuses the aid of a potential rescuer on the grounds of potential injury to her 'modesty,' and drowns (184).

Although it is hard to see how Williams's wish for escapism in the face of political injustice could really have been satisfied in such an unconsoling tale of betrayed children on the run from history and unjust power, the tale does suggest how compelling it was for progressive writers in the 1790s to meditate on the value and viability of innocence, especially that of children, and perhaps still more that of girls. Wollstonecraft's response in *The Wrongs of Woman*—another tale of a betrayed and excluded woman and her attempts to protect and nourish the rational capacities of a daughter—was to insist on the need for children as well as adults to engage critically and creatively with history. The most significant of these within the novel is Jemima's history, which stimulates the thoughts of the heroine, Maria, to 'take a wider range.' Previously, she has 'been rendered incapable of sober reflection' through the loss of her child at the hands of a ruthless husband—'the act of atrocity of which she was the victim.'[5] Having absorbed the lessons of Jemima's past, Maria finds that she is able to begin to forge a future in which they can both escape their prison. Maria's narrative is her way of passing on the lessons that she has drawn from Jemima's history, which she intends as the foundation of an education designed to set her daughter free from infantine incapacity into emancipated thought, unfolding her powers of critical judgement: 'From my narrative, my dear girl, you may gather instruction, the counsel, which is meant rather to exercise than influence your mind.'[6]

The figure of the under-developed and brutalized child haunts *The Wrongs of Woman* as a spectral threat to her planned nurturance of her infant daughter's intellectual growth. Maria's motivation in writing her history is her sense of the hunger and abandonment of her lost child, for whom, unable to offer her the nourishment of her 'burning bosom,' she feels 'maternal apprehension.'[7] Her anxiety is heightened by Jemima's account of her childhood sufferings. With 'no bosom to nestle in, no kindred warmth to foster me,' Jemima remembers herself as a 'weak and rickety babe' whose face bore the marks of neglect and starvation, 'furrows of reflection and care,' so that she resembled 'a little old woman, or a hag shrivelling into nothing,' as if all her infant promise had been lost and the ravages of age had supplanted the freshness of childhood (103). The reader recalls this history of premature decay and thwarted potential later on, when Maria gives her account of discovering an illegitimate daughter: the living evidence of Maria's husband's pre-marital promiscuity and negligence, fathered on a servant whom he later discarded and who, 'thrown on the town,' died a pauper. The child, weak and rickety, like the young Jemima, 'could hardly support herself' and her face is marked by 'the wrinkles produced by the peevishness of pain' (149). Maria's decision to nurture this abandoned child presages her transformative recognition of Jemima as a 'fellow-creature' who is part of the 'paradise' of love that she is conjuring up with Darnford, so that the three form a blissful quasi-familial triad: 'the world contained not three happier beings' (101). Maria's promise, after hearing Jemima's history, to 'procure' her the 'better fate' that she merits is accompanied with a 'maternal benediction,' in which Jemima and Maria's lost daughter seem equally the object of blessing (121–22). Jemima is thus in a sense another daughter to Maria, as well as another mother to Maria's child.

When William Godwin published *The Wrongs of Woman* as part of his edition of Wollstonecraft's *Posthumous Works*, his placing of her fragmentary *Lessons* directly after the sketched ending in which Maria decides to 'live for [her] child' indicates the extent to which he saw her unfinished primer for a daughter as continuous with this novel's politicized focus on nurturing the mind of an infant girl (203). This was a perception that Wollstonecraft evidently shared. With its dedicatory note identifying Wollstonecraft's *Lessons* as 'the first book of a series which I intended to have written for my unfortunate girl,' Wollstonecraft signals to the reader the connections between *Maria*, *Lessons* and her own real struggles to construct a viable future for herself and her daughter, Fanny Imlay. Like Maria, Wollstonecraft felt the pain of her daughter's lack of a loving father, although she has Maria argue for the greater wisdom that a mother can pass on to a little girl:

> The tenderness of a father who knew the world, might be great; but could it equal that of a mother – of a mother, labouring under a portion of the misery, which the constitution of society seems to have entailed on all her kind? It is, my child, … only such a mother, who will dare to break through all restraint to provide for your happiness…. (124)

Maria's emphasis on her child's unfolding rational powers, and their necessity in order to break through the restraints imposed upon the oppressed, serves as her motivation for the memoir of her life that she writes for her child. Rather than confirming historical suffering as an 'entailed' inheritance that her daughter is powerless to escape, she hopes to give her the ability to be the author of her own life, as far as is possible. Wollstonecraft's sense of the support that a father could add to this maternal care for a daughter drew on her own experience of the breakdown of her relationship with Fanny's father, Gilbert Imlay. The letters to Imlay that Godwin placed before *The Wrongs of Woman* in the *Posthumous Works* often mention Fanny and reflect on the growth of the bond between mother and baby, and the baby's burgeoning intelligence. In a letter written on 26 December 1794, Wollstonecraft laments that the absent Imlay is forsaking something of infinite value through his absence, since it means that he will not see Fanny's 'little mind unfold[ing] itself.'[8] Three days later, she refers again to what he is missing because of his absence from his child: 'I grow sad very often when I am playing with her, that you are not here, to observe with me how her mind unfolds, and her little heart becomes attached. – These appear to me to be true pleasures – and still you suffer them to escape you, in search of what we may never enjoy.'[9] On 15 January 1795, Wollstonecraft invites Imlay to marvel at his daughter's tenacity and energy of mind: 'You would laugh to see her; she is just like a little squirrel; she will guard a crust for two hours; and after fixing her eye on an object for some time, dart on it with an aim as sure as a bird of prey – nothing can equal her life and spirits' (97–8). By 4 October 1795, Wollstonecraft had finally realized that Imlay was never going to return to her and the child; that he had formed a new attachment and wished to obliterate their history as a family: 'Every emotion yields to an overwhelming flood of sorrow – and the playfulness of my child distresses me. – ... you talk of the ties which bind you to me and my child. – Tell me, that you wish it, and I will cut this Gordian knot.'[10] Although she longed for the connection to endure, Wollstonecraft hated the idea of dependence, and her letter signals her willingness to relinquish her claims on Imlay. The decision was not without cost, however, as the next letter reveals: a suicide note, written just before Wollstonecraft threw herself into the Thames, it shows her making arrangements for her daughter to be fostered by another family in Paris. She survived the attempt, and eventually recovered.

Wollstonecraft's *Lessons* is a kind of wish fulfilment in answer to the struggles and tragedies of *The Wrongs of Woman* and the letters to Imlay:

in place of the absent, abusive, and even murderous fathers of these histories of abandonment, *Lessons* presents us with an idealized family scene, in which the father and the mother lovingly and playfully work together to elicit the potential of their little daughter. The 'new impulse' capable of transforming the world that Godwin claimed for Wollstonecraft's other posthumous works is clearly discernible in this work for very young readers.[11] Godwin in fact comments that he sees the *Lessons* as connected to 'the affectionate and pathetic manner in which Maria Venables addresses her infant' in *The Wrongs of Woman*. He effectively presents Wollstonecraft's primer as a kind of coda to her novel fragment, a narrative similarly born out of 'the agonising and painful sentiment with which the author originally bequeathed these papers, as a legacy for the benefit of her child.'[12] Again, the references to legacy and bequest suggest Godwin's awareness that Wollstonecraft was continuing to focus, even in the midst of her own despair at a woman's life, on the promise of 'futurity.' Even as she herself lost hope for a viable future, the *Lessons* show Wollstonecraft mapping out the means by which her daughter might empower herself, chiefly by learning to see herself as an active thinker, not primarily as an obedient subject. The means by which Wollstonecraft communicates this confidence in her own powers to her fictional baby daughter is through deep affection and steady, consistent nurturance, 'enlightened maternal affection' as Wollstonecraft calls it in *A Vindication of the Rights of Woman*. The maternal voice is crucial in eliciting the child's sense of self, and forms a kind of inheritance upon which the child can draw in future.[13]

By the fifth lesson in her primer, Wollstonecraft's fictional little girl is four, and is faced with the challenge of relating to a new baby brother. The mother-narrator encourages her to see herself as newly powerful in comparison to the new-born, but also to feel compassion for the baby, since she was once equally 'feeble' and 'helpless.'[14] The child is helped to see how far she has come since these helpless beginnings, and coaxed to perceive her displacement from the mother's breast as a mark of her graduation from that feeble state of total dependence, a first step towards becoming empowered to look after herself. Accordingly, any assistance that the little girl needs is provisional: her mother will tie her frock for her only 'till you are stronger;' and as she grows physically, she also grows intellectually.[15] The unequal status of the child and her parents is not absolute and permanent, since they were themselves once children, something that Wollstonecraft is careful to point out through the mother-narrator as she introduces the idea of growth, telling her daughter: 'Papa and I were children, like you.'[16] At the moment, she needs her parents to think for her. Even at this early stage, however, she is encouraged to think for herself as much as she can, to extrapolate from what she is told to increase her understanding.

Parental authority is likewise presented in *A Vindication of the Rights of Woman* as something that must be ceded as a daughter's mind gains strength: 'the Almighty Father of all has implanted an affection in me to serve as a guard to you whilst your reason is unfolding; but when your mind arrives at maturity, you must only obey me, or rather respect my opinions, so far as they coincide with the light that is breaking in on your own mind.'[17] In contrast with Hannah More, Wollstonecraft views this 'irradiation' as wholly desirable and natural. In line with the enlightenment and emancipation that she had argued for in the *Vindication*, the parents' right to command the child's obedience in *Lessons* is temporary, ebbing away as the child learns to think independently. In the final extant lesson, she is assured of her progress in becoming a thinking being, capable of forming moral ideas through the use of her reason. When her mother is suffering from a headache, the little girl does not think to be quiet until her father explains that her noisiness is making the pain worse; but once told, she is able to remember and draw her own inferences on a later occasion. Wollstonecraft's maternal narrator affectionately shows her child how far she has already advanced towards self-awareness and consideration for others, forming her own moral ideas from observation and reflection:

> You say that you do not know how to think. Yes; you do a little. The other day papa was tired; he had been walking about all the morning. After dinner he fell asleep on the sopha. I did not bid you be quiet; but you thought of what papa said to you, when my head ached. This made you think that you ought not to make a noise, when papa was resting himself ... You were going out; but thinking again, you came back to me on your tiptoes. Whisper – whisper. Pray mama, call me, when papa wakes; for I shall be afraid to open the door to see, lest I should disturb him ... That was thinking. When a child does wrong at first, she does not know any better. But after she has been told that she must not disturb mama, when poor mama is unwell, she thinks herself, that she must not wake papa when he is tired. Another day we will see if you can think about any thing else.[18]

Notably, this is the first time in the *Lessons* that the fictional girl is given her own speech: with the power to think (the word is repeated six times, and 'thought' once), to reflect, and to form a plan of action founded on this independent thought, she becomes a more fully formed character. Given a history of the growth of her own mind by her nurturing mother, she is assured that she is on the road to becoming a thinker, a moral philosopher. Wollstonecraft's radical sexual politics, although left implicit, are as discernible in the *Lessons* as in *A Vindication of the Rights of Woman*: she wishes to reinstate in girls' education what she had earlier called 'the birthright of man, the right of acting according to the direction of his own reason.'[19]

One of Wollstonecraft's main influences in the *Lessons* is Anna Letitia Barbauld, who evokes the open, imaginative, and enquiring child also envisioned in Wollstonecraft's primer. Barbauld's own *Lessons for Children* (1778–9) invents the intimate conversational style and pedagogical method later adopted in Wollstonecraft's *Lessons*, and it seems clear that Wollstonecraft consciously echoes the movement traced by Barbauld from single words to simple stories, although with the difference that in place of Barbauld's fictional child, 'Charles,' Wollstonecraft chooses to focus on an unnamed girl. But Barbauld's *Hymns in Prose for Children* (1781) is the more important source for Wollstonecraft's emphasis on the observant, imaginative, and relational intelligence that she nurtures in the child of *Lessons*. Barbauld's 'child of reason' is essentially a progressive being, able to grow and learn as it observes and reflects; and strikingly, this is an ungendered and innate ability, which only needs to be recognized and nurtured by the adult parent or teacher.[20] That this benevolent parent is modelled on a distinctly maternal God is significant: one who 'is the parent of all,' of '[a]ll the men, and all the women who are alive in the wide world,' and whose 'hand is always stretched out over us' in a gesture of motherly protectiveness and affection, extending this nurturing care equally to '[l]abourers spent with toil, and young children, and every little humming insect.'[21]

This maternal imagery is consistently related in Barbauld's writings to the embryonic powers of mind in the human child. Using a nexus of association stretching back to her early poem, 'A Summer Evening's Meditation' (published in 1773), infant, mother, and God seem constantly interrelated in the *Hymns in Prose*. In her 1773 poem, Barbauld writes of her perception of her own mind as containing 'An embryo GOD; a spark of fire divine,' able through acts of meditation and mental exploration to travel out imaginatively to

> solitudes of vast unpeopled space,
> The desarts of creation, wide and wild;
> Where embryo systems and unkindled suns
> Sleep in the womb of chaos....[22]

It is as if Barbauld's mind to some extent equals or even exceeds that of God, able to conceive of and to 'people' space that is as yet uncreated. This poetic potential—the potential to deepen experience imaginatively so as to transform our vision of what the universe is and might be—is folded within the child at birth, ready to be fed and to grow. Barbauld touches on these ideas in her audacious address to an unborn child, 'To a Little Invisible Being Who Is Expected Soon to Become Visible' (1796), where she invokes the 'powers expanding slow' in the 'Germ of new life,' and reflects:

> What powers lie folded in thy curious frame, –
> Senses from objects locked, and mind from thought!
> How little canst thou guess thy lofty claim
> To grasp at all the worlds the Almighty wrought!

Even as an 'infant bud of being,' Barbauld insists on the child's 'lofty claim' of its right to rise and 'fill the air,' temporarily 'locked' within and as yet undeveloped by contact with the sensory world, but ready to be released into action.[23] Similarly, in 'Hymn X' of *Hymns in Prose*, the child is compared to an acorn, physically tiny, yet embodying sublime powers implanted by nature: 'Such an acorn, whose cup can only contain a drop or two of dew, contained the whole oak. All its massy trunk, all its knotted branches, all its multitude of leaves were in that acorn; it grew, it spread, it unfolded itself by degrees, it received nourishment from the rains, and the dews, and the well-adapted soil, but it was all there.'[24] Just as the acorn is able to unfold through its increasing contact with rain, dew, and soil, the child is nourished by 'instruction,' which 'feed[s] the mind, and make[s] it unfold its hidden powers' (253). These powers of mind, of thought, and of imagination, linked by Barbauld to the contemplation of God's immortal powers at work in the natural and human world, are to be venerated, not suffered to decay through neglect: 'Respect in the infant the future man. Destroy not in the man the rudiments of an angel' (254).

Barbauld's point is that the child's mind connects it to the divine presence through its inborn powers of progressive growth; but the 'respect' that she urges also links her 'child of reason' to the revolutionary language of universal rights. If the child invoked in 'Hymn X' is a being through whom God speaks, to be accorded respect for its God-given powers of mind, the sick child wept over by the enslaved African woman in 'Hymn VIII' is no less angelic in potential: as Barbauld emphasizes there, slaves and kings are all equally part of the 'families of men' (249). Later, in her anonymously published *Address to the Opposers of the Repeal of the Corporation and Test Acts* (1790), she is more explicit, linking the rise of 'the spirit of Enquiry' and 'Philosophy,' which prompts the growth of 'light and knowledge,' to the birth of a liberty that extends its reach to 'every class of men,' including 'the poor African, the victim of hard impenetrable avarice' (277). Thus, she argues, '[m]an, *as* man, becomes an object of respect,' and equality ceases to be a mere theory, 'brought home to men's business and bosoms' (276). Echoing her imagery of embryonic potential lying dormant, but ready to develop if nurtured, in 1790 Barbauld sees the Revolution as an unlocking of bonds that have held back growth: the 'minds of men' now 'swell and heave beneath oppression, as the seas within the Polar circle, when, at the approach of Spring, they grow impatient to burst their icy chains' (278). The consequence of this painful labour, however, is a new birth, in which 'Man, the creature of God' replaces 'Nobles, the creatures of Kings.' Barbauld hopes for a 'reign of Peace,' 'from shore to shore,/Till *Wars* shall cease, and *Slavery* be no more' (277, 278, 281). Although Barbauld is more circumspect about articulating this egalitarian philosophy in *Hymns in Prose* nine years earlier, it is notable that the only mention of God punishing human beings is in relation to the unfamilial treatment of enslaved or conquered people meted out by the 'monarch' who behaves as if he is beyond criticism: 'boast not thyself as though there were none above thee: – ... his powerful arm is always over thee; and if thou doest ill, assuredly he will punish thee' (249).

Evenings at Home (1792–6), co-written with Barbauld's brother, John Aikin, is openly political in tone and subject matter and aims to unfold children's capacities to enquire into inequality through reflection on historical events and personages as well as through social observation and contemplation of natural history. Through the conversations and dialogues that elicit the 'spirit of Enquiry' that Barbauld associates with the nurturing of God-given powers of mind and with the growth of liberty, children are respected and encouraged as autonomous, conscious thinkers. The aim is to foster their ability 'to learn to form ideas with precision, and to express them with accuracy,' as the father tells his son in 'The Art of Distinguishing.' As in the personal history that Maria relates to her daughter in Wollstonecraft's *Wrongs of Woman*, the father seeks to exercise rather than to influence the child's mind, so he is willing to cede the point when the boy indicates his preference for a lively description of a horse in action rather than a dry taxonomy: 'I believe I should have done the same at your age. Remember, however, that [...] I have not given you a definition to teach you what a horse is, but to teach you to *think*.'[25] This philosophical and political education is centred on the issues of the day in 1792–6, when Britain was at war with France, which makes *Evenings at Home*'s unambiguously anti-martial and anti-imperial ideas, mediated through stories and dialogues about birds and animals, heroism and patriotism, still more striking. Home and family are emphatically continuous here with the public and political realm.[26] Although most of the pieces in the collection were written by John Aikin, they are indebted to the vision of liberty and humanity articulated in Barbauld's political writings. Her *Sins of Government, Sins of the Nation* (1793) is a particularly rich source for Aikin's dialogues about the reality of war as opposed to the dehumanizing rhetoric of warmongers, and for those dealing with the concepts of nation and patriotism. Her critique of the inversion of the 'natural course of our feelings' which prompts Britons to rejoice in the misfortunes of their French neighbours draws on her ethic of connectedness: her extension of the concept of 'family' to include 'all the men, and all the women who are alive in the wide world' in *Hymns in Prose*.[27]

This moral and political vision is communicated to the child readers of *Evenings at Home* via a reflection on natural history, and specifically the question of whether animals can be said to act as social beings, or whether this is the preserve of humanity. In Aikin's 'The Rookery,' a father explains to his son that among rooks, society is 'a sort of league for mutual aid and defence, but in which every one is left to do as he pleases, without any obligation to employ himself for the whole body,' and is therefore often riven by conflicts and competition for resources. A beehive, on the other hand, 'is the true image of a commonwealth,' in which each individual seeks to 'obtain some benefit for the *whole body*, not to give particular advantages to a *few*.'[28] This is implicitly a criticism of the monopolizing of resources by rich people, the drones of human society. It is, however, equally reminiscent of Barbauld's analysis in *Sins of Government* of how governments exploit narrow local attachments to justify hostile policies towards neighbouring nations: 'We must act in opposition to the

peacemakers; we must ... blow the coals of discord, otherwise their commerce will revive, and ... then they might be more flourishing than ourselves.' Barbauld sees this policy as motivated not by laudable feelings of
connection to others close to us, but by greed:

> Thus do we extend our grasping hands from east to west ... and in our self-
> ish monopolizing spirit are almost angry that the sun should ripen any pro-
> ductions but for our markets, or the ocean bear any vessels but our own
> upon its broad bosom. We are not ashamed to use that solecism in terms
> *natural enemies*, as if nature, and not our own bad passions, made us ene-
> mies; as if that relation, from which, in private life, flows confidence, affec-
> tion, endearing intercourse, were in nations only a signal for mutual
> slaughter.[29]

Aikin's dialogue, 'The Price of a Victory,' engages closely with this
vision of the corruption of natural bonds through the debasement of language in government propaganda. Oswald's jubilant announcement of
the news of a military victory—'We have got a complete victory, and have
killed I don't know how many thousands of the enemy'—is challenged by
his father, who invites him to review the words that he is using without
due reflection. In place of Oswald's term, 'the enemy,' the father substitutes the phrase 'human creatures' and asks whether their destruction is
something to rejoice over. Although Oswald admits that his father has
raised a just objection, he reasons that 'it is right that our country has
gained a great advantage;' but the father responds that desirable as it is
that their country should prosper, it can only be right if this is achieved
'without injuring the rest of mankind.' War seldom yields 'real advantages'
for any nation, since it always produces 'dreadful evils' that cannot be celebrated by any humane person.[30] He points out that the battle whose victory is being unthinkingly celebrated has entailed the deaths of 'ten
thousand men,' and nearly as many wounded, and when Oswald persists
in distinguishing between the casualties of 'the enemy' and the British
army, stresses again that 'they are *men* on both sides' (53). To the 10,000
dead and wounded soldiers, another 30,000 casualties—those bereaved or
left mutilated—have to be added. When he lights his celebratory candles
that evening, the father suggests, Oswald should therefore 'think what
they cost' (54). Aikin's representation of this sober calculation of the damage inflicted by war on families, and by implication on the 'endearing
intercourse' that should connect all human beings *as* human beings, comes

very close to repeating Barbauld's 'translation' of war propaganda into accurate language in *Sins of Government*:

> We devote a certain number of men to perish on land and sea, and the rest of us sleep sound, and, protected in our usual occupations, talk of the events of war as what diversifies the flat uniformity of life … We should, therefore, do well to *translate* this word war into language more intelligible to us. When we pay our army and our navy estimates, let us set down—so much for killing, so much for maiming, so much for making widows and orphans, so much for bringing famine upon a district....[31]

In order to humanize the language of 'enemies,' 'advantage,' and 'victories' used unthinkingly in discussions of war, and to bring home to Oswald the real suffering that it involves, Aikin's fictional father tells him the history of one soldier, Walter, as one that represents the history of thousands more in the past. Naming this individual man means that Oswald can no longer see him as, in Barbauld's words in *Sins of the Nation*, 'a small imperceptible part of a human machine, called a Regiment.'[32] The details of his ordinary, slow death, and its effect on his loved ones, make it clear that history as reported in newspapers, focusing on the military victory of a day or the heroes of the hour, is a misrepresentation of the real story of war as it affects the mass of human beings caught up in it. Barbauld insists in *Sins of Government*:

> We must fix our eyes, not on the hero returning with conquest, nor yet on the gallant officer dying in the bed of honour, the subject of picture and of song, but on the private soldier, forced into the service, exhausted by camp-sickness and fatigue; pale, emaciated, crawling to an hospital with the prospect of life, perhaps a long life, blasted, useless and suffering. (313)

In line with Barbauld's admonition, Aikin's adult character does not spare his child the details of Walter's wounds, his mutilated body, the eventually fatal damage done to his health and to that of his fiançee, and the ways that this destruction of an individual comes home to his friends and family. Oswald's silence at the end of this description is telling. That he has nothing to say to this 'history' suggests the ways in which Aikin's 'translation' of propaganda and abstractions into embodied, human terms serves to reshape the child's understanding of the ideas and words of war, to the extent that he no longer has a language in which he can respond. Nonetheless, this silence leaves an opening for children reading the

dialogue to discuss and reflect on what they have read, and for their powers of mind—their empathetic moral imagination—to unfold and grow as
a consequence, as the fictional boy's implicitly do.

Samuel Taylor Coleridge's vision of family in 'Fears in Solitude' and
'Frost at Midnight' (1798) seems profoundly influenced by Barbauld's
polemic and Aikin's dialogue. Echoing the family settings of many of the
stories and dialogues in *Evenings at Home*, 'Fears in Solitude' reflects on
the inhumanity of war from the point of view of the 'small and silent dell':
the place of familial intimacy and the 'bonds of natural love,' where it has
seemed possible to 'dream of better worlds.'[33] Breaking in on this idyllic
scene, the threat of violent invasion by the 'enemy' is, Coleridge argues, a
just punishment for Britain's own unneighbourly violence towards 'distant
tribes;' but rather than reflecting soberly on the consequences of this
neglect of 'the forms of nature,' Britons have

> been clamorous
> For war and bloodshed; animating sports,
> The which we pay for as a thing to talk of,
> Spectators and not combatants![34]

Barbauld and Aikin emphasize the ways in which the debased and
dehumanized language of war becomes interwoven with the pleasures of
narrative history, as Barbauld's 'Things By Their Right Names' also shows,
with its child protagonist who delights in a story of murder until he realizes
that his father is really describing a battlefield. This is echoed in Coleridge's
conviction that war has been made into entertainment at the expense of a
sense of feeling for all 'human brethren,' a loss of connectedness that has
affected children as much as adults:

> Boys and girls,
> And women, that would groan to see a child.
> Pull off an insect's leg, all read of war,
> The best amusement for our morning meal![35]

The result is that every child and adult become 'fluent' in 'all our dainty
terms for fratricide,' reading descriptions of battles as if they were 'empty
sounds to which/We join no feeling, and attach no form.'[36]

That reference to 'fratricide' suggests how deeply Coleridge still
adheres, even in the midst of his 'filial fears' for his country, to the sense

that the 'enemy' is in fact a man and a brother; that revolutionary France is, as Barbauld put it in her *Address to the Opposers of the Repeal of the Corporation and Test Acts*, a 'sister nation' 'nursed at the breast of liberty,' like her older sibling, Britain.[37] As we see in 'Frost at Midnight,' published alongside 'Fears in Solitude,' Coleridge persists in cultivating an ethic of fellow-feeling that is fundamentally inimical to a narrowly defined patriotism, and that is founded on his contemplation of his child. His infant son's 'gentle breathings' inspire a sense of hope associated with the child's undefended openness, his responsiveness to beauty, and his connection to a more meaningful language than the 'empty sounds to which/We join no feeling, and attach no form.' Coleridge hopes that his child will be able to 'see and hear/The lovely shapes and sounds intelligible' of a God who fraternizes all beings, 'Himself in all, and all things in himself.'[38] Eight years earlier, Barbauld had imaged the progress of liberty, led by philosophy, as an Arctic spring of 'increasing light and knowledge,' in which the frozen waters 'swell and heave beneath oppression … impatient to burst their icy chains.'[39] Similarly, Coleridge represents his infant son, even before the warmth of the sun has 'capp'd' the points of the icicles with 'pendulous drops,' reaching up towards the light of the moon, 'stretch[ing] and flutter[ing] from thy mother's arms,/As thou would'st fly for very eagerness.' Through his child, Coleridge is able to reflect on the frozen silence of his political isolation in a period of Government reaction, realizing his longing for connection with other living beings—a 'companionable form/With which I can hold commune'—as well as to see beyond the history of his own unhappy childhood to a hoped-for liberation of his child's powers of imagination, thought, and speech.[40]

Coleridge's spiritualized vision of the possibilities of childhood may seem remote from Maria Edgeworth's much more secular understanding of how adults can learn from children's perceptions and responses, a recurring theme in her *Practical Education*, also published in 1798. But again, Edgeworth is preoccupied by the questions about the burden of history that engage so many of the radical and reformist writers who focus on children and childhood in fiction, poetry and philosophy of the 1790s. *Practical Education*'s emphasis on the unfolding of children's capacity for enquiry and invention demonstrates Edgeworth's confidence in children's powers of mind, and the transformative effects of their ways of seeing. She is keen that children should think and feel for themselves, and 'exercise their invention upon all subjects,' from fiction and scientific technology to historical events.[41] Edgeworth's wariness of the potential perversion of children's truthfulness by adult authority pervades her approach to their natural responses. She especially values the strong reactions that children have to cruelty and suffering in historical accounts, commenting:

> the simple morality of childhood is continually puzzled and shocked at the representation of the crimes and the virtues of historical heroes. History, when divested of the graces of eloquence, and of that veil which the imagination is taught to throw over antiquity, presents a disgusting, terrible list of crimes and calamities; murders, assassinations, battles, revolutions, are the memorable events of history. The love of glory atones for military barbarity; treachery and fraud are often dignified with the names of prudence and policy; and the historian, desirous to appear moral and sentimental, yet compelled to produce facts, makes out an inconsistent, ambiguous system of morality. (202)

Rather than perpetuating misery by forcing children into pious and unthinking veneration for the heroes of national history, Edgeworth recommends that parents or teachers 'should never force any system upon the belief of children; but [should] wait until they can understand all the arguments on each side of the question.' She therefore urges that children should be given the time and space to reflect: 'When the young reader pauses to think, allow him time to think, and suffer him to question the assertions which he meets with in books with freedom' (421, 202). Edgeworth thus joins Wollstonecraft, Barbauld, and Aikin in seeing this freedom to engage critically with historical event and political reality as a means of progress. As Barbauld puts it in her *Civic Sermons to the People* (1792), this freedom of enquiry enables citizens to reflect on the 'uses of Government' and thus empowers them to 'judge what is misshapen, monstrous, and out of proportion, and what is well contrived, beautiful, and harmonious.'[42] As citizens of the future, children are necessarily a part of the culture of enquiry that these reformist writers hoped would outlive the repression of the 1790s.

William Godwin explicitly connects the unfolding of children's powers of thought and imagination with the eradication of 'despotism' and 'public misery' in his collection of essays, *The Enquirer* (1797). Written at a time when Godwin was reading or rereading all of Wollstonecraft's works, including her writing for children, Godwin echoes her emphasis on nurturing children's minds and encouraging them to see themselves as thinkers, exercising their inventive capacity to social ends. He focuses on the importance of learning 'to think, to discriminate, to remember and to enquire,' since a more passive and conventional education, he argues, produces only 'common talents,' when what is needed is 'genius': the power to be creative and inventive.[43] This is not, for Godwin, an innate gift so much as the conscious cultivation of enquiry, of a freshness of vision that cuts through the veil of normalization:

> Tyranny grows up by a kind of necessity of nature ... poverty, fraud, violence, murder, and a thousand evils follow in the rear. These cannot be extirpated without great discernment and great energies. Men of genius must rise up, to show their brethren that these evils, though familiar, are not therefore the less dreadful ... It is thus only that important reforms can be produced.

As a 'friend to general happiness,' Godwin looks to children for this defamiliarized insight into the sources of 'public misery,' seeing the 'rising generation' as potential 'saviours of the human race.'[44] He is conscious, however, that the 'present order of society' threatens to thwart the fulfilment of this promise (17). Like Wollstonecraft in *The Wrongs of Woman*, Godwin is troubled by the damage inflicted on the minds and talents of working-class children, neglected, brutalized, and wasted:

> Examine the children of peasants. Nothing is more common than to find in them a promise of understanding, a quickness of observation, an ingenuousness of character, and a delicacy of tact, at the age of seven years, the very traces of which are obliterated at the age of fourteen. The cares of the world fall upon them. They are enlisted at the crimping-house of oppression. They are brutified by immoderate and unintermitted labour. Their hearts are hardened, and their spirits broken, by all that they see, all that they feel, and all that they look forward to. (16–17)

Godwin's description recalls Jemima's evocation of her childhood self as a miserable and broken creature resembling 'a little old woman, or a hag shrivelling into nothing.'[45] Social injustice and inequality constitute, Godwin declares, 'the great slaughter-house of genius and of mind ... the unrelenting murderer of hope and gaiety, of the love of reflection and the love of life.'[46]

Godwin's response to this problem was not direct, but it was sustained. Over the next two decades, he devoted himself largely to writing for children that would seek to foster this love of reflection and of life. Many of his published works as part of his Juvenile Library imprint were histories, either personal—of Lady Jane Grey, of William Mulready, the artist—or national (England, Greece, and Rome); several of these explored the question of the survival of critical enquiry under conditions of struggle or outright oppression. Other, unpublished pieces show Godwin exploring the ways in which children's thinking powers can be exercised and strengthened through the pleasures of play, observation, and conversation. One of these, Godwin's *Juvenile Accomplishments or the Amusements of Salt Hill* (1806), is written for boys who have begun to take a 'step towards manhood,' with the aim of 'excit[ing] their ambition & ... correct[ing] their judgment,' through a mixture of 'histories' and 'sketches of reasoning.'[47] Although his characters are relatively privileged boys aged between 9 and 11 attending a school for 'young gentlemen,' what they learn through the debating game that they play is to express their own thoughts rather than 'delivering the sentiments of another.' Since the story is set in the 1770s, the great issue of the day is the American Revolution, although they quickly realize that they will do better to debate 'the politics of history,' since this involves events that are finished and therefore easier to consider from all angles. Their rhetorical skills are imperfect to begin with, but their ambition to understand and discuss is strong: 'Politics was the flame at which they saw all the world catch fire, & they could not be cold.' The fragment ends with an extended debate on whether greatness is hereditary or a matter of self-generated merit, which concludes with the boys agreeing that 'people of honourable birth usually monopolize to themselves the best education,' and that 'abilities & merit' are not passed down 'in any mysterious way.' To argue that the 'fine ethereal flame of genius is conveyed down with the proper particles of the blood' is, the boys concur, a nonsense: merits and abilities are a matter of education, although 'great merit will often make its way in spite of a bad and neglected education.' While Godwin sets his juvenile debates in a school rather than a domestic setting, his evident interest in shaping the future behaviour and attitudes of his fictional boys as they progress in their careers is an expression of his hope, and that of Aikin and Barbauld, that their more open-minded, egalitarian ideas will gradually effect larger social change, making them a means of perpetuating the 'love of reflection' in themselves and others.

A very different manuscript fragment, also dating from 1806, seeks to foster a sense of joy in fellow-feeling through ecstatic evocations of scenes of nature.[48] Written in the form of a familiar, affectionate letter to a small boy, recounting the 'history of a country walk,' Godwin begins with straightforward, if lively, descriptions of the rural scenes the two have witnessed and experienced—of sheep seen from a distance against a green field, of a rookery, sitting together by a river, observing the 'peace & pleasure among the inhabitants of the water, as well as of the earth & air.'[49] But the piece ends with an extended and rapturous evocation of 'the great invisible principle, acting every where, which maintains the life of every thing around us.'[50] This, Godwin tells his child, is 'the secret meaning of all the things you have seen this morning: it is a delightful subject: it is more than delightful: it will make you serious, & at the same time happy, whenever you think of it.' The invisible life force is associated by Godwin with thought: 'That thing in a man which thinks, we call the spirit or soul of a man: we can never see it, but there it is: when he dies, we can see nothing go from him: but his soul is gone, & he lives no more.' Although trees and flowers do not think, we 'imagine our general spirit as pervading inanimate nature, & communicating life & vigour to the whole vegetable world: this we call the Great Spirit, or God.'[51] For Godwin, this creative and intellectual power unites all living beings in fraternity: 'every thing about me lives, & when I observe of them that they like me have life & health, & are continually experiencing those changes which are indications of health, I can almost say to the tree & the shrub, Thou art my brother!'[52] Again, this vision of joyous equality and relationship could only have been intended to encourage the child reader to cultivate hopeful, compassionate, and empathetic feeling for others, as fellow expressions of this will to life and beauty. From a 'history,' once more, a child is led to contemplate future transformation through a renovated perception of the present.

The work of these radical and reformist writers, whether reflecting on the state of childhood as a potential source of future social transformation or focusing on children's innocence as an imaginary consolation for the traumas of revolution and repression, is marked by the awareness that complete immunity to oppressive realities—war, inequality, slavery, colonialism—is never really possible, even in fantasy. Mary Wollstonecraft, Anna Barbauld, John Aikin, Maria Edgeworth, and William Godwin end by creating a very different understanding of children, not as innocent, isolated beings, but as future citizens, who need to be equipped and informed to take an active and transformative part in society. In unfolding the powers of children's minds, including those of girls, to become autonomous, conscious thinkers—the open and imaginative, knowledge-seeking 'child of reason' invoked in Barbauld's *Hymns in Prose*—they seek to revolutionize Burke's conservative idea of 'family affections,' placing their hopes for the future in a rising generation rather than in the inherited social order of Burke's 'canonized forefathers.'[53]

NOTES

1. Edmund Burke, *Reflections on the Revolution in France* (London: J. Dodsley, 1790), 49, 327.
2. Hannah More, *Strictures on the Modern System of Female Education*, 2 vols. (London: T. Cadell & W. Davies, 1799), II, 134–5.
3. Helen Maria Williams, *Paul and Virginia, translated from the French of Bernardin de Saint-Pierre* (London: G. G. Robinson, 1795), xi–xii, iii.
4. *Paul and Virginia*, 5. Subsequent references appear parenthetically.
5. Wollstonecraft, *Mary and The Wrongs of Woman*, ed. Gary Kelly (Oxford: Oxford University Press, 1980), 120, 76.
6. Wollstonecraft, *Wrongs*, 124. See Alan Richardson's discussion of this passage in *Literature, Education, and Romanticism: Reading as Social Practice, 1780–1832* (Cambridge: Cambridge University Press, 1994), 188; and more recently, Malini Roy's discussion of Maria's revolutionary history in 'Mary Wollstonecraft's Childish Resentment: The Angry Girl, the *Wrongs* and the *Rights of Woman*,' 29–30: James Holt McGavran (ed.), *Time of Beauty, Time of Fear: The Romantic Legacy in the Literature of Childhood* (Iowa City: University of Iowa Press, 2012), 20–39.
7. Wollstonecraft, *Wrongs*, 75. Subsequent references appear parenthetically.
8. *Posthumous Works of the Author of "A Vindication of the Rights of Woman"*, ed. William Godwin, 4 vols. (London: J. Johnson & G. G. & J. Robinson, 1798), III, 78.
9. *Posthumous Works*, III, 86.
10. *Posthumous Works*, IV, 8–9.
11. *Posthumous Works*, I, Preface [ii].
12. *Posthumous Works*, II, 173–4.
13. Wollstonecraft defines 'enlightened maternal affection' in *A Vindication of the Rights of Woman* as distinguishing the 'good mother,' who is able to '[dart] the keen eye of contemplation into futurity,' and capable of using 'sense' and 'independence of mind' to nurture a child while never forgetting 'the common relationship that binds the whole family on earth together': a revolutionized bond akin to Richard Price's enlightened patriotism in *A Discourse on the Love of our Country* (1789). *A Vindication of the Rights of Men with A Vindication of the Rights of Woman and Hints*, ed. Sylvana Tomaselli (Cambridge: Cambridge University Press, 1995), 243.
14. *Posthumous Works*, II, 180.

15. Ibid., 188.
16. Ibid., II, 189.
17. *A Vindication of the Rights of Woman*, 247.
18. *Posthumous Works*, II, 195–6.
19. *A Vindication of the Rights of Woman*, 247.
20. *Hymns in Prose for Children*, in *Anna Letitia Barbauld: Selected Poetry and Prose*, eds William McCarthy and Elizabeth Kraft (Peterborough, Ont.: Broadview Press, 2002), 245.
21. *Hymns in Prose*, 241, 244.
22. 22. 'A Summer Evening's Meditation,' in *Anna Letitia Barbauld: Selected Poetry and Prose*, ll.56, 94–97.
23. 'To a Little Invisible Being Who Is Expected Soon to Become Visible,' in *Anna Letitia Barbauld: Selected Poetry and Prose*, ll. 1, 5–8, 12, 7, 11, 6. William McCarthy describes the baby in this poem as needing to 'break free in order to claim its rights as a rational being': see McCarthy, *Anna Letitia Barbauld: Voice of the Enlightenment* (Baltimore: The Johns Hopkins University Press, 2008), 390. He dates the poem to Spring 1796 (note 4, 643).
24. *Anna Letitia Barbauld: Selected Poetry and Prose*, 252. Subsequent references appear parenthetically. 'Hymn X' was a later addition, first published in the 1814 edition of *Hymns in Prose*, although its consonance with the ideas of 'To a Little Invisible Being' suggests that it may date from the 1790s.
25. *Evenings at Home; or, the Juvenile Budget Opened*, 6 vols. (London: J. Johnson, second edition, 1794), II, 136.
26. In a richly detailed and perceptive account of the radical politics of *Evenings at Home*, Michelle Levy argues that for Aikin and Barbauld the family is at the heart of the improvement of the nation: see *Family Authorship and Romantic Print Culture* (Basingstoke/New York: Palgrave Macmillan, 2008), 14, 24.
27. *Anna Letitia Barbauld: Selected Poetry and Prose*, 241.
28. *Evenings at Home*, I, 82, 83, 84.
29. *Anna Letitia Barbauld: Selected Poetry and Prose*, 310.
30. *Evenings at Home*, IV, 51.
31. *Anna Letitia Barbauld: Selected Poetry and Prose*, 312.
32. *Anna Letitia Barbauld: Selected Poetry and Prose*, 313.
33. Coleridge, *Fears in Solitude, Written in 1798, During the Alarm of an Invasion. To Which Are Added, France, an Ode, and Frost at Midnight* (London: J. Johnson, 1798), 'Fears in Solitude,' ll. 2, 177, 26.
34. ll. 51, 24, 90–93.
35. ll. 32, 101–104.
36. ll. 108, 110, 112–13.

37. l. 195; Barbauld, *Address*, 279.
38. 'Frost at Midnight,' ll. 50, 63–4, 67.
39. Barbauld, *Address*, 276–77.
40. ll. 81, 84–5, 19–20.
41. *Practical Education*, ed. Susan Manly, in *The Novels and Selected Works of Maria Edgeworth*, 12 vols., Gen. Eds. Marilyn Butler and Mitzi Myers, Consulting Editor W. J. Mc Cormack (London: Pickering & Chatto, 1999–2003), XI, 6.
42. Barbauld, *Civic Sermons to the People, Number II* (London: J. Johnson, 1792), 23.
43. Godwin, *The Enquirer* (London: G. G. & J. Robinson, 1797), 6, 10.
44. *Enquirer*, 10–11.
45. Wollstonecraft, *Wrongs*, 103.
46. Godwin, *Enquirer*, 17.
47. Bodleian Library, Oxford: MS Abinger. c. 25, Preface. (The manuscript fragment is either unpaginated or inconsistently paginated throughout.)
48. Bodleian Library, Oxford: MS Abinger. c. 24.
49. MS Abinger. c. 24, 10, 5.
50. MS Abinger. c. 24, 13.
51. MS Abinger. c. 24, 11–13.
52. MS Abinger. c. 24, 18.
53. Burke, *Reflections*, 49.

CHAPTER 9

Mediocrity: Mechanical Training and Music for Girls

Donelle Ruwe

The excellence of musical performance is a decorated screen, behind which all defects in domestic knowledge, in taste, judgment, and literature, and the talents which make an elegant companion are creditably concealed.
—*Hannah More,* Coelebs in Search of a Wife *(1808–1809, rpt. 1995, Bristol: Thoemmes, 111)*

Mrs. W. is constantly urging us to take pains, and pay every attention to whatever we attempt to acquire; but she is very anxious that we should distinguish between mere accomplishments, and that sterling knowledge which furnishes and enlarges the mind. Even accomplishments, she says, are chiefly to be valued as they tend to refine the taste, and extend the views: and I have often heard to observe, that life is too short to allow us to devote much of it, to any thing that may not directly or indirectly become useful *to ourselves or others. She once knew a young lady, who had devoted her whole life to learning to play on the harp. She*

I thank the Northern Arizona University Faculty Grants Program for supporting my research on this essay.

D. Ruwe (✉)
Northern Arizona University, Flagstaff, AZ, USA
e-mail: Donelle.Ruwe@nau.edu

© The Author(s) 2018   163
A. O'Malley (ed.), *Literary Cultures and Eighteenth-Century Childhoods*, Literary Cultures and Childhoods,
https://doi.org/10.1007/978-3-319-94737-2_9

succeeded, as might be expected, in her object—that of playing on the harp
better than any of her friends: but what then! 'What a terrible mistake,'
said Mrs. W, 'for a being sent into the world to prepare for immortality!'
—Mrs. Ann Taylor and Jane Taylor, Correspondence Between a
Mother and Her Daughter at School *(1817, London: Taylor and*
Hessey, 56)

Music with its much vaunted capacity to soothe disturbed emotions and
inspire feelings of rapture and sublimity was a valued art form in the long
eighteenth century, but as these quotes aptly demonstrate, girls were
strongly discouraged from working to achieve virtuosity in music performance.[1] As Gillen D'Arcy Wood explains, virtuosity in its historical sense
suggests both 'a luxury exhibit and a mechanical mode of performance,'
and as such, virtuosity is far removed from domestic accomplishments,
which are valued as proper employments of private time.[2] British pedagogical writers of the period typically link music training to wasteful,
mind-numbing practice and self-centered behaviour despite the fact that
music training as a regimen of practice corresponds to successful self-
discipline, time management, the creation of beauty, and psychological
interiority—highly privileged skills.[3] The ideal of rational education and
the sublime potential of music cannot be easily reconciled with the grim
realities of instrumental music education: music proficiency requires years
of mechanical practice and technical exercises. Fears of the virtuoso were
particularly acute when they were inflected through the concerns of
rational educators and Dissenters. Maria Edgeworth, for example, argues
in *Practical Education* (1798) that rational thought is in opposition to
effective music performance, for an active and alert mind hinders any
mechanical operation. In tasks requiring manual dexterity, writes
Edgeworth, 'we go on habitually without thought. Thought would
probably interrupt the operation, and break the chain of associated
actions.'[4]

Music as a female accomplishment is riddled with contradictions. It
encourages expressiveness and private time (the time spent in practice),
and it was a treasured aspect of domestic life for many women, as evi-
denced by networks of female copyists and sheet-music exchange circles.[5]
And yet, how private or pleasurable can music practice really be? It is noisy,
repetitive, and often unpleasant. Music precludes conversation since one
cannot converse and read music simultaneously. Further, music often

brings the middle-class girl's public and private roles into conflict, for even home musicales and evening entertainments place girl performers under public scrutiny. Music expertise might enhance a girl's marriageability, but only so long as her performance is good but not too good. In other words, a virtuoso is undesirable, even unseemly, but a poor musician is unattractive. Most Enlightenment-era criticism of music as an accomplishment focuses not on music training per se but on *excessive* music training and issues of public performance. For these writers, the highest acceptable level of music performance for girls is mediocrity, just enough facility to play pleasing, simple airs.

This chapter shifts our focus from virtuosity to the gendered rhetoric of mediocrity. I explore pedagogical texts and children's books, determining what happens when mediocrity is the goal of a girl's music practice. By focusing on mediocrity, I expose ideological contradictions in the construction of music education: in particular, the illogical attitude that artlessness is the pinnacle of a girl's performance style, but that this artlessness can be achieved without mechanical practice. I study the anxiety experienced by music professionals when mediocrity is a student's goal: in such cases, *master* teachers are not required for students to achieve basic competency, and standardized lessons are more cost-effective than individualized ones. Finally, if we accept that the regimen of practice is a safe zone for the development of female assertiveness (given that the work of achieving mediocrity is a socially sanctioned, private space of female labour), I ask why women writers of pedagogical novels, epistolary fictions, and educational tracts—even those whose backgrounds include work with music professionals—do not address the potential of music in a girl's developmental process.

IMAGINARY DICHOTOMY: ART AND ARTLESSNESS

Discussions of music pedagogy in educational works evoke questions at the heart of Romantic aesthetics. Is art an untutored, spontaneous expression of deeply felt emotion, or is it the product of labour and craft? How can the Romantic ideal of natural genius be reconciled with the necessity for mechanical labour, apprenticeship, and imitation? Should girls even strive for greatness if greatness requires a single-minded devotion to the work? While literary production can be naturalized as if it is merely an extension of speech, it is much harder to present performance on a musical instrument as untutored. When pedagogical writers depict the education of an instrumentalist, they must either acknowledge the necessity of mechanical practice or conceal the reality that proficiency takes years of technical training. When the music student is a girl, the tension between mechanical practice and artlessness is even more pronounced.

We know from recent studies on contemporary musicians that the amount of time spent practicing music (rather than inherent talent) determine a student's ability to perform at the highest levels. To reach grade five music competency, for example, students must put in an average of 1200 hours of practice.[6] In a famous study comparing amateur and professional pianists, Swedish psychologist K. Anders Ericsson discovered that amateurs practice no more than 3 hours a week, averaging 2000 total hours by age 20. By contrast, professional musicians reach 10,000 hours by age 20.[7] Ericsson's conclusion is clear: 'the differences between expert performers and normal adults reflect a life-long period of deliberate effort to improve performance in a specific domain.'[8] Deliberate practice as described by Ericsson is an investment of resources and time: it must be designed for the task and the learner, it requires continuous feedback, it is highly demanding mentally, and it is not fun. The resources necessary for deliberate practice and 10,000 hours of training by age 20 were simply not available to the typical eighteenth-century girl, particularly when the chosen instrument was a piano that might need to be shared with siblings or schoolmates. The problematic logistics of piano practice crop up in multiple moral tales and pedagogical tracts in this era. For example, Jane Taylor's girl's school novella, *Sketches from a Youthful Circle*, presents an altercation between two girls over the scheduling of practice time. When so many students receive lessons, it is 'necessary that each young lady should have a particular hour for music,' and it is very difficult to find another opportunity.[9] There is no way for the girls in Taylor's youthful circle to get 10,000 hours of practice; they are, perforce, striving for mediocrity as the pinnacle of achievement. Further, as the repeated complaints of education reformers such as Mary Wollstonecraft make clear, girls' education is disorganized and haphazard. Such conditions are not amenable to the rigour of deliberate practice.

Jean-Jacques Rousseau and Stéphanie-Félicité Ducrest de Saint-Aubin, Comtesse de Genlis, two prominent Enlightenment-era education philosophers, novelists, and music teachers, propose very different approaches to music training for girls. Rousseau, who began his working life as a music teacher and copyist and authored *Dissertation on Modern Music* (1743), sidesteps the issue of mechanical practice entirely by depicting music training of girls in *Emile* (1762) as an untutored and natural explo-ration.[10] By contrast, Madame de Genlis's novel *Adèle et Théodore, ou Lettres sur l'éducation* (1782, translated as *Adelaide and Theodore*), which was a rebuttal of Rousseau's educational program, exhaustively details the rigours of mechanical training and structured practice. Genlis was an exceptional musician, and her expertise as a teacher was well known: her 1802 introductory guide to harp playing, *Nouvelle méthode pour appren-dre à jouer de la harpe en moins de six mois de leçons*, went through several editions, and her technique as a harpist was written about by others.[11]

Rousseau's ideal music education consists of natural gifts that develop through undirected exploration resulting in artlessness, a natural simplic-ity seemingly produced without effort. *Emile*'s Sophy is introduced to basic fingering technique, but thereafter music training is directed by her own sense of beauty and a desire to make pretty sounds:

> Sophy has natural gifts; she is aware of them, and they have not been neglected; but never having had a chance of much training she is content to use her pretty voice to sing tastefully and truly; . . . . She has had no singing master but her father, no dancing mistress but her mother; a neighbouring organist has given her a few lessons in playing accompaniments on the spinet, and she has improved herself by practice. At first she only wished to show off her hand on the dark keys; then she discovered that the thin clear tone of the spinet made her voice sound sweeter; little by little she recog-nised the charms of harmony; as she grew older she at last began to enjoy the charms of expression, to love music for its own sake. But she has taste rather than talent; she cannot read a simple air from notes.[12]

Rousseau's approach to Sophy's music education is fantastical at best. He avoids grappling with the necessity of sustained practice to achieve musical facility. Sophy learns without serious study or logical method, but readers are to assume that her natural expressiveness makes her music charming. Her voice, in particular, is an instrument that is best left untutored in favor of a natural songbird quality. To argue for an untrained voice is one thing, but it is quite another to indicate that one naturally understands how to play a virginal, harpsichord, harp, or guitar, the main instruments used by women in the mid-eighteenth century. Rousseau does concede that instru-mental music requires training, but no more than a few lessons, and he minimizes their effect on Sophy. Although she 'has improved herself by practice,' Rousseau depicts her practice as frivolous, as the undisciplined product of feminine vanity. She is motivated to 'show off her hand on the dark keys,' and her spinet playing is merely an enhancement of her true talent, an untutored singing voice.

While Rousseau's depiction of musicianship as a naturally occurring phenomenon is extreme and impractical, many music teachers did attempt to naturalize music teaching and used images of nature in their music teaching guides. For example, the anonymous 1814 *The Power of Music, in which is Shown, by a Variety of Pleasing and Instructive Anecdotes, the Effect it Has on Man and Animals* offers multiple animal narratives involving music.[13] In Charles Dibdin's *Music Epitomized: A School Book: In Which the Whole Science of Music Is Explained*, music-note reading is explicitly linked to plant growth: triple meter, for example, is presented as twigs sprouting in multiples of three from rows of branches, and another illustration uses the image of a tree to demonstrate 'the length of notes as they grow out of each other' (Figs. 9.1 and 9.2).[14]

By contrast, Madame de Genlis is no fan of 'natural' talent. She insists that music performance requires extensive practice. When Genlis's alter ego in *Adelaide and Theodore*, the Baroness d'Almane, explains her music teaching methodology, she emphasizes mechanical exercises. Unlike Rousseau, she does not promote a fantasy about natural abilities being enough to create pleasing sound, and her detailed descriptions of practice fit all of the criteria of deliberate practice as established by Ericsson:

> To arrive at perfection either on the harp or harpsichord, . . . [children] ought to practice a twelvemonth, first with one hand, then with the other . . . They should by turns execute all the shakes and most difficult passages that are to be met with, using the left hand most, which is in fact more awkward than the right, and has less strength. This requires at the beginning so little attention from the scholar that it cannot weary her: on the other hand, expecting her to read music, to place her hands properly to finger well, and to put treble and base together, requires much application, and is difficult and tiresome; . . . No master will adopt my method, because by following it they cannot make their scholar in five or six months play by rote several tunes; and I must confess there are many parents who would be very little pleased to see their daughters, after a year's instruction, only able to repeat a few passages. But . . . in less than three months she will surpass those who have learned three years in the common way.[15]

Through this rigorous system, the Baroness' young daughter Adelaide masters rudimentary music technique and builds strength and dexterity. However, the intensive mechanical practice required by Genlis was too

Fig. 9.1 'Triple Time' from Charles Dibdin's *Music Epitomized*, 8th edition. (Courtesy of Toronto Public Library, Osborne Collection of Early Children's Books, Toronto, Canada)

much for even her most ardent admirers, such as Margaret Chinnery, who adopted virtually all of Genlis's pedagogical techniques with the exception of her approach to music. As Chinnery writes, this method requires children to give too 'large a portion of time... devoted to a study rendered

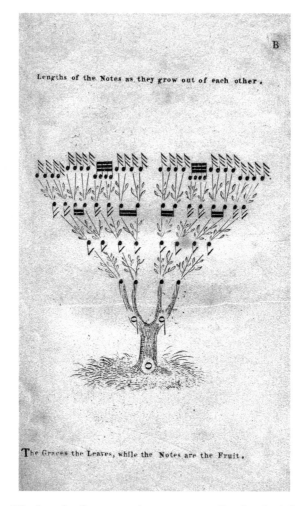

Fig. 9.2 'The length of notes as they grow out of each other' from Charles Dibdin's *Music Epitomized*, 8th edition. (Courtesy of Toronto Public Library, Osborne Collection of Early Children's Books, Toronto, Canada)

merely mechanical by their being left in ignorance of the cause and meaning of what they are required to execute.'[16]

Though parents might have reservations about such an extreme focus on mechanical skills, Rousseau's methodology (which romanticizes music performance as a naturally occurring ability) would, if actually put into practice, ensure incompetent performance. Artlessness cannot be an approach to music teaching. Rather, artlessness is an appearance that is gained through extensive deliberate practice. Genlis's mode is mechanical in approach but much more effective in the long run.

This section of my chapter opened with passages from French works because British pedagogical writers offer almost no positive descriptions of music education. In England, the teaching of music had not been a serious field of inquiry since its virtual banishment from schools during the Reformation. John Locke felt that it was a trifling waste of a gentleman's time.[17] Charles Allen's 1760 treatise on female education argues that although music is 'one of the most genteel qualifications which a young lady can possess,' it should only be an amusement, a solace, and an inspiration, for if a girl practices too hard, it leads to crass professionalism and curtails the time spent in achieving 'a *complete education.*'[18] A young lady should not 'arrive at the highest degree of perfection in this, or in any other accomplishment. It is no shame for a young lady to be outdone in music by an opera-singer.'[19] Allen implies that music virtuosity is unseemly, linked to those of weak virtue (opera-singers), and ornamental rather than moral. In other words, mediocrity, not virtuosity, is a girl's proper goal. The anonymous 1778 *Euterpe; or Remarks on the Use and Abuse of Music, as Part of Modern Education* advises girls to learn only the rudiments of note reading so as 'to sing easy, plain, simple tunes by inspection, and not the artificial manner of spelling a song on the keys of their harpsichord.'[20] In *Plan for the Conduct of Female Education in Boarding Schools* (1797), Erasmus Darwin claims that girls who spend too much time on trivial accomplishments and exhibit in public 'extinguish the blush of youthful timidity.'[21] None of these authors encourage the commitment to music practice propounded by Genlis.

BRITISH MUSIC TEACHERS AND THE CHIROPLAST DEBATE

To discover a passion for technique practice in British texts of the period, we must turn to the pedagogical writings of professional musicians. Debates about how to teach instrumental music to children were rigorous and reached a particular heyday in England with the 1814 invention of the chiroplast by Johann Bernhard Logier (1777–1846). Logier was born in Germany, settled in England in 1791, and eventually became the music director of Dublin's Royal Hibernian Theatre. The chiroplast was

Fig. 9.3 Plate from Logier's *First Companion to the Royal Patent Chiroplast*, printed with permission of the Harry Ransom Center, University of Texas Austin

a mechanical contraption that fit over a piano keyboard. It moved laterally, holding wrists and hands in the proper position (see Fig. 9.3).[22] Logier was an astute businessman and built an entire industry around his patented chiroplast. He promoted a complete music teaching system and offered professional training to music teachers (who paid 100 guineas to learn how to implement his method). His teacher's manual, *The Companion to the Chiroplast*, included fee schedules for individual and group lessons, the costs of purchasing or renting chiroplasts, and recommendations for using advanced students as secondary instructors.[23] One of the more controversial elements of the chiroplast was that it allowed piano to be taught in group lessons so long as an instructor had multiple pianos fitted with the contraption.[24] Logier's suggestion that music instruction could be managed in more cost-effective ways and, thus, become more accessible to the less affluent masses has striking parallels to other early education reform movements such as the Lancaster system. Logier taught with his method in England, Ireland, and Berlin, and chiroplasts sold particularly well in Russia. An improved version of the chiroplast was still being marketed in 1877.

The chiroplast method, with its standardized methodology and mechanical training, emphasizes the mass production of music skills, and it lends itself to the discourse of mediocrity rather than to virtuosity. One aesthetic-commercial aspect of mediocrity is that it is reproducible and transmittable. It does not promote individual excellence (as does the culture of virtuosity). A vigorous pamphlet war over Logier's method debated the merits of individual versus group lessons, individualized expression over mechanical uniformity, and rational and emotional engagement versus muscle memory. Underlying all of these debates was a profound anxiety about the commercialization of music teaching, the rise of a professional artisan class, and the purpose of music in the lives of girls.

To promote his system, Logier staged demonstrations in Dublin and London of working-class girls using the chiroplast. These demonstrations included oral examinations of the students' knowledge of music theory. Logier invited a committee of professors from the newly established Philharmonic Society of London to attend and evaluate his system.[25] One of these professors, Henri De Monti, published an excoriating review of Logier's system. Monti's tract, *Strictures on Mr. Logier's System of Musical Education*, provides a front-row view of Logier's methodology, which Monti condemns as a 'System of Musical Quackery.'[26] Here are Monti's first impressions upon entering Logier's demonstration room in April 1817:

> I was struck with astonishment, at seeing one grand and ten square pianofortes, with their tops off, (probably to ensure the best effect,) so disposed, that the backs of the performers were of necessity turned to the audience.

> 'Whatever these great Masters may teach,' said I to myself, 'they certainly evince but little care and solicitude for the forming and preserving correct and delicate ears in their Pupils.' (7–8)

Monti describes how 'eleven piano-fortes were struck at once by about thirty young Ladies; and the horrible discords of the wretchedly-tuned instruments overwhelmed my poor auditory nerves' (9). Monti's observation is probably fair, for the difficulties of tuning early nineteenth-century pianos so that they were all on the same pitch were all but insurmountable, and any large group of pianos would not have perfectly synchronized pitches.[27] Monti also finds that the chiroplast's physical effects are temporary. The upper part of the oblong frame keeps the wrist of the performer so confined that it cannot be raised. Children 'thus manacled' have no choice in how to play and do not learn musical judgment, unlike those who are individually taught and may follow 'the judicious example and instructions of an experienced Master' (17).

Beyond these technical issues, Logier's system troubles Monti, for it does not respect class barriers and treats music teaching as a factory process with a cheap mass-distribution system rather than as a specialized art requiring a synergy between master and student. Monti complains that group lessons are so inexpensive that parents from 'inferior stations' are 'seduced' by the 'cheapness of the bauble,' and their children intermingle promiscuously with those of 'superior rank' (44). He then imagines some poor governess in a boarding school who will 'commence teaching *a la Logier*, and by dint of vociferation, and the brandishing of her rod, and skipping to and fro nimbly among the array of Pupils and Pianos, make more money in one hour, than she could otherwise obtain in a whole week' (45). These fantasies of an unstoppable chain of ill-taught women teaching poorly in turn require, of course, a matching fantasy in which a well-trained male musician rides to the rescue. Monti reassures his readers that 'intelligent, honest, and independent men' will investigate Logier's system and protect the unsuspecting public from his quackery (46).

Monti criticizes not only the performance aspects of Logier's system but also his approach to music theory which, according to Monti, emphasizes rote memorization:

> Mr. Logier talks loudly of his scholars, some of them very young children, being capable to analyze the works of the greatest musicians. But what kind of analysis does Mr. Logier mean? Does he teach his Pupils how to examine

a piece of music, with the eyes of a learned critic? How to appreciate, first, its melody, its expression, its energy, its tendency and fitness to excite or to allay such and such passions? (48)

For the music theory portion of the demonstration, Logier's students identified the intervals between notes in a diatonic scale. Logier was delighted at his pupils' correct answers, but Monti found that when he put forth 'a very simple question to one of them, *viz*, What interval was there from G sharp to A flat? The young Lady did not seem to understand me' (9). In point of fact, Monti asked a trick question. There is no interval between G sharp and A flat, for they are different names for the same pitch.

Monti's attempts to discredit Logier are representative of music professionals who disapprove of the mechanization of the 'art' of teaching. If the music master's expertise can be distributed through workbooks and student monitors, then the master teacher has lost his monopoly over his specialized profession.[28] Logier's students are taught in groups, so there is minimal individualized teaching, no passing down of craft from master to pupil. Muscle memory is taught through machines. Logier's distribution of knowledge comes dangerously close to factory work, to a form of alienated labour in which the hands of the musician-in-training are literally separate from the mind of the musician. And, to add insult to injury, Logier's students come from different social and economic stations and are indiscriminately placed together in a single room and taught the same lessons, regardless of rank and ability. Monti's scathing report about Logier's system indicates that the stakes were high for the fledgling Philharmonic Society, which was attempting to establish itself as the arbiter of the standards of the music profession. Logier refuted Monti's claims in a pamphlet of his own in which he names various professors who undersigned the committee's report but had never attended a demonstration, and he presents his correspondence with the prestigious Sir George Thomas Smart (who had had a positive experience at a Logier demonstration and conceded that his fees were not out of line).[29]

Many musicians and teachers praised Logier's system for the efficiency that Monti found so very objectionable. For example, the anonymous tract *Advice from an Eminent Professor on the Continent, To a Nobleman in this Country, on the Manner in which his Children should be Instructed on the Piano-forte* (1818) argued that Logier's system was useful precisely because it did not require a master to teach basic knowledge and technique, and that the 'jealous' territorialism of British music professors was the only reason that it had not been adopted in England.[30] For all that the commotion over the chiroplast would suggest that Logier was an invention peddler and self-promoter, he was actually a solid music theorist who authored one of the century's best introductions to music theory. Logier's *System of the Science of Music: Logier's Comprehensive Course in Music, Harmony, and Practical Composition* was still in print as late as 1976. In 1817 Logier teamed up with Friedrich Kalkbrenner, who was widely considered the preeminent pianist of the age, to found an academy in London where music theory and piano playing could be taught with the help of the chiroplast.[31]

Mediocrity, as a proper female level of achievement, is discussed in several of the written defenses of Logier, but in these texts mediocrity is used to defend mechanical practice and is no longer associated with virtuosity. W. Nixon's *A Guide to Instruction on the Piano-Forte: Designed for the Use of Both Parents and Pupils; in a Series of Short Essays, Dedicated to the Young Ladies of the Musical Seminary* (1834) quotes Logier on the title page regarding the rapid attainment of 'a good position of the hand, correct finger, and graceful execution, by the shortest means.'[32] Nixon, like Genlis and Logier, contends that a formal system is especially essential for students who wish to be ordinary players because they will spend less time practicing and must maximize its effectiveness.[33] Nixon suggests that 'natural ability' impedes progress, for it instills improper playing habits that must be unlearned.[34] Nixon's refutation of 'natural ability' and effulgent praise of structured exercises suggests the degree to which the discourse of a Romanticization of natural gifts was locked into a binary opposition with the discourse of mechanical training.

RATIONAL EDUCATORS AND THEIR OPPOSITION TO MUSIC TRAINING

None of this growing body of professional literature made its way into the writings of British women pedagogues who were in the forefront of public discussions of education. Writers like Hannah More, Mary Wollstonecraft, and Maria Edgeworth were not musicians. Though dedicated to raising the standards of women's education, they failed to promote a system for music teaching. When these writers address the teaching of music, it is wrapped up in troubling issues, such as the bad influence of foreigners, the irreligious nature of music, the element of public display which is damaging to female modesty, the alignment of music with ornamental rather than rational accomplishments, and the necessity of monotonous practice to achieve mediocrity. If the purpose of Enlightenment-era rational education is to create a flexible, thoughtful mind that is prepared to learn quickly, create astute analysis, employ a sympathetic imagination, and assimilate new knowledge, then clearly the acquisition of mechanical skills and teaching methods that rely upon rote memorization are a bad thing. British pedagogical writers use music performance and practice as an easy marker for moral corruption, linking music to a host of sins from vanity to laziness. In *Moral Tales* (1802), Maria Edgeworth creates a self-absorbed and foppish flute-playing tutor named Mr. Supine to exemplify the worst sort of guardian to be left in charge of young men.[35] Jane Taylor's moral novella, *Display* (1823), uses music performance as a running motif for frivolousness and false pride.[36]

For most British pedagogical writers, the central problem with music education for girls is that mastery takes far too long to achieve, and a girl's time is better spent in rational activities such as reading. To quote an 1809 children's poem by Mary Lamb, 'A benefit to books we owe / Music can ne'er dispense; / The one does only *sound* bestow, / The other gives us *sense*.'[37] This poem, 'To a Young Lady, on Being too Fond of Music,' reminds girls that even if they achieve the 'utmost summit' of musicality, their skill will not repay their pains, the loss of youth, or the time that could have been spent in 'nobler studies.'[38] Hannah More's *Coelebs in Search of Wife* (1808–1809) contains an entire chapter about the ridiculousness of women who take music too seriously and who do not understand that the moral duties of wife and mother take precedence:

> I look upon the great predominance of music in female education,' said Mr. Stanley, 'to be the source of more mischief than is suspected; not from any evil in the thing itself, but from its being such a gulf of time, as really to leave little room for solid acquisitions. I love music, and, were it only cultivated as an amusement, should commend it. But the monstrous proportion, or rather disproportion, of life which it swallows up . . . has converted an innocent diversion into a positive sin.[39]

The chapter ends when a young miss runs off with Signor Squallini, the Italian music master. As the Squallini reference indicates, sometimes anti-music attitudes reflect xenophobia. Edgeworth's 1798 *Practical Education* questions the value of having a daughter 'turned into an automaton for eight hours in every day for fifteen years, for the promise of hearing her... pronounced the first private performer at the most fashionable, and most crowded concert in London.'[40] Such single-mindedness runs counter to a girl's future role as a mother and educator, and the length of time required for dexterity means that few people are excellent. Instead, they become 'mere machines' and the 'slaves of custom.'[41] Few girls, writes Edgeworth, ever 'get beyond a certain point of mediocrity.'[42]

Superficial music mastery by British girls in pursuit of a husband is exemplified by the Calcutta trade in keyboard instruments. Sailors invested in musical instruments to be sold in India to the growing Anglo population, and British women aboard ships (who were attempting to market themselves to single men in the colonies) needed access to instruments in order to maintain their music-playing abilities.[43] During a voyage to India in 1764, Robert Clive 'was driven practically insane by the efforts of a would-be harpsichord player' who practiced the same two tunes for four hours daily.[44] Here is one key difference between music and other arts. Because music makes noise, a musician intrudes into the space of others in a way that the silent work of the writer and watercolorist does not.

Rousseau-influenced authors clung to the fantasy that artlessness could be decoupled from mechanical practice. Wollstonecraft is conflicted between the positive expressive qualities of music and the negatives of monotonous practice. In *Thoughts on the Education of Daughters* (1787), Wollstonecraft writes that although listening to music is a 'rational and delicate pleasure,' music performance is an exterior accomplishment, like art and dress, and does not improve the mind.[45] Wollstonecraft defaults to Rousseau's position and states that she prefers simple, artless melodies and 'expression to execution.'[46] Little Harry in Thomas Day's *Sandford and Merton* (1783–1789) can barely keep his eyes open when girls play piano with a high degree of polish, but the simple country airs of a good girl are enthralling.[47] Music training is presented as a vicious circle: music is a pleasure if it is simple and artless, artlessness requires dedicated practice, and dedicated practice takes away time from rational and moral accomplishments.

Charles Dibdin, the popular composer, theatre writer, and author of *A Musical Tour Through England* (1788), disputed the rational educator's concerns in *A Letter on Musical Education, by Mr. Charles Dibdin; Addressed to a Father, and through him to those Parents whose Particular Pleasure is in the Accomplishment of their Children* (1791). Dibdin insists that music is 'one of the most rational accomplishments,' and, as with other rational skills, musicianship 'cannot be acquired but by degrees.'[48] Dibdin's idea of music training echoes Genlis's insistence that children must master rudimentary fingering exercises before attempting complex passages. Too many music teachers, he argues, aim to have students perform showpieces by rote and care nothing about their students' understanding of music: '[t]he regular progression of rules, which in music as in language ought to commence with the most familiar articles, and not attempt any thing like perfection but gradually, and by degrees, are totally neglected, and Miss, the very first day, sits down to play abstruse passages out of Hayden [sic] and Pleyel.'[49] Girls learn dazzling tricks and 'play arpegeos [*sic*] and consecutive octaves . . . but not one single favourite air' (19). Since their music education emphasizes surface appearance without deeper understanding, these girls abandon music once they are married and never find music a pleasure in and of itself. The time spent in rote training does not translate into a life-long accomplishment providing comfort and pleasure. Dibdin's argument, thus, refutes Wollstonecraft's suggestion that music appreciation is a discrete activity from music practice and performance. Dibdin suggests that structured music training teaches girls not only how to perform music but also how to appreciate it.

A Case Study of Music for Girls: Adelaide O'Keeffe's *Dudley*

The moral tales and novels of most British rational educators such as Wollstonecraft, More, and Taylor dismiss the value of music education for children, and the only comprehensive treatment of music education for children that I have found in a British novel of the long eighteenth century occurs in Adelaide O'Keeffe's three-volume *Dudley* (1819). Modeled after Genlis's *Adelaide and Theodore, Dudley* is an epistolary novel depicting a comprehensive educational regime.[50] O'Keeffe presents five positive or negative exemplary narratives of music education: piano lessons that, through unhealthy time-consuming practice, kill a young girl; a music teacher who strains the voice of her pupil by requiring her to rehearse artificially high notes; a girl who is encouraged to learn to sing by mimicking birdsong; three impoverished sisters who are allowed to study music only after they have mastered homemaking skills; and, finally, a young effeminate boy who must be discouraged from flute playing.

In *Dudley*, six correspondents detail the ongoing education of children. The main correspondents are the widower Sir Eliot Howard, his widowed sister Jane, and their widowed half-sister Caroline, Countess Alford. The novel begins when the newly widowed Sir Eliot flees to the Isle of Tenerife with his infant daughter Claudy. His sister Jane (whose husband and children died several years prior to the events in *Dudley*) is Claudy's substitute mother and teacher. O'Keeffe uses the backstories of Caroline and Jane as salutary lessons about education. The half-sisters had been educated quite differently by their mothers. Caroline went to an elegant boarding school and excels in the ornamental arts, particularly piano and singing. By contrast, Jane had a primarily domestic education and feels inferior to her more polished half-sister. When Jane became a mother, she resolved to give her children a better mixture of 'the solid and the ornamental.'[51] 'Aim at perfection in all you do,' she urged her daughter and son, and her daughter obsessively practiced the piano, gained 'astonishing proficiency' (1.226), became 'a tall pale shadow, supported by irons,' and sunk under a consumption, a 'victim of [Jane's] system of tuition' (2.148). Jane's son, a genius at languages, suffered from a nervous debility resulting in a 'confirmed state of idiotism' (2.149). Both of Jane's children died young, killed off by virtuosity.

When Eliot asks Jane to take care of Claudy and Dudley (a clergyman's child whom Eliot adopts), Jane chooses a different educational approach.[52] This time she follows Rousseau's dictate that physical activity should be emphasized in the early stages of a child's life. Jane decides that Claudy will spend seven years in healthful activity before any formal studies. Claudy, unlike Jane's daughter, will never gain 'astonishing proficiency' at the piano, but she will not destroy her health in pursuit of virtuosity, either. Claudy will, perhaps, achieve mediocrity at the piano, but she will not be allowed to focus on any single academic or ornamental pursuit.

Given the novel's association of virtuosity with child death, it is not surprising that scenes of formal music training are depicted as horrific torture, as when Caroline, Countess Alford gives Claudy music lessons:

> Claudy [was] standing at Lady Alford's knee, seemingly endeavouring at some great effort, which the latter was encouraging her to accomplish. The child looked weary and exhausted, her mouth was open, her neck stretched out, her face white, her eyes red. Not at first comprehending the cause, I expressed my alarm, when Caroline carelessly replied, 'Oh, you Eliot! Claudy is learning to sing; this is her fourth lesson, and she has already reached up to G. (2.323)

Claudy is overcome by her exertions and can only be restored by contemplating a nest of Capirote songbirds:

> A few notes were given by way of prelude after which followed, for upwards of twenty minutes, the richest strains of music that ever met the human ear: the children. . . now sat listening to it with evident pleasure, marking by their looks and raised fingers, the varying cadence, the sweet piping sound, the swell, the thrill, and the fall of notes. (2.325–26)

Claudy's father tells her that he would rather hear any bird for five minutes than the best singers in the universe, no matter how well trained. In an allusion to Rousseau's music training of Sophy, Claudy's father explains that Claudy should learn music in the same way that the birds learn: 'if you can catch a little tune by ear, and warble it in your own simple fashion, as this bird does, all is well, but very superior scientific singing should be avoided' (2.326). Claudy is not encouraged to strive for the virtuosity of a 'St. Cecelia' (2.325). She is to be mediocre in her accomplishments. Sadly, O'Keeffe provides no practical methodology or rationale for teaching music. She only repeats Rousseauian clichés about artlessness and nature. Claudy, like Sophy, will sing like a songbird but will have no understanding of music theory and performance.

In another parallel to Rousseau's *Emile*, O'Keeffe's *Dudley* educates a child with the specific intent to make the child a suitable domestic partner for a particular future spouse. Sophy's entire education is intended to make her a suitable wife for Emile; in O'Keeffe's novel, however, it is a lower-ranking boy who must be taught to be a proper husband. When Eliot discovers that Dudley is learning the flute so that he might accompany Claudy's piano songs, he bans music from the boy's education and teaches Dudley the manly skill of fencing instead (2.331). Though Eliot's rationalization is that music is a superficial art, an equally compelling though unstated cause of his prohibition is the nature of 'accompanied keyboard music,' a type of composition in which the keyboard (usually played by women) has the lead part, and the accompaniment parts are written out for single-voiced instruments (usually performed by men). As Howard Irving explains, men's instruments, which in the long eighteenth century were the flute, violin, trumpet, and other single-voiced instruments, were used to enhance the sound of a harpsichord.[53] Women's instruments, the harpsichord and the piano, were notoriously hard to keep in tune and often poorly designed with a weak tone. The accompaniment parts featured droning violin chords and sustained flute notes which filled out the thready tones of the harpsichord and piano. From 1750 to 1820, accompanied keyboard music was the dominant form of music published for domestic consumption. Since Eliot plans for Dudley to marry his daughter, it is imperative that the physically weak, less wealthy, effeminate boy not play second fiddle to the wealthier, stronger girl.[54] When Eliot prohibits Dudley from playing the flute, he is trying to masculinize him. Eliot's awareness that music is feminized presages the feminization of domestic music (in contrast to the masculinized world of music professionals) that begins in the Victorian era and which continues to this day.

While the story of Jane's daughter's virtuosity and Claudy's painful vocal training are cautionary tales for upper-class readers about the dangers of virtuosity, Adelaide O'Keeffe offers an exemplary narrative of mediocrity in music for middle-class readers (especially the impoverished middle class). Dudley's sisters are kept at home to save money, their parents 'being fully capable of teaching them' everything they need to know 'to render them worthy wives and mistresses of families' (2.271). Only after 'absolutely necessary' domestic skills are learned can they study ornamental accomplishments. The girls may choose between drawing, languages, and music, but only 'one style, one tongue, and one instrument' (2: 274). One girl opts for music, and because harp lessons are too expensive, she settles on the piano. For this family, both cost and space must be considered before selecting a musical instrument. As Hannah More notes in *Coelebs in Search of Wife*, music training is hardly practicable in a large family: 'six girls daily playing their four hours apiece' on a family's single instrument require them to 'be at it in succession, day and night, to keep pace with their neighbours.'[55]

Although the Irish, probably Catholic, and European-educated O'Keeffe has more in common with the artisan class than the pedagogical writers whose Anglican or Dissenting backgrounds and orientation toward rational education made them suspicious of music, O'Keeffe's novel shares the generic British distrust of music education.[56] O'Keeffe was intimately connected to the professional artisan class that consisted of actors, artists, artisans, and dancers, all of low economic level and dependent upon their work for a livelihood.[57] O'Keeffe was an amanuensis for her father, the blind comic-opera composer John O'Keeffe, and was well aware of the tenuous living afforded to professional musicians. Money was a continual problem for the O'Keeffe family. Theatres, publishers, and the British crown owed John and Adelaide pensions, royalties, and annuities, but the money did not always come, and when it did, it was rarely on time. Most of these annuities stopped after John O'Keeffe's death, leaving Adelaide almost destitute.

In reading these writers who question the value of music training for girls, I am struck by what is missing: discussions of how music training and performance can increase a girl's self-confidence.[58] The piano is a massive piece of furniture that is not easily moved from room to room. Piano playing is the noisiest and most intrusive female accomplishment of all (indeed, the piano is classified as a percussive as well as a string instrument). Music practice, thus, is the opposite of self-effacement in that it intrudes on the domestic space physically through both bulk and sound. Further, the time spent in practice gives girls uninterrupted privacy for thought and emotional expression. Since early keyboard instruments were hard to keep in tune, music training for girls might include the sort of labour that is today expected of professional instrument technicians.[59] However, none of the British education writers address music training as confidence building, not even Adelaide O'Keeffe, the daughter of a composer. Apparently the writings of music professionals such as Genlis, Dibdin, Logier, and others who insisted upon a science of music teaching that emphasized a steady building of skills and knowledge had no influence on British pedagogical writers such as the Taylors, Wollstonecraft, More, and O'Keeffe. These writers, who would typically be opposed to Rousseauian approaches to teaching girls, default time and again to his fantastical vision of an artlessness achieved without mechanical practice.[60]

NOTES

1. Two persistent philosophical theories of emotion and music are expressivism (music expresses the emotional intentions of the artist) and arousalism (music arouses emotions in listeners). See Andrew Kania, 'Music,' *The Routledge Companion to Aesthetics*, 3rd edition, ed. Berys Gaut and Dominic McIver Lopes (Abingdon and New York: Routledge, 2013): 404–14.

2. Gillen D'Arcy Wood, *Romanticism and Music Culture in Britain, 1770–1840: Virtue and Virtuosity* (Cambridge: Cambridge University Press, 2010), 152.

3. See D'Arcy Wood's discussion of the rational educators' response to virtuosity in *Romanticism and Music Culture*, especially 151–65. For a classic discussion of music and British domestic culture, see Richard Leppert's *Music*

and Image: Domesticity, Ideology and Socio-Cultural Formation in Eighteenth-Century England (Cambridge: Cambridge University Press, 1988).

4. Maria Edgeworth and Richard Lovell Edgeworth, *Practical Education.* 2 vols. (London: Johnson, 1798), 304.

5. Jane Austen is a case in point. She practiced piano daily, performed for her family in the evenings, and had a circle of amateur musician friends with whom she exchanged music. At her death she owned about 1500 pages of music, some half of it copied in her own hand. See D'Arcy Wood, *Romanticism and Music Culture in Britain*, 153.

6. Geoff Colvin overviews multiple studies on the importance of practice time versus innate talent in *Talent Is Overrated: What Really Separates World-Class Performers from Everybody Else* (Penguin: New York, 2008), especially 17–19. Grade five music listed in the ABRSM standards include pieces such as J. S. Bach's 'Prelude in E Minor' and Mozart's 'Allegretto'—this music requires a high level of skill but not extraordinary talent. http://us.abrsm.org/en/our-exams/piano/piano-grade-5/ ABRSM is the UK's largest music education body and the world's leading provider of music exams, offering assessments to more than 630,000 candidates in 93 countries every year.

7. Malcolm Gladwell, *Outliers: The Story of Success* (New York: Little, Brown, and Co. 2008), 47–48.

8. Reprinted in Colvin, 63.

9. Jane Taylor, *Sketches from a Youthful Circle.* 2nd ed. Preface. Ann (Taylor) Gilbert (London: Darton, 1836), 173.

10. For a discussion of Rousseau's music philosophy and its connection to his other writings, see John T. Scott, 'The Harmony between Rousseau's Musical Theory and his Philosophy,' *Journal of the History of Ideas*, 59.2 (April 1998): 287–308.

11. Casimir Baecker, one of Genlis's adopted children whom she had instructed since the age of eight, was a renowned harpist and composer. Baecker's and Genlis's harp performances inspired M. Alexandre de Laborde's 1806 publication *Lettre à madame de Genlis sur les sons harmoniques de le harpe*. For a detailed analysis of Genlis's many connections to professional musicians, see Denise Yim's 'An Early Nineteenth-Century Correspondence between Two Friends: the Unpublished Letters of Madame de Genlis to her English Admirer Margaret Chinnery,' *Australian Journal of French Studies* 35 (1998): 308–32, especially 316–18. For discussion of Genlis's influence on British pedagogical writers, see Donelle Ruwe's 'The British Reception of Genlis's *Adèle et Théodore*, Preceptive Fiction, the Professionalization of Handmade Literacies,' *Women's Writing* 25.1 (2018): 5–20.

12. Jean-Jacques Rousseau, *Emile*, trans. Barbara Foxley (London: Dent, 1993), 427.

13. Anon. *The Power of Music. In which is Shown, by a Variety of a Pleasing and Instructive Anecdotes, the Effects it Has on Man and Animals* (Harris: London, 1814).

14. Mr. [Charles] Dibdin, *Music Epitomized: A School Book: In Which the Whole Science of Music Is Completely Explained*. 8th ed. revised and corrected by J. Jousse (London: Goulding, [18--]).

15. Madame la Comtesse de Genlis, *Adelaide and Theodore; or Letters on Education*. Trans. anon. 2nd ed. (London: Bathurst, 1784), 1: 54–55.

16. Reprinted in Denise Yim, 'Madame de Genlis's *Adèle et Théodore*: its Influence on an English Family's Education.' *Australian Journal of French Studies* 38 (2001): 141–57. 155.

17. John Locke, *Some Thoughts Concerning Education and of the Conduct of the Understanding*, ed. Ruth W. Grant and Nathan Tarkov (Indianapolis: Hackett Publishing, 1996), 150–52.

18. Charles Allen, *The Polite Lady, or a Course of Female Education in a Series of Letters, from a Mother to her Daughter* (Philadelphia: Printed for Matthew Carey, 1798 [1760]), 21, 24. Elizabeth Natalie Morgan discusses Allen's insistence on submissive behavior for girls in her dissertation 'The Virtuous Virtuosa: Women at the Pianoforte in England, 1780–1820' (UCLA, 2009), 44–46.

19. Allen, *The Polite Lady*, 23–24.

20. Reprinted in Howard Irving, 'Music as Pursuit for Men: Accompanied Keyboard Music as Domestic Recreation,' *College Music Symposium* 30, no. 2 (1990): 126–37. 136.

21. Erasmus Darwin, *A Plan for the Conduct of Female Education in Boarding Schools* (Derby: Johnson, 1797; Fascism ed. New York: Johnson, 1968), 13.

22. Plate from *The First Companion to the Royal Patent Chiroplast, or Hand-Director: a New Invented Apparatus for Facilitating the Attainment of a Proper Execution on the Piano Forte*, printed for the author, no date.

23. Logier's detailed schedule of fees in this 1818 pamphlet includes the following suggestions: for two days a week, a pupil in a party of 12 paid 10 guineas per quarter; in a party of 16, 7 guineas; in a party of 24, 5 guineas. Entrance cost 1 1/2 guineas, and ladies who did not wish to purchase a chiroplast could hire them for a guinea per quarter.

24. I use the word 'piano' as a generic term encompassing the piano and its precursors, the forte-piano and piano-forte.

25. Music teaching and performance had become a recognized profession with a professional organization founded in 1813, the Philharmonic Society of London. This society sponsored concerts and commissioned new works by major composers. As the anti-Logier pamphlets indicate, the society also attempted to police the profession.

26. Henri Monti, *Strictures on Mr. Logier's System of Musical Education* (Glasgow: Turnbull, 1817), 3. All further references to Monti appear parenthetically.

27. England suffered from discordant pianos to a greater extent than other European countries. Continental tuning methods were more accurate, but England did not adopt these methods until later in the nineteenth century.

28. In England in 1750–1850, the routes to becoming a professional musician, such as apprenticeships or chorister training, required musical studies beginning at an early age. The most widespread method was the private lesson, but cost and availability made extensive private study unavailable to most aspiring musicians. See Deborah Rohr's *The Careers of British Musicians, 1750–1850* (Cambridge: Cambridge University Press, 2001), especially 62–85.

29. Johann Bernhard Logier, *A Refutation of the Fallacies and Misrepresentations Contained in a Pamphlet, Entitled 'An Exposition of the New System of Musical Education,' published by a Committee of Professors in London* (London: Hunter, 1818), 3.

30. Anon. *Advice from an Eminent Professor on the Continent, To a Nobleman in this Country, on the Manner in which his Children should be Instructed on the Piano-forte*, translated by a Lady of Rank (1818), 26.

31. Camille Saint-Saëns recalled using a chiroplast in Kalkbrenner's studio. Important musicians who adopted the chiroplast include Louis Spohr, inventor of the violin chin rest, and Johann Gottlob Friedrich Wieck, father of Clara Schuman. The contemporary pianist and historian of piano technique, Natalia Strelchenko (1976–2015), notes that the chiroplast encouraged a classical-era finger technique characterized by fluidity and a light touch that favored the action of the Viennese piano. This technique was superseded by ones associated with high Romanticism and the Beethoven Broadview piano in which the weight of the arm is used to produce sounds associated with dramatic, emotive works. See Natalia Strelchenko's demonstration of the chiroplast, 'Lecture-Recital Part 3—Chiroplastic Machine. Wrist Technique,' https://www.youtube.com/watch?v=u8wfCGALLIE

32. W. Nixon, *A Guide to Instruction on the Piano-Forte: Designed for the Use of Both Parents and Pupils; in a Series of Short Essays, Dedicated to the Young Ladies of the Musical Seminary* (Cincinnati: Drake, 1834).

33. Ibid., 6.

34. Ibid., 11.

35. Maria Edgeworth, *Moral Tales for Young People.* 2 vols. (London: Johnson, 1802).

36. Jane Taylor. *Display: a Tale.* 11th ed. (London: Taylor and Hessey, 1823).

37. Mary Lamb, 'To a Young Lady on Being too Fond of Music,' in Charles Lamb and Mary Lamb, *Poetry for Children: To Which are Added Prince Dorus and Some Uncollected Poems by Charles Lamb*. ed. Richard Herne Shepherd (New York: Scribner, 1889), 154. Emphasis in original.
38. Ibid., 153.
39. More, *Coelebs*, 110.
40. Maria Edgeworth and Richard Lovell Edgeworth, *Practical Education* 305.
41. Ibid., 303, 305.
42. Ibid., 304.
43. Ian Woodfield, 'The Calcutta Piano Trade in the Late Eighteenth-Century,' in *Music and British Culture, 1785–1914: Essays in Honour of Cyril Ehrlich*, ed. Christina Bashford and Leanne Langley (Oxford: Oxford University Press, 2000), 1–21.
44. Ibid., 5.
45. Mary Wollstonecraft, *Thoughts on the Education of Daughters*, fascism. ed. (1787; Bristol, England: Thoemmes Press, 1995), 42.
46. Ibid., 43.
47. Thomas Day, *The History of Sandford and Merton* (Peterborough, Ont.: Broadview Press, 2010).
48. [Charles] Dibdin, *A Letter on Musical Education* (London: Printed by Dibdin, 1791), 7, 10.
49. Ibid., 9.
50. *Dudley* was well received though its sales were not astounding. See sales figures in the Longman ledgers, available in the Corvey Project database *British Fiction, 1800–1829* [http://www.british-fiction.cf.ac.uk/publishing/dudl19-52.html, accessed 2004]. In 1824 a French translation by the Baroness de Montolieu was published, which O'Keeffe found to be 'too freely translated' (340). Adelaide O'Keeffe, 'Memoir,' in *O'Keeffe's Legacy to His Daughter*, edited by Adelaide O'Keeffe (London: For the Editor, 1834), xi–xxxviii.
51. Adelaide O'Keeffe, *Dudley*, 3 vols. (London: Longman, 1819), 2.148. Henceforward, all citations to *Dudley* are in-text citations.
52. The French translation gives the two children equal billing: *Dudley et Claudy, ou, L'Ile de Ténérife*, which further connects the book to *Adelaide and Theodore*. Adelaide O'Keeffe, *Dudley et Claudy: ou, L'Ile de Ténérife*. Trans. Madame de Montolieu (Paris: Arthus Bertrand, 1824).
53. See Irving, 'Music as Pursuit,' 126–37.
54. *La Belle Assemblée* found the unevenness in the masculine and feminine qualities of Dudley and Claudy to be the novel's main flaw: 'the union brought about between the robust, romping Claudy, and the little sickly Dudley' is not 'to be found amongst the chapter of probabilities.' Review

of *Dudley*, by Adelaide O'Keeffe. *La Belle Assemblée* 20 (Oct 1819): 184–85 (184).

55. More, *Coelebs*, 111.

56. For a full discussion of Adelaide O'Keeffe's works and pedagogical approach, see Donelle Ruwe, *British Children's Poetry of the Romantic Era: Verse, Riddle, and Rhyme* (Houndmills: Ashgate, 2014), especially 108–38. O'Keeffe might have known Dibdin's writings on music. Dibdin was still working in the theatres in the early 1780s, about the time that John O'Keeffe's career began, and John O'Keeffe had performed in some of Dibdin's plays in Dublin. See Roger Fiske, *English Theatre Music in the Eighteenth Century* (London: Oxford University Press, 1973), 357. In his *Recollections*, John O'Keeffe discusses attending Dibdin's one-man entertainment in the Strand in 1792, the 'Sans Souci,' in which Dibdin told stories, sang songs, and created characters with humorous accents. Adelaide was 16 and living with her father at that time.

57. Nancy B. Reich defines the artisan class in 'Women as Musicians: A Question of Class,' *Musicology and Difference: Gender and Sexuality in Music Scholarship*. ed. Ruth A. Solie (Berkeley: University of California Press, 1993).

58. For a recent study indicating how music classes help with self-esteem, see Nikki S. Rickard, Peter Appelman, and Richard James, 'Orchestrating Life Skills: The Effect of Increased School-Based Music Classes on Children's Social Competence and Self-Esteem,' *International Journal of Music Education* 31, no. 3 (2013): 292–309.

59. Thomas Williamson's traveler's handbook *East India Vade-Mecum* recommends that young women should learn to repair and tune their own keyboard instruments. See Woodfield, 'The Calcutta Piano Trade in the Late Eighteenth-Century,' 15.

60. Wollstonecraft opens Chapter 5 of *A Vindication of the Rights of Woman* with an attack on Rousseau's education of Sophy: he gives 'mock dignity to lust' and 'guarantees a system of cunning and lasciviousness.' See *A Vindication of the Rights of Woman*, ed. Carol H. Poston. 2nd edition (New York: Norton, 1988), 78. See Mitzi Myers's analysis of Rousseau's opposition to female-associated tasks such as socializing children in 'Little Girls Lost: Rewriting Romantic Childhood, Righting Gender and Genre.' *Teaching Children's Literature: Issues, Pedagogy, Resources*. ed. Glenn Edward Sadler (New York: MLA, 1992), 131–42.

CHAPTER 10

From Wild Fictions to Accurate Observation: Domesticating Wonder in Children's Literature of the Late Eighteenth Century

Richard De Ritter

In the preface to his *L'Ami des Enfants* (1782–83), Arnaud Berquin assures parents that his collection of tales, dialogues, and 'moral dramas' is fit 'to become a proper reading book for children.'[1] To justify this claim, Berquin describes what his text includes—but not before announcing what it excludes:

> Instead of those wild fictions of the Wonderful, in which [children's] understanding is too commonly bewilder'd, they will here see only what occurs or may occur within the limits of their families. The sentiments with which the work abounds, are not above the level of their comprehension. It introduces them, accompanied by none, except their parents, the companions of their pastimes, the domestics that surround them, or the animals they are accustomed to behold.[2]

Berquin's text proved to be a phenomenally popular work of children's literature.[3] Its 'concern for realism' meant that it effectively became a 'manifesto for the moral tale[s]' that were so popular in the final decades

R. De Ritter (✉)
University of Leeds, Leeds, UK
e-mail: R.DeRitter@leeds.ac.uk

© The Author(s) 2018

A. O'Malley (ed.), *Literary Cultures and Eighteenth-Century Childhoods*, Literary Cultures and Childhoods,
https://doi.org/10.1007/978-3-319-94737-2_10

of the eighteenth century.[4] As John Dunkley has noted, the success of Berquin's text lay in its capacity to satisfy children's interest in 'the world around them' while offering 'something which parents would accept and encourage, in the hope of forming both morals and taste.'[5] As the preface suggests, the expulsion of 'the Wonderful' underpins the book's reassuring reputation. In this instance, 'the Wonderful' is a daunting prospect that threatens to derail the development of children's understanding. While Berquin's text was predicated upon communal models of reading— in which both parents and children would participate—the 'wild fictions' he castigates are markedly anti-social, carrying their young readers beyond 'the limits of their families' and those objects and people that they 'are accustomed to behold.' By contrast, Berquin's moral tales are based in an intimate sociability. Pitched at the level of the child's comprehension, the sentiments that these stories promote sit happily within the familiar borders of the child's life, delineated by their parents, their friends, their servants, and their animals.

The contracted range of Berquin's text aligns it with what has been identified as the rationalizing mode of late eighteenth-century writing for children. The parameters for critical discussions of this material were firmly established in the early twentieth century, when F. J. Harvey Darton described the period's children's literature as enacting a 'quarrel between rationalism and imagination.'[6] This binary opposition was further enforced in the 1980s, most notably within Geoffrey Summerfield's *Fantasy and Reason: Children's Literature in the Eighteenth Century*. There, Summerfield argues that children's literature came to be dominated by a conception of 'education as an ascent toward rationality.' The result was an emphasis on the values of 'enlightenment, science and commerce' at the expense of 'the metaphors, the multivalences, [and] the poetic resonances' of fantasy.[7] More recently, Alan Richardson has questioned the exclusivity of the terms used by critics such as Summerfield, although he too identifies a distinctive 'rationalist tradition' of children's literature, in which the child 'is never to lose its sense of self-possession, never to suspend its carefully inculcated habits of rational thought for a moment of pleasing (or frightful) wonder.'[8] The work of Mitzi Myers poses a welcome revision to the tendency to regard 'rationalist' writing as consisting of one-dimensional didacticism. For Myers, the derisive commentary that such writing has attracted since its publication is ineluctably linked to the fact that it is, predominantly, the work of female authors. Myers suggests that far from being reductive or stifling, the rationalizing discourse of women's writing for children ushered in 'technical as well as thematic innovations,' including a 'redefined realism grounded in everyday objects and accessible achievements.'[9]

In the wake of Myers's feminist reassessment, subsequent work on eighteenth-century children's literature has tended to abandon the binary logic of previous critics, offering a richer, arguably less polemical, assessment of its merits.[10] Accordingly, rather than resurrecting an antagonistic framework in which reason and rationalism are pitched against wonder and the imagination, this chapter focuses on the productive relationships between these terms. While writers such as Berquin may deride the 'wild fictions of the Wonderful,' I argue that experiences of wonder are central to, and firmly embedded within, the form and content of putatively 'rationalist' works of children's literature. Similarly, while Berquin's limited sphere of observation—in which children 'see only what occurs or may occur within the limits of their families'—implies a corresponding contraction of the imagination, this chapter demonstrates that a focus on the observable world is far from antithetical to imaginative and sympathetic expansion. Focusing on examples from the works of Charlotte Smith, John Aikin and Anna Letitia Barbauld, and Priscilla Wakefield, the following discussion re-evaluates the status of wonder in the period's writing for children. To varying extents, these authors shared Berquin's antipathy towards forms of wonder that 'bewilder'd' the understanding. Such violent effects were inimical to their pedagogic agendas, which emphasized the careful cultivation of children's minds. Nevertheless, they recognized the role that affective experiences could play within their ostensibly rationalist schemes of education, and were mindful of producing works that were, in Charlotte Smith's words, 'attractive to children.'[11] Consequently, these authors re-orientated wonder: they removed it from the discombobulating effects of 'wild fictions' and relocated it within the realm of the empirically verifiable, where it could provide the basis of children's moral and intellectual development. Effectively, they domesticated wonder, harnessing its potential as an educational force. Rather than the unpredictable imaginative transport caused by 'wild fictions,' these authors suggest that wonder can be experienced through localized acts of observation, which intensify children's consciousness of the world around them. In turn, this heightened awareness generates self-reflection, enabling children to see themselves as social and moral subjects. In this respect, this domesticated version of wonder becomes imbued with ethical potential, prompting children to examine their relationships with others. Ultimately, while writers in the 'rationalist tradition' frequently begin by focusing on what Myers refers to as 'everyday objects,' they subsequently work outwards, demanding that readers both exercise and expand the limits of their sympathetic imagination.

STRANGE THINGS AND FAMILIAR MATTERS: LOCATING WONDER

In her recent monograph *Eighteenth-Century Fiction and the Reinvention of Wonder*, Sarah Tindal Kareem examines a familiar narrative which posits that, over the course of the eighteenth century, the production of wonder by supernatural means 'lost its effect' in the face of a 'newly secular age.'[12] Kareem draws upon the work of Jane Bennett, who uses the term 'disenchantment tales' to refer to narratives of Western progress in which modern society is blighted by a sense of loss. For proponents of this historical story, 'the inevitable price for rationalization or scientization is,' Bennett writes, 'the eclipse of wonder at the world.'[13] The notion that an age of wonders was 'snuffed out by an age of reason' has also been subjected to scrutiny by Lorraine Daston and Katherine Park in their influential study, *Wonders and the Order of Nature*.[14] As all of these thinkers suggest, the trajectory of wonder in the eighteenth century is too complex and diffuse to be summarized as 'a wholesale shift from credulity to skepticism' caused by the progress of science and secularization.[15] Nevertheless, it has proved an influential narrative—one whose presence can be discerned in many accounts of the development of children's literature. It is not difficult to see why. Charles Lamb's complaint that 'the old classics of the nursery' were displaced by moral and didactic works has taken on axiomatic status in critical work on children's literature. His infamous letter of 1802 refers to Anna Letitia Barbauld and Sarah Trimmer as authors whose works dispense with imaginative delight and present instead '[k]nowledge ... in the *shape* of *knowledge*.' 'Science has succeeded to Poetry no less in the little walks of children than with men,' he writes, encapsulating the 'sense of loss' that Bennett attributes to such 'disenchantment tales.'[16] Similarly, as I began by observing, many writers of the period expressed hostility to what Berquin refers to as 'wild fictions of the Wonderful' which 'bewilder' children's understanding. A typical example can be found in Elizabeth Hamilton's *Letters on the Elementary Principles of Education* (1801–1802), which outlines 'the danger of inflaming the imagination, and kindling the passions, by a detail of fictitious wonders.' Like Berquin, Hamilton suggests that an 'early taste for the wonderful' is psychologically damaging, distorting children's sense of the probable and disrupting 'sound reasoning.'[17] The kind of works that Hamilton has in mind are 'stories of giants and enchanters, of Fairies and Genii,' which provide 'unnecessary stimulus to [the] imagination' and, correspondingly, 'retard the progress of the other faculties of the mind.'[18] These sentiments are echoed by Sarah Trimmer in *The Guardian of Education* (1803), where she comments disapprovingly on those books 'which are fit to fill the heads of children with confused notions of wonderful and supernatural events, brought about by the agency of imaginary beings.'[19] Such comments can be located within the 'ideological battle' in which middle-class writers 'sought to expunge vicious plebeian influences from the nursery environment.'[20] From this perspective, the wonderful is rendered suspicious, threatening to create confusion and tumult in the minds of children. Such explicit hostility to these effects may explain the tendency to interpret this tradition of writing as advocating didacticism at the expense of imaginative exploration. But this judgement is complicated by the recognition that what these writers condemn are *fictitious* wonders, which they align with the marvellous and the supernatural.[21] A closer examination of the concept of wonder in the eighteenth century reveals that this is just one manifestation of wonder among many.

As Peter Swaab has recently noted, wonder is a 'complex word' denoting a concept that is both 'ambiguous and troubling.'[22] As a noun, a 'wonder' can signify phenomena 'encountered externally': what Samuel Johnson's *Dictionary* calls 'strange thing[s]' that are 'more or greater than can be expected.'[23] But it can also refer to the affective state that such wonders inspire. Encompassing '[a]dmiration; astonishment; amazement; [and] surprise,' the emotional state of wonder ranges from an overpowering sensation that 'restrict[s] our mental mobility' to a mood that forms a spur to activity, initiating a quest to fill the vacuum of one's ignorance.[24] Sarah Tindal Kareem alludes to this variety of meanings when she conceives of wonder 'as a finely gradated spectrum that moves from astonishment through curiosity toward radical doubt.'[25] With their focus on 'wild fictions' which obstruct 'sound reasoning', the writers referred to above evoke a form of wonder that prompts 'astonishment': a stupefying sensation that inhibits 'attentive enquiry.'[26] In these instances, fictitious wonders instigate a state of self-alienating uncertainty that verifies Daston and Park's suggestion that wonders 'register the line between the known and the unknown.'[27] In this liminal guise, the state of wonder threatens to usher children away from the comfortingly familiar scope of the home—'the limits of their families,' as Berquin puts it. Wonder—and the 'strange things' by which it is inspired—represents otherness: a threat not just to children's understanding, but to the security of the domestic environment they inhabit.

However, while the hostility of these writers appears to confirm the demise of supernaturally induced wonder in the eighteenth century, other, less disorientating and potentially educative forms of wonder continue to exist. As Daston and Park argue, wonder was not expelled by an age of reason; rather it 'shifted its objects and altered its texture almost beyond recognition.'[28] In her reassessment of the realist mode of the eighteenth-century novel, Kareem suggests that wonder is cultivated 'as a rational response to the ordinary;' this idea is equally relevant to a range of eighteenth-century writing for children.[29] Decades before rationalist children's literature had emerged as an identifiable literary mode, the pioneering bookseller John Newbery employed the persona of Tom Telescope to author his *Newtonian System of Philosophy* (1761).[30] As its subtitle indicates, the abstract scientific principles discussed in this work are 'familiarized and made entertaining' by reference to 'Objects with which [its readers] are familiarly acquainted.' The book's contents range from the limits of the solar system to 'the consideration of things with which [its readers] are more intimately acquainted,' with its protagonist asking his auditors to enquire into the causes of various natural phenomena: 'How was that Mountain lifted up to the sky? How came this crystal Spring to bubble on its lofty brow, or that large River to flow from its massy side?'[31] While these features of the landscape may be familiar, the text insists that they 'are not, on that account, the less wonderful'—an assertion that it substantiates by exploring the geological processes that produce such natural occurrences.[32] Three decades later, a story in John Aikin and Anna Barbauld's *Evenings at Home* echoes the methodology of Newbery's *Newtonian System* by demonstrating how even 'matters familiar among ourselves' can become 'wonderful' if they are examined in sufficient detail.[33] An attentive enquiry into the 'nature and properties' of apparently mundane objects will, Aikin and Barbauld suggest, have a defamiliarizing effect, revealing the wonders latent in the phenomena of everyday life.[34] This is given an explicitly religious inflection in Newbery's *Newtonian System*, which insists that 'a man may, even at home, and within himself, see the Wonders of God in the Works of Creation.'[35] In these instances, the evocation of wonder does not result in the paralysis of astonishment feared by Berquin and Hamilton. Rather, wonder is revealed to be an 'interrogative' passion, reminding us that, as a verb, to wonder is 'to be desirous to know or learn.'[36] In this respect, experiences of wonder have a 'temporal trajectory' that sees individuals move from a state of ignorance to one of knowledge.[37] Moreover, the identification of wonder within the ordinary and the familiar marks its domestication, suggesting how it might be harnessed as a mode of encouraging children to undertake an attentive, and even critical, view of their immediate surroundings.

In light of this, it is possible to reconsider the implications of Berquin's suggestion that his writing will only expose children to 'what occurs or may occur within the limits of their families.' What sounds like an introspective retreat into a rigidly circumscribed environment may also harbour the potential for experiences of educative wonder. While Johnson's *Dictionary* asserts that wonder is produced by encounters with 'strange things,' writers such as Newbery, Aikin, and Barbauld propose that it is evoked when ordinary things are made strange via a process of rational investigation. If the home represents a refuge from the 'wild fictions of the wonderful,' it also contains the potential for what might be referred to as domestic forms of wonder that prompt children to re-examine their relationship with the world around them. In what follows I draw upon three examples of writing from the 1790s. I focus first on how Charlotte Smith navigates her way between competing forms of wonder in her 1796 work, *Rambles Farther*: a text that revolves around an authoritative maternal figure who teaches children to observe their local environment in an accurate, even scientific, manner. Maintaining this line of enquiry, I turn to a short piece from Barbauld and Aikin's *Evenings at Home*, which further demonstrates the defamiliarizing effects of wonder. Finally, I explore Priscilla Wakefield's *Mental Improvement* (1794): a text that demonstrates how wonder can unsettle the boundaries by which domesticity is defined. These authors suggest that, rather than disrupting 'sound reasoning' or 'bewilder[ing]' the understanding, wonder can prove conducive to reason and enable children to imagine themselves as citizens of the world.

Seeing Every Object 'As It Really Is': *Rambles Farther* and *Evenings at Home*

Published in 1796, Charlotte Smith's *Rambles Farther* is the sequel to the previous year's *Rural Walks*. Both texts are fictionalized dialogues, which are frequently interspersed with poetry.[38] They focus on the educational practices of the widowed Mrs Woodfield, who raises her own children and their conceited cousin Caroline, who is educated out of her petulant ways by the end of *Rural Walks*. In the preface to *Rural Walks*, Smith cites Berquin's *L'Ami des Enfants* as the model for her own writing for children, and his influence is evident in both of her perambulatory works.[39] The third dialogue of *Rambles Farther*—which is entitled 'Wonders'—is set at the coast, where Mrs Woodfield is visiting a friend, along with her daughters (Elizabeth and Henrietta) and another dispossessed child, the orphaned Ella Sedley. The coastal setting provides much that is novel and interesting to the children, and the dialogue progresses from a discussion of the sea's flora and fauna to its mythological inhabitants: nereids, sirens, and mermaids. Such matters cause an unexpected surge of nostalgia in Mrs Woodfield, as she recalls her former affection for the 'wild and improbable' parts of the *Arabian Nights*.[40] She continues:

> Part of the pleasure we feel from these fictions arises from our love of the marvellous, and part from the agreeable recollection of the stories we used to listen to in the happy days of our childhood. You, Elizabeth, have been rather taught to see every object around you as it really is, than to be either pleased or frightened by the fables which, when I was in the nursery, were admitted there. (1,65)

Mrs Woodfield's admission represents a strange and uncertain moment: one that articulates the rationalizing movement away from the marvellous even as it acknowledges its allure.[41] This contradiction is displayed so openly—and so ambivalently—that the suggestion that Elizabeth will neither be 'pleased [n]or frightened' by such fables, feels like a deprivation as much as a liberation from a bewildered and inflamed imagination. Within Smith's text, the expulsion of the marvellous hinges upon the kind of accurate observation that keeps individuals anchored to the world around them. By observing 'every object around [them] as it really is,' Mrs Woodfield's daughters remain immune to the 'credulity' that Elizabeth Hamilton fears. Indeed, Smith's empirical emphasis recalls Berquin's reassurance that within his book children will 'see only what occurs or may occur within the limits of their families.'[42] For Smith, however, this commitment to accurate local observation leads to forms of wonder that facilitate both the acquisition of knowledge and, ultimately, reverence for God.

As the dialogue draws to an end, Mrs Woodfield signals the importance of possessing sufficient leisure time to cultivate a disciplined, and suitably reverential, response to the natural world. In this respect, Smith's text foregrounds the middle-class ideology that is implicit to works within the rationalist tradition of children's literature.[43] As they look upon the sea, Mrs Woodfield explains to Elizabeth that 'the fisherman and the sailor who live upon it ... see nothing extraordinary in it' (1:68–69). Rather than considering 'the wonders contained in its bosom,' these labouring-class individuals are 'unused to make reflections of any kind' (1,68, 69). Their observations concern nature as a space of work, rather than a site of contemplation. Thus, while 'a man, whose living depends on the sea or the traffic upon great rivers, knows perfectly well when to look for high tides,' he remains ignorant regarding 'the phænomenon that produces them' (1:70). In contrast to these 'unenlightened villager[s]' (1,70), the middle-class children Smith addresses are free from the demands of labour. Consequently, they are able to see nature as an object of wonder, rather than an economic resource, as Mrs Woodville explains:

> But those, my Elizabeth, who have greater opportunities of information, and more leisure for reflection, learn to look up with greater reverence and admiration towards the great first cause, who has spread before us, whither-soever we turn, the wonders of his wisdom, and who undoubtedly meant them all to contribute to the happiness of that being, on whom ... he has bestowed the greatest portion of reason. (1:71)

Smith revisits the idea that Newbery expresses in *The Newtonian System*, in which wonder facilitates a mode of religious adoration. If wonder initially arises from an 'ignorance of causes,' it is heightened and given purpose by the quest to remedy that lack of knowledge.[44] Reason and imaginative delight work in tandem here: those who have sufficiently cultivated their observational powers find that wonders are in fact constantly before them, 'whithersoever [they] turn.' Simultaneously, however, those wonders serve as signifiers of God, the 'first great cause,' whom we can only 'look ... towards.'[45] Wonders are thus simultaneously 'before us,' and tantalizingly beyond us.

Within *Rambles Farther*, Smith begins to familiarize the 'wonderful,' by bringing it into the immediate orbit of the daily lives of her readers. While her strategy recalls Berquin's focus on what children can 'see ... within the limits of their families,' Smith's model of 'experiential learning' also alerts us to the fact that some modes of vision are more far-reaching than others.[46] With the right degree of cultivation, what individuals see before them can lead to speculations that range far beyond their immediate geographical location. A similar dynamic is explored in John Aikin and Anna Barbauld's popular, six-volume collection of 'miscellaneous pieces,' *Evenings at Home; or, the Juvenile Budget Opened*. There, however, what Smith calls 'the wonders of [God's] wisdom' (1:71) are overshadowed by an investigation into 'the wonderful art of man.'[47] In this respect, Aikin and Barbauld's influential text plays a vital role in the domestication and rationalization of wonder in writing for children. While they dispense with the marvellous and the fantastic, they remain invested in the stimulating effects of wonder, which they relocate within the industrial and commercial landscape of contemporary Britain. Far from inducing bewilderment and credulity, the altered texture of wonder within their work enables children to become 'penetrating observers of their own society,' demonstrating 'the transformative potential of rational discourse.'[48] Nowhere is this more evident than in Barbauld's short piece, 'On Manufactures.'[49]

This dialogue begins with the father responding to the question posed by his son, Henry: 'Pray what is a Manufacture?' (2:97). Over the course of his answer, the father reflects upon the etymology and usage of the word, as well as on Britain's status as a 'commercial nation' (2:104). The 'commercialist ethos' of Aikin and Barbauld's brand of middle-class Dissent shines through, as the father explains how British industry is underpinned by 'a friendly intercourse with foreign nations' (2:104).[50] The conversation then turns to the subject of mechanical ingenuity, at which point the father refers to Sir Richard Arkwright, whose inventions revolutionized the textile industry in the late eighteenth century.[51] This provides an opportunity to offer a brief lesson on social mobility ('in this country every one is free to rise by merit' [2:109–110]), before focusing on Arkwright's achievements. It is at this point that the text's reorientation of wonder becomes most apparent:

> *Fa.* ...Arkwright used to say, that if he had time to perfect his inventions, he would put a fleece of wool into a box, and it should come out broad cloth.
>   *Hen.* What did he mean by that; was there any fairy in the box to turn it into broad cloth with her wand?
>   *Fa.* He was assisted by the only fairies that ever had the power of transformation, Art and Industry: he meant that he would contrive so many machines, wheel within wheel, that the combing, carding, and other various operations should be performed by mechanism, almost without the hand of man. (2:110–111)

With its unequivocal expulsion of the fantastic and the supernatural, this moment is emblematic of the reconfiguration of wonder in rationalist writing for children. Eschewing 'the agency of imaginary beings' (as Sarah Trimmer puts it), this short dialogue celebrates the agency of human industry.[52] For Barbauld, the metamorphosis of raw materials into finished products provides a source of fascination fitting for an age of 'rationalization' and 'scientization.'[53] Her subjects are not the fairies of Henry's imagination, but those of modern, commercial Britain: the fairies of 'Art and Industry.' Nevertheless, Barbauld maintains a sense of imaginative interest by employing what Michelle Levy identifies as 'an Enlightenment strategy of demystification': a pedagogical mode that delves beyond superficial appearances in order to compel children to re-examine their assumptions about the world around them and the objects within it.[54] This process could be accused of fostering a clinical, disenchanted mode of vision; here, however, it has the paradoxical effect of conferring an almost magical power upon the transformative capacities of technological production. While the dialogue praises the physical form and productive potential of the human hand ('those two instruments you carry always about with you' [2:107]), in this instance it celebrates the eradication of human labour: such is the wonder of Arkwright's technological innovations, the operations described are 'performed by mechanism, almost without the hand of man.' Paradoxically, then, Barbauld's celebration of human industry risks succumbing to a kind of commodity fetishism in which, as Marx puts it, 'the products of men's hands' are 'endowed with a life of their own.'[55]

This idea is manifested more explicitly as the dialogue turns to the manufacture, and origins, of linen: 'who would suppose, on seeing the green stalks of a plant, that it could be formed into a texture so smooth, so snowy-white, so firm, and yet so flexible as to wrap itself and adapt itself to every movement of the body?' (2:112). The human labour required to form 'the green stalks of a plant' into 'lawns and cambrics' is tacitly acknowledged, but is overshadowed by the active presence of the fabric, which 'wrap[s]' and 'adapt[s] itself' to the contours of the human body (2:114). For all that the text operates according to a logic of demystification, it invests commodities with an autonomous power, rendering them alien. In this respect, *Evenings at Home* relies not so much upon a tactic of demystification, as one of 'defamiliarisation,' by which the familiar is made strange.[56] This has the effect of transforming seemingly trivial objects into subjects of reflection and contemplation, as Henry demonstrates when he articulates his surprise at the origin of his clothes: 'I think if I had not been told, I should never have been able to guess that my coat came off the back of the sheep' (2:111).[57] While wonder is traditionally associated with an 'ignorance of causes,' here the principle is reversed: Henry's surprise is the product of the explanatory power of his father's rational discourse.[58] In turn, this grants him a heightened awareness of the material and economic structures that shape the world around him. Commenting on Barbauld's *Lessons for Children* (1778–79), William McCarthy notes that such revelatory moments seldom result in 'transcendental solitude;' rather, they reinforce the fact that 'people always live together, in some form of mutual dependence.'[59] While wonder may be a subjective affective state, it is also a social phenomenon, with the potential to forge sympathetic and even ethical relationships between individuals. This is explored in more depth in the final text I discuss: Priscilla Wakefield's *Mental Improvement*.

THE WONDERS OF ART AND NATURE: PRISCILLA WAKEFIELD

Wakefield was the highly successful author of 16 books for children.[60] Her prominence within the period dominated by 'rational' writing for children was recognized in the 1930s by F. J. Harvey Darton, but she has since suffered critical neglect, despite enjoying considerable success in her lifetime. The influence of Aikin and Barbauld is apparent in her work, particularly within her 1794 publication, *Mental Improvement: or the Beauties and Wonders of Nature and Art, Conveyed in a Series of Instructive Conversations.* As its title suggests, this text is structured around a series of conversations involving the Harcourt family, which consists of two parents and their four children, Sophia, Cecilia, Charles, and Henry, aged between 9 and 16. They are also frequently accompanied by Augusta, a motherless neighbouring child, whose occasionally ignorant and prejudiced views do not quite conform to the enlightened rationalism that animates the Harcourt family.

Like Smith's *Rambles Farther*, Wakefield's *Mental Improvement* encourages children to engage in a form of learning based upon the principles of observation and reflection. '[F]rom the early dawn of reason,' Wakefield asserts, children 'should be accustomed to observe every thing with attention, that falls under their notice.'[61] In the text's preface, she expresses concern that many young people may be 'unacquainted either with the materials, of those things they daily use, or the methods of manufacturing them' (1:i-ii). Rejecting the systematic rigours of 'classical learning,' she proposes a model of education that blends 'instruction … with amusement,' and that encourages children to engage actively with the world around them (1:ii). A 'judicious instructor,' she notes, 'will find matter for a lesson among those objects, that are termed common or insignificant' (1:i). Engaging with the world in this way reveals what *Mental Improvement*'s subtitle refers to as 'the Beauties and Wonders of Nature and Art.' Rather than the 'strange things' described by Samuel Johnson, Wakefield asserts that the wonders of modern life are things with which her readers are intimately acquainted: perceiving their enchanted status simply requires individuals to exercise their powers of observation and rational reflection. In turn, the affective state that these objects inspire is far from the kind of wonder that, in Stephen Greenblatt's words, 'depends upon a suspension or failure of categories' and leads to a moment of 'paralysis.'[62] As I will suggest, in Wakefield's text such moments of suspension are almost always resolved: objects are inevitably placed within sense-making frameworks and seldom stand 'alone [and] unsystematized.'[63] Rather than the disorientating stasis of astonishment, this mood of wonder resembles what Kareem refers to as a 'durational affect' that corresponds to 'the passage from unknowing to knowing rather than a single epiphanic moment.'[64] The end point of this state is comprised of religious adoration and an enhanced sense of one's own ethical status.

The preface of *Mental Improvement* alludes to Aikin and Barbauld's *Evenings at Home*, both in its content and its mode of defamiliarization, by which the common and the quotidian are rendered strange:

> Would any child suppose, that the cloth, of which her frock is made, is composed of the fibrous parts of a green plant; or that the paper she draws upon, is the same substance wrought into a different form; that the transparent glass that she drinks out of, was once a heap of sand and ashes; or that the ribbon she wears, is the produce of an insect? (1:ii)

Wakefield's text does not seek to overpower its readers by exposing them to awe-inspiring spectacles: rather, it gradually works outwards, letting the microcosmic give way to the macrocosmic on a journey of rational reflection. This strategy challenges the assumption that an attention to detail is symptomatic of confinement and limitation. As Jacqueline Labbe notes, it is generally assumed that detail 'draws the eye inward and downward, not upward and outward,' and emphasizes 'the body over the mind.'[65] Indeed, the items that Wakefield brings to her reader's attention are bound up with intimate, bodily rituals: dressing, drinking, and writing. But what begins as an inward-looking and embodied focus on details proceeds to an imaginative move outwards, and the assumption of a broader, more panoramic perspective; under Wakefield's defamiliarizing gaze, something as simple as a child's frock becomes an object of philosophic reflection. Indeed, when the origins of her clothes are explained later on in the text, the previously incredulous Augusta confesses to feeling ashamed of her former ignorance, noting: 'it is wonderful to me, to think that this piece of linen ever grew in a field' (2:9). It is a moment that neatly encapsulates the manner in which Wakefield's text brings wonder into the home, awakening the awareness of the children who live there. Her exploration of 'the nature of the materials of what we wear and use' (1:7) challenges the idea that the family home is a bounded, static site. Instead, by reminding her readers of the processes of commerce and manufacture that go into the production of household commodities, Wakefield constructs a version of domesticity that exists in a complex negotiation with the world at large. In doing so, she demands that her readers reconsider their relationship to consumer culture.

An example of this arises when Augusta asks about the origins of a 'fine pearl necklace' (1:133) that she has received as a gift. This leads to an account of pearl-diving in the East Indies, which causes one of the children to lament '[t]he dangers the poor diver incurs, to obtain a mere bauble.' In response, her mother announces that '[t]he real value of pearls and diamonds is small, because they do not contribute to the support or comfort of the life of man; but whilst people of fortune will lavish great sums upon such insignificant things, there will always be found people whose necessities will impel them to obtain them at the risk of their lives' (1:137). It is a lesson in the distinction between use and exchange value that derives almost directly from Adam Smith's *The Wealth of Nations* (1776).[66] Smith's economic principle becomes the basis of Wakefield's middle-class morality, enabling her to inform her readers about the human labour invested in luxurious commodities.[67] What begins as a question about the origins of a necklace soon morphs into a meditation on the economic ties that bind English consumers with geographically distant human beings. The obvious disparity between these two groups feeds into what Fiona Price labels Wakefield's 'deep-seated dislike of luxury,' and demonstrates how meditations upon particular objects give rise to an expansive ethical imagination.[68]

In this respect, Wakefield's writing appears equally indebted to Adam Smith's earlier major work, *The Theory of Moral Sentiments* (1759). Smith's comments in a chapter on 'universal benevolence' are particularly relevant to the mode by which Wakefield operates:

> Though our effectual good offices can very seldom be extended to any wider society than that of our own country; our good-will is circumscribed by no boundary, but may embrace the immensity of the universe. We cannot form the idea of any innocent and sensible being, whose happiness we should not desire, or to whose misery, when distinctly brought home to the imagination, we should not have some degree of aversion.[69]

In Wakefield's work, children are introduced to what Smith calls the 'immensity of the universe' through a combination of detailed examination and parental information. When initially encountered, children understand items such as pearls and diamonds as decontextualized commodities with no visible history. The education they subsequently receive defamiliarizes these objects: their origins are quite literally 'brought home' into the domestic environment in a manner that excites the sympathy of Wakefield's young protagonists.

The rationalist version of wonder that I have been outlining plays a key role in this process, acting as the catalyst for the production of imaginative sympathy. An example of this occurs when *Mental Improvement*'s Mr Harcourt announces that the family will spend the evening discussing the whale: a conversational topic that, he suggests, 'will be new and wonderful' to the company (1:9). The discussion soon turns to the actions of the sailors who 'brave every danger' as they hunt whales in the Arctic. Upon hearing this, Cecilia, the youngest daughter of the Harcourt family, enters the conversation:

CECILIA.
I cannot think what use they can be of, to tempt people to go so far for them.

MR. HARCOURT.
You will find that they supply several useful articles for our convenience. Your stays, for example, would not be so well shaped without whalebone.

CECILIA.
Are the bones that stiffen our stays really the bones of whales?
(1:10)

Wakefield's relentlessly pragmatic text enacts a characteristic shift in scale, juxtaposing the 'danger' of whale-hunting with the 'convenience' of the whalebone stays that support the young ladies' corsets. Cecilia's thoughts are compelled to turn from 'the most obscure corner of the globe' to the stays that rest upon—and even shape—the surface of her body (1:9). Once again, wonder is not caused by 'novelty' but by the recognition of the radical otherness of that which appeared familiar. By these means, the 'things' that the Harcourt family 'daily use' are visibly implicated in an economic network that extends across the globe, opening children's minds to other modes of existence. As the elder Harcourt daughter notes after hearing about the 'dangers' of whale-hunting (1:12): 'I shall never see a piece of whalebone, but I shall think of the labours and difficulties of the poor Greenland sailors' (1:23–24). While the Harcourt daughters remain aware—and in awe—of the origin of their whalebone stays, what they celebrate is the human labour of acquisition. Throughout *Mental Improvement*, Wakefield suggests how the evocation of wonder helps to develop a mode of associative logic that ensures that domestic objects are never entirely divorced from their original context. In turn, this cultivates a form of imaginative sympathy that transcends national boundaries and provides Wakefield's text with a conscience. It ensures that her young readers, like the Harcourt children, are not complacent consumers, but are aware of the global formations that shape their domestic existence.

According to Jane Bennett, '[t]o be enchanted is to be struck and shaken by the extraordinary that lives amid the familiar and everyday.' Rejecting 'the image of modernity as [a] disenchanted … place of reason,' Bennett reiterates the importance of an affective engagement with the world, claiming that 'the mood of enchantment may be valuable for ethical life.'[70] With its emphasis on a form of imaginative sympathy that connects English children with individuals labouring in distant climes, Wakefield's *Mental Improvement* seems to confirm Bennett's thesis. Similarly, the acts of defamiliarization that Wakefield, Aikin, and Barbauld employ prompt an affective and intellectual response, leading to a critical re-evaluation of objects and processes that might otherwise be taken for granted. Simultaneously, however, the expulsion of what Berquin refers to as the 'wild fictions of the Wonderful' makes texts like *Mental Improvement* appear to be agents of 'disenchantment.' Even as Charlotte Smith's Mrs Woodfield recognizes the 'pleasure' of 'marvellous' fictions, she rejects them in favour of 'see[ing] every object … as it really is.' While wonder retains its ability to incite momentary astonishment, the children that inhabit these texts are guided by parental figures to gain the knowledge required to move beyond bewildered amazement towards a state of informed admiration. This is a form of wonder that finds coherence within, but also expands, the 'limits of [children's] families.' Far from being destroyed by an increasing adherence to rational thought, this manifestation of wonder is both produced and sustained by reason. It is this quality that sees a newly domesticated form of wonder thrive in what has long been understood to be a period of purely rational writing for children.

NOTES

1. Arnaud Berquin, *The Children's Friend; Consisting of Apt Tales, Short Dialogues, and Moral Dramas; All Intended to Engage Attention, Cherish Feeling, and inculcate Virtue, in the Rising Generation*, trans. Rev. Mark Anthony Meilan, 8 vols. (London: John Stockdale, 1786), 1:22.
2. Ibid., 1:16–17.
3. As Geoffrey Summerfield rather unflatteringly notes, *L'Ami Des Enfants* 'spread like a plague in the nurseries and apartments of Europe.' Geoffrey Summerfield, *Fantasy and Reason: Children's Literature in the Eighteenth Century* (London: Methuen, 1984), 103.
4. M. O. Grenby, *Children's Literature* (Edinburgh: Edinburgh University Press, 2008), 69.
5. John Dunkley, 'Berquin's *L'Ami Des Enfants* and the Hidden Curriculum of Class Relations,' *Journal for Eighteenth-Century Studies* 16 (1993): 187.
6. F. J. Harvey Darton, *Children's Books in England: Five Centuries of Social Life*, 3rd ed., rev. Brian Alderson (Cambridge: Cambridge University Press, 1982 [1932]), 99.
7. Summerfield, xiii, xiv, xiii.
8. Alan Richardson, *Literature, Education and Romanticism: Reading as Social Practice, 1780–1832* (Cambridge: Cambridge University Press, 1994), 57–60, 58, 57.
9. Mitzi Myers, 'Wise Child, Wise Peasant, Wise Guy: Geoffrey Summerfield's Case Against the Eighteenth Century,' *Children's Literature Association Quarterly* 12 (1987): 109.
10. For examples of recent studies, see M. O. Grenby's *The Child Reader, 1700–1840* (Cambridge: Cambridge University Press, 2011); Lissa Paul's *The Children's Book Business: Lessons from the Long Eighteenth Century* (New York: Routledge, 2011); and Donelle Ruwe's *British Children's Poetry in the Romantic Era: Verse, Riddle, and Rhyme* (Basingstoke: Palgrave Macmillan, 2014).

11. Charlotte Smith, *Rural Walks: In Dialogues. Intended for the use of Young Persons*, 2 vols. (London: T. Cadell Jun. and W. Davies, 1795), 1:v.

12. Sarah Tindal Kareem, *Eighteenth-Century Fiction and the Reinvention of Wonder* (Oxford: Oxford University Press, 2014), 1.

13. Jane Bennett, *The Enchantment of Modern Life: Attachments, Crossings, and Ethics* (Princeton: Princeton University Press, 2001), 8.

14. Lorraine Daston and Katherine Park, *Wonders and the Order of Nature 1150–1750* (New York: Zone Books, 2001), 361.

15. Kareem, *Eighteenth-Century Fiction and the Reinvention of Wonder,* 17; Daston and Park, *Wonders and the Order of Nature*, 361.

16. *The Letters of Charles Lamb to which are added those of his sister Mary Lamb*, ed. E. V. Lucas, 3 vols. (London: J. M. Dent and Methuen, 1935), 1:326; Bennett, *The Enchantment of Modern Life*, 8. A considered account of Lamb's letter is offered in Lissa Paul's *The Children's Book Business*, 100–03. Paul's account draws on William McCarthy's *Anna Letitia Barbauld: Voice of the Enlightenment* (Baltimore: Johns Hopkins University Press, 2008), 445–46.

17. Elizabeth Hamilton, *Letters on the Elementary Principles of Education*, 3rd ed. 3 vols. (Bath: G. and J. Robertson, 1803), 1:404, 405–06.

18. Ibid., 1:406, 407.

19. Sarah Trimmer, *The Guardian of Education* 2 (1803): 185.

20. Andrew O'Malley, *The Making of the Modern Child: Children's Literature and Childhood in the Late Eighteenth Century* (London: Routledge, 2003), 125, 124.

21. Indeed, what Meilan translates as 'wild fictions of the Wonderful' appear in the original French as 'ces fictions extravagantes & de ce marveilleux bizarre.' See Berquin, *L'Ami des Enfants*, 24 vols. (London: M. Elmsley, 1782–83), 1: vi.

22. Peter Swaab, '"Wonder" as a Complex Word,' *Romanticism* 18 (2012): 270.

23. Samuel Johnson, *A Dictionary of the English Language . . .*, 2nd edn., 2 vols. (London: J. and P. Knapton et al., 1755–56).

24. Johnson, *Dictionary*; T. G. Bishop, *Shakespeare and the Theatre of Wonder* (Cambridge: Cambridge University Press, 1996), 7.

25. Kareem, *Eighteenth-Century Fiction and the Reinvention of Wonder*, 8.

26. Daston and Park, *Wonders and the Order of Nature*, 317.

27. Ibid., 13.

28. Ibid., 362.

29. Kareem, *Eighteenth-Century Fiction and the Reinvention of Wonder*, 22. Similarly, in a discussion of Romantic aesthetics Matthew Scott argues that '[w]onder is . . . an emotion that is to be associated not only with the extraordinary itself, but also with the extraordinary aspects of the ordi-

nary.' See Matthew Scott, '"A manner beyond courtesy": Two Concepts of Wonder in Coleridge and Shelley,' *Romanticism* 18 (2012): 237.

30. Newbery's authorship of this text has never been proved but, as John Rowe Townsend notes, he was probably its 'author as well as publisher.' See John Rowe Townsend, 'John Newbery and Tom Telescope,' in *Opening the Nursery Door: Reading, Writing and Childhood 1600–1900*, ed. Mary Hilton, Morag Styles and Victor Watson (London: Routledge, 1997), 83.

31. [J. Newbery?], *The Newtonian System of Philosophy: Adapted to the Capacities of young Gentlemen and Ladies, and familiarized and made entertaining by Objects with which they are familiarly acquainted . . .* (London: J. Newbery, 1761), 62.

32. Ibid.

33. John Aikin and Anna Letitia Barbauld, 'Travellers' Wonders,' in *Evenings at Home; or, the Juvenile Budget Opened. Consisting of a Variety of Miscellaneous Pieces, for the Instruction and Amusement of Young Persons*, 6 vols. (London: J. Johnson, 1792–96), 1:31.

34. Ibid.

35. Newbery, *Newtonian System*, 97.

36. On wonder as interrogative, see Kareem, *Eighteenth-Century Fiction and the Reinvention of Wonder*, 9; and Scott, '"A manner beyond courtesy": Two Concepts of Wonder in Coleridge and Shelley,' 229. On wonder as a verb, see the *OED*, 'wonder, v.', 2.

37. Kareem, *Eighteenth-Century Fiction and the Reinvention of Wonder*, 9.

38. For an account of Smith's distinctive brand of children's literature, see Elizabeth A. Dolan, Introduction to *The Works of Charlotte Smith*, vol. 12, *Rural Walks, Rambles Father, Minor Morals, A Narrative of the Loss of the Catherine*, ed. Elizabeth A. Dolan (London: Pickering and Chatto, 2007), xii–xviii.

39. Smith writes that Berquin's text succeeds in being 'attractive to children, yet not uninteresting to others farther advanced in life.' Smith, *Rural Walks*, 1:v.

40. Charlotte Smith, *Rambles Farther: A Continuation of Rural Walks: In Dialogues. Intended for the Use of Young Persons*, 2 vols. (London: T. Cadell Jun. and W. Davies, 1795), 1:64. Subsequent references are made parenthetically.

41. As M. O. Grenby has noted, similar gestures appear in the work of late seventeenth-century Puritan writers who '[recount] their childhood love of romances only to repudiate it.' See *The Child Reader*, 104.

42. Berquin, *The Children's Friend*, 16.

43. However, it is worth noting that while they arguably embody middle-class ideology, the protagonists of Smith's writing for children are often in dif-

ficult financial circumstances. As Elizabeth Dolan notes, characters such as Mrs Woodfield 'place themselves on a continuum with the poor people they encounter,' rather than viewing them as objects of charity. See Elizabeth A. Dolan, *Seeing Suffering in Women's Literature of the Romantic Era* (Aldershot: Ashgate, 2008), 168.

44. Daston and Park, *Wonders and the Order of Nature*, 314.

45. Smith may be alluding to Alexander Pope's *An Essay on Man* (1734), which describes how man 'But looks through Nature, up to Nature's God.' She quotes this line in her *Conversations Introducing Poetry: Chiefly on Subjects of Natural History. For the use of Children and Young Persons*, 2 vols. (London: J. Johnson, 1804), 2:7. See also Pope, *An Essay on Man*, in *The Major Works*, ed. Pat Rogers (Oxford: Oxford University Press, 1993), IV. l. 332 (307).

46. Dolan, *Seeing Suffering in Women's Literature of the Romantic Era*, 182.

47. Aikin and Barbauld, 'On Manufactures,' in *Evenings at Home*, ii, 100. Subsequent references are made parenthetically.

48. Michelle Levy, 'The Radical Education of *Evenings at Home*,' *Eighteenth-Century Fiction* 19 (2006): 134, 140.

49. The authorship of the pieces within *Evenings at Home* remains open to discussion. Perhaps the best guide we have is provided by Aikin's daughter Lucy, who attributes just 14 of the work's 99 pieces to Barbauld. See McCarthy, *Anna Letitia Barbauld*, 323–24, 629 n. 47. Michelle Levy speculates that Barbauld may have played a bigger role in the composition of *Evenings at Home* and usefully suggests that we should look beyond the attribution of individual authorship and understand the work as the expression of the 'collectively held views' of Aikin and Barbauld. See Levy, 'The Radical Education of *Evenings at Home*,' 131. However, for ease of expression, this chapter follows Lucy Aikin's attributions.

50. Daniel E. White, 'The "Joinerina": Anna Barbauld, the Aikin Family Circle, and the Dissenting Public Sphere,' *Eighteenth-Century Studies* 32 (Summer, 1999): 515.

51. As the text notes, Arkwright had died relatively recently, in 1792.

52. Trimmer, *The Guardian of Education* 2 (1803): 185.

53. Bennett, *The Enchantment of Modern Life*, 8.

54. Levy, 'The Radical Education of *Evenings at Home*,' 132.

55. Karl Marx, *Capital: A Critique of Political Economy, Volume One* (1867), trans. Ben Fowkes (London: Penguin in association with New Left Review, 1990), 165.

56. Darren Howard, 'Talking Animals and Reading Children: Teaching (dis) Obedience in John Aikin and Anna Barbauld's *Evenings at Home*,' *Studies in Romanticism* 48 (2009): 655.

57. A similar moment features in Richard Johnson's earlier *Juvenile Rambles*, in which the sight of some 'pretty little lambkins' leads to a reflection on the production and trade of wool, which creates 'employment for a vast number of people, through whose hands it passes till it at last comes upon your back.' See [R. Johnson], *Juvenile Rambles, Through the Paths of Nature; in which Many Parts of the Wonderful Works of the Creation are brought Forward and made Familiar to the Capacity of every Little Miss and Master, who wishes to becomes Wise and Good* (London: E. Newbery, [1786]), 9, 11.

58. Daston and Park, *Wonders and the Natural World*, 314.

59. William McCarthy, 'Mother of All Discourses: Anna Barbauld's *Lessons for Children*,' *Princeton University Library Chronicle* 60 (1999): 211.

60. See Bridget Hill, 'Priscilla Wakefield as a Writer of Children's Educational Books,' *Women's Writing* 4 (1997): 5–6.

61. Priscilla Wakefield, *Mental Improvement: or the Beauties and Wonders of Nature and Art, Conveyed in a Series of Instructive Conversations*, 2 vols. (London: Darton and Harvey, 1794), 1:i. Subsequent references are made parenthetically.

62. Stephen Greenblatt, *Marvelous Possessions: The Wonder of the New World* (Oxford: Clarendon Press, 1991), 20.

63. Ibid.

64. Kareem, *Eighteenth-Century Fiction and the Reinvention of Wonder*, 9.

65. Jacqueline M. Labbe, *Romantic Visualities: Landscape, Gender and Romanticism* (Basingstoke: Palgrave, 1998), 3.

66. As Smith notes in his discussion of this subject, a 'diamond . . . has scarce any value in use; but a very great quantity of other goods may frequently be had in exchange for it.' See Adam Smith, *An Inquiry into the Nature and Causes of the Wealth of Nations* (1776), ed. R. H. Campbell, A. S. Skinner and W. B. Todd, 2 vols. (Oxford: Clarendon Press, 1976), 1:45. Wakefield's familiarity with Smith is made explicit in the opening pages of her *Reflections on the Present Condition of the Female Sex; with Suggestions for its Improvement* (London: J. Johnson; Darton and Harvey, 1798).

67. Wakefield's text can be seen within the context of the tendency to place 'the middle classes at [the] moral and productive centre' of the 'social and class order' of the late eighteenth century. See O'Malley, *The Making of the Modern Child*, 124.

68. Fiona Price, *Revolutions in Taste, 1773–1818: Women Writers and the Aesthetics of Romanticism* (Farnham: Ashgate, 2009), 100.

69. Adam Smith, *The Theory of Moral Sentiments* (1759), ed. D. D. Raphael and A. L. Macfie (Oxford: Clarendon Press, 1976), 235.

70. Bennett, *The Enchantment of Modern Life*, 4, 3.

CHAPTER 11

'To Communicate Energy': Eliza Fenwick Cultures the New-World Child

Lissa Paul

In the spring of 1829, British author and teacher Eliza Fenwick (1766–1840) began advertising for the school for girls she was about to open in Niagara. As she had done when starting similar schools in Bridgetown Barbados, New Haven Connecticut, and New York City, she pitched her defining brand: her ability 'to inspire [in her students] a taste for knowledge and to cultivate the power of acquiring it' (*Niagara Farmer's Journal*, 22 April 1829). What is noteworthy in Eliza's ad is her emphasis on the teacher/student dynamic: a new-world variation on the educational philosophy she had been evolving over a 40-year period, beginning when she had been an up-and-coming young author in the heady days of pedagogical and political reform in 1790s London. As I follow Eliza's moves from England to Barbados to North America, I'll explain how she adapted her teaching to each new location and how, in concert with the communities of women with whom she networked, she was able to provide for herself and her family without male support. Unlike contributions by men—whose legacies are typically preserved in the public sphere (their names surviving on buildings or street signs or corporations)—cultural contributions made by women in the private sphere are

L. Paul (✉)
Brock University, St. Catharines, ON, Canada
e-mail: lpaul@brocku.ca

© The Author(s) 2018

211

A. O'Malley (ed.), *Literary Cultures and Eighteenth-Century Childhoods*, Literary Cultures and Childhoods,
https://doi.org/10.1007/978-3-319-94737-2_11

harder to define and harder to sustain. Eliza's innovative teaching, I'll argue, did live on through the lives of the young people she taught in the early nineteenth century, surviving in the communities in which she lived and ultimately contributing to the development of the social fabric of those communities.

By the time Eliza composed the ad for her new school in what was then Upper Canada, she was a long way physically, socially, culturally, and intellectually from her old-world life in England. There she had been the author of a well-received first novel, *Secresy* (1795), wife of John Fenwick (1757–1823), mother of their two young children, Eliza Ann (born 1789) and Orlando (born 1798), and an active participant in the intellectual, political, and literary circles surrounding Mary Wollstonecraft and William Godwin. By the time of her arrival in 1829, in the colonial town of what is now Niagara-on-the-Lake, she was a 63-year-old grandmother with four young grandchildren to support on her own. And she was launching a new school for girls. It was her third colonial venture in school owning and operating. Long separated from John (she had left him around 1800 and he died in 1823), her own children were dead. Her son, Orlando, had died at 17 in Barbados in 1816, her daughter, Eliza Ann Rutherford, more recently in 1828, in New York, leaving her four young children (Eliza's grandchildren) essentially orphaned as their father, William Rutherford, had abandoned the family years earlier in Barbados.

Eliza had not intended to become self-supporting. As a young woman in England, she only began thinking seriously about earning her own living after, as her friend Henry Crabb Robinson (1775–1867) explained, she had been reduced 'to poverty from affluence' because of the political and financial recklessness of her husband John.[1] Before taking on the school business, Eliza had tried the other options open to intellectual women at her time, all of which proved useful in her colonial enterprises. In England, besides shopkeeping (she had managed Godwin's book shop for a few months, between November 1807 and January 1808) and working as a governess in London and in a town near Cork, Ireland, she also took up writing for children. Between 1804 and 1813, she had authored or edited an astonishing total of at least 12 books, including *Visits to the Juvenile Library* (1805), *Songs for the Nursery* (1805), and *Rays from the Rainbow* (1812).[2] Although Eliza's route from literary London to Upper-Canadian schoolteacher was circuitous, following the traces of her journey reveals how she carried her pedagogical philosophy with her and how she transplanted it in the 'new world.'

COMMUNICATING ENERGY

The school business was the employment option Eliza Fenwick adopted seriously rather late in life, and it was only at the urging of her daughter, Eliza Ann. Always a reluctant actress but a dutiful daughter, Eliza Ann had gone to Barbados to take up a steady gig in a new theatre company in order to earn enough money to help fund her younger brother's education. Within a year of arriving (she appeared in the first performance of the Theatre Royal in Bridgetown in 1812), Eliza Ann had identified a niche in the market, one that would enable her to quit her job as an actress and provide an opportunity for a partnership with her mother in the ownership and operation of a school for girls. What Eliza Ann saw was that her mother's expertise as an English governess and author of educational books for children would make her school a desirable option for rich colonial plantation owners looking for alternatives to sending their daughters to England for their education. It was in that period—around 1813— as mother in the 'old world' and daughter in the new contemplated a plan for developing a financially and socially secure future, that they also began to sketch what a 'new-world' educational ethos might look like.

While Eliza Ann was planning her career change from actress to teacher in Barbados in 1813—during which time she also married and had a child—Eliza was in Lee Mount, Ireland, working as a governess and financing (with her daughter's help) the end of her son Orlando's education nearby at school in Cork. Eliza was relatively happy with her situation, as she wrote in letters to her friend, author Mary Hays (1759–1843), but she was also picking up tips on pitching a viable programme of education for the daughters of the rich, a programme that would balance the ornamental (their focus) with the intellectual (her focus). In the period when Eliza Ann raised the possibility of a running an elite school for girls together in Barbados, Eliza was thinking, hard, about what an idealized educational environment might look like. In an unpublished section of a letter to Mary Hays, written in February 1813, Eliza sketched her vision: 'To be able to fix a willing delighted attention,' she wrote, 'to communicate energy, to perceive ideas shooting expanding and maturing under your guidance & culture and to receive an intelligent need of affection & gratitude in return for your labours from yr [your] pupils is a vision of very agreeable promise I grant you.'[3]

As Eliza Ann was planning to open her new Seminary for Young Ladies in Barbados in January 1814, the evidence that she was in close

communication with her mother is visible in the 'coming soon' announcement that appeared on 28 December 1813 in the *Barbados Mercury
Gazette*. In what we might now call a 'mission statement' for the school,
Eliza Ann—echoing, almost verbatim, the lines her mother had written to
Mary—promises that the 'chief endeavor' of the new school would be 'to
fix the attention of her Pupils by gaining their affections,' and 'to cultivate
the better feelings of the heart,' while encouraging 'the development of
youthful understanding.'

For eighteenth-century scholars, Eliza's lines to Mary and the matching lines from Eliza Ann's advertisement ring as an echo of the famous
lines from John Thomson's 1728 poem, 'Spring.' The section comparing
children to plants in need of a gardener's care begins:

> Delightful task! To rear the tender Thought,
> To teach the young Idea how to shoot,
> To pour the fresh instructions o'er the Mind,
> To breathe the inspiring Spirit, and to plant
> The generous Purpose in the glowing Breast.[4]

The late Julia Briggs wrote eloquently about the influence of Thomson's
ideas on educational discourse in the 1790s, and the way they played out
against John Locke's late seventeenth-century perceptions of children as
essentially young plants in need of a gardener's expert care. 'The goal of
the nursery,' says Briggs, 'was to optimize good growth.' She then glosses
Thomson's phrase 'delightful task,' as something that 'expresses the pleasures of cultivation, whether of children or of plants—perhaps even of
feelings.'[5] The basic sense, however, was that teachers taught what children were supposed to learn. As Briggs says pointedly, what children were
denied in the gardening model was 'agency.' So even though there was a
kinder, gentler view of pedagogical practice, 'the distribution of power
remained unchanged.'[6] Teachers constructed the agenda and children
were supposed to receive it, to bend to willingly into the required shape.

What is new in Eliza's 1813 spin on Thomson's image is that instead of
conceptualizing education as a hierarchical top-down system, she emphasized a dynamic relationship between teacher and student. Rather than the
cultivation of slow growth, Eliza's version of intellectual ideas of 'communicating energy,' of 'shooting, expanding and maturing' reads more
like a fireworks display. In the language of neuroscience, Eliza's vision
reads like the processes of the brain in the act of thinking, that is, in the act

of synaptic transmission: the moment when the chemical signals jump across the gap between the synaptic transmitters and the synaptic receivers. It's a moment when cascades of reactions light up the brain with electrical activity. For Eliza, thinking in an educational context was more like that: active, vital, dynamic and involving an exchange between student and teacher.

Eliza's vision of education as a reciprocal relationship between teacher and student was not, of course, completely original. It was an adaptation and application of the pedagogical principles developed by people who had been active in the intellectual circles Eliza had inhabited in the 1790s, especially in the new language focusing on the instructor's responsibilities in the process, in being the kind of person who lights the spark that inspires an intellectual relationship. Glimpses of that kind of reciprocal relationship are in, for example, Ellenor Fenn's *Cobwebs to Catch Flies* (1783) and in Anna Barbauld's *Lessons for Children* (1787–1788). William Godwin, in his essay 'Of the Communication of Knowledge,' from *The Enquirer*, explicitly foregrounds the significance of the teacher/student interaction when he observes that 'study with desire is real activity: without desire it is but the semblance or mockery of activity,' and that the first object of instruction 'is to give the pupil a motive to learn.'[7] Godwin's emphasis on the relationship, on providing pupils with 'a motive to learn,' is what Eliza carried with her to the 'new world.'

EDUCATING FOR THE USEFUL AND THE ORNAMENTAL IN THE CARIBBEAN

The Seminary for Young Ladies in Bridgetown in its eight years of operation (1814–1822) did offer both useful (what we might term a liberal arts emphasis on languages and literature) and ornamental (art, music, and dance) instruction for the daughters of the rich. It looks as if Eliza handled the business of the school (the hiring of teachers and the collection of fees) and the instruction in literature and music, leaving her daughter to focus on one of the marquee accomplishments of her own education as an actress: music and dance. The ads for their school in the *Barbados Mercury Gazette* focus consistently on both the public examinations (for the display of the useful education acquired by the young ladies) and on the school ball (for the display of the ornamental). Both public events were also clearly used as marketing tools for their educational brand. Eliza provides a particularly charming description of one of their last annual school balls. 'A school Ball,' she writes, 'is certainly a pleasing & interesting spectacle, & ours in particular, for the children begin this branch of their education very early, & the little groups, all in one elegant costume of white sattin trowsers [*sic*], with lace, gauze or book-muslin frocks, tastefully trimmed, appear like fairies.'[8] The two American schools Eliza and her daughter attempted to run together, first in New Haven, then in New York, operated on the same principles that had informed their first colonial school: an emphasis on the student/teacher dynamic, and on offering both useful and ornamental education to the young ladies in their charge.

The Barbados school closed in 1822, ostensibly because Eliza Ann's declining health required—as she was told by her doctors—a cooler climate. The decision to close the school was difficult. The two women had been running it successfully on their own since 1818 when Eliza Ann's husband, William Rutherford, left for England just as she was giving birth to their fourth child. Like Eliza's husband John Fenwick a generation earlier, William Rutherford turned out to be a liability, as, like his father-in-law, he was given to drink and gambling. After William Rutherford left, Eliza and her daughter had to use the money they had earned in running the school (a mark of their success) to pay off his debts. Even in the overtly conservative world of early nineteenth-century Barbados, the fact that the two women could do so demonstrated that they had achieved both social and financial success in their shared enterprise, their first Seminary for Young Ladies.

In the end, however, it was not only Eliza Ann's declining health that prompted the move to New Haven. The island itself was in decline. Although the British abolition of the slave trade in 1807 had stopped British ships from transporting enslaved people from Africa to Barbados, it was still a slave-dependent island, with an enslaved majority black population outnumbering the ruling white minority by five to one. The infrastructure was beginning to collapse and the threat of a slave uprising was never far away, especially as the local memory of the Easter 1816 rebellion that had shut down the island for two weeks lingered. Although slavery was not abolished by the British parliament until several years later, in 1833, the tide of public opinion was slowly turning towards abolition in the 1820s and the anxiety in the minority white population was increasing. But besides the political instability in Barbados, the move to New Haven had also been prompted by the ever-present threat of disease, especially yellow fever, particularly lethal in young people. Eliza's own teenaged son

Orlando had died of the disease in 1816 and her four young grandchildren would be among the most vulnerable population if they stayed.

The reason I've provided such a detailed account of the health, safety, and political reasons prompting the closure of the successful Seminary for Young Ladies is so that I can explain the migration of Eliza's progressive pedagogical ideas across the Atlantic. Ideas—in some ways, obviously—move with people, but how and why those ideas move and how they change as they move is rarely subject to investigation. In moving from Barbados to the United States in July of 1822, Eliza and her daughter had executed a well-planned exit strategy. By deciding to move to New Haven in the first place, they knew they would arrive with an established network of connections in place. Because trade between New Haven and Bridgetown had been extensive through the eighteenth century, trading families from Barbados had already settled there, so Eliza knew that she would arrive to a warm welcome. The other smart thing Eliza and Eliza Ann did in preparation for their departure was to recruit a few students from the Caribbean to travel with them and seed the American iteration of their Seminary for Young Ladies. Despite their careful plans and initial warm welcome, they found that they could not sell their brand of useful and ornamental education to the Americans as easily as they had initially assumed. Adaptation was not a straightforward process.

ADAPTING TO AMERICA

An advertisement that Eliza and her daughter ran in the *American Mercury* of Monday 26 August 1822 announced their intention to set up their new school on fashionable State Street, one of the original 'nine squares' on which the town of New Haven was built. 'Mesdames Fenwick and Rutherford,' as they styled themselves, promoted their new venture to prospective parents, saying that they would 'give an annual public examination,' during which 'the young Ladies' would be 'questioned in the presence of their friends, on the progress of their studies,' and, to display 'the accomplishment of Dancing,' they would also hold 'a public School Ball.' In the heart of conservative New Haven, however, dancing was not as desirable an accomplishment as it had been in England or Barbados, as an explanatory notice in the *Connecticut Herald* of Tuesday 18 November 1823 would seem to suggest: 'Mrs. Fenwick and Mrs. Rutherford,' begins the ad, 'hope it will not be considered as an improper innovation on the custom at present established here, that their Ball is prepared for, and appropriated entirely to the Exhibition of the Dancing of the Pupils; in order for their parents and friends may have an opportunity of judging of their progress in the accomplishment, and in the grace and propriety of their deportment.' The dancing curriculum does appear demanding, and despite her declining health, Eliza Ann gave 'lessons in Minuets, Quadrills [*sic*], Scotch Reels, Irish Planxties, Spanish dances, Fancy Ballets.'[9] As the international range of dances demonstrates, Eliza Ann was essentially bringing European culture to the colonies.

Whether the display of dancing was what the locals considered 'improper' or whether it was something else that prompted the citizens of New Haven to reject Eliza's brand of schooling is not clear. But not long after the scandal, Eliza and her daughter found themselves the subject of false malicious gossip that eventually ran them out of town. As the two women had arrived in New Haven with four young children but no husband, father or male family member of any kind in sight, the children were rumoured to have been fathered by different men, and Eliza accused of having run a house of ill repute in England. Although the allegations were baseless, it was too late for the school, especially one that pitched itself as catering to the daughters of the conservative elite. Eliza, Eliza Ann, and the children picked up and started again in New York in 1825.

It would be easy to dismiss Eliza's attempt to transplant her school brand as a failure, but there is evidence that her pedagogical gifts did influence at least two students in New Haven, both of whom sustained lifelong connections with Eliza and her family. One young woman, Sarah Butler (1806–1888), met the man she would marry, Alexander Duncan (1805–1889), at one of the first New Haven school balls, probably in 1823. Ultimately the Duncans became Eliza's benefactors, first supporting the education of her granddaughter, Bessie Rutherford, and then Eliza herself after she ultimately retired in 1838. Eliza died at their home in Rhode Island in 1840. Another of Eliza's students, Theodora (Dora) Barrell, also sustained an enduring relationship with Eliza's family after being a student at the New Haven school. Both Eliza and Eliza Ann attended Dora's wedding to Ferdinand Massa in 1826. The fact that education was important to the Barrell/Massa families survives in a carefully preserved artefact, now held in the archives at Columbia University in New York: an early translation of Locke's 1767 *Thoughts Concerning Education*, published in 1708 in French as *De L'Education des enfans Traduit de l'Anglois*. Correspondence between Eliza's descendants and Dora Massa's continued long into the nineteenth century.[10] The telling point is that despite the brief and difficult time Eliza and her family spent in New Haven, the evidence of her pedagogical influence remains traceable in the connection with two of her identifiable pupils, Sarah Butler Duncan and Theodora Barrell Massa.

The last Seminary for Young Ladies Eliza and Eliza Ann ran together was in New York City, at 663 Broadway. By the time they ran their ad for the school on 20 May 1825, in the *New York Evening Post*, they were clearly used to selling their brand. Like the ads in Barbados and New Haven, their New York ad again specified that their 'public examinations' were designed 'to excite an emulation in the minds of the pupil, to merit the approbation of their friends.' Despite the fact that dancing was still on offer at the school, there was no mention of a school ball. The school was short-lived as Eliza Ann's health increasingly declined. She died in 1828, marking the end of the mother-daughter partnership in the school business. Faced with her own grief at the loss of her beloved daughter, and at the prospect of being solely responsible for her four grandchildren (then aged between 10 and 15), Eliza temporarily opened a kind of high-end boarding house in New York as a way of earning enough to support her grandchildren. As luck would have it, however, it was through one of her New York neighbours, Elizabeth Baldwin Morgan, that Eliza found her way to a new school with a new partner in Upper Canada.

SETTLING IN UPPER CANADA

Elizabeth Morgan's sister, Mary Baldwin Breakenridge (1791–1871), was, like Eliza, also recently bereft. Her husband, lawyer John Breakenridge, had just died in Niagara leaving her pregnant with their fifth child. That is how the two women, one young, Mary Breakenridge, and one old, Eliza Fenwick, both with young children to support, were connected. It was Elizabeth Morgan who realized that her sister Mary could open a viable school for girls in Niagara in the property belonging to her late husband, as long as she had Eliza's experience and expertise to the enterprise. The school in Niagara would be a fresh start for both recently bereaved women, its existence testimony to the unsung network of emotional and intellectual support alive among women committed to creating viable futures for their children against all odds. As an experienced teacher by that time, Eliza had honed her pitch and her views. The explosive 'shooting, expanding and maturing' desire for communicating intellectual energy in the teacher/student dynamic was still there, but it had morphed into something more generous, more welcoming, more inclusive, as we might say now.

The ad for the new Seminary For Young Ladies in the 1829 issue of the *Niagara Farmer's Journal* still reads as an eloquent commitment to a community of women to the girls and promises that together they will 'create an interest in the affection of their pupils, as the surest means of stimulating them to exertion,' and that 'during school hours,' they will keep their charges 'constantly and energetically employed—to inspire them with a zeal for excelling in their studies.' That is how, of course, the 'shooting, expanding and maturing' of intellectual life endures. But in the interests of making sure that their new school would appeal broadly to a wide range of pupils, both women also made it clear in the ad that they were able to attend to the needs of individual students who might need more support. '[W]here timidity of disposition or slowness of capacity render a child incapable of excelling others,' they wrote, 'still by noticing with approbation every step towards improvement' they would be able 'to delight her with the consciousness of excelling her former self.'[11] A twenty-first-century reader might be inclined to praise the inclusive ethos of the school.

Because Eliza had been in the school business for more than 15 years by the time she arrived in Upper Canada, she knew that in order to run the enterprise successfully the people she hired had to share her progressive agenda. By chance, a job description survives in a letter she sent in 1830 to her New York friend, John Moffat, for the kind of teacher she needed in order to support her stated educational ethos. With its emphasis on intellectual accomplishment and a mutually respectful teacher/student relationship, her sketch of the ideal candidate looks distinctly modern:

> We require particularly Writing & arithmetic & a competent knowledge of Geography & English Grammar. If possessing other accomplishments (Drawing for instance) so much the better and we wish to find one who had sense enough to be a steady disciplinarian and a temper patient & amiable enough to make herself loved as well as respected. We use neither whips, rods or canes—No blows are ever struck.[12]

With her assertion that 'no whips, rods or canes' are used in her school and that 'no blows are ever struck,' Eliza silently shadows lines from one of her own books for children, *Visits to the Juvenile Library*, published by Benjamin Tabart in 1805. In the novel, it is the (enslaved) nanny Nora who portrayed education as analogous to the kinds of punishments to which enslaved people were typically subjected: 'all the terrors of rods, canes, dark closets, and stocks.'[13] Eliza's clear rejection of the rights of teachers to inflict physical or psychological punishments on students stands as testimony to the fact that her faith in education as liberating—the antithesis of being enslaved by ignorance—was as strong in her 1830 lived experience as it had been in her 1805 fictional construct.

In her letter to John Moffat, Eliza was also explicit that the teacher she required for her Niagara school would not be a 'disciple of Miss Fanny Wright.' Eliza's request reveals a lot about her up-to-date knowledge of the news of the day, social history, and degrees of separation. Although Fanny Wright's name has now all but completely faded from pedagogical history, she was in her own time known as a progressive educator. Scottish-born, she was regarded as a reformer, an abolitionist, and as a supporter of equal education for the rich and the poor, for boys and for girls, the free and the enslaved. She had recently given a series of promotional speeches in New York and had earned a kind of celebrity status. Fanny Wright (1795–1852), however, also had a connection with someone Eliza had known, literally from birth, in England: Mary Godwin Shelley. One of the philanthropic, innovative things that Fanny Wright had attempted was a utopian community, Nashoba, in Tennessee, on which enslaved people could, in theory, work the land and free themselves. Mary Shelley became a supporter after receiving a letter from Fanny Wright invoking her parents, William Godwin and Mary Wollstonecraft, as the inspiration for her calls to abolition, women's rights, and social reform.[14] Fanny Wright ought to have been exactly the kind of person with whom Eliza would feel kinship, especially given the personal connection through Mary Shelley and her parents. In retrospect, it is, of course, dangerous to make assumptions about what Eliza was implying in her rejection of Fanny Wright's disciples, but given Eliza's experience in adapting to new environments, I suspect that she wanted to ensure that the teachers she hired would not offend the daughters of the elite (and essentially conservative) families to whom she was selling her school brand.

There is one more clear expression of Eliza's ability to adapt 'old-world' pedagogical practices to the 'new world': she managed to repackage the school balls she had so loved in Barbados for her Niagara clientele. In a letter to the Moffat family, dated 13 October 1831, she explained that she had planned not as a school ball, but as she termed it, a 'coterie' to be held in conjunction with the school. She organized the date (20 October

1831), the times, the venue, the music, the food, and the participants. She charged each young lady 'a small subscription of a quarter dollar' to cover expenses, and in order to control the occasion, she reserved to herself 'the exclusive right of inviting young gentlemen.' The event went well. 'The damsels were all in plain white frocks without any ornaments,' she explained, and she praised them for being 'very handsome.' The twenty-four young men she invited, the 'elite of the community,' came as well. Eliza was pleased with the party, especially as everything went to plan. 'They began and ended dancing punctually,' she explained, and added that she had never seen 'better manners nor more cheerful countenances.'[15]

Despite the success of the school, the Seminary for Young Ladies in Niagara came to an end too, around 1833. Mary Breakenridge was frequently ill, but, unlike Eliza, she had a lot of family support. Her brother, William Warren Baldwin, was one of the leading citizens of what was then York (it didn't become Toronto until 1834), and she and her family were simply cared for by her brother and his family. Eliza, however, still had to work for a living. So with the close of the school in Niagara, her colonial quest for total financial independence ended. Between 1833 and her retirement in 1838, she was the mistress of the boarding house for the boys of Upper Canada College, the prep school for the nascent University of Toronto (still King's College at the time, having received its charter in 1827).

Like the schools Eliza had run in Barbados, New Haven, and New York, the Niagara school had been successful, but unsustainable. A hauntingly disparaging comment made about girls' schools in Upper Canada by Charles Duncombe survives in his 1836 'Report on Education.'[16] There he describes 'female institutions' as 'ephemeral' and explains that:

> because in most cases every thing depends upon the character and enterprise of a single individual. A school may be at the height of prosperity one week, and the next week entirely extinct. Communities seem almost entirely dependent upon chance, both for the character and perpetuity of female schools. (39)

Charles Duncombe, as it happens, had been one of the correspondents of William Warren Baldwin's son Robert (ultimately a famous politician in his own right)[17] at a time when Eliza would have been close to the Baldwin family. If Duncombe discussed the Niagara Seminary for Young Ladies with the Baldwins, nothing survives in the archive. Duncombe does, however, support an intellectual course of study in his report, and he echoes phrases that ring close to the sentiments expressed by Eliza channeling those of Mary Wollstonecraft. As the object of female education he explicitly names both 'the physical, intellectual and moral education of children' and 'the care of the health and the formation of the character of the future citizen' (41). The qualities of the women he imagines will be entrusted with the task of being companions, friends, and educators of the next generation, chime perfectly with Eliza's plan for educating the girls in her schools. And that was the plan she had developed in concert with Mary Wollstonecraft, William Godwin, Mary Hays, and the other philosophers, educators, and publishers of her late-enlightenment circle in London. The qualities Eliza identified in her ideal teacher also match the ones Duncombe sketches. He too suggests that a teacher of girls and young women should be characterized by 'her warm sympathies, her lively imagination, her ready invention, her quick perception,' as well as her 'patient attention, calm judgment, steady efficiency and habitual self-control' (41–2). He also names 'those qualities of the head and the heart' as those replacing the 'weeping, vapid, pretty plaything' as the 'model of female loveliness' (42). He champions the study of mathematics, as well as 'pursuits designed to cultivate the taste and imagination, such as rhetoric, poetry, and other branches of polite literature' (44). Duncombe's report has other characteristic phrases that seem to have come from the rhetoric of the promotional materials for Eliza's schools, especially in the attention to the teacher/student relationship, in the capacity of all children to learn. His lines in the report read:

> As the care of the intellect is the business of teachers, we find that some success always attend these efforts. However dull the child or incompetent the teacher, at the end of each year it will be found that every child has learned something, and the memory at least if no other faculty is to some extent cultivated. (47)

The idea that even the 'dull child' can be educated resonates perfectly with the 1829 advertisement for the Niagara Seminary for Young Ladies, with its promise that despite timidity or disposition or slowness, which might render a child incapable of excelling others, even the slow child would be able to find delight in her 'consciousness of excelling her former self.'[18] Whether or not Eliza actually influenced Duncombe's report, I can't confirm. At best, I can set the ideas against each other and know that Charles

Duncombe and Eliza Fenwick had common friends and were in the same place at the same time. Although I've tried to demonstrate through this chapter that Eliza succeeded in her desire to 'communicate energy' to the young women she taught, to see their ideas 'shooting, expanding and maturing,' in the end, ideas, like fireworks, are ephemeral.

NOTES

1. The note appears in an 1829 annotation to an 1808 letter written to Henry Crabb Robinson by Eliza Fenwick. Crabb Robinson also says in his note that Eliza had an 'unhappy marriage to a wild Irishman [it does not appear that John was Irish] of good heart but no conduct.' HCR correspondence 1808 #116: 7 January 1808 and February 1829. Eliza had written the original note to Henry Crabb Robinson asking for funds to help her daughter prepare for the stage. Crabb Robinson papers are held in Dr. Williams's Library, London, UK.
2. In an unpublished letter dated 10 June 1832, to John Moffat (1788–1865), a New York silversmith and friend, Eliza says that in London she had worked for the publisher Sir Richard Phillips and that he had 'engaged [her] assistance in his many enterprises of translations from French & compilations, chiefly of school books.' She does identify herself as one of Phillips's authors using the pseudonym 'Rev'd David Blair.' Although she is known as the person who edited *The Class Book* for Phillips she also says that she compiled 'many others under the same & other important names,' but there are no extant records that I've been able to find identifying which books she compiled. Phillips used a range of pseudonyms for his schoolbooks, in a prescient attempt to establish a brand identity in the educational book business. 'Goldsmith,' for example, was the name associated with his geography books. All the letters I cite in this chapter are my own transcriptions of the manuscript originals, most of which are in the New-York Historical Society (NYHS) Fenwick Papers (MS211). A. F. Wedd edited a volume of Fenwick's letters to her ancestor, Mary Hays, published as *The Fate of the Fenwicks: 1798–1828*. London: Methuen, 1927. As there were errors and omissions, I made fresh transcriptions. I also transcribed the unpublished letters and fragment in the archive written to members of the family of John Moffat.
3. Eliza Fenwick to Mary Hays, 1 February 1813. Unpublished. Fenwick Family Papers (MS211) New-York Historical Society (NYHS). All transcriptions are mine. The folders in the three boxes of manuscript material have recently been put into two boxes. As the files are arranged in date order, the material is in the file matching its date.

4. Thomson, James. *The Seasons. Containing, Spring. Summer. Autumn. Winter.* Philadelphia: Jacob Johnson, 1795. Ll. 1149–53.
5. Briggs, Julia. "'Delightful Task!" Women, Children and Reading in the Mid-Eighteenth Century.' *Culturing the Child, 1690–1914: Essays in Memory of Mitzi Myers,* ed. Donelle Ruwe (Lanham, Maryland: Scarecrow Press, 2005. 67–82), 70.
6. Ibid.
7. Godwin, William. *The Enquirer* (London: Simpkin and Marshall, 1923), 69–70.
8. Eliza Fenwick to Mary Hays, 15 April 1821.
9. *Connecticut Herald,* 3 May 1824.
10. The Barrell Family Papers (1751–1829) are held at Columbia University Libraries in New York. The information about Dora's marriage to Ferdinand Massa is in that archive, as well as the information that Eliza and Eliza Ann attended their wedding in 1826.
11. *Niagara Farmer's Journal,* 22 April 1829.
12. Eliza Fenwick to John Moffat, 19 April 1830. Fenwick Family Papers (MS 211). NYHS.
13. Eliza Fenwick, *Visits to the Juvenile Library; Or Knowledge Proved to be the Source of Happiness* (London: Tabart, 1805), 15.
14. Mary Shelley, in response to Fanny Wright's 'fan letter,' requesting support: 'The memory of my Mother has been always been the pride & delight of my life; & the admiration of others for her, has been the cause of most of the happiness I have enjoyed. Her greatness of soul & my father's high talents have perpetually reminded me that I ought to degenerate as little as I could from those from whom I derived my being' (12 September 1827): http://theamericanreader.com/12-september-1827-mary-shelley-to-frances-wright/. See also Celia Morris Eckhardt, *Fanny Wright: Rebel in America* (Cambridge Mass.: Harvard UP, 1984).
15. Eliza Fenwick to the Moffat family (20 October 1831). Fenwick Family Papers (MS211). NYH.
16. Charles Duncombe, *Doctor Charles Duncombe's Report Upon the Subject of Education, made to the Parliament of Upper Canada, 25th February 1836. Through the Commissioners Doctors Morrison and Bruce, appointed by a Resolution of the House of Assembly, 1835 to Obtain information on the subject of Education.* Toronto: M. Reynolds, 1836. Subsequent citations appear parenthetically.
17. Baldwin Family Papers. Toronto Public Library. L12 1801–1843 15 September 1836: A 42 number 171.
18. *Niagara Farmer's Journal,* 22 April 1829.

Shifting Representations and Meanings of Childhood

In the Margins: Children and Graphic Satire in the Eighteenth Century and Early Nineteenth Century

Sebastian Mitchell

It is now widely accepted there was a significant shift in attitudes towards young children in Britain in the middle of the eighteenth century.[1] One can see evidence of this social and cultural transformation in the material developments from the 1750s onwards, with the growth of the numbers of toys and games to be found in affluent households. Their presence suggested an increasing emphasis on the idea that childhood, and especially early childhood, should be regarded as much as a period of enjoyment as of one of education.[2] Children, however, also played a significant role in the psychological and social developments of sentimental discourse in this period, the notion that the bedrock of a fully functioning civil society was the capacity of its members not only to sympathise and identify with the predicament of others, but also to be able to exhibit such feelings when circumstances deemed it necessary. In Britain, this enthusiasm for emotional responsiveness had significant origins in the journalism of Addison and Steele, and received further conceptual justification in the moral philosophy of Francis Hutchison, David Hume, and Adam Smith.

S. Mitchell (✉)
University of Birmingham, Birmingham, UK
e-mail: J.H.S.MITCHELL@bham.ac.uk

© The Author(s) 2018
A. O'Malley (ed.), *Literary Cultures and Eighteenth-Century Childhoods*, Literary Cultures and Childhoods,
https://doi.org/10.1007/978-3-319-94737-2_12

Philosophical discussion on how the passions lead us under optimal conditions to the property-owning society of the modern state had its corollary in the middle-ranking habit of assessing one's friends and acquaintances in terms of their responses to supposedly evocative works and scenes.[3] James Boswell records how the celebrated speech coach, Thomas Sheridan, and his wife took to calibrating the affective capacities (and hence the degree of refinement and civility) of their social circle by how they reacted to the sublime and melancholy prose poetry of the supposed ancient Gaelic bard, Ossian. The Sheridans, Boswell reports, were using Ossian as a 'thermometer by which they could judge the warmth of every body's heart.'[4] By the 1770s, the forthright expression of feeling had become a prominent aspect of popular artistic expression in novels, romances, and verses. And in visual culture, a central means by which indulgent feeling is conveyed is through the depiction of children in affecting portraits, in pitiful scenes of impoverishment, in charming images of play, and in the personification of specific emotional states.

The principal means by which such affecting imagery was produced and circulated in prodigious numbers throughout the second half of the century was via stand-alone visual prints. Such appealing images could be collected, stored in portfolios, glued into scrapbooks, framed and hung on walls as affordable means of decoration, or even in some cases pasted onto walls as a collage-style wallpaper.[5] The emergence and proliferation of affecting imagery in British print culture in the second half of the eighteenth century coincided with a similarly steep rise in the production and consumption of satirical imagery. The common material reason for the production of these images is the development of a substantial independent domestic print industry with an active market for such pictures. And it is tempting to conceive of these types of prints as operating as the obverse of one another, with graphic satire providing a dark distorted mirror to the charm, charity, and indulgent feelings typical of the sentimental, a barbed version of contemporary society in general and of its elite members in particular, defined by their foolish, vicious, venal, and self-serving characteristics. And if one were then to consider the separation of childhood into a distinct sphere of activities and expectations from that of adulthood, then one might expect to see a similar separation in the representation of children, with a preponderance in sentimental prints, and relatively few in graphic satire.

As this chapter will show, this proves to be a reasonably accurate assessment of the weight of representation of children in these respective visual fields, yet it is my intention in what follows to examine some of the ambiguities and cross-currents in these areas and to consider, in particular, the representation of children in graphic satire in this period. The sentimental as an expression of feeling can result in some troubling forms of visualisation; and by the same token the satirical can utilise some of the familiar associations of children from sentimental discourse, such as those of innocence, charity, pity, and the sanctity of the family. Given his prominent role in the development of English visual satire, his endeavours to establish an indigenous English print industry (as a response to the dominance of imported prints from continental Europe in the early part of the eighteenth century), and indeed, his labours in the service of impoverished children through his unstinting support for the Foundling Hospital in London, one might well expect such a discussion to commence with an account of William Hogarth. However, the chapter will close rather than open with a consideration of this artist; and I trust the reasons for doing so will become apparent in due course, but suffice to say at this stage that Hogarth produced in his visual satires a complex and nuanced set of depictions of children, and seemed intent on synthesising the very different capacities of the sympathetic and satirical in the representation of one small boy.

As modern print historians are keen to stress, printmaking was almost always a commercial undertaking with a number of parties collaborating in the production of a given image, and with no plate being prepared unless there was a reasonable prospect of turning a profit from the sale of the resulting image.[6] If aesthetic distinctiveness was a consequence of limited reproducibility, then this was also perceived as a commercial disadvantage, precisely because copper plates wore out after even modest use, and had to be either recut or replaced. However, the economic imperatives of print production also meant that as a medium it was exceptionally sensitive and responsive to the vagaries of general taste, and the standard calculation for print publishers, then, was to produce images which could be readily recognised as belonging to a particular genre, but which possessed sufficient distinctiveness to render them more desirable as objects of consumption than their immediate competition.

We can see examples of such mainstream affecting images of children in the prints after the works of the artist Richard Morton Paye. Valentine Green's attractive version of Paye's *Child of Sorrow* (1773), for example, shows a small child laying her head on what appears to be the ledge of a sarcophagus. She meets the viewer's gaze with the appearance of resigned melancholy. The spectator is no doubt meant to infer from the setting that the mournful child is contemplating the loss of a near relative, perhaps a parent or a sibling, but she also seems to exemplify the passion from which she is ostensibly afflicted, such that the design has a pleasing instructive aspect, that true sorrow should be reflective and reserved, rather than demonstrative and overwhelming. As Samuel Johnson observes in his *Dictionary of the English Language* (1755), 'sorrow' is a state 'not commonly understood as the effect of present evil, but of lost good.'[7] In Charles Howard Hodges's mezzotint after the same artist's *Children Spouting Tragedy* (1785) (Fig. 12.1), a group of children appear to be enacting the dénouement of a tragedy, either from classical drama or a modern play with a classical setting. The child in the centre is declaiming

Fig. 12.1 Charles Howard Hodges after Richard Morton Paye, *Children Spouting Tragedy*, 1785, mezzotint, 45.4 × 55.5 cm. (Courtesy of the Lewis Walpole Library, Yale University)

(striking a standard pose for tragic peroration), the girl to her left bows her head and weeps, and a young boy lies at her feet, as though playing the slain hero. The image functions on the basis of a disjuncture between the events which the children are improbably attempting to convey, and the inadequacy of their comprehension to do so effectively. 'Spouting' in the print's title is used in a transitive and figurative sense to indicate that the juvenile performers utter their lines without contemplating their meaning, and the entire image serves as a visual pun: the typical activity of 'play' in childhood becomes the performance of a stage play, which by dint of the actors' age and inexperience they are singularly unqualified to perform. The picture's emotional effect seems to be that of wry and gentle indulgence, to provoke a certain knowingness in the adult audience, that the grown-up world will become the stage in which child actors will eventually appreciate how unchecked desires and passions may result in catastrophe.

One can argue that sentimentalism is an inherently unstable discourse in that it always has a tendency to slip from the sympathetic and the charitable to notions of desire which have instead personal gratification as their principal objective; and it is one of the subtle and memorable aspects of Laurence Sterne's *A Sentimental Journey Through France and Italy* (1768), a work which Tim Clayton points out was 'the singular most popular source for prints' in this period.[8] The sympathetic and sensitive travelling of the book's protagonist, Parson Yorick, depends on his barely sublimated sexuality and the transactional nature of some of his emotional encounters. One might also suggest that what lends a given print of children its distinctiveness is its capacity to inflect upon the inherent instability of a discourse which ostensibly celebrates feeling as a central means for arriving at evaluative judgements and as an appropriate basis for interacting with one's fellow subjects. However, when it comes to the visual depiction of children within the general ambit of sentimental expressiveness, the works of the most successful English artist of the second half of the eighteenth century, Sir Joshua Reynolds, not only provide an extensive anatomy of the ambiguities and contradictions in the affective representation of children, but also seem intent in some pictures to press such imagery to the point of conceptual collapse.

Reynolds produced throughout his career in the region of 200 pictures featuring children (out of a total of about 1700 paintings including portraits and subject paintings), and because of his standing as the leading English artist of the second half of the eighteenth century, many of these images were subsequently produced as prints.[9] Popular images included mother and child portraits, such as James Wright's mezzotint in 1768 of the Duchess of Marlborough, a notable aristocratic beauty, and her infant daughter, Lady Caroline Spencer, and portraits of individual children, such as in J.R. Smith's print of *Master Crewe as Henry VIII* (1776), an image of diminished bravado, lauded by Horace Walpole for its 'humour and satire' in the distillation of 'Holbein's swaggering and colossal haughtiness of Henry VIII to the boyish jollity of Master Crewe.'[10] However, Reynolds also produced fancy paintings of children, that is, images which often have the appearance of portraits, but are intended as exemplifications of particular qualities associated with childhood, or are depictions of a given type rather than a specific child. As Martin Postle points out, fancy painting provided Reynolds with an experimental licence, allowing for both technical innovation and the exploration of the ideological precepts of portraiture.[11] Two of Reynolds's most challenging images of children in this genre are a set of pendant portraits he produced in the 1770s, as these images play uncomfortably with conceptions of children as subjects of universal sympathy and as objects of sexual commodification.

Both pictures, *Cupid in the Character of a Link Boy* and *Mercury* (portrayed as a cut purse), were engraved by John Dean in 1777 (Figs. 12.2 and 12.3). As with Reynolds's depiction of Master Crewe as Henry VIII, the pictures suggest an exercise in deflation and miniaturisation, but in this instance, it is Roman mythology rather than Tudor history which is the source material.

As David Mannings observes, the classical allusions and references are skilfully introduced. Cupid is shown with a torch, which he sometimes carries in both classical and renaissance imagery, rather than his more common bow and arrows.[12] The depiction of Mercury as a thief has an antecedent in Ovid's *Metamorphoses*, where the winged messenger steals Apollo's cattle when the oracular god of the sun has been distracted by amorous thoughts. A link boy was a child paid to guide clients through darkened city streets with his torch. Reynolds imagines the boy's wings sprouting from the back of his threadbare jacket (with a prominent hole in the right sleeve at the elbow). The cutpurse Mercury is also a young child with limp wings protruding from his felt bonnet; and he holds an empty stolen purse in his left hand. The purse's intricate embroidery is in stark contrast to the thief's plain hat and frock. The hard evidence of Mercury's criminal proclivities nestles in his hand, but the link boy's propensity for crime remains implicit. From an eighteenth-century perspective, both boys can be conceived as part of a demi-monde which placed them outside

Fig. 12.2 John Dean after Sir Joshua Reynolds, *Cupid in the Character of a Link Boy*, 1777, mezzotint, 38.9 × 27.4 cm. (Yale Center for British Art, Paul Mellon Fund)

the reciprocal expectations of sympathetic discourse. The proliferating numbers of abandoned poor children could be readily dismissed as fledgling criminals. As Dorothy George pithily observed, just so many 'villains ripening for the gallows.'[13]

Mannings begins his account of these paintings by suggesting that 'whereas some of Reynold's fancy pictures are sentimental, others are witty, playful or erotic.'[14] The circumspect nature of this statement and the use of a prepositional 'or' where we would expect the conjunctive 'and' indicate the extent of modern sensitivities over such imagery. The torch which the small boy in *Cupid in the Character of a Link Boy* grips in his right hand has an obvious phallic connotation. The torch indicates the role that such street children played in guiding their clients to various sexual assignations in dark streets and closes, but the picture also suggests

Fig. 12.3 John Dean
after Sir Joshua
Reynolds, *Mercury*,
1777, mezzotint,
39 × 27.4 cm. (Yale
Center for British Art,
Paul Mellon Fund)

such children are objects of sexual gratification (as indicated by the neat but prominent hole in the sleeve of the boy's jacket). And the phallic symbolism of *Cupid in the Character of a Link Boy* is complemented by the empty slit purse in *Mercury*, with a sense of the boy having been discarded once the sexual act has been performed. The ostensible 'wit' in such depictions is in the connection between an understanding of the nature of the lives of such children and the tradition of its representation, but also in the expectation that the cognoscenti will be alert to the role of boys (*pueri*) in Roman erotic literature. As Amy Richlin has observed, Latin poets, such as Pliny, Seneca, Petronius, and Martial, produced lustful verses after the example of Greek epigrams; and the focus of desire in such compositions is usually the socially marginal figure of the young slave. These boys, she states, 'are never viewed as potential adults who will become freedmen, carry on business or government, have children, or grow old. The *pueri* in these poems are "sex objects" in the starkest sense.'[15]

One can see that the appeal to potential purchasers of such prints is the sophistication and skill in the construction of their imagery; and, indeed, one cannot discount the possibility that some bought the prints principally because of their pederastic overtones. But it is also possible to regard these paintings and subsequent prints as providing a commentary on the discursive limitations of any indulgent sentimental version of childhood. Indeed, one might regard the pictures as suggesting that it is absurd to treat such malign urchins in anything approaching sympathetic terms (the link-boy cupid has the jagged tar-black wings of the daemon, rather than the pristine white feathers of an angel). Yet Reynolds's fancy paintings seem to resist drawing such a hard-and-fast distinction between the pathetic and impoverished young as deserving recipients of universal sympathy, and those street children who remain resolutely beyond the pale. The children in these fancy pictures still appear pitiful in their damaged state, still deserving of compassion beneath their ingenious and darkly ludic treatment.

We can understand, then, that images of children form a substantial component of the English print market from the middle of the eighteenth century onwards. Those images are also varied from the straightforward sentimental and indulgent to images which explore the limitations of such a child-centred discourse, and the nature of the sexual exploitation of street children. So, given the range of images of childhood available in the print market, the question arises as to whether children are significantly present within the rapidly expanding area of graphic satire in this era. For the purposes of answering this question, I examined a range of graphic works, but the core of the analysis was an inspection of the complete runs of unmounted Roys of satirical prints, held by the British Museum, for three prominent British artists in the late eighteenth century and early nineteenth century (a 'Roy' is a single print struck on a full sheet of Royal-sized paper, 25 × 20 inches). These printmakers were James Gillray (1756–1815), Thomas Rowlandson (1757–1827), and William Heath (1794–1840).

Gillray produces the largest number of satirical prints of the three artists, followed by Rowlandson and then Heath. Gillray also used more images of children or items related to childhood than the other two.[16] In Gillray's satirical works, about 1 in 30 of the prints alludes to childhood; this figure drops to 1 in 40 for Rowlandson; and I could only find one image of children in the run of Heath's unmounted Roys. On the evidence of this survey, children have four central functions in graphic satire in this period: first, as spectators to the main events; second, as victims of cruel parents or of unjust social policies (and sometimes a mixture of both); third, as offering a demonstration of defining parental characteristics (so portrayed as a miniature version of their father or mother); and fourth, as adults portrayed as though they were infants and children for purposes of disparaging their conduct. Children do often appear as marginal figures, both in the sense that they are situated at the periphery of the image, and are supportive of the main action of the print. However, there are also notable exceptions to this general rule.

From the 1760s onwards, there are surprisingly few children in the inspected prints whose sole purpose is to serve as spectators to the main events (whereas the use of children for this purpose is extremely common in prints of landscapes and rural views). Rowlandson does depict children looking on at entertaining behaviour in his domestic satires. In his *Batchelor's Fare, Bread, Cheese and Kisses* (1814), for example, a young serving girl stands in a doorway, spying on a canoodling couple (and thereby intriguingly replicates the viewer's own indulgent gaze). Children understandably are present when family life is being examined. Rowlandson produced an engaging pair of domestic prints in 1809, *The Comforts of Matrimony: A Good Toast* and *The Miseries of Wedlock: The Tables Turned* (both 1809). The former is a contented family scene with a husband toasting bread next to the stove with adoring wife and three contented small children; the latter depicts turbulent domestic relations, with the children now imperilled as their parents violently argue over supper. A young girl tugs her mother's dress in an attempt to restrain her. In the midst of this dispute, a chair is knocked backwards with the middle child desperately clinging onto it. The overturning table (a metaphor for upturned family circumstances) is about to land, along with the crockery and cutlery, on top of the startled infant.

Perhaps surprisingly, there are no children featured in Rowlandson's ribald erotica, apart from the occasional decorative cupid, though there is a vague sexual allusion in one noteworthy political satire with a suggestion of neglected maternal responsibilities. Rowlandson produced a series of pointed visual attacks on Georgiana, Duchess of Devonshire, for her energetic support and active campaigning for the Whig party during the General Election in 1784. One of these, *Political Affection* (1784) (Fig. 12.4), satirises the duchess by suggesting her enthusiastic politicking is the by-product of unnatural nurturing instincts. The duchess ignores her infant son; he stands at her side, crying with his arms raised, while she suckles a very large bear in a white nursing dress (Charles James Fox in ursine guise).[17] Either in conscious imitation of this episode, or because he

Fig. 12.4   Thomas Rowlandson, *Political Affection*, 1784, etching, 24.5 × 35 cm. (General Collection, Beinecke Rare Book and Manuscript Library, Yale University)

coincidentally happened upon the same device, Gillray depicts the Countess of Strathmore and Kinghorne as suckling two cats rather than a large improbably frocked bear in *The Injur'd Count* (1786). The neglected boy, standing at her side, mournfully reflects that 'I wish I was a cat; my mama would love me still.' The print alludes to an earlier scandal in which the countess had separated from her first husband, the Earl of Strathmore and Kinghorne, and had been impregnated by one of her lovers. Her reputation had been tarnished in a series of articles in the *Morning Post* from April 1777 onwards. It became common knowledge that she was fond of cats, and that she harboured an inexplicable animosity towards her son (she admitted at the start of her memoir in the early 1790s that she was guilty of 'an unnatural dislike' of her eldest child).[18]

Lady Strathmore was also the target of Gillray's vicious satire, *Lady Termagant Flaybum Going to Give her Step Son a Taste of her Desert after Dinner* [...] (1786) (Fig. 12.5). The print shows the countess seated languidly in an armchair in the dining room (the remnants of dinner and

Fig. 12.5 James Gillray, *Lady Termagant Flaybum Going to Give her Step Son a Taste of her Desert after Dinner* [...], 1786, hand-coloured etching and stipple engraving, 43 × 54 cm. (Courtesy of the Lewis Walpole Library, Yale University)

wine can be seen in the background). The countess, or Lady Flaybum, has dishevelled hair and exposed breasts. She has a birch rod in her right hand. To her left, a maid holds a distressed-looking boy aged about 12. The maid is unbuttoning and removing the boy's breaches in preparation for him to be flagellated by his mother (the reason for the description of the boy as a 'Step Son' is unclear, but perhaps it is intended to play on the common association of cruelty of stepmothers). The implication is that the countess is doubly unnatural in her relation to the child, not only lacking the ties and obligations of parental affection, but indeed, seeking some post-prandial sexual gratification from the boy's chastisement.

Vic Gatrell points out that both prints were propagandistic travesties of Lady Strathmore's actual circumstances. The countess had fled from a sustained campaign of abuse by her domineering second husband, Andrew

Robinson Stoney Bowes, a libertine who had married her for her for-tune.[19] Bowes had been convicted and fined for cruelty against her in May 1786; and the prints were part of his ongoing campaign against his wife, a desperate attempt to secure legal advantage by further traducing her (Gillray also produced a print in 1786 of a pitiful Bowes being helped into court at the King's Bench). The countess was vindicated in the courts at the end of the decade, but *Lady Termagant Flaybum* continued to sell well through the 1790s, and Gillray successfully recycled the device of a female flagellant for a print in 1795.[20] At best, the depiction of the countess indi-cates public indifference to her circumstances; and at worst, the prints suggest a pervasive misogyny in eighteenth-century English society, where the default position was to conceive of women, especially aristocratic women, who failed to conform to social and political norms as being gov-erned by perverse instincts.[21] However, the depiction of a sadistic act towards an actual child, rather than politicians portrayed as children or being childish, is unusual in the period's graphic satire.

More common than images of children being abused or neglected by their parents are those which show them passing from conditions of rela-tive ease and comfort to those of abject poverty, because of prevailing social and political circumstances. These are often presented as a general complaint about the treatment and fate of servicemen, part of a narrative of personal sacrifice in the national interest. Indeed, the figure of the impoverished military man with starving children often regularly appears in the period's children literature. Gillray's *John Bull's Progress* (1793) (Fig. 12.6), for example, has four consecutive panels, entitled 'John Bull Happy,' 'John Bull Goes to War,' 'John Bull's Property in Danger,' and the ironical concluding frame, 'John Bull's Glorious Return.' The print was produced when Britain was fighting with its allies against revolution-ary France in continental Europe. The first panel shows a plump John Bull in his armchair with pitcher before the hearth; his wife is at a spinning wheel behind him; and two young healthy boys play with a bird in a wicker basket. The final panel shows the archetypical Englishman returning from the military campaign. He is emaciated; he stands on a crutch in the door-way (having lost an eye and a leg). His family now lives in a hovel; and his two young children are deranged from hunger. The only unmounted satir-ical print depicting children by William Heath in the British Museum col-lection makes a similar point on the treatment of returning servicemen and their families. Heath's *Military Progress (Slow Movement); or, The Review of Merit* (1822) is a box strip of eight frames, which recounts the tale of an

Fig. 12.6 James Gillray, *John Bull's Progress*, 1793, hand-coloured etching, 31 × 38 cm. (Courtesy of the Lewis Walpole Library, Yale University)

English officer in a marching regiment during the Napoleonic wars. The officer is shown in an early frame meeting his future wife at a ball, then about to depart for France, saying farewell to his wife and young daughter at Dover. The penultimate frame depicts the family living in poverty once the officer has returned from war. The half-pay officer sits dejectedly in a bare room, while his daughter scrubs the floor and his son weeps by his side. In the final image, he is glimpsed through the barred window of a debtors prison. His wife is being pushed away for the door by a callous gaoler; she holds an infant, while the two older children wave their arms and cry in distress.

While children appear relatively infrequently in print satire, it is rather more usual by the 1780s to encounter prints where politicians and other public figures are treated as though they were children, or being associated with childish things. The increasing prominence of such imagery would in itself suggest a consolidation of the ideological demarcations between the respective expectations of adulthood and childhood. Gillray's *A Block for the Wigs; or, The New State Whirligig* (1783) (Fig. 12.7), for example, satirises the ineffectualness of the coalition government. Fox, Burke, and North and other ministers pointlessly whirl around on a merry-go-round, with the king depicted as a wig block in the carousel's centre. In *Westminster School; or, Dr Busby settling accounts with Master Biffy and his Playmates* (1785), Gillray casts Fox as the celebrated Richard Busby, the long-standing and politically adept headmaster of Westminster School during the Commonwealth and Restoration. Fox-as-Busby is on the point of birching William Pitt and his supporters, all depicted as errant pupils in the school hall (Dorothy George describes this as a propagandist print, 'misrepresenting the actual state of politics').[22]

If the onset of the Napoleonic wars did not extinguish criticism of the British political elite by English satirists, then the main targets certainly shifted from the turpitude and hypocrisies of domestic politicians to the

Fig. 12.7 James Gillray, *A Block for the Wigs; or, the New State Whirligig*, 1783, etching, 25 × 34 cm. (Yale Center for British Art, Paul Mellon Collection)

French foe in general, and to Napoleon in particular. Images of children were utilised as part of this visual campaign. Napoleon's four-year-old nephew makes an appearance in Gillray's panoramic *Grand Coronation Procession of Napoleone* (1805). The print satirises the pompousness of the ceremony without quite dispelling the notion that the coronation must have possessed a certain majesty. Near the front of the parade, the Prime Minister's wife, a stout matronly Mme Talleyrand, leads Charles-Louis, son of Louis I, the emperor's brother. The print, however, scurrilously implies that the emperor is the boy's true father. The caption describes the child as 'the heir apparent, in ye path of glory,' and his strutting suggests that he has inherited a good portion of his father's hauteur and ambition. Rowlandson's *Nursing the Spawn of a Tyrant; or Frenchmen Sick of the Breed* (1811) depicts one of Napoleon's real children, with the suggestion that he has inherited a rather more sinister trait. On hearing the news that the young empress, Marie Louise, had given birth to a son, Rowlandson depicts the infant as his father's perfect miniature, whose first action on being born is to assault his mother with a dagger and to pitch an orb at her. The empress exclaims (while Napoleon looks on approvingly from behind a drape in the background) 'the very shamm and spit of its Tyrant Father – nay now I look again he is the very picture of his Grandfather the Devil.'

The devil is Napoleon's father rather than his grandfather in a sequence of European prints at the time of the Leipzig campaign, and the collapse of the empire. Rowlandson contributed an English version, *The Devils Darling* (1814) (Fig. 12.8) in which a tightly swaddled infant Napoleon is being nursed by a large dark gloating Satan. Napoleon is often portrayed as though he were a child; and this is evidently in part a consequence of the scale on which he is regularly caricatured. As Tim Clayton and Sheila O'Connell have pointed out, Napoleon was 5′ 6″, the average height for a European man in this era. They argue that the idea that he was diminutive took hold in English satirical prints as a shorthand for belittling the French ruler after the Peace of Amiens broke down in 1803.[23] Gillray draws on Jonathan Swift's *Gulliver's Travels* (1726) on two occasions to satirise Napoleon and contemporary circumstances. The first two parts of *Gulliver's Travels*, 'A Voyage to Lilliput,' in which Gulliver is a giant amongst the minute Lilliputians, and 'A Voyage to Brobdingnag,' in which Gulliver is tiny compared to the giant Brobdingnagians, were often read by children, and hence associated with childhood from the early eighteenth century onwards; an abridged version of Swift's book appeared in 1727, along with various chapbook editions later in the century.[24] Gillray's *The King of Brobdingnag, and*

Fig. 12.8 Thomas Rowlandson, *The Devils Darling*, 1814, hand-coloured etching, 34 × 24 cm. (Image courtesy of Bonhams)

THE DEVILS DARLING.

Gulliver (1803), after a design by Thomas Braddyll, shows George III as the giant king holding the consul in the palm of his hand. Napoleon is supposed to be Gulliver, but has the appearance of a toy soldier. The king quotes the observation of Swift's giant monarch after Gulliver had celebrated British constitutional arrangements in utopian terms, that 'I cannot but conclude you to be one of the most pernicious, little odious reptiles that nature ever suffered to crawl on the surface of the Earth.' George Cruikshank offers a surprisingly poignant perspective on the enemy's children in *French Conscript for the Years 1820, 21, 22, 23, 24 & 25* (1813). His print is a comment on the increasingly young age at which soldiers were conscripted into the French army after the heavy losses in the Russian campaign. He envisages an infant army in which very small children struggle to march in their preposterously oversized uniforms, hats and helmets.

And one little boy, naked from the waist down (so presumably not yet potty trained), stands on his toes in a vain attempt to clean his musket, and wistfully proclaims that 'I want to go home to my mamme.'

In the course of their discussion on the development of the discursive capacity of poetry through the eighteenth century, John Barrell and Harriet Guest suggested that there was a distinctive shift in the expressive capabilities of that particular medium which followed from Adam Smith's ideas on the requirements of specialisation for economic efficiency. In this argument, poetry is understood to move from being a medium which can provide a cogent and plausible discussion of economic relations to one in which verse has to relinquish such real-world authority. Poetry is confined to lamenting the detrimental effects of the increasingly commercial nature of British society (such as in Oliver Goldsmith's *The Deserted Village*, 1770), rather than making any significant contribution to the debate about the nature of the economy.[25] And we might momentarily consider whether we can detect a similar taxonomic separation within print culture in the late eighteenth century and early nineteenth century. If children have not been excluded from graphic satire by the later part of the eighteenth century, then there use, in the main, would seem to be of an abstract nature, a representative of a type, an exemplification of the follies of the adult world; and in this respect, they usually appear in the peripheral spaces, supplementary and supportive to the print's main narrative and purpose. It seems that the marginalisation of children within print satire coincides with the period in which depictions of children take centre stage in sentimental imagery, even as the limits of such sympathetic representation are being tested in Reynolds's subject works. That separation suggests that children increasingly belonged, at least conceptually, to a discrete phase of innocence and unsullied potential for goodness, while the visual satire became a matter of exposing the defectiveness of the adult world in its myriad guises. Yet, if one were to see a separation in the depiction of children as being analogous to that of poetry and political economy, then one might expect to discover a point of conflation of the sentimental and satirical *prior* to the emergence of distinct genres, where the child would be realised in a more rounded form; and it does seem that we can detect exactly that kind of discursive convergence in work of the leading English visual satirist of the early and middle part of the eighteenth century, William Hogarth.

Mark Hallett has argued convincingly that the woodcut engraving which Hogarth used as the title-sheet vignette for his aesthetic treatise,

The Analysis of Beauty: Written with a View of Fixing the Fluctuating Ideas of Taste (1753), should be interpreted metonymically for Hogarth's career as a whole. The image shows a serpentine line (the line of beauty) encased in a glass prism, and set on a plinth with the word, 'Variety,' inscribed upon it. Hogarth had begun his career as an artist as a 15-year-old apprentice to an engraver of silver plate, and by his early 20s he had established himself in London as an independent copper-plate engraver, producing illustrations for books and billhead receipts. When not at work as a young man, he studied painting at St Martin's Lane Academy, and then with the English decorative painter, Sir James Thornhill (his future father-in-law). Hallett observes that the modern appreciation of Hogarth rests largely on his satirical *œuvre*, and this emphasis has obscured his contributions to other fields of artistic endeavour. 'Variety,' Hallett believes, serves as a fitting epitaph for the artist in terms of his visual proliferation, but also in terms of the areas in which he practised. In addition to being a brilliant satirist, Hogarth was, he says, 'an unusually innovative and ambitious figure in a number of other artistic fields, including those of portraiture, history painting and art theory.'[26]

We can, however, turn this proposition on its head, and suggest that one of the animating and transformative aspects of Hogarth's graphic satire is its encompassing vision whereby the expectations and styles of other genres, old-master painting, history painting, and conversation pieces, would be drawn upon for the construction of a wide-ranging form of social critique. If Hogarth's satiric vision was by turns jaded, remorseless, and comic, then the modern world still had to be realised in all its immanence, and part of that project was to conceive in a direct and uncompromising fashion how children fitted into such an inclusive social schema. Forty out of 240 Hogarth's graphic works feature children.[27] The significance of children within Hogarthian satire can be straightforwardly assessed on positional grounds: whereas they often appear to the side of later satirical images, Hogarth has them in active roles and often situated right in the middle of the picture. His early satirical painting, *The Christening* (c. 1727–1728, and etched by Joseph Sympson Jr. in the early 1730s), for example, depicts an affluent family gathered in a grand house for this ceremony. The picture is clearly intended as a reflection of hypocrisy, vanity, sexual immorality, and professional misconduct in high society. A fop ostentatiously admires himself in a mirror on the paintings right-hand side, and the clergyman, who is supposed to be conducting the proceedings, is distracted by the décolletage of the young woman standing next to him. The picture has a pervasive sense of stillness, as though the figures are self-consciously maintaining their respective poses. The exception to this vain tableaux is a small boy in an elegant silken dress with his back turned in the central foreground. He has just reached up and tipped over the improvised christening bowl, spilling the baptismal water. The young boy and his actions are thus central to the scene (presumably the other characters will respond in the next moment to this disruption). The boy is also an ambiguous figure. His conduct can be read as being indicative of the general discord and neglect of the household, as a further sign of the collective transgression of religious ceremony and belief, or as an infuriated response to the conduct of these privileged worldly adults.

Even when children are portrayed in Hogarth's graphic works as the indisputable victims of cruelty or neglect, they still seem to have a more central and dynamic role when compared with the work of later satirists. *Gin Lane* (1751) (Fig. 12.9) is a scathing commentary on the destructive effects of the widespread availability of cheap gin, especially on society's poorer members. The scene's location is the impoverished area of St Giles, to the west of Bloomsbury. The print associates the excessive and addictive consumption of gin with an array of social horrors. It depicts a carpenter and his wife pawning their tools and cookware to be able to purchase more spirits. In the background, a body of a woman is being laid in a coffin with a child wailing beside her; a man walks jauntily with a child skewered on a spear-like implement; the upper storey of a tenement is collapsing from neglect; a man hangs from the rafters (presumably having committed suicide in ruined despair); and to the right a drunken riot is underway with a stool about to be broken over somebody's head. On the frame's right-hand edge, a woman ladles gin into her child to subdue his or her cries. In the foreground, an emaciated sightless ballad-seller weakly grips a gin flask. In the centre of this nightmarish image of sodden London is an addled mother (Madam Geneva as a demotic Britannia).[28] She is so inebriated that she lets her infant slip from her lap to fall to his almost certain death in the street below. The startled inverted child is the most eye-catching element of this packed scene. His fall indicates that it is poor mothers and children who suffer most from excessive alcohol consumption, but the figure of the tumbling disorientated child also seems to suggest that English society, as a whole, is spiralling towards some awful chaotic terminus.

Fig. 12.9 William Hogarth, *Gin Lane*, 1751, engraving and etching, 38.9 × 32.1 cm. (Courtesy of the Lewis Walpole Library, Yale University)

Moll's young son in the final plate of *A Harlot's Progress* (1732) (Fig. 12.10) is similarly situated at the centre. He sits directly beneath his mother's coffin dressed in elaborate oversized mourning dress. In an episode

Fig. 12.10 William Hogarth, *A Harlot's Progress*, Plate 6, 1732, etching and engraving, 31.6 × 39 cm. (Courtesy of the Lewis Walpole Library, Yale University)

which reveals the sexual shenanigans and the counterfeit self-serving behaviour of the adult mourners, his presence is consistent with the overall theme of the picture, of abiding indifference to the death of his 23-year-old mother from venereal disease; but the small boy is also insulated from the vanities, compulsions, and double-dealings of the adults. Oblivious to their conduct, he plays with a toy, a spinning top, tongue placed on his upper lip as he concentrates intently on this task. In the final scene of Hogarth's *Marriage A-la-Mode* (1745), the dying lady's child is presented to her by her nurse, while the lady's hypocritical father removes her wedding ring even before she has expired. The child has a pox mark on his cheek and callipers on his legs (a sign of inherited corruption); and once again, the response to the parent is ambivalent. The boy's embrace of his dying mother can be regarded as a gesture of anger as much as of affection.

Lower-order children also often play an active role in Hogarth's cosmopolitan scenes. In his light-hearted commentary on the tensions between the preciousness of high culture and rowdiness of low culture, *The Enraged Musician* (1741), the children contribute to the cacophony and general disorder which so infuriates the professional violinist and composer. He gazes angrily and exasperatedly out of his ground-floor window, hands clapped across his ears to muffle the din. An infant's cries accompany the shouts of his mother. A small well-dressed young girl holds a rattle while gazing at a young boy who shamelessly urinates into a hole in the street (his desultory approach to his studies indicated by his slate lying discarded on the ground behind him). To his left, a young jovial drummer boy provides the regular beat for the street's ad-hoc orchestra, with hawkers' cries, a horn player, a bassoonist, and the top notes supplied by the sound of a cleaver being sharpened on a grinding wheel.

Street children are both a more menacing and seductive presence in the fourth plate of *The Rake's Progress* (1735), *The Rake Arrested Going to Court*, or at least they are by the second state of the print. In this episode, Tom, the spendthrift son of a miserly merchant, and central figure in this series, is arrested by a bailiff for debt. In Hogarth's painting and the print's first state, a short figure stands by a chair looking on at the events (he may be about to steal Tom's cane). In the print's second state, this figure has been replaced by a group of boys gambling with dice and cards (with one of their number now lifting Tom's handkerchief). The introduction of the gang fills a previously underpopulated space in the frame, but it also underscores the point that Tom has squandered much of his fortune at the gaming table, as these children ape the vices of their elders and betters. Hogarth's bleakest depiction of the destructive capabilities of childhood, however, is in the first panel of his popular series, *The Four Stages of Cruelty* (1751, made available as both line engravings and woodcuts).

In *The First Stage of Cruelty* (Fig. 12.11), a group of boys are shown taking delight in torturing animals. In the print's background, a link boy (torch in hand), the subsequent subject of Reynolds's fancy painting, looks on as his companion cauterises a bird's eyes with a needle which has just been heated in the torch's flame. In the middle of the print, young Tom Nero, the protagonist of this merciless narrative, is inserting an arrow into the anus of a terrified, howling dog. Nero will graduate in cruelty from animals to humans in adult life. He is shown in the third panel being arrested having slit the throat of his faithful lover and accomplice, Anne Gill. In the final frame, the ironically entitled 'The Reward of Cruelty,'

Fig. 12.11   William Hogarth, *First Stage of Cruelty, The Four Stages of Cruelty,* 1751, etching and engraving, 38.7 × 32.4 cm. (Yale Center for British Art, Gift of Patricia Cornwall)

the body of the executed Nero is shown being dissected at the Barber-Surgeons' Hall. His entrails tumble onto the ground at the front of the anatomical theatre, and a dog, the original victim of Nero's boyhood viciousness, is on the point of consuming his cold discarded heart (perhaps as a sentimental negation), in what Roy Porter memorably described as an act of 'canine *lex talionis*.'[29]

If Hogarth's depictions of lower-order children seem to accord with a general disdain for such urchins as so many criminals ripening for the gallows, then their presence in these prints also suggests that if society is going to be subjected to a full sceptical analysis, then its younger members cannot be excluded on grounds of inappropriateness. Of course, these critical images are produced at a point where the ideological separation between the worlds of adult and children had not become so thoroughly entrenched that it became almost impossible to include such damning representations of children within graphic satire (Gillray produced only two in his entire career: a print on the Paris massacres of 1792, where the *sans-culottes* are depicted as a family of cannibals with the two children partaking of the gruesome feast, and a depiction in 1809 of the politician and pamphleteer William Cobbett as a boy setting animals on one another). The conceptual advantage of Hogarth's encompassing satirical vision is that it allowed for a more nuanced approach to the relationship of children to adults, and a rather more candid account of children's potentialities when compared to later caricatures. The difficulties and complexities of this early stage of life are engagingly exhibited in the third plate, *Evening* in Hogarth's series, *The Four Times of Day* (1738) (Fig. 12.12).

This muted scene shows a family of the middling sort strolling home in the twilight, having attended a performance at the Sadler's Wells Theatre (the episode is set in the countryside of Islington, on the northern edge of the eighteenth-century city). The social perspective is horizontal with Hogarth considering in this image the conduct of his own class. In the foreground, the husband, a dyer by profession (with hands stained blue in some early copies to indicate this), looks distracted. He is accompanied by his ample pregnant wife (sometimes with her cheeks and breast coloured an impassioned crimson); and the family's collie, also heavily pregnant, lopes along in front of them. The husband carries the youngest child, who is asleep on his shoulder. In the middle ground, a cow is being milked, and the horns of the beast appear to protrude from the top of the husband's bewigged head. The trick of perspective suggests, then, that the wife has cuckolded her husband. To the right, there is a surprisingly peace-

Fig. 12.12   Bernard Baron after William Hogarth, *Evening, The Four Times of Day*, 1738, etching and engraving, 45.4 × 37.5 cm. (Yale Center for British Art, Paul Mellon Collection)

ful view of a tavern, given the uproarious behaviour which usually accompanies Hogarth's depictions of such hostelries. We see Londoners sitting in this rural setting, smoking, and enjoying a drink. The harmonious connection between town and country is indicated by the tavern's sign, a portrait of 'Sir Hugh Myddelton,' the seventeenth-century engineer, who constructed canals and waterways to transport water to London from the surrounding countryside (the family walk alongside a canal). The most dramatic part of this scene, however, is the squabble between the two older children, just to the left of the picture's centre. The sister, fan in hand, berates her younger brother. He is in tears at her onslaught. He clutches a gingerbread man in his right hand (and we can reasonably surmise that the dispute is over this dainty). In his left hand, he holds the strap of his father's brass-knob walking cane with the shaft placed between his legs.

The critical consensus on this image is that it is a satire on reversed and, therefore unnatural, sexual and domestic relations, where the dominance of the large sensual wife over her passive long-suffering husband is re-enacted in the relationship of the two older children, with the boy dissolving into womanly tears when bullied by his precocious sister.[30] There are, no doubt, some accidental, or at least iterative, elements to this scene. David Bindman points out that the proof's first state lacks the scolding girl. She was introduced subsequently, because the engraver, Bernard Baron, complained to the artist that 'this boy has no apparent cause to Wimper.'[31] But even setting that aside, it remains difficult to resolve the image into a tidy and complete interpretation of a parody of inverted middle-class sexual relations. In her recent comprehensive account of the painting on which this print is based, Elizabeth Einberg suggests that the young boy employs his father's cane as an ad-hoc toy, 'riding it as a hobby-horse.'[32] As that may be, it is difficult *not* to interpret the upright stick positioned between his legs as a phallus. If such an image seems to anticipate Reynolds's subject painting of the link boy with torch in hand, then it also remains distinct from it, insofar as Hogarth's child cannot plausibly be regarded as an erotic object.

One might be tempted to interpret the walking stick as a kind of symbol of displaced sexual potency from father to son; or it could be seen as the unpredictable nature and direction of erotic stimulation. In any event, the satirical content of the print as a whole appears to be tempered, as though the various visual devices and tricks of perspective are employed to reveal the inner tensions of this unremarkable family of the middling sort, realised here in almost documentary terms, as though the spectator has just caught sight of the parents and children on their long walk home. If the late-afternoon bucolic setting is intended to provide a contrast to the domestic circumstances of these Londoners, then the pastoralism cannot be entirely dismissed as a salving aspect which belongs to the family, as much as it provides an instructive contrast to it. The small weeping boy near the picture's centre looks like an early sentimental emblem; yet beyond the print's immediate satirical target of deceptive middle-station probity, the scene suggests a more general observation on the psychological and sexual tensions of family life. And as an image, *Evening* seems to reach beyond its own historical moment, indeed reaches beyond its own satirical remit, to remind us of that Freudian insight from the early twentieth century, that the complexities and contradictions of emotions and desire are manifest in us all from the earliest age.[33]

NOTES

1. See, for example, Hugh Cunningham, *Children and Childhood in Western Society since 1500* (London: Longman, 1995), 54; James Christen Stewart, *The New Child: British Art and the Origins of British Childhood, 1730–1830* (Berkeley: University of California, 1995), 82; Roy Porter, *English Society in the Eighteenth Century* (London: Penguin, 1990), 266–68; and Marcia Pointon, *Hanging the Head: Portaiture and Social Formation* (New Haven: Yale University Press, 1993), 177. Ivy Pinchbeck and Margaret Hewitt offer a more sceptical view on the overall effect of such changes in attitude in their *Children in English Society*, 2 vols. (London: Routledge & Kegan Paul, 1969, 1978), I, 298–312.
2. See J.H. Plumb, 'The New World of Children in Eighteenth-Century England,' *Past and Present* 67 (1975): 64–95; John Brewer 'Childhood Revisited: The Genesis of the Modern Toy,' *History Today* 30 (1980): 32–9; and Sebastian Mitchell, 'But Cast Their Eyes on These Wretched Little Beings: The Innocence and Experience of Children in the Late Eighteenth Century,' *New Formations* 42 (2001): 115–30.
3. For modern discussions on the significance of the passions for notions of social formation in eighteenth-century Britain, see Lawrence E. Klein, *Shaftesbury and the Culture of Politeness: Moral Discourse and Cultural Politics in the Early Eighteenth Century* (Cambridge: Cambridge University Press, 1994); Terry Eagleton, *The Ideology of the Aesthetic* (Oxford: Blackwell, 1990), 31–69; and Juliet Shields, *Sentimental Literature and Anglo–Scottish Identity, 1745–1820* (Cambridge: Cambridge University Press, 2010). Alasdair MacIntyre demonstrates how David Hume recon-

ciles the passions with the requirements of a property-owning society in his *Whose Justice? Which Rationality* (London: Duckworth, 1988), 301–25. David H. Solkin's *Painting for Money: The Visual Arts and the Public Sphere* (New Haven: Yale University Press, 1992) remains an important account of the relationship of feeling to economic circumstances.

4. James Boswell, *London Journal 1762–1763*, ed. Gordon Turnbull (London: Penguin, 2010), 133.

5. For an overview of print collection, display, and storage, see Antony Griffiths, *The Print Before Photography: An Introduction to European Printmaking 1550–1820* (London: British Museum Press, 2016), 411–45.

6. See, for example, Timothy Clayton, *The English Print, 1688–1702* (New Haven: Yale University Press, 1997), 3–25; and Griffiths, *The Print Before Photography*, 9, 70–7, and 223–33.

7. 'Sorrow,' in Samuel Johnson, *Dictionary of the English Language* […], 7th ed., 2 vols., (London: Rivington, 1785), II [n.p].

8. Clayton, *The English Print*, 253.

9. Figures derived on the basis of a survey of the images in David Mannings, *Sir Joshua Reynolds: A Complete Catalogue of his Paintings*, 2 vols. (New Haven: Yale University Press, 2000). Mannings also lists the prints after the Reynolds paintings.

10. Horace Walpole, *Anecdotes of Painting in England [....] Collected by the Late George Vertue*, ed. by Ralph N. Wornum, 3 vols (London: Bohn, 1849), I, p. xvii, n. 2. The quotation is from a note to the advertisement for the fourth edition of the *Anecdotes* in which Walpole uses the picture of Master Crewe as a means of rebutting charges of plagiarism levelled against the artist. Walpole suggests here that the picture is exemplary of Reynolds's style and originality, 'the exuberance of his invention will be the grammar of future painters of portraits.'

11. See Martin Postle, *Sir Joshua Reynolds: The Subject Paintings* (Cambridge: Cambridge University Press), 60–61; and Martin Postle *Angels and Urchins: The Fancy Picture in 18th-Century Art* (London: Daig, 1998), 5.

12. David Mannings, 'Cupid as a Link Boy' and 'Mercury as a Cut Purse,' in *Reynolds*, ed. Nicholas Penny (London: Royal Academy of Arts, 1986), 264–5.

13. M.D. George, *London Life in the Eighteenth Century* (Harmondsworth: Penguin, 1966), 239.

14. Mannings, 'Cupid as a Link Boy' and 'Mercury as a Cut Purse,' 264.

15. Amy Richlin, *Garden of Priapus: Sexuality and Aggression in Roman Humor* (Oxford: Oxford University Press, 1992), 34.

16. The approximate numbers of prints for each artist in the British Museum collection, once duplicates have been removed, are as follows: there are 2000 images by Gillray of which 1200 are unmounted Roys; 1300 by

Rowlandson of which 650 are unmounted Roys; and 620 by Heath of
which 550 are unmounted Roys. These figures were derived by counting
on site and by cross-checking with the British Museum online catalogue.

17. See also Anja Müller's account of unnatural suckling in graphic satire for
political purposes in her *Framing Childhood in Eighteenth-Century
Periodicals and Print* (Aldershot: Ashgate, 2009), 53–60.

18. Mary Eleanor Bowes, *The Confessions of the Countess of Strathmore* (London:
Locke, 1793), B1r. Paragraphs obliquely referring to the conduct of the
Countess of Strathmore began to appear in *The Morning Post*, 23 December
1776. Andrew Robinson Stoney complained about the traducing of her
reputation and subsequent insinuations against him to the paper's editor.
An overview of the dispute and the vitriolic exchange of letters between
both parties was published in *The Morning Post*, 20 January 1777.

19. Vic Gatrell, *City of Laughter: Sex and Satire in Eighteenth-Century London*
(London: Atlantic, 2006), 331–44.

20. Gillray, *Lady Termangant Tinglebum: The Lovely Flagellation* (1795). The
print is revised version of an earlier caricature. Lady Termangant
Tinglebum's victims are supposed to be young women. Only a flagellant's
legs are visible in this caricature.

21. See Diana Donald's discussion of the depiction of aristocratic 'sexual
adventurism' in her *The Age of Caricature: Satirical Prints in the Reign of
George III* (New Haven: Yale University Press, 1996), 100–03.

22. Mary Dorothy George, *Catalogue of Political and Personal Satires:
Preserved in the Department of Prints and Drawings in the British Museum,
Vol. VI, 1784–1792* (London: British Museum Press, 1938), 222.

23. See Tim Clayton and Sheila O'Connell, *Bonaparte and the British: Prints
and Propaganda in the Age of Napoleon* (London: British Museum, 2015),
109–11.

24. See Peter Hunt, *An Introduction to Children's Literature* (Oxford: Oxford
University Press, 1994), 42. For the novel's publication history, see
Jonathan Swift *Gulliver's Travels*, ed. David Womersley (Cambridge:
Cambridge University Press, 2012), ciii, and 647–49. See also David Francis
Taylor's account of Gillray's use of Swift's text against the background of
domestic anxieties, 'Gillray's Gulliver and the 1803 Invasion Scare,' in *The
Afterlives of Eighteenth-Century Fiction*, ed. Daniel Cook and Nicholas
Seager (Cambridge: Cambridge University Press, 2015), 193–211.

25. See John Barrell and Harriet Guest, 'On the Uses of Contradiction:
Economics and Morality in the Eighteenth-Century Longer Poem,' in *The
New Eighteenth Century: Theory, Politics, Literature*, eds. Felicity Nussbaum
and Lara Brown (London: Methuen, 1987), 121–43. See also Sebastian
Mitchell, 'Oliver Goldsmith's *The Deserted Village*: Past, Present and Future,'
English: Journal of the English Association, 55.212 (2006): 123–39.

26. Mark Hallett and Christine Riding, *Hogarth* (London: Tate Publishing, 2006), 14.

27. Figures determined on the basis of a survey of the images in *Hogarth's Graphic Works: First Complete Edition*, 2 vols, ed. Ronald Paulson (New Haven: Yale University Press, 1965).

28. See Paulson, *Hogarth's Graphic Works*, I, 207. On the iconography of Madam Geneva, see Patrick Dillon, *The Much-Lamented Death of Madam Geneva: The Eighteenth-Century Gin Craze* (London: Review, 2003), especially 4–23.

29. Roy Porter, *Bodies Politic: Disease, Death and Doctors in Britain, 1650–1900* (London: Reaktion, 2001), 49.

30. See Paulson, *Hogarth's Graphic Works*, I, 180; Sean Shesgreen, *Engravings by Hogarth* (New York: Dover, 1973), no. 44; and Hallett and Riding, *Hogarth*, 135.

31. David Bindman, *Hogarth and his Times: Serious Comedy* (London: British Museum Press, 1997), 86.

32. Elizabeth Einberg, *William Hogarth: A Complete Catalogue of the Paintings* (New Haven: Yale University Press, 2016), 175.

33. I have in mind Freud's essay on infantile sexuality; see Sigmund Freud, *On Sexuality: Three Essays on the Theory of Sexuality and Other Works*, trans. James Strachey (London: Penguin, 1991), 88–126.

CHAPTER 13

Redefining the Gothic Child: An Educational Experiment?

Jessica R. Evans

Scholars often view Ann Radcliffe (1764–1823) as 'The Great Enchantress' whose novels helped to establish and develop the Gothic mode.[1] As for her private life and beliefs, biographers and critics alike agree that while there is a scarcity of information, it is generally believed that Radcliffe was taught at a female school by Sophia Lee (1750–1824), author of the Gothic novel *The Recess* (1785), and her sister Harriet Lee (1757–1851), both of whom were actively involved in the instruction of children.[2] Radcliffe was known to be a recluse in her adult life. Nevertheless, I argue that she actively participated in the 1790s debates concerning what constituted a proper female education through her writing and employed the Gothic mode as a way of transforming her child characters, including those in adolescence, through their pedagogical upbringing. While I discuss multiple texts, I focus on Radcliffe's *The Mysteries of Udolpho* (1794), which is representative of how women writers during this time used depictions of children as ways of exploring various educational theories.

The link between pedagogy and the Gothic mode may seem unusual to modern-day readers, but the relationship is quite real. Novel reading, especially of Gothic literature with its ties to romance, was controversial.[3]

J. R. Evans (✉)
Columbia State Community College, Columbia, TN, USA
e-mail: jevans23@Columbiastate.edu

A. O'Malley (ed.), *Literary Cultures and Eighteenth-Century Childhoods*, Literary Cultures and Childhoods,
https://doi.org/10.1007/978-3-319-94737-2_13

261

As Jacqueline Pearson observes, 'The argument about women's reading centred on the novel, with novel-reading one of the most contested areas in cultural debate.'[4] Pearson goes on to discuss how Gothic literature in particular played an important role in the controversy over women's reading.[5] Margaret Maxwell points out that 'generally speaking, before the mid-eighteenth century their [children's] recreational reading was the same as that perused by their elders.'[6] In *The Guardian of Education*, Sarah Trimmer (1741–1810) cautions her readers of the dangers of fairy tales and romance, warning against their potentially adverse effects on children.[7] However, it is in writing Gothic literature that Radcliffe deals with topics such as childhood development and the continuance of female education into adulthood. Since girls were usually prepared for their roles within the domestic sphere, they often did not undergo the specialized training that boys would in their adolescent years.[8] Radcliffe, though, provides Emily St. Aubert in *The Mysteries of Udolpho* as an example of a well-educated young woman who furthers her learning outside of her home.

The 1790s saw not only a taste for Gothic novels but also an obsession and ongoing debate over female education.[9] Many women writers published their views on the inadequacies of current teaching methodologies and on what a proper education for girls ought to look like.[10] Most female authors—from the conservative Hannah More (1745–1833) to the radical Mary Wollstonecraft (1759–1797)—viewed childhood as the opportune time to begin one's religious instruction. In *Strictures on the Modern System of Female Education* (1799), More considers education's goal as instilling a devout Christian faith in pupils, especially girls (whose domestic future would be much more limited), to prepare them for the vicissitudes of life.[11] At the most radical end of the spectrum lie Wollstonecraft's *A Vindication of the Rights of Woman* (1792) and her unfinished novel *Maria: or, The Wrongs of Woman* (1798) in which she laments the current state of education with its over-reliance on sensibility as well as its emphasis on an accomplishment-based pedagogy for young girls.[12] As we will see, Radcliffe combines More's religious instruction as a means of comfort and strength with Wollstonecraft's desire for both reason and sensibility to guide a young adolescent through both puberty and adulthood. In Radcliffe, we see a blending of both Rousseauvian values—the pastoral and isolated surroundings for the ideal childhood schooling of Emily St. Aubert—and Lockean concepts—the need for reason as the foundational building block of a proper education.[13]

Radcliffe's decision to emphasize Emily's schooling, then, seems to ask readers to consider *The Mysteries of Udolpho* in the context of contemporary pedagogy. Betty Rizzo lays the groundwork with her brief but important observation of how education is a theme and statement in Gothic novels: 'The standard plot of the female gothic at its best—as in Ann Radcliffe—provided an allegorical road map showing women their dilemma and the way out—through education.'[14] How, then, does Radcliffe, 'The Great Enchantress,' employ the Gothic mode in order to contribute to the 1790s debate on female education through her depictions of childhood?

To answer this question, we must consider the lengthy exposition of the novel where Radcliffe devotes well over 100 pages to describing the adolescent Emily St. Aubert's life with her father and especially their educational tour across France. Radcliffe chooses to begin her novel with a depiction of Monsieur St. Aubert: his preferences, childhood, and choices. The reader soon discovers that St. Aubert prefers the country to the city, benevolence to ambition, and intellectual equality in marriage to marrying for money.[15] St. Aubert loves literature, considering knowledge to be a treasure and 'parental duties' a joy (2). We find out that his library 'was enriched by a collection of the best books in the ancient and modern languages' (2–3). As Emily's father and educator, St. Aubert's background and philosophy on life along with his erudition are significant parts of the curriculum that he shares with his daughter. St. Aubert attempts to mould Emily into the best possible version of both a rational and a sentimental being, and he does so by teaching her lessons on the beauties of nature, the knowledge of literature, and the use of reasoning. The emphasis on St. Aubert's literary knowledge and his preference for picturesque landscapes to city life exemplify Rousseauvian philosophy, while his benevolent attitude is meant to mark him as the ideal educator.

Of course, the ideal instructor must have an exemplary pupil, and St. Aubert's daughter reads frequently, draws, plays music, studies birds and plants, and appreciates the beauty of nature (3). Ann Shteir explains that '[i]n the history of botanical culture, daughters worked alongside their fathers, and girls' botanical interests developed within botanical families.'[16] By teaching Emily botany, St. Aubert follows a more progressive trend of the eighteenth century where girls benefited from learning science (as opposed to the ornamental education of female accomplishments). Although Emily has a 'native genius,' Radcliffe makes it clear that her intellect is still 'assisted by the instructions of Monsieur and Madame St.

Aubert' (3). Emily's pastoral childhood is Rousseauvian in nature, but St. Aubert's emphasis on reason and on the need to control imagination places his pedagogy in the Lockean school as well. Although Madame St. Aubert is clearly a co-educator, Radcliffe is much more concerned with St. Aubert as the primary teacher. The reason for this could be that Radcliffe appears to suggest that fathers should be actively involved in their daughters' schooling (similar to how Locke and Rousseau viewed the importance of the father in a boy's education). Furthermore, by depicting St. Aubert as the primary educator, Radcliffe allows her heroine to receive a more 'masculine' education. Emily benefits from a male instructor instead of an 'academy' for ladies—where superficial accomplishments, such as dancing and etiquette, were the primary focus. In *A Vindication of the Rights of Woman* (1792), Wollstonecraft criticizes the current state of female education, in which 'women are not allowed to have sufficient *strength of mind* to acquire what really deserves the name of virtue.'[17] Radcliffe seems to echo Wollstonecraft's views:

> As she [Emily] advanced in youth, this sensibility gave a pensive tone to her spirits, and a softness to her manner, which added grace to beauty, and rendered her a very interesting object to persons of a congenial disposition. But St. Aubert had too much good sense to prefer a charm to a virtue; and had penetration enough to see, that this charm was too dangerous to its possessor to be allowed the character of a blessing. He endeavoured, therefore, to strengthen her mind; to enure her to habits of self-command; to teach her to reject the first impulse of her feelings, and to look, with cool examination, upon the disappointments he sometimes threw in her way. (5)

Since Radcliffe clearly prefers reason and 'strength of mind' to the susceptibility of emotions or the threat of acute sensibility, her pedagogical values coincide with Wollstonecraft's. Also like Wollstonecraft, Radcliffe distrusts the promotion of charms and superficial accomplishments (for example, grace, beauty, and manners) over the development of intellectual accomplishments (strength of mind, reason, and understanding). Radcliffe considers the emphasis on the superficial as pernicious to women (causing them to be vain and shallow) and as a desperately flawed version of female education.[18] St. Aubert desires Emily to attain this strength of mind and to be able to 'self-command' or, in other words, to take care of herself and use reason to make sense out of disappointments and difficult situations. Again, this coincides with Wollstonecraft, who views herself as a woman who is empowered by reason: 'Thanks to that Being who [...] gave me sufficient strength of mind to dare to exert my own reason, till, becoming dependent only on him for the support of my virtue, I view, with indignation, the mistaken notions that enslave my sex' (49). Emily will need to use her reason to confront her strong sensibilities and overactive imagination. It is her rational and 'masculine' education provided by her father that prepares her for the mysterious and terrifying encounters at Udolpho.

Like the young, affluent men of the eighteenth century, Emily must go on her version of the Grand Tour in order to complete her schooling. Radcliffe's emphasis on Emily's Grand Tour should not be overlooked. With an inclination to travel herself, Radcliffe wrote *A Journey Made in the Summer of 1794* and published it the following year.[19] In *The Mysteries of Udolpho*, Radcliffe incorporates her own interest in travelling as a part of her female protagonist's schooling. She allows Emily to benefit from travelling abroad by coming out of the private sphere of the home into the public sphere, depicting this as an instructional opportunity. She journeys with St. Aubert and her love interest, Valancourt, learning from them as well as sharing her own observations on the nature and landscape that surround them. Emily's continual reflections on what she sees as she travels is a way of her internalizing the educational experience of visiting foreign lands and learning from other cultures.[20] Therefore, Radcliffe boldly gives Emily a cultural experience typically reserved only for young men and shows how Emily is capable of becoming strengthened and improved from such a journey.[21]

Emily's ability to appreciate her Grand Tour and to recognize the beauties of nature also demonstrates her superior taste. Gary Kelly considers Radcliffe's fiction 'novels of description' and claims that 'the emphasis in the descriptive passages is on the heroine's "taste."'[22] However, Emily's excellent 'taste' in the sublimity of nature is part of her schooling. In the first part of the novel, it is taught to her by St. Aubert, and she later applies her lessons to help navigate and survive the precarious situations she finds herself facing. Her taste helps her to distinguish between proper and improper situations as she travels with Montoni to his mansion and he attempts to force her into accepting the marriage offer of Count Morano. Radcliffe's 'novels of descriptions' are about more than just taste; they are novels of education, linking good 'taste' to proper pedagogy that assists Emily in her coming of age. William Stafford asserts: 'Mary Wollstonecraft, Mary Robinson, Charlotte Smith and Ann Radcliffe present sensibility and appreciation of picturesque nature as alternative status-markers, indicators of spiritual superiority which regularly elevate the sensitive and refined woman above the socially superior and classically educated male.'[23] It does not appear as though Emily's classical literary background is lacking at all. Hence, her talent for appreciating nature may illustrate her ability to excel even more in her educational journey.

In fact, Radcliffe may be hinting at Emily's superiority, especially if we consider how Emily and Valancourt share much of the Grand Tour together with the same guide, St. Aubert. Emily stays true to the lessons she learned about appreciating the beauty and sublimity of nature, enabling her to find strength in difficult times (such as when she is practically held captive in Montoni's mansion). Valancourt, on the other hand, distances himself from nature and becomes engrossed in a society of individuals who corrupt his good morals and values. Emily, not Valancourt, becomes the ideal for her readers to emulate. Radcliffe thus implies that Emily is capable of benefiting just as much, if not more, from an educational Grand Tour as a man.

After her Grand Tour, Emily undergoes trials and tests of her mind, fighting the perils of an active imagination. The death of her beloved father and instructor leaves Emily without a protector and forces her to start practising what her father has taught her—how to use philosophy and the love of nature to soothe wounds of grief. According to Margarita Georgieva, 'all gothic children have to deal with loss,'[24] and Emily must suffer the loss of both her mother and father, the separation from her love, Valancourt, and the death of Madame Montoni (St. Aubert's sister). When her father dies, Emily is without a teacher and becomes the graduated pupil, who is not yet ready to become an educator herself. As Emily faces the mental tortures of Udolpho and considers the potential dangers of living under Montoni's 'protection,' Radcliffe makes it clear that Emily must rely on her reason and find strength of mind in order to combat the seductive powers of imagination and sensibility:

> [Emily] greatly feared he [Montoni] had a heart too void of feeling to oppose the perpetration of whatever his interest might suggest .... To these circumstances, which conspired to give her alarm, were now added those thousand nameless terrors, which exist only in active imaginations, and which set reason and examination equally at defiance .... Her heart, as it gave her back the image of Valancourt, mourned in vain regret, but reason soon came with a consolation which, though feeble at first, acquired vigour from reflection. (240)

Looking at this passage from a pedagogical perspective and with an aware-ness of the 1790s debates over female education, we can make several important observations. To begin, Emily fears the heartlessness of Montoni. Clearly, a Gothic heroine, who must be sensitive toward the feelings of others, would be afraid and even threatened by someone who is without sensibility exerting control over her. Radcliffe, like Wollstonecraft, is not opposed to sensibility and seems to desire that her readers agree with Emily that the heartless Montoni is to be feared and, perhaps, even-tually pitied. Nevertheless, too much sensibility is a problem, and a reli-ance on feelings alone is something that neither Radcliffe nor Wollstonecraft desire for women.[25] Emily is terrorized just as much if not more by her own imagination and acute feelings than by the cruelty of Montoni. Emily's 'active imagination,' when given free rein, 'set reason and exami-nation equally at defiance' (240). Emily is not practising what she has learned from St. Aubert's training: the need to use reason to acquire a certain 'strength of mind.' Although her heart is at war with her reason, Emily eventually does rely on her mind along with the powers of reflection to overcome her fears and find a certain amount of peace. Thus, Radcliffe implies that reason, examination, and reflection are the antidotes to overly active imaginations and overpowered sensibility.

Emily also applies her religious faith alongside her study of nature to combat her mental terrors. Radcliffe writes, 'Thus, she [Emily] endeav-oured to amuse her fancy, and was not unsuccessful. [...] She raised her thoughts in prayer, which she felt always most disposed to do, when view-ing the sublimity of nature, and her mind recovered its strength' (242). Emily finds peace and comfort in her faith, and Radcliffe is not alone in including religion within her protagonist's education. During the late eighteenth century, religion was frequently a major aspect of the peda-gogical curriculum for children. Much of Hannah More's argument on education is based on the inculcation of religious instruction.[26] Nevertheless, some writers did not include religion in their pedagogical treatises and, like Richard and Maria Edgeworth with their influential work *Practical Education* (1798), were criticized, typically rather harshly, for the omission, by, among others, Sarah Trimmer in *The Guardian of Education*.[27] We see Emily's connection to religion throughout the novel; she even considers the serenity of life as a nun, and it is in the convent that she finds comfort after the loss of her father. Radcliffe was, most likely, influenced by her own devout religious beliefs, and, as common sense would have it then, a moral education for Radcliffe would be faith based.[28]

Radcliffe allows the reader to infer that any proper education would include religion, yet Emily's childhood does not centre upon attending mass or learning her catechisms. Her schooling resembles what the Edgeworths proposed in *Practical Education*. Radcliffe again blends pedagogical theories together in Emily, creating an educational experiment that withstands even Gothic situations and obstacles.

Typical of the Gothic narrative, Emily is surrounded by mysteries at Udolpho: Who plays the lute? Is Montoni a murderer? What is behind the veil? What is her actual identity? Is she the daughter of the tragic Marchioness?[29] As Andrew Smith and Diana Wallace observe, female writers of Gothic novels tended to offer rational explanations for the seemingly 'supernatural' events in their stories, while male writers, like Matthew Lewis and William Beckford, left supernatural occurrences unexplained.[30] Radcliffe follows this convention of the female Gothic, especially with her resolution of the mysterious black veil in Udolpho. Emily thinks she sees the remains of a murdered person when she lifts the black veil covering a decomposing body, but later on, it is discovered that what Emily had actually uncovered was simply a wax sculpture (662). Radcliffe allows Emily's overactive sensibility to cloud her perceptions, causing Emily more emotional trauma than she would have experienced had she relied on her reason.

Radcliffe's near-obsession with the sublime is well known; that she was influenced by Edmund Burke is another fact.[31] However, her use of the sublime in connection with education has yet to be adequately addressed by literary scholars. Georgieva lays the groundwork for understanding the potential relationship between the sublime and childhood education:

> The idea of the sublime and its relation to the beautiful, the awful and the terrible also had a complex influence on the writing for and about children. Edgeworth considered simplicity as 'a source of the sublime peculiarly suited to children' and noted their 'accuracy of observation,' as well as the 'distinctness of perception' in children and their sincerity, which 'are essential to this species of sublime.' (*Practical Education*, 33:147)[32]

If we take this relation between the child and the sublime a step further, we can see that Radcliffe may actually be connecting the sublime to the child's schooling. Emily's connection to nature starts when she is young, working in the greenhouse or taking excursions in the valley. St. Aubert employs these activities as part of his pedagogy; the sublime can also be found in these instructional exercises. We must not forget Emily's terrifying yet pleasing experience with the flute and poem that occurs during one of her outings in the woodland. The beautiful nature and the mysterious, almost ominous, happenings around her are enlivened by her active imagination. Emily's love of sublime nature starts in childhood, and her connection to and appreciation of the sublime help define her character.

As a *Bildungsroman*, the novel's ending informs the reader about whether the protagonist will benefit from her experiences and become a fully mature and beneficial member of society or whether she will sink under the oppressive circumstances that surround her. Radcliffe gives her long-suffering heroine a much overdue happy ending with Emily marrying her true love Valancourt: '[Emily and Valancourt] were, at length, restored to each other—to the beloved landscapes of their native country,— ... to the pleasures of enlightened society' (672). Valancourt and Emily's homecoming restores them not only to each other but also to the beauty of their homeland. Again, Emily finds happiness in nature, but Radcliffe does not stop there. Emily still desires to improve her mind and live in an 'enlightened society.' She has now successfully overcome her sensibility enough that her feelings enhance her reason and vice versa. Rousseau and Locke are put in harmony with one another. More's religious instruction and Wollstonecraft's liberating concepts come together to depict an idealized vision of the perfectly mature young woman. Emily's education is, therefore, complete, and she can now create her own intellectual society where hearts and minds work together instead of against each other.

Emily transitions from adolescence to adulthood, returning to her childhood home as its mature owner and symbolically taking the place of her parents. Emily and Valancourt enjoy specific characteristics of their new home together at La Vallée—their pedagogical paradise:

> O! how joyful it is to tell of happiness, such as that of Valancourt and Emily; to relate, that, after suffering under the oppression of the vicious and the disdain of the weak, they were, at length, restored to each other—to the beloved *landscapes* of their native country,—to the securest felicity of this life, that of aspiring to *moral* and labouring for *intellectual improvement*—to the pleasures of *enlightened society*, and to the exercise of the *benevolence*, which had always animated their hearts; while the bowers of La Vallée became, once more, the retreat of goodness, wisdom, and domestic blessedness! (672, my italics)

Radcliffe establishes that Emily and Valancourt have escaped oppression. Rizzo, especially, discusses how the Gothic mode depicts the threats of patriarchal tyranny toward women in particular.[33] Emily and Valancourt experience oppression in that they are both denied the right to follow their feelings, yet Emily arguably suffers more since Montoni denies her the agency to apply St. Aubert's instruction. For instance, Emily can easily discern (much better than Montoni) that Count Morano is not a proper match for her; she also correctly realizes the inappropriateness of certain situations Montoni places her in, such as keeping her as his ward even after Madame Montoni has died. Emily is not allowed to act on her observations using the skills she acquired via her schooling. Radcliffe cries out against Emily's physical oppression (held captive in Montoni's mansion) as well as her mental oppression (restricted from applying her education). In contrast, at La Vallée, Emily is free from oppression both intellectually and physically.

Radcliffe emphasizes the characteristics that make La Vallée an educational paradise: appreciation of nature, moral improvement, intellectual development, an enlightened community, and benevolence. As noted earlier, her landscape descriptions that sometimes seem to overwhelm the reader serve as a way of teaching her heroine. In La Vallée, Emily finds a place where she can continue to practise her lessons on nature and its sublimity but also, as can easily be inferred, employ the landscape around her to teach future generations (most likely her own children). In addition to nature, Radcliffe emphasizes both moral and intellectual improvement. For Radcliffe, *moral* would encompass right and wrong, the differences between vice and virtue, and so forth, signifying the development of one's character and reputation, while *intellectual* improvement would emphasize the exercising of a person's understanding and employing the mind.[34] Radcliffe is not alone in her emphasis on improving women's intellectual development. In *A Vindication of the Rights of Woman*, Wollstonecraft desires that women be treated 'like rational creatures, instead of flattering their *fascinating* graces … I wish to persuade women to endeavour to acquire strength, both of mind and body' (13, italics in original). Wollstonecraft wants women of all ages to exercise their understanding and attain strength of mind; objectives Radcliffe shares with her in *The Mysteries of Udolpho*.

This desire to improve the current state of women's education was expressed in the works of other major female writers of the time as well. Elizabeth Inchbald ends her sentimental novel *A Simple Story* (1791) with a clearly didactic message, faulting the tragic heroine's father, Mr. Milner, for not bestowing on his daughter 'A PROPER EDUCATION' (written in upper-case letters on a line of its own).[35] Maria Edgeworth also desired for girls to attain effective instruction that emphasized reason and strength of mind. In her first published work, *Letters for Literary Ladies* (1795), Edgeworth defends young women's rights to be taught literature and how to employ reason. This sentiment stayed with her even to her last work *Helen* (1834), where the protagonist must learn to acquire fortitude and strength of mind in order to obtain a happy ending. Jane Austen implies these lessons as well. For example, in *Pride and Prejudice* (1813), Jane and Elizabeth Bennet exercise their understanding while their younger sisters do not. Elizabeth pleads with Mr. Collins to treat her as a 'rational creature' instead of as 'an elegant female,' seemingly echoing Wollstonecraft from several years earlier.[36] Thus, the vision of La Vallée as a place where moral and intellectual development thrives demonstrates Radcliffe's desire to enter in and identify what constitutes a proper education, for both men and women.

Now that Emily is a fully mature individual, it is her responsibility to become a beneficial member of her community. Emily and Valancourt find themselves amidst 'the pleasures of enlightened society' (672).[37] Emily appears as an equal partner in her marriage with Valancourt, demonstrating the importance of attaining equality in marriage. Before they are married, *he* must live up to *her* standards, or she will renounce him forever. During the 1790s, women writers, like those under discussion, advocated for marriage equality. An unequal match was not only unhappy for the wife and husband but also for the children since it did not set a good example for the next generation. A well-known advocate for sexual equality, Wollstonecraft writes, 'Contending for the rights of woman, my main argument is built on this simple principle, that if she be not prepared by education to become the companion of man, she will stop the progress of knowledge and virtue; for truth must be common to all, or it will be inefficacious with respect to its influence on general practice' (*A Vindication* 4). Though not as bold as Wollstonecraft, Edgeworth also emphasizes equality in marriage. In *Belinda* (1801), Mr. and Mrs. Percival's exemplary marriage is clearly contrasted with Lady Delacour's unhappy and ornamental one.[38] Mrs. Percival is well educated. Both she and her husband teach their children in a setting similar to Radcliffe's La Vallée. Belinda must learn from Lady Delacour's mistake and Mrs. Percival's example in order to reject unfit suitors, like Sir Philip Baddely, and eventually accept a man who is her equal, Clarence Hervey. Like Edgeworth and Wollstonecraft, we can see how Radcliffe adds her voice to the conversation concerning women's equality in marriage.

A society of enlightened individuals offers Emily support as well. When surrounded by moral and intelligent people, she is strengthened in her own intellectual development but also benefits from the sound advice she receives from her husband or other members, who benefit from her advice in turn. The concept of needing a moral, intellectual community is prevalent in the works of Radcliffe's female contemporaries as well. For example, in Edgeworth's *Belinda*, the eponymous protagonist must distinguish between the corrupting company of Harriet Freke and the improving community of Mr. and Mrs. Percival. Likewise, in *A Vindication of the Rights of Woman*, Wollstonecraft vehemently desires for women to improve their social status and become equal members of that society instead of belonging to a group of 'mindless' women. By belonging to an educated society, Emily and Valancourt will not only personally benefit from a support system but will also bring up their future children within this society of moral thinkers.

As part of this community, Emily must exercise her knowledge and sentiment to help those in need. La Vallée becomes a place where benevolence flourishes.[39] Emily and Valancourt's generous and kind hearts are demonstrated throughout the novel. Valancourt's monetary gift to a poor woman and her family that he meets on his journey with Emily and St. Aubert is an excellent example of a type of sensibility that Emily desires in a spouse. Emily's kindness toward her aunt and her natural inclination to eschew monetary gain in favour of familial love and duty is another example. It is not surprising that Emily and Valancourt will continue to offer benevolence at La Vallée.

Radcliffe is not alone in assigning benevolence or generosity as a necessary pedagogical practice. In fact, throughout the eighteenth century, writers emphasized and promoted generosity as a trait to be emulated by both adults and children alike. Andrew O'Malley observes that '[t]he emphasis on charity in children's books of the period coincides with attempts by the middle classes to disrupt traditional patronage, aristocratic dispensing of monies, and state sponsored charities with individually motivated acts of giving.'[40] In her instructional stories, Edgeworth frequently depicts the kindness and generosity of children in a positive light, and she notably would allow child characters to be capable of even helping adults.

Mary V. Jackson claims, 'Maria Edgeworth respected children enough to wish not to lie to them or distort the truth "for their own good" … in cases where the upper orders committed wrongs. Among Maria's tales for the very young are several that expose the greed, cruelty, or thoughtlessness of the respectable and affluent.'[41] Edgeworth's desire to teach young children to be benevolent at a young age can be seen clearly in her story 'The Birth-Day Present.' Laura, a young girl, sees a child's efforts at weaving lace to earn money destroyed by an idle footman, and Laura proves herself to be kind, humble, and benevolent by giving her own money to help the child (without ever waiting to be thanked for her generosity). Her sister Rosamond learns from Laura that true generosity and kindness are more important than external beauty.[42] In 'Simple Susan,' the eponymous child protagonist's charity toward others is what enables her to save her own family.[43] Radcliffe, like many writers for children in the eighteenth century, saw benevolence as a necessary characteristic to instill in a child through schooling.

Some scholars have questioned whether Emily learns anything at all. Richard S. Albright, for example, writes, 'It is easy to see why the novel has so often been read as a story of an inner journey—or perhaps not a journey at all, for "journey" implies "progress" and whether any occurs in *Udolpho* is debatable—but read at least as a narrative of inner space.'[44] Likewise, David Durant argues against reading Radcliffe's fiction as novels of education and claims that they should be considered as conservative.[45] He even asserts that Emily never truly matures and remains instead a child.[46] However, Emily does become a fully mature adult. She receives a rational-based education that assists her on the Grand Tour as well as in the Gothic situations that surround her. Emily applies her education to overcome obstacles and eventually becomes an ideal educator herself. *The Mysteries of Udolpho* is a *Bildungsroman,* and it is not a 'conservative gothic' but a complex mixture of both conservative and liberal values posited as the perfect blend for educating girls. There is most certainly progress: Emily's educational journey. It is an inner journey (developing Emily's mind), but it can be seen through her actions and thoughts. Emily must learn to conquer her fears, solve mysteries, and become the rational and sentimental adult that her father hoped she would be. Her story shows her 'coming of age' and the progress she makes toward replacing her parents as intellectual pedagogues. With this case study of *The Mysteries of Udolpho*, we see that Radcliffe is not simply writing and defining a Gothic narrative, but she is also writing and defining what she believes constitutes proper female pedagogy through her depiction of Emily as a Gothic child of education.

Many writers found the Gothic mode, or at least its conventions, an innovative way to bring their primary concerns over education into the period's ongoing conversation. Persecuted heroines, patriarchal villains, limited resources, and physical and psychological dangers appear in a vast array of novels from Frances Burney's *Evelina* (1778) and *Cecilia* (1782) to Mary Wollstonecraft's *Maria: or, The Wrongs of Woman* (1798) and Mary Hays's *The Victim of Prejudice* (1799).[47] Gothic conventions find their way into the narrative structure, illustrating the plights of women's situation indeed. Looking at Radcliffe's *The Mysteries of Udolpho* as an exemplary text shows how approaching these novels within a pedagogical perspective associated with the 'coming of age' narrative can bring a better understanding of both the text itself and the culture surrounding its publication.

Like many eighteenth-century writers, Radcliffe makes it clear that she has attached a moral to her novel.[48]

> O! useful may it be to have shewn, that, though the vicious can sometimes pour affliction upon the good, their power is transient and their punishment certain; and that innocence, though oppressed by injustice; shall, supported by patience, finally triumph over misfortune! And, if the weak hand, that has recorded this tale, has, by its scenes, beguiled the mourner of one hour of sorrow, or, by its moral, taught him to sustain it—the effort, however humble, has not been in vain, nor is the writer unrewarded. (672)

Radcliffe's stated moral, that evil will be punished and good will prevail, is joined by a plea for the importance of a rational female education. In this, Radcliffe's Gothic tale joins, perhaps unexpectedly, the efforts of Wollstonecraft's *A Vindication of the Rights of Woman*, More's *Strictures on the Modern System of Female Education*, Edgeworth's *Letters for Literary Ladies*, and others. Read through the lens of the period's debates over female education, the story of Gothic child Emily St. Aubert reveals how a properly educated girl can undertake many challenges and arise a victorious woman if given the intellectual training that is required.[49]

NOTES

1. See Rictor Norton, *Mistress of Udolpho: The Life of Ann Radcliffe* (London: Leicester University Press, 1999); Deborah D. Rogers, *Ann Radcliffe: A Bio-Bibliography* (Westport, Conn.: Greenwood Press, 1996); Robert Miles, *Ann Radcliffe: The Great Enchantress* (Manchester: Manchester University Press, 1995); and Aline Grant, *Ann Radcliffe: A Biography* (Denver: A. Swallow, 1951).
2. See Rebecca Garwood on 'Sophia Lee (1750–1824) and Harriet Lee (1757–1851)' (Chawton House Library).
3. See also Jacqueline Pearson, *Women's Reading in Britain, 1750–1835: A Dangerous Recreation*, (Cambridge University Press, 1999).
4. Jacqueline Pearson, *Women's Reading in Britain, 1750–1835*, 196.
5. Ibid., 100.
6. Margaret Maxwell, 'The Perils of the Imagination: Pre-Victorian Children's Literature and the Critics,' (*Children's Literature in Education* 5.1 [1974]: 45).
7. Sarah Trimmer, ed. *The Guardian of Education*, 5 vols. (London: J. Johnson, 1801–1805). See also Andrew O'Malley's *The Making of the Modern Child* (New York: Routledge, 2003) and M. O. Grenby's '"A Conservative Woman Doing Radical Things": Sarah Trimmer and *The Guardian of Education*,' in *Culturing the Child: 1690–1914*, ed. Donelle Ruwe (Lanham, MD: The Children's Literature Association and The Scarecrow Press, INC., 2005).
8. See Andrew O'Malley, *The Making of the Modern Child*, (Routledge, 2003).
9. For other discussions and critical approaches to Gothic novels, see Eve Kosofsky Sedgwick *The Coherence of Gothic Conventions* (New York: Methuen, 1986); Jerrold E. Hogle, ed., *A Cambridge Companion to Gothic Fiction* (Cambridge: Cambridge University Press, 2002); Terry Castle, *The Female Thermometer: Eighteenth-Century Culture and the Invention of the Uncanny* (New York: Oxford University Press, 1995); Diana Wallace and Andrew Smith, *The Female Gothic: New Directions* (New York: Palgrave Macmillan, 2009); Rictor Norton, ed., *Gothic Readings: The First Wave, 1764–1840* (London: Leicester University Press, 2000); Diane Long Hoeveler, *Gothic Feminism: The Professionalization of Gender from Charlotte Smith to the Brontës* (University Park, PA: Pennsylvania State University Press, 1998); Dale Spender, *Mothers of the Novel: 100 Good Women Writers Before Jane Austen* (London: Pandora, 1986); Nelson C. Smith, 'Sense, Sensibility, and Ann Radcliffe,' *Studies in English Literature, 1500–1900* 13, no. 4 (1973): 577–590; Yael Shapira, 'Where The Bodies Are Hidden: Ann Radcliffe's 'Delicate' Gothic,' *Eighteenth-Century Fiction* 18, no. 4 (2006):

453–76; and Patricia Whiting, 'Literal and Literary Representations of the Family in *The Mysteries of Udolpho*,' *Eighteenth-Century Fiction* 8, no. 4 (July 1996): 485–501.

10. Catharine Macaulay (1731–1791) even calls it an 'absurd notion' to educate girls differently than boys. See Catharine Macaulay, *Letters on education. With observations on religious and metaphysical subjects.* (London: printed for C. Dilly in the Poultry, 1790). Likewise, Wollstonecraft's admirer Mary Hays (1759–1843) decries the belief of women's inferiority, arguing for changes to women's education. See Eleanor Ty's 'Introduction' to *The Victim of Prejudice*, xv. (Peterborough, ON: Broadview Press, 1998).

11. Hannah More, *Strictures on the Modern System of Female Education*, 1799 (Oxford: Woodstock Books, 1995).

12. Mary Wollstonecraft, *A Vindication of the Rights of Woman*, 1792, Ed. Miriam Brody (London: Penguin, 2004); and *Maria: or, The Wrongs of Woman*, 1798 (New York: Norton, 1975).

13. John Locke, *Some Thoughts Concerning Education*, (London: printed for A and J. Churchill, at the Black Swan in Pater-Noster-Row, 1705); Jean-Jacques Rousseau, *Emile or On Education*, 1762, trans. and ed. Allan Bloom (New York: Basic Books, 1979). Margarita Georgieva also points this out in *The Gothic Child* (London: Palgrave Macmillan, 2013), 79: 'Similarly, Radcliffe's *Udolpho* (1794), Roche's *Clermont* (1798), and Crandolph's *Mysterious Hand* (1811) are all about fathers whose chief employment is teaching their daughters in a countryside setting using a model inspired by a combination of Lockean and Rousseauvian ideas of education.'

14. Betty Rizzo, 'Renegotiating the Gothic,' *Revising Women: Eighteenth-Century 'Women's Fiction' and Social Engagement*, ed. Paula R. Backscheider (Baltimore: The Johns Hopkins University Press, 2000), 62. See also Margarita Georgieva, *The Gothic Child* (London: Palgrave Macmillan, 2013). While not explicitly concerned with issues of education, Margarita Georgieva's discussion of the characteristics of the Gothic child is worth noting here: the child's exposure to the death of a loved one, the child's subjection to an adult's experiments at raising him or her, the impact of parental figures, the role of mystery, and the relation to sublimity. Miriam Leranbaum also recognizes that education plays an important part in this novel. See Miriam Leranbaum, "Mistresses of Orthodoxy': Education in the Lives and Writing of Late Eighteenth-Century English Women Writers,' *Proceedings of the American Philosophical Society* 121, no. 4 (Aug. 1977): 281–301, 300.

15. Ann Radcliffe, *The Mysteries of Udolpho*. 1794. (Oxford: Oxford University Press, 1998), 1–2. References are to this edition, and will appear parenthetically.

16. Ann B. Shteir, *Cultivating Women: Cultivating Science*, (Johns Hopkins University Press, 1996), 4.
17. Mary Wollstonecraft. *A Vindication of the Rights of Woman*. 1792. ed. Miriam Brody. (London: Penguin, 2004), 28 (my italics). Parenthetical references are to this edition.
18. The need for a rational heroine who uses logic to dispel 'supernatural' events and provide logical explanations is one of the trademarks of Maria Edgeworth's protagonist in *Belinda* (1801). See Robert Miles's *Radcliffe: The Great Enchantress* for a discussion of how Radcliffe uses the explanations of the supernatural. Miles is interested in the sensibility of the heroine as well.
19. Ann Radcliffe, *A journey made in the summer of 1794, through Holland and the western frontier of Germany, with a return down the Rhine: to which are added, observations during a tour of the lakes of Lancashire, Westmoreland, and Cumberland*. 1795.
20. See Jayne Elizabeth Lewis, "No Colour of Language': Radcliffe's Aesthetic Unbound,' *Eighteenth-Century Studies*, 39, no. 3 (2006): 377–90. Lewis provides an application of aesthetic and linguistic theories to Radcliffe's descriptions.
21. In Jean-Jacques Rousseau's *Emile* (1762), the eponymous protagonist must wait to marry his true love until he completes his two-year-long Grand Tour.
22. Gary Kelly, *English Fiction of the Romantic Period 1789–1830* (London: Longman, 1990), 52.
23. William Stafford, 'The Gender of the Place: Building and Landscape in Women-Authored Texts in England of the 1790s,' *Transactions of the Royal Historical Society* 13 (2003): 317–318.
24. Margarita Georgieva, *The Gothic Child* (London: Palgrave Macmillan, 2013), 89.
25. In 'Renegotiating the Gothic,' Betty Rizzo makes a similar observation: 'Writers like Radcliffe and Wollstonecraft, who may be seen as suspicious of sensibility in women, are, in fact, only suspicious of sensibility unregulated by reason, and rightfully so' (99). For an excellent discussion on reason and sensibility (with special attention to Radcliffe's other well-known Gothic novel *The Italian*), see the rest of Rizzo's essay. Dale Spender's *Mothers of the Novel* also makes many brief but valid observations of Radcliffe's preference for both reason and sensibility. However, I am much more concerned with tying reason and sensibility with Emily's education and contextualizing that within the 1790s, looking at Emily as a Gothic child of education.
26. See also Patricia Demers, *The World of Hannah More*, (Lexington: University Press of Kentucky, 1996).

27. Maria and Richard Edgeworth, *Practical Education*, 1798 (London: Pickering & Chatto, 2003), 282–83. See also Sarah Trimmer, ed. *The Guardian of Education*, 5 vols. (London: J. Johnson, 1801–1805).

28. See Robert J. Mayhew, 'Latitudinarianism and the Novels of Ann Radcliffe,' *Texas Studies in Literature and Language* 44, no. 3 (2002): 273–301. Mayhew provides an in-depth look at Radcliffe's religious educational background. In the article, Mayhew posits that '[t]he element of Radcliffe's 'old-fashioned society' that is the key to her writing lies in her religious beliefs. It would appear that Radcliffe was imbued with the tenets of the so-called Latitudinarian school of Anglicans' (274). Mayhew attempts to tie in the landscape descriptions in Radcliffe's novels with the Latitudinarian connection to nature and its relation to proving the existence of God. Mayhew also discusses the Latitudinarian belief in reason and a distrust of the supernatural. See also Rictor Norton's *Mistress of Udolpho: The Life of Ann Radcliffe* where he argues that Radcliffe may actually be more of a Unitarian Dissenter than a strictly religious Anglican, thereby connecting her with more radical female contemporaries, such as Wollstonecraft, Inchbald, and Hays.

29. See Georgieva's last chapter 'The Sublime Child' from *The Gothic Child* (2013).

30. See Diana Wallace and Andrew Smith, *The Female Gothic: New Directions* (New York: Palgrave Macmillan, 2009).

31. See Edmund Burke, *A Philosophical Enquiry into the Origin of Our Ideas of the Sublime and Beautiful* (1757) and even his *Reflections on the Revolution of France* (1790). Also, see Bonamy Dobrée, who claims that 'Radcliffe's debt to Burke is profound' (*The Mysteries of Udolpho*, Oxford: Oxford University Press, 1998, 675).

32. Georgieva, *The Gothic Child*, 191.

33. See Rizzo, 'Renegotiating the Gothic.'

34. According to Samuel Johnson's *Dictionary*, *moral* was typically defined as '1. Relating to the practice of men towards each other, as it may be virtuous or criminal; good or bad ... 2. Reasoning or instructing with regard to vice and virtue ... 3. Popular; customary; such as is known or admitted in the general business of life,' Samuel Johnson, *A Dictionary of the English Language*, vol. 2, London: printed for J. F. and C. Rivington, L. Davis, T. Payne and Son, et al., 1785,150. *Moral* could also be used to distance humans from physical influences or differentiate themselves from animals. See Jenny Davidson, *Breeding: A Partial History of the Eighteenth Century* (New York: Columbia UP, 2009), especially 96. Also according to Johnson's *Dictionary*, *intellectual* as an adjective could be defined as '1. Relating to the understanding; belonging to the mind; transacted by the understanding ... 2. Mental; comprising the faculty of understanding;

belonging to the mind ... 3. Ideal; perceived by the intellect, not the senses ... 4. Having the power of understanding,' 1068. Emily had to continually exercise her understanding throughout her journey, and it is this intellectual improvement that would most likely be referenced and promoted as a necessary part of female pedagogy.

35. Elizabeth Inchbald, *A Simple Story*, (Oxford: Oxford University Press, 2009), 338.

36. Jane Austen, *Pride and Prejudice*, (Oxford: Oxford University Press, 2008), 83.

37. Johnson's *Dictionary* defines *enlighten* as '1. To illuminate; to supply with light ... 2. To quicken in the faculty of vision ... 3. To instruct; to furnish with the increase of knowledge,' 698–99. It is interesting to note that when Emily becomes part of this enlightened society, she is freed from superstition; she has learned her lesson and prefers a rational outlook and the company of others who share this outlook as well.

38. Maria Edgeworth, *Belinda*. 1802. (Oxford: Oxford University Press, 1999).

39. Johnson's *Dictionary* defines *benevolence* as '1. Disposition to do good; kindness; charity; good will,' 247.

40. Andrew O'Malley, *The Making of the Modern Child*, 125.

41. Mary V. Jackson, *Engines of Instruction, Mischief and Magic: Children's Literature in England from Its Beginnings to 1839* (Lincoln: University of Nebraska Press, 1989), 163.

42. Maria Edgeworth, 'The Birth-Day Present,' *The Norton Anthology of Children's Literature*, ed. Jack Zipes et al. (New York: W. W. Norton & Co., 2005), 2111–21.

43. Maria Edgeworth, 'Simple Susan,' *The Parent's Assistant* (London: Pickering & Chatto, 2003).

44. Richard S. Albright, 'No Time Like the Present: *The Mysteries of Udolpho*,' *Journal for Early Modern Cultural Studies* 5, no. 1 (2005): 49–75, 53.

45. David Durant, 'Anne Radcliffe and the Conservative Gothic,' *Studies in English Literature, 1500–1900* 22, no. 3 (1982): 519–530, 519–520.

46. David Durant, 'Anne Radcliffe and the Conservative Gothic,' 528.

47. Frances Burney, *Cecilia, or Memoirs of an Heiress*. 1782. (Oxford: Oxford University Press, 2009) and *Evelina*. 1779, 2nd ed., ed. Susan Kubica Howard, (Toronto: Broadview, 2000). Mary Hays, *The Victim of Prejudice*. 1799. (Peterborough, ON: Broadview Press, 1998).

48. In *Belinda* (1801), Edgeworth ends by specifically challenging her readers to figure out the moral.

49. I would like to thank Lisa Zunshine, Andrew O'Malley, Alfred Lutz, and Judith Prats for their feedback and encouragement through the various stages of this work.

CHAPTER 14

Lemuel Haynes and 'Little Adults': Race and the Prehistory of Childhood in Early New England

Jennifer Thorn

Philip Greven has described the Congregational minister, theologian, and writer Jonathan Edwards as 'the most articulate rationalizer and defender of eternal punishment in American history,' and Edwards's writings abound in evidence both of this view and of the steady severity with which he applied his central truth, original sin, to his society's thinking about children.[1] 'As innocent as children seem to be to us, yet, if they are out of Christ, they are not so in God's sight, but are young vipers, and are infinitely more hateful than vipers,' Edwards affirms in *Some Thoughts Concerning the Present Revival of Religion in New England* (1742).[2] In that work, Edwards defended the Great Awakening of the 1730s and 1740s, in which he was a central figure, against critics whose rejection of the legitimacy of the region's religious revivals evinces an unease that is not unlike Greven's with Edwards's readiness to preach hellfire to children. The chapter 'Ministers blamed for speaking terror to those who are already under great terrors,' in which Edwards's (in)famous remark about child-vipers appears, steadily and vividly presents the peril of damnation as the

J. Thorn (✉)
Saint Anselm College, Manchester, NH, USA
e-mail: jthorn@anselm.edu

© The Author(s) 2018   281
A. O'Malley (ed.), *Literary Cultures and Eighteenth-Century Childhoods*, Literary Cultures and Childhoods,
https://doi.org/10.1007/978-3-319-94737-2_14

inescapable condition of both children and adults. But, at the same time, this insistence on the common vulnerability of all people has a levelling potential: all people—regardless of age, gender, race, class, or even the religion into which they are born—are doomed to burn unless they receive God's grace.[3] Edwards does not speak gently to children, instead condemning as negligent those who would shield children from the threat of damnation. 'Why should we conceal the truth from them? Will those children that have been dealt tenderly with, in this respect, and lived and died insensible of it, till they come to feel it in hell, ever thank parents, and others, for their tenderness, in not letting them know what they were in danger of?,' he writes—a remark that interestingly carries a rationale not only for the cruelty that Edwards's critics see but also for the potential acceptance of pious children's superiority to impious adults, of children's right to meet to pray and talk apart from adults, and of the rhetorical authority of child preachers.[4]

Edwards's subordination of the hierarchical relationship of adult and child to that of those who are 'in Christ' and 'out of Christ' rhetorically replaces a hierarchy of the letter with one of the spirit. The levelling tendency of making original sin the linchpin of social organization is also implied by Edwards's posthumously published *The Christian Doctrine of Original Sin Defended* (1758). '[A]ll which are in Christ … have the benefit of his obedience,' Edwards writes: the souls of all of the saved, regardless of the social rank, ethnicity, age, or gender of their material bodies, are dissolved in the shared *corpus mysticum* of Christ, in which there is no difference. And, as correlate, 'all that are in Adam have the sorrowful fruit of his disobedience.'[5] Edwards draws back from the radical potential of this view, using Indians as a test case. '[W]ill any pretend, that all mankind have actually been partakers of this new fund of light?,' he asks. His tone implies his sense of the obviousness of his next point: the 'many millions of Indians, on the American side of the globe' could not receive these 'benefits' before Christian Europeans arrived on the scene.[6] But even here, the tension Edwards evinces between racialized bodies in and out of Europe and that of tainted human nature affirms the primacy of the latter.

This chapter examines an important case of the unintended and short-lived consequences of the Puritan non-differentiation of childhood and adulthood for early New England's theory and practice of racial differentiation and inclusion. Placing the life and writings of the Congregational minister and one-time pauper Lemuel Haynes in a continuum with

Calvinist works that preceded his own, the chapter describes a kind of loophole implied by the Puritan call for submission to God above all things, one that enabled Haynes's rise to social prominence; his 1788 placement in the West Parish Congregational Church of Rutland, Vermont, made him the first black pastor of an all-white congregation in America. Haynes' childhood shows the real-world levelling potential of the Calvinist emphasis on original sin; he was readily seen by his neighbours in Granville, Connecticut, as a pious child of a familiar, even formulaic, kind, sincerely warning children and adults alike of the always-imminent possibility of damnation, a piety that indirectly led to remarkable social mobility—education, ordination, and leadership of an all-white church.[7] His legibility as pious, that is, enabled a legibility as 'child' that might otherwise have been denied him.

The importance of Haynes's biography and writings to the history of American childhood is at odds with the sternly anti-levelling import of his writings as a pious adult and his conservative practice as a father and minister, a seeming contradiction that deepens the significance to the field of American childhood studies. Haynes himself could value his own ardent self-subordination to God as a sinner only as a response to original sin; he could not consciously value its enabling of a crack in New England's racial biases to let him rise, write, preach, and lead. Haynes's life and writings help us grapple with the instability, fragility, and imbrication of eighteenth-century hierarchies of age and race, a fluidity shut down in the early nineteenth century by the hardening of ideas about both race and childhood. It was in this later era, in 1818, that the white congregation he had served for 30 years asked him to leave. Though the reason for this removal was allegedly doctrinal differences, it is likely that it also reflected, if indirectly, the changed climate regarding race, religion, and childhood. As original sin lost its grip on mainline Protestantism, the possibility of rhetorically and materially empowering child preachers faded; in nineteenth-century America, 'children' would serve different purposes in relation to the conceptualization of goodness and evil, innocence and guilt.

Describing the methodological challenges posed by Puritan elegies, the themes and form of which are not easily accessed via traditional aesthetics, Jeffrey Hammond warns against 'the literary historian's chief occupational hazard: a sense of superiority to the people whose writings are providing his or her livelihood,' a hazard best countered, in his view, by 'a rigorous effort to understand and empathize with the people who inhabited that culture.'[8] The role of original sin in the attitudes toward children of seventeenth-century Puritans and their eighteenth-century evangelical heirs requires just this rigour and empathy, for understandings of children's place in social hierarchy rested upon this belief and its sometimes paradoxical implications. I will suggest here, first, the importance of attending to original sin and the prospect of damnation as the conceptual foundation for the reciprocal duties enjoined upon social superiors and inferiors in Puritan society. Such translation of the assumption of universal spiritual frailty into identities of race, class, gender, and age was fraught and, especially in the middle decades of the eighteenth century, subject to reinterpretations of the Fifth Commandment, mandating children's subordination to their parents, that can seem surprising today.

Puritans understood original sin not as inherent in individuals' identities but as a dire condition inescapably afflicting all humanity that required, so to speak, salvific dissolution in the shared *corpus mysticum* of Christ. This shared affliction made the state of individual souls a shared and, at least rhetorically, generic responsibility of all. That is, Puritan readings, and Great Awakening re-readings, of original sin drew from the assumption of a generic, damned human nature the demand that all sinners both act to save others and open themselves to others' efforts to save them. This model of human nature and sociality tied the identity of social superiors very closely to their inferiors in that the credibility of their claims to be Christian and their hopes of avoiding hell depended both on their recognition that they shared a corrupt human nature with their dependents and on their use of their privilege to protect dependents from damnation.

If this rhetorical linkage of social superiors and inferiors in some ways effaced distinctions between them, so much more so did the loophole opened by the acknowledgement that spiritual hierarchy was not the equivalent of, and mattered much more than, social hierarchy. This loophole meant that social inferiors—including children and 'Negroes,' the groups of dependents included in eighteenth-century understandings of 'family' that are under scrutiny in this chapter—could be recognized, and justified, as spiritual superiors to their social betters. Jonathan Edwards did not mince words as he spoke to families about what prioritizing salvation might, and should, mean. The social position of householder did not guarantee his worthiness to be obeyed, Edwards wrote in *Thoughts on the Revival*: 'For unconverted parents are as likely to poison the souls of their family in their manner of training them up, as unconverted ministers are to poison their people.'[9] For this reason, pious children of impious parents should not be faulted for 'pray[ing] openly that [their] mother[s] and father[s] may either be converted, or taken away and sent to hell quickly, before their guilt is greater.'[10] The moral danger posed by unconverted heads of household to their dependents is so great that 'it would be well for all mankind were they dead.'[11]

Children were not the only dependents in households requiring religious instruction; as Harry Stout notes, after the 1620 founding of Plymouth and the 1630 founding of the Massachusetts Bay Colony, all unattached newcomers to New England were required to affiliate themselves with a family, through which they would receive religious instruction.[12] Most towns required household catechizing by law; many wrote their own catechisms (often largely adapted from others). This emphasis on family as site of religious instruction and social order persisted into the eighteenth century, as did the legal definition of 'family' as a household led by a master and mistress, including all hired servants, indentured servants, slaves, and apprentices. In 1706, Cotton Mather, the prolific Puritan minister and writer, of the same generation as Jonathan Edwards's minister-father, Timothy Edwards, published a pamphlet that figures prominently in recent accounts of early New England 'family slavery.'[13] These analyses note that 'The Negro Christianized: An Essay to Excite and Assist that Good Work, the Instruction of Negro-Servants in New England' counters racial determinism in its rejection of the 'Brutish insinuation' that 'Negroes' lack 'Rational Souls' even as it unquestioningly accepts that slavery is fully compatible with church and civil law.[14] In making this argument, 'The Negro Christianized' also reveals the imbrication of the identities of both 'Negro-Servants' and 'Householders' in terms that both do and don't single out 'Negro-Servants' as a distinctive category of the dependents over whom 'Householders' presided.

The reality of original sin, the threat of damnation, binds the two groups, Mather tells his audience: 'uninstructed Negroes' will haunt those masters who left them ignorant and unsaved, 'summoning [them] to answer before the Tribunal of God, for suffering them to perish.'[15] Salvation cannot be achieved in isolation: 'If you withhold Knowledge from your Black People, they will be Destroy'd' and 'their Destruction will be very much at your Doors; you must answer for it.'[16] Salvation requires not only passive avoidance of sin but active protection of all vulnerable dependents: 'if you use no means to save that Soul, thy Soul shall certainly smart for it' (18). Unconverted slaves, servants, apprentices, and children have the same power to condemn the householder to eternal damnation because their spiritual state is taken as reflective not of their individual actions but of the householder's acceptance of his duty toward them. 'Are they worthy to be called Christians, who are content tho' a part of their Families remain Heathen?': though Mather speaks here explicitly of 'Negro-Servants,' he could as well be speaking of children (5). Dependents are thus stripped not of responsibility for their own actions, but of the credit or blame that their actions might elicit. If householders' children, or their 'well-instructed and well-dispos'd English servants' help catechize 'Negro-Servants,' that virtue reflects only upon their father, just as does the blame for such servants' impiety or bad behaviour (29, 22). Mather goes so far as to ask his slaveholding audience to imagine their slaves in peril of (spiritual) death as if they were 'crying to you, in terms like those of the Child whom a Lion was running away withal; Help! Help! I am yet alive!' (15).

The entangling of the fates of superiors and inferiors evident in *The Negro Christianized* resembles the Puritan explanations for dependents of the Fifth Commandment in the abstraction of the duty of deference owed to all according to their places. In the section of catechism included in *The New England Primer*, the explanation of the Fifth Commandment that children (and servants, slaves, and apprentices) learning to read would have recited repeatedly states that 'The fifth commandment requireth the preserving the honour, and performing the duties belonging to every one in their several places and relations, as superiors, inferiors, or equals.'[17] This gloss on filial piety in a sense makes everyone 'a child' owing appropriate behaviour to social superiors and inferiors; 'every one,' including the fledgling reader, is owed some kind of 'honour.' Cotton Mather explained the Fifth Commandment both as part of the catechism in *The Negro Christianized* and in the collection of pious children's holy deaths that he added to a popular English children's book imported into New England beginning in the 1670s. James Janeway's *A Token for Children, Being an Exact Account of the Conversion, Holy and Exemplary Lives and Joyful Deaths of Several Young Children*, first printed in two parts in London in 1671 and 1672, offered its readers accounts of 13 pious children who, in the 1650s, had experienced spiritual crisis and resolution, positively influenced parents and peers, and died dramatically holy deaths. For its first New England printing in 1700, Cotton Mather anonymously added 'modern' accounts of children's piety and death, in the 1680s through the 1720s, in towns in Massachusetts including Scituate, Salem, and Southold. Here, Mather's rhyming gloss on the fifth and sixth commandments—requiring filial piety and forbidding murder—leaves quite a lot of room for interpretation:

> In their *Fit places*, every one,
> I should with all *Fit Honours* own.
> That *Life* none may unjustly Loose,
> Means I should all with *Kindness* use.[18]

What exactly is the letter of behaviour that would let a child or dependent perform the spirit of the law urged here? The answer given by the book in which this verse appears would seem to involve choosing obedience to God over obedience to parents and social authorities. Indeed, in Janeway's *Token*, as in the new *Token* that Mather added to it, children would seem to display '*Kindness*' sometimes by telling unconverted adult neighbours that they will burn in hell and weeping copiously in front of siblings who have not yet found God, to express their mortal concern for their souls. Obedience becomes a mandate for disobedience, of a circumscribed kind. Mather's gloss on the Fifth Commandment in *The Negro Christianized* rephrases it so as to affirm the imperative of black servants' and slaves' obedience of their masters—and also leaves unparticularized the actions by which the deference regarded to all people would be shown. Mather states the Fifth Commandment simply as 'Honour thy Father and Mother' (with a terrible oblivion, overlooking the ways that New England's labour practices and its particular practices of slaveholding obstructed and distorted black family life) and explicates it thus: 'I must show all due Respect unto Every One; and if I have a Master or Mistress, I must be very dutiful unto them.'[19] Thus both of Mather's explanations of the Fifth Commandment do not particularize what is meant by 'due Respect,' what are the 'Fit places' that 'every one' rightly inhabits.

With the Bible, Janeway's *Token for Children* was the bestselling book in seventeenth-century New England; it sold steadily well into the nineteenth century. Though its title, like that of the *Token for the Children of New-England* that Mather wrote anonymously and had bound with it from 1700, implies an audience of children, many of the celebratory biographies state directly their value to adults. Thus in Janeway's *Token*, the description of Susannah Bicks notes that 'the power and eminency of religion did shine in her so clearly' that she 'may well be proposed as a pattern not only to children, but to persons of riper years;' and in Mather's new *Token*, 'grown up people might learn and take example from' Elizabeth

Butcher.[20] Gillian Avery explains the appeal of the two *Tokens* in terms of both content and form. Not only did these stories feature child protagonists for 'the first time … in any literary work'; 'in Janeway were thirteen children manifestly more holy than their elders, some of them as young as five years old, gloriously holding the stage. And there was dialogue and domestic detail, too.'[21] This mid-seventeenth-century and early-eighteenth-century approval of the potential fitness of pious children to minister to less pious adults is extended in Jonathan Edwards's strong mid-eighteenth-century response, in *Thoughts on the Revival of Religion in New England* (1742), to those who would ban children from forming their own prayer meetings, seeing their lack of adult supervision as inappropriate:

> We that are grown persons, have defects in our prayers that are a thousand times worse in the sight of God, and are a greater confusion, and more absurd nonsense, than their childish indiscretions. There is not so much difference before God, between children and grown persons, as we are ready to imagine; we are all poor, ignorant, foolish babes in his sight: our adult age does not bring us so much nearer to God, as we are apt to think.[22]

Original sin dissolves distinction—here, between adult and child—and requires relationship with others. Children who moved by fear of damnation to act to save themselves and others 'ought by no means to be discouraged or discountenanced.'[23] Children's spiritual potential and potential for authority is the same as that of adults.

The life and writings of Lemuel Haynes, born in Connecticut in 1753, as the fervour of the Great Awakening began to fade, illustrate both an important mid-century potential for an ambiguous empowerment of children and non-whites via the slippage between these two kinds of hierarchy—a potential that emergent ideas about childhood and race would shut down in the early nineteenth century. His life and writings both extend and depart from precedent Puritan understandings of 'family instruction,' social and spiritual hierarchy, the duties of fathers and masters, and the duties of dependents.

When the child Lemuel Haynes (1753–1833) began to voice concern about the state of his soul, he did so because he had received religious family instruction from David and Elizabeth Rose in three capacities. He was at once a child sharing family time with the affectionate adults who raised him—and also a child labourer purchased into indenture at the age of five months for a term of 21 years by a farming family that wanted his labour—and also a biracial pauper being trained to Christianity by the white Christian adults who educated him both as a term of his indenture and as an evangelical Christian duty. Though the complexity of the kinds of social inferiority that marked his initial relationship to the Roses raises questions about how to understand both his childhood piety and his adult life as a minister, it is the latter that most strongly suggests shifts in the history of early American childhood. Haynes's precocious piety is easily legible as such by those familiar with the psalters, hymnals, and didactic texts that children and dependents encountered as part of family instruction. Like Elizabeth Butcher and the other exemplary children of the *Token for the Children of New-England*, the child Lemuel Haynes was fearfully aware of the possibility of death and damnation. As if fresh from the *New England Primer* alphabet's reminder that 'Youth forward slips, Death soonest nips,' he composed, as a child, the epitaph for a three-year-old neighbour whose grave was the first in the town's cemetery—'I was the first came here to die: / Children and youth, prepare to die.'[24] Thunder frightened him, as a reminder of God's mighty power to destroy, a habitual fear to which the Roses responded by singing Isaac Watts's hymn 'God the Thunderer' with him, the last two stanzas of which vividly, even violently, imagine the final judgement:

> What shall the wretch the sinner do?
> He once defy'd the Lord;
> But he shall dread the thund'rer now,
> And sink beneath his word.
>
> Tempests of angry fire shall roll
> To blast the rebel worm
> And beat upon his naked soul
> In one eternal storm.[25]

Haynes himself chose this hymn for these occasions, suggesting that, even as a child, he could have agreed with Edwards's self-defence against critics who felt he should soften his sermons' focus on the prospect of hell: it is 'like blaming a surgeon, because when he has begun to thrust in his lance, whereby he has already put his patient to great pain, and he shrinks, rather than applauding his persistence to the core of the wound' in order to save the patient's life.[26] God's role as judge and punisher and fear of hell again informed Haynes's spiritual journey, when, as a young adult, he saw the Aurora Borealis. Thinking that it indicated that the Day of Judgement had come, he experienced the conversion—the emotionally intense experience of acceptance by and surrender to God—he had long hoped for.[27]

In this way, the scripts that taught children how to recognize piety and that sometimes permitted their elevation over adults in its name seem continuous with Haynes's Calvinist childhood; and the ambiguous empowerment they offered can seem fulfilled in his youthful piety and the upward mobility it enabled. This source of his success—the Puritan and Great Awakening focus on the equal danger of hell faced by children and adults and the recognition of the potential for spiritual authority in children—makes it surprising to find the adult Haynes deriving rhetorical and social authority as a parent and minister in terms that marginalize children and that award adults the credit or blame for children's characters. The adult Haynes's steady self-presentation as the parent and minister who bears complete responsibility for his dependents, children and congregants, thus surprisingly makes him resemble Mather's 'householder,' possessor of 'A Despotick Power which gives thee numberless Advantages, to call [dependents], and lead them into the Way of the Lord.'[28] This resemblance is ironic in light of Mather's confidence that religious instruction would make 'Negro-servants' more obedient and docile—categorically, then, never 'householders' themselves.[29] It is also ironic that Haynes, who, it would seem, benefited from the Great Awakening encouragement of autonomous child piety—views like Edwards's that 'our adult age does not bring us so much nearer to God, as we are apt to think'—seems in his letters and sermons to regard child piety as reflective not of the spiritual state of the children themselves but of their superiors.[30] His long career thus suggests the closing of a loophole through which dyadic relationships of superiors and inferiors could be, at least sometimes, flipped so that inferiors became, in limited circumstances, superiors—a loophole that possibly might have enabled shifts not only in understandings of children's duty of obedience to adults but also in understandings of 'Negroes'' duty of deference to whites—a duty that would seem, to modern eyes, to be contradicted by Haynes's leadership of the First Congregational Church of Rutland, Vermont for 30 years.

Haynes's indenture ended when he turned 21, but he remained part of the Roses' household, returning there after he was discharged, with typhus, from the militia after two years of service. Soon after that return, when asked to choose a sermon to read aloud in family instruction, he read one that he had written himself without revealing its authorship. The Roses' delight on learning that a sermon they had thought was by Jonathan Edwards was in fact by young Lemuel led them to encourage him to pursue training for ordination, after which he served for 2 years as an interim minister in Torrington, Connecticut, and then was sent in 1788, aged 40, to Rutland, Vermont, where he would preside over the First Congregational Church for 30 years. He took with him his white wife, Elizabeth Babbitt, ten years his junior, a schoolteacher he had helped through a spiritual crisis culminating in her conversion. Their ten children were all born in Vermont. Cooley dwells delightedly on the family instruction over which Haynes presided, quoting long dialogues between Haynes and his children about the meaning of Bible verses in support of his claim that it was here 'that his character shone the brightest.'[31] That these transcripts identify Haynes by name when his children are almost without exception identified only by initials creates the sense that the children were understood by Cooley as generic background to Haynes's glory (280–86). It also makes us imagine Cooley admitted to the domestic space of family instruction for the specific purpose of watching Haynes perform the role of paternal religious instructor—an awareness of this behaviour as a role that suggests its diminishing self-evidence. Haynes's children play a similarly effaced role in the epitaph he wrote for his own tombstone: 'here lies the dust of a poor hell-deserving sinner, who ventured into eternity trusting wholly on the merits of Christ for salvation. In the full belief of the great doctrines he preached while on earth, he invites his children, and all who read this, to trust their eternal interest on the same foundation' (312).[32] Urging piety on 'his children, and all who read this,' the 80-year-old Haynes makes the two groups analogous: the authority of this injunction derives from his righteous, and generic, humility; from a reminder of the worldly authority of ministers; and from real and metaphoric fatherhood.

Haynes's correspondence with Cooley focused steadily on his children's spiritual state, often in terms that make their piety or disbelief a credit to or debit against him. Only half of his children seem to have converted, a rate that casts in doubt Cooley's praise of '[m]orning and evening worship, as it had been conducted in his family' as 'a foretaste of heavenly joys' (308).[33] Statements about their faith and submission to God by one of Haynes's sons and about one of his daughters tellingly erode the distinction between submission to God and to a father-minister. One of Haynes's sons remarked after his death, 'May I never be guilty of any act that shall

tarnish his memory,' imagining the point of virtuous behaviour as preservation of his father's reputation rather than submission to God (280).
Cooley notes that Haynes was 'consol[ed]' at his daughter Olive's death
bed in 1823, when she was 25, by having 'receiv[ed]' from her dying lips
assurance that Christ was her "all"'—a consolation that seems to have
been short-lived (259). Despite this 'evidence of being one of God's
adopted children' as she died, he worried all his life that he had 'felt no
more anxiety for the welfare of her soul' while she was alive and could have
led her to still greater piety (258, 280). This inability or unwillingness to
refer children's spiritual success or failure to their own ledgers, so to speak,
is also seen in his correspondence with Cooley, in comments on children's
sickness or death. Haynes's 14-year-old daughter is so sick that he has
'doubts of her ever recovering,' he tells Cooley in a letter of October 3,
1802, a dire situation that he responds to as if it were his responsibility,
and thus his struggle: 'God is correcting us … I find I deserve chastise-
ments' (88).

A similar contrast with the two *Tokens*—a similar presentation of children facing death as other than the protagonists of their own stories—can
be found in a letter to Cooley of September 15, 1797, that explained the
recent deaths in the congregation of 15 'chiefly children' as divine punishment of 'our neglect of family religion— … we take so little care to educate our children in religion' (82). In letters like these, Haynes seems
unconsciously to be using children as generic props in a struggle centred
elsewhere, an adult struggle in which they can only ever be props. He
makes use of his experience of 'the decease of my own child' to understand
the hope that many parents feel for reunion with children 'at the judgment' (260). He advises a bachelor clergyman in a nearby parish that
unless he married, 'he could not feel that sympathy in their joys and sor-
rows which he would if he had a family of his own'—a lack of sympathy
that would negatively impact his spiritual authority with his congregants
and thus his ability to do his (worldly) job as pastor (128).

In September 1797, Haynes preached a funeral sermon in his church in
Rutland entitled 'The Important Concerns of Ministers and the People of
Their Charge,' which made the scriptural text, 1 Thessalonians 2:19, the
basis for a detailed assertion of the special spiritual duties and powers of
ministers, urging deference to them and presenting their care of congregants as appropriately fear-inspiring. Both ministers and congregants must
face judgement, Haynes notes first. Although their earthly domains are
separate in life, they may hope to meet in heaven, where congregants'

piety and salvation will bring 'peculiar joy and satisfaction' to their minister, crowning and completing his work (322, 328). He stresses throughout the lengthy sermon, which dwells much on doctrine and little on the life of the departed Rev. Abraham Carpenter, the 'distinct societies' of ministers and congregants during life, a kind of separate spheres of 'householders' and dependents (323). Haynes describes the final judgement as a kind of test of *noblesse oblige* in which superiors and inferiors are judged, and judge each other, in terms of their compliance with their respective duties of protection and obedience. In terms reminiscent of Mather's warning that 'unconverted Negroes' would condemn a 'householder' to hell, Haynes asserts that congregants' evidence assessing ministers on the grounds of doctrine, clarity and humility in preaching, and practice will raise or condemn them in the afterlife: God will 'closely attend' to '[t]he deportment or examples of ministers among their people[,] … their private visits, exhortations, and reproofs, holy desires and wrestlings for the souls of their hearers' (325). When Haynes finally refers to Abraham Cowley and his family, 9 pages into the 12-page sermon, he does so only to make Cowley an exemplum of the powerful minister-father whose words and actions can redeem or damn his dependent congregation: 'The influence of a faithful or unfaithful minister is such as to effect unborn ages' (326). This assertion of the cultural capital of ministers shows more than a little wishful thinking; church attendance in Puritan and evangelical congregations declined steadily over the eighteenth century, the Great Awakening and successor revivals notwithstanding. Haynes assures Cowley's widow and children that the departed husband/father 'still lives in another state, and is more useful to the universe than he could be in this world,' effacing the validity of all relationships to the departed except that of obedient convert or disobedient sinner (331). The pleasure in the afterlife that Cowley's grieving family should seek seems to be neither God's nor their own, but Cowley's: will they be 'a crown of rejoicing to the departed'?, Haynes asks (331). Similarly, the wrath in the afterlife that they should fear seems to be not God's, but Cowley's: 'Can you, dare you meet him at the bar of Christ in impenitence?' (331). Thus for Mather, Edwards, and Haynes, Calvinists all, the terrifying imminence of divine judgement is a given; all urge lives lived in the light of death. But though all three accept their hierarchical societies, only Haynes seems to see no potential slippage between the letter and the spirit of obedience to God's law—only Haynes essentializes the elevation of ministers and fathers above dependents, taking the former's superior holiness and power as a given.

Haynes's language verges on implying that God requires householders to possess dependents so that they can demonstrate their full devotion to God by demoting them. In the funeral sermon to Abraham Cowley, Haynes describes Cowley's rejection in heaven of the claims of his wife and children to entrance. If they are unworthy, he would happily 'join with the Judge of all in saying, Depart!' (331). On his own deathbed, Haynes complied with the model of father-ministers' virtue voiced here, one that showed love for dependents only by demanding full focus on their readiness for judgement. A daughter 'who was not a professor of religion' asked the dying Haynes to pray for her once he got to heaven, and 'a kind of holy indignation seemed to kindle in his features, and he said, "No! no! no!" expressing great displeasure at this unscriptural suggestion' (308). His last words were, 'I love my wife, I love my children, but I love my Saviour best of all' (309). In his biography of Jonathan Edwards, George Marsden comments thus on the painful paradox through which Calvinists were compelled both to strive to please God and to recognize that they could never do so: '[s]eldom has there been a spiritual discipline where so much effort was put into recognizing the worthlessness of one's own efforts.'[34] This discipline demanded, in effect, a permanent rejection of self by self. In Haynes's letters and sermons, and in the late eighteenth- and early nineteenth-century New England in which they were written, that righteous discontent seems to require in a newly stark way the making of human connections specifically to be able to cast them off. This willed isolation-unto-God may reflect Haynes's particular history, circumstances, and character, but it speaks also to the exhaustion or diminishing efficacy of Calvinist assumptions in the face of what John Wood Sweet has called the 'diverse and competitive religious culture of eighteenth-century New England.'[35]

For John Wood Sweet, even as culturally various peoples (Indigenous, African, European) were brought into new kinds of relationships by the colonial promise of Christian community, and even as extant relationships were understood differently because of its various and ambivalent force, this 'cultural convergence ... also helped to invent "racial" identities,' a process he tracks across the long eighteenth century.[36] This chapter has tracked an analogous process through which the differentiation of children and adults came to matter more. Extending the Puritan non-differentiation between children and adults, the Great Awakening allowed, even pushed, children and adults to interact in new ways—to understand submission to God as mandating a kind of defiance of, as well as deference to, familial hierarchy. In the years just after the Great Awakening, Lemuel Haynes acquired authority to preach to his superiors (first adults, then whites) via this script. But even as Haynes's writings resemble Edwards's in lamenting the death of children and rejoicing in their conversion, they show no trace of Edwards's, and the mid-century Awakening's, sense of childhood piety as a desirable response to the supreme danger of pride, or its intense focus on children's religious experience and comportment. Haynes's prioritization of other kinds of spiritual danger reflects, perhaps, the impossibility of an affiliation with children, real or imagined, providing rhetorical authority to a late eighteenth-century biracial man and former pauper, as it could and did to a mid-century white evangelical like Jonathan Edwards. Relatedly, Edwards's ability to present some children as adults' superiors indicates a kind of privilege; his social position is secure enough that such 'slumming' cannot derail it.

For Steven Mintz, it was only in the early nineteenth century that a declining birth rate, middle-class prosperity, social uncertainty, and the Romantic challenge to original sin brought about the 'invention' of 'middle-class childhood.' This new American ideal of 'childish innocence,' 'sheltered from adult realities,' 'free from labor and devoted to schooling,' had as its correlate new expectations of middle-class motherhood.[37] Haynes's defensive arrogation of family instruction and the near invisibility of his wife in Cooley's reminiscences and Haynes's letters may suggest another kind of pressure on Calvinist assumptions and practices that had become unsustainable. Nineteenth-century domestic ideals equated church and home in ways that both resemble family instruction and indicate its secularization. The Transcendentalist abolitionist, reformer, and Unitarian minister Theodore Parker saw home as a kind of church, 'the dearest spot in the world,' because it is there that mothers do God's work of awakening the soul. Parker saw God as 'the ever-loving, long-suffering Mother, who watches over us with unwearied patience, who punishes us only for our good, who hates our sins even as our mothers hated them in the fullness of their love for our better selves, and who will fold us all, blest and forgiven at last, upon the bosom of Eternal Love.'[38] The Congregationalist minister and writer Horace Bushnell similarly saw '[h]ome and religion' as 'kindred words; names both of love and reverence; home, because it is the seat of religion, religion, because it is the sacred element of home.' Bushnell understood families as 'so many little churches, only they are as much better, in many points, as they are more private, closer to the life of infancy, and more completely blended with the common affairs of life.'[39] But in these churches, the religion preached and practised was, in a real sense, domesticity—the nurturing care of children by mothers with the leisure to provide that care. Because aspects of this 'religion' pervade western culture today, it may be Haynes—the pioneering African-American who was the first in the nation to head an all-white church, the first to receive an honourary degree from Middlebury College, whose sons became a doctor and a lawyer—who seems the most archaic of the three Calvinist thinkers about the capacity for spiritual authority of dependents that has been considered here.

NOTES

1. Philip Greven, *Spare the Child: The Religious Roots of Punishment and the Psychological Impact of Physical Abuse* (New York: Vintage, 1992), 21. It is safe to say that Puritan attitudes toward childhood are not regarded positively within the field of childhood studies. The tone with which Steven Mintz describes the preference for their Indian captors' society of some reluctantly redeemed early eighteenth-century Puritan children reifies a familiar image of New England Puritans as culpably demanding and cold: 'Treated with great kindness by the Indians ... and freed of the work obligations imposed on colonial children, many young people found life in captivity preferable to that in New England.' John Zornado sees New England Puritanism as 'ideological[ly] oppressi[ve],' teaching children self-hatred and submission in order to preserve political hierarchy. The allegations leveled against the Puritans, explicitly or by implication, are that their failure to regard childhood as a distinctive and even valuable period of life made them both deluded and cruel. Thus John Demos faults Puritan culture for 'show[ing] little sense that children might somehow be a special group, with their own needs and interests and capacities. Instead they were viewed largely as miniature adults.' Even more moderate historians of childhood such as Gillian Avery seem to presume, perhaps unconsciously, that perceptions of older and younger people that do not oppose these groups as adults and children do a grave disservice to the younger people, as in her approving detection 'in the last three decades of the [eighteenth] century a dawning realization that children ought to be approached in a different way from adults.' Puritan children—as presented in texts written by Puritan adults—do not seem even to be legible as children. See also Holly Brewer's assertion that the Puritans' seeming non-differentiation of child and adult reflected not perception but emphasis: as she writes, '[i]t is not that children were not recognized as having distinct needs from adults. ... It was more that the distinction between children and adults was less

important' than would be the case later. Steven Mintz, *Huck's Raft: A History of American Childhood* (Cambridge: Harvard University Press, 2006), 8; John Zornado, *Inventing the Child* (New York: Routledge, 2006), 18; John Demos, *A Little Commonwealth: Family Life in Plymouth Colony*, 2nd ed. (New York: Oxford University Press, 2000), 58; Gillian Avery, *Behold the Child: American Children and Their Books* (Baltimore: Johns Hopkins University Press, 1994), 28. Holly Brewer, "Children and Parenting" in *A Companion to Colonial America*, ed. Daniel Vickers (Malden, MA: Blackwell Publishing, 2003), 251.

2. Jonathan Edwards, *Edwards on Revivals: Containing a Faithful Narrative of the Surprising Work of God in the Conversion of Many Hundred Souls in Northampton, Massachusetts, A.D. 1735; Also Thoughts on the Revival of Religion in New England, 1742, and the Way in which it Ought to be Acknowledged and Promoted Jonathan Edwards, Thoughts on Revival* (New York: Dunning and Spalding, 1832), 242. William Wordsworth's poem 'Ode on Intimations of Immortality from Recollections of Early Childhood' includes the phrase 'trailing clouds of glory.'

3. In some ways, Anna Mae Duane's discussion of the way that Calvinism imbricates racial hierarchy with the subordination of children to adults runs parallel to the argument offered here. She notes that 'according to the binary logic that generates so much of Puritan cosmology, if Indians are outcast because they are rebellious children, then *any* rebellious child bears a perilous resemblance to the outcast and dangerous Indians'—a view that certainly does the racist work of infantilizing Indians and that certainly makes children's obedience foundational to social order, as she claims. But this analogy also poses problems addressed variously in practice, the possibility that pious Indians could deserve greater social authority than corrupt white people and that pious children could deserve greater social authority than corrupt adults. Anna Mae Duane, *Suffering Childhood in Early America: Violence, Race, and the Making of the Child Victim* (Athens: University of Georgia Press, 2010), 37.

4. Edwards, *Some Thoughts*, 242.

5. Jonathan Edwards, *The Christian Doctrine of Original Sin Defended; Evidences of Its Truth Produced, And Arguments to the Contrary Answered* (Worcester, MA: printed for Isaiah Thomas, 1798), 251.

6. Ibid., 251.

7. See John Saillant's discussion of the 'combination of exploitation and sentiment' evident in white householders' attitudes toward black child servants and apprentices: it 'also offered a familial and religious language of affection, benevolence, sentiment, and virtue that African Americans used as leverage for respect and security in a white society.' John Saillant, *Black Puritan, Black Republican: The Life and Thought of Lemuel Haynes, 1753–1833* (New York: Oxford University Press, 2003), 12.

298   J. THORN

8. Jeffrey Hammond, *The American Puritan Elegy: A Literary and Cultural Study* (New York: Cambridge University Press, 2000), 4.
9. Edwards, *Thoughts on Revivals*, 352.
10. Ibid., 352.
11. Ibid., 353.
12. Harry S. Stout, *The New England Soul: Preaching and Religious Culture in New England* (New York: Oxford University Press, 2011), 22.
13. William Dillon Piersen, *Black Yankees: The Development of an Afro-American Subculture in Eighteenth-Century New England* (Amherst: University of Massachusetts Press, 1988), 25.
14. [Cotton Mather], *The Negro Christianized: An Essay to Excite and Assist that Good Work, The Instruction of Negro-Servants in Christianity* (Boston: printed by B. Green, 1706). For examples of readings of this pamphlet in relation to seventeenth- and eighteenth-century understandings of race, see Winthrop Jordan; Dana Nelson; and Frank Shuffelton.
15. Mather, *The Negro Christianized*, 16.
16. Ibid., 16, further references appear parenthetically.
17. *The New-England* Primer (Boston: printed by Edward Draper, 1777).
18. James Janeway, *A Token for Children, Being an Exact Account of the Conversion, Holy and Exemplary Lives and Joyful Deaths of Several Young Children; To Which Is Added, A Token for the Children of New-England* (Boston, printed by Timothy Green for Benjamin Eliot, 1700), 32.
19. Mather, *The Negro Christianized*, 41.
20. Janeway, *A Token for Children*, 106, 163.
21. Avery, *Behold the Child*, 33, 31.
22. Edwards, *Thoughts on the Revival of Religion*, 260.
23. Ibid., 260.
24. *The New England Primer, Improved for the More Easy Attaining the True Reading of English* (Boston: printed for Wharton and Bowes, 1764); Timothy Mather Cooley, *Sketches of the Life and Character of the Rev. Lemuel Haynes, A.M.* (New-York, Harper & Brothers, 1837), 268.
25. Isaac Watts, *Psalms, Hymns, and Spiritual Songs of the Old and New Testament: Faithfully Translated Into English Metre*, 2d ed. Ed. Thomas Prince, (Boston: printed by Thomas and John Fleet), 1773.
26. Edwards, *Edwards on Revivals*, 237–8.
27. Cooley, *Sketches of the Life*, 41.
28. Mather, *The Negro Christianized*, 10.
29. Ibid., 22.
30. Edwards, *Edwards on Revivals*, 260.
31. Cooley, *Sketches of the Life*, 280. Further references appear parenthetically.
32. Haynes is buried in the Lee-Oatman Cemetery in South Granville, New York.

33. In a letter to Cooley of April 10, 1810, Haynes permitted himself to boast that 'three of my wicked children, I hope, love God' (93). All ten of his children had been born by then; the oldest child was in her mid-20s and the youngest perhaps seven years old. A letter to Cooley of April 27, 1820, confided that 'three daughters and two sons' had experienced conversion (ibid., 211). Further references appear parenthetically.

34. George M. Marsden, *Jonathan Edwards: A Life* (New Haven: Yale University Press), 28.

35. John Wood Sweet, *Bodies Politic: Negotiating Race in the American North, 1730–1830* (Philadelphia: University of Pennsylvania Press, 2006), 108.

36. Ibid., 106.

37. Mintz, *Huck's Raft*, 77.

38. Theodore Parker, *The Collected Works of Theodore Parker*, volume 2. Ed. Frances Power Cobbe (London: Trubner & Co, 1865), v.

39. Horace Bushnell, *Christian Nurture* (New York: Charles Scribner, 1871), 406.

Index[1]

---

[1] Note: Page numbers followed by 'n' refer to notes.

© The Author(s) 2018   301
A. O'Malley (ed.), *Literary Cultures and Eighteenth-Century
Childhoods*, Literary Cultures and Childhoods,
https://doi.org/10.1007/978-3-319-94737-2

.

Printed by Printforce, the Netherlands